D0444348

# Discover

# **Spain**

Experience the best of Spain

This edition written and researched by
**Brendan Sainsbury,**
**Stuart Butler, Anthony Ham, Isabella Noble, John Noble,**
**Josephine Quintero, Regis St Louis, Andy Symington**

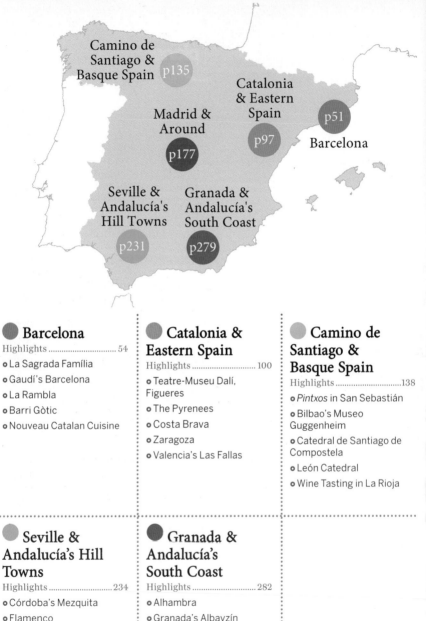

# Contents

## Plan Your Trip

## Discover

⬤⬤⬤

### Barcelona  51

⬤⬤⬤

### Catalonia & Eastern Spain  97

⬤ ### Madrid & Around

# Contents

## Discover Spain

## In Focus

## Survival Guide

# This Is Spain

From soulful flamenco and daring architecture, to delicious food and avant-garde cities, Spain could be Europe's most exotic country. Wherever you venture you'll discover a beguiling land with a mix of stirring and often curious traditions, live-for-the-moment hedonism and a willingness to embrace the future with a relentlessly adventurous spirit.

## Spain's dynamic cities are temples to all that's modern and cool.

Madrid, Barcelona, Valencia and Seville have become bywords for that peculiarly Spanish talent for living the good life, at full volume and all night long. At the same time, most cities promise a daytime feast of more sedate but nonetheless exceptional sites, from world-class art galleries and graceful Islamic-era monuments to *barrios* (neighbourhoods) overflowing with medieval charm, and zany Gaudí flights of fancy.

## Spaniards have turned eating and drinking into an art form.

From the culinary flamboyance of *pintxos* (Basque tapas) in San Sebastián to steaming seafood-infused paella served under the Valencian sunshine, Spanish food has an enviable reputation. In fact, if you really want to experience the best of Spain the way to do it is not to rush through an endless succession of tourist sights, but rather to slow the pace down and make eating the centrepiece of your day.

## Spain is a reflection of its past.

Poignantly windswept Roman ruins, cathedrals of rare power and incomparable jewels of Islamic architecture speak of a country where the great civilisations of history have always risen, fallen and left behind their indelible mark. More recently, what other country could produce such rebellious and relentlessly creative spirits as Salvador Dalí, Pablo Picasso and Antoni Gaudí and place them front and centre in public life? Here, grand monuments to the past coexist alongside architectural creations of such daring that it becomes clear that Spain's future will be every bit as original as its past.

> **Spain is a beguiling mix of stirring and often curious traditions.**

Flamenco dancer
GREG GERLA/GETTY IMAGES ©

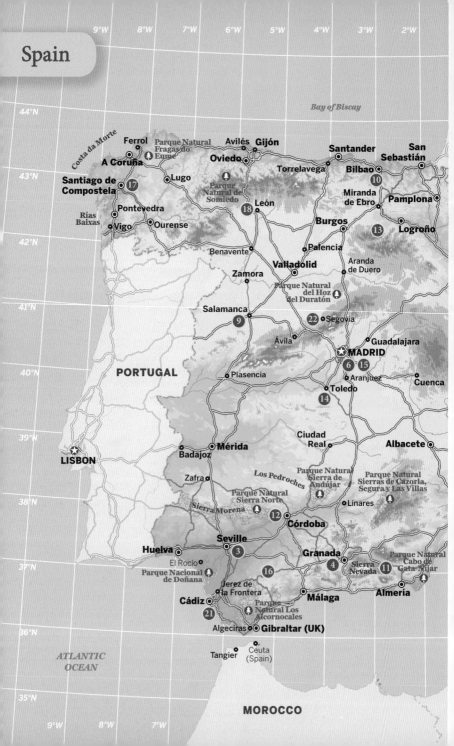

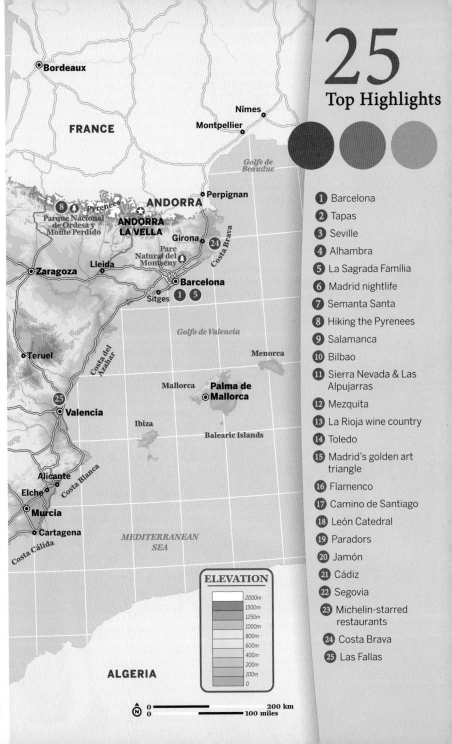

# 25
## Top Highlights

1. Barcelona
2. Tapas
3. Seville
4. Alhambra
5. La Sagrada Família
6. Madrid nightlife
7. Semanta Santa
8. Hiking the Pyrenees
9. Salamanca
10. Bilbao
11. Sierra Nevada & Las Alpujarras
12. Mezquita
13. La Rioja wine country
14. Toledo
15. Madrid's golden art triangle
16. Flamenco
17. Camino de Santiago
18. León Catedral
19. Paradors
20. Jamón
21. Cádiz
22. Segovia
23. Michelin-starred restaurants
24. Costa Brava
25. Las Fallas

# 25 Spain's Top Highlights

# Barcelona

Home to cutting-edge architecture, world-class dining and vertiginous nightlife, Barcelona (p51) has long been one of Europe's most alluring destinations. Days are spent wandering the cobblestone lanes of the Gothic quarter, basking on Mediterranean beaches or marvelling at Gaudí masterpieces across the city. By night, Barcelona is a whirl of vintage cocktail bars, gilded music halls, innovative eateries and dance-loving clubs, with the party extending well into the night. There are also colourful markets, hallowed arenas (such as Camp Nou where FC Barça plays), and a calendar packed with traditional Catalan festivals. Park Güell (p80)

1

ROSS DURANT PHOTOGRAPHY/GETTY IMAGES ©

## Tasting Tapas

One of the world's most enjoyable ways to eat, tapas is as much a way of life as it is Spain's most accessible culinary superstar. These bite-sized bar snacks are the accompaniment to countless Spanish nights of revelry and come in seemingly endless variations on the theme. In Andalucía, expect the best jamón or fine Spanish olives. In San Sebastián (p150) and elsewhere in the Basque Country (where they call tapas *pintxos*) tapas are an elaborate form of culinary art.

# Soulful Seville

Nowhere is as quintessentially Spanish as Seville, a city of capricious moods and soulful secrets which has played a pivotal role in the evolution of flamenco, bullfighting, baroque art and Mudéjar architecture. Blessed with year-round sunshine and fuelled culturally by a never-ending schedule of ebullient festivals, everything seems more amorous here, a feeling not lost on legions of 19th century aesthetes who used the city as a setting in their romantic works of fiction. Head south to the home of Carmen and Don Juan and take up the story. Plaza de España, Seville (p249)

## The Best...
## Fiestas

**LAS FALLAS, VALENCIA**
Possibly the country's noisiest festival, Las Fallas is an explosion of fireworks and burning effigies. (p129)

**FERIA DE ABRIL, SEVILLE**
Eating, drinking, dressing up (both you and your horse) and lots and lots of flamenco. (p43)

**LOS SANFERMINES, PAMPLONA**
Run, very fast, away from a pack of marauding bulls. (p161)

**CARNAVAL, ANDALUCÍA**
Cádiz puts on its fancy dress clothes for the most riotous Carnaval celebration in Spain. (p42)

WALTER BIBIKOW/GETTY IMAGES ©

13

# The Best...
## Post-Islamic Architectural Wonders

**LA SAGRADA FAMÍLIA, BARCELONA**
Gaudí's masterpiece and icon of Barcelona in all its Modernista splendour. (p72)

**MUSEO GUGGENHEIM, BILBAO**
The astonishing Frank Gehry–designed symbol of the new Bilbao. (p148)

**CIUDAD DE LAS ARTES Y LAS CIENCIAS, VALENCIA**
Valencia's showpiece avant-garde complex by world-renowned local architect Santiago Calatrava. (p128)

**BAEZA, ANDALUCÍA**
Andalucía's finest Renaissance collection, tucked away in little-visited Jaén province. (p314)

## Alhambra

The palace complex of Granada's Alhambra (p290) is close to architectural perfection. It is perhaps the most refined example of Islamic art anywhere in the world, not to mention the most enduring symbol of 800 years of Moorish rule in what was known as Al-Andalus. From afar, the Alhambra's red fortress towers dominate the Granada skyline, set against a backdrop of the Sierra Nevada's snow-capped peaks. Up close, the Alhambra's perfectly proportioned Generalife gardens complement the exquisite detail of the Palacio Nazaríes.

④

## La Sagrada Família

One of Spain's top sights, the Modernista brainchild of Antoni Gaudí remains a work in progress more than 80 years after its creator's death. Fanciful and profound, inspired by nature and barely restrained by a Gothic style, Barcelona's quirky temple (p72) soars skyward with an almost playful majesty. The improbable angles and departures from architectural convention will have you shaking your head in disbelief.

⑤

## Madrid Nightlife

Madrid (p205) is not the only European city with nightlife, but few can match its intensity and street clamour. There are wall-to-wall bars, small clubs, live venues, cocktail bars and mega-clubs beloved by A-list celebrities all across the city, with unimaginable variety to suit all tastes. But it's in Huertas, Malasaña, Chueca and La Latina that you'll really understand what we're talking about. Outdoor cafes on Calle de las Huertas

## Semana Santa

Return to Spain's medieval Christian roots in the country's dramatic Easter celebrations (p43). Religious fraternities parade elaborate *pasos* (figures) of Christ and the Virgin Mary through the streets to the emotive acclaim of the populace; the most prestigious procession is the *madrugada* (early hours) of Good Friday. Seen for the first time, it's an exotic and utterly compelling fusion of pageantry, solemnity and deep religious faith. The most extraordinary processions are in Castilla y León, Castilla La Mancha and Andalucía, but if you choose one, make it Seville. Semana Santa procession, Seville (p240)

# Hiking the Pyrenees

Spain is a walker's destination of exceptional variety, but we reckon the Pyrenees (p122) offer the most special hiking country. The Parque Nacional de Ordesa y Monte Perdido is one of the high points (pun intended) of the Pyrenees. Centred on Monte Perdido (3348m), it offers plenty of opportunities for tough excursions along great rock walls and glacial cirques, accompanied by the occasional chamois. Even better, there are limits on the number of people in the park at any one time. Parque Nacional de Ordesa y Monte Perdido (p122)

SANTIAGO BADON/GETTY IMAGES ©

## The Best... Nightlife

**MADRID**
Nights that never seem to end, with bars, clubs and great live music. (p205)

**VALENCIA**
Barrio del Carmen nights are famous throughout Spain. (p131)

**SITGES**
Where Barcelona comes to let its hair down; a huge gay scene and unforgettable Carnaval. (p349)

**SALAMANCA**
Feel-good nights beneath floodlit Renaissance buildings. (p191)

## Renaissance Salamanca

Luminous when floodlit, the elegant central square of Salamanca, the Plaza Mayor (p224), is possibly the most attractive in all of Spain. It is just one of many highlights in a city whose architectural splendour has few peers. Salamanca is home to one of Europe's oldest and most prestigious universities, so student revelry also lights up the nights. It's this combination of grandeur and energy that makes so many people call Salamanca their favourite city in Spain. Plaza Mayor (p224)

# The Best...
## Areas for Hiking

**SIERRA NEVADA**
Extraordinary scenery and wildlife, and mainland Spain's highest terrain.
(p310)

**PARQUE NACIONAL DE ORDESA Y MONTE PERDIDO**
Where the Pyrenees truly take your breath away.
(p122)

**PICOS DE EUROPA**
Magnificent mountain scenery and wild bears.
(p165)

**LAS ALPUJARRAS**
Rural Andalucía at its best amid gorgeous valleys.
(p310)

DESIGN PICS / KEN WELSH / GETTY IMAGES

## Bilbao, Spain's Northern Gem

It only took one building, a shimmering titanium fish called the Museo Guggenheim, to turn Bilbao (p144) from a by word for industrial decay into a major European art centre. But while it's this most iconic of modern buildings that draws the visitors it's the hard working soul of this city that ends up captivating and let's face it there's plenty to be entranced by: riverside promenades, clunky funicular railways, superb *pintxos* bars, an iconic football team and a clutch of quality museums. Foyer of Frank Gehry's Museo Guggenheim (p148)

## Sierra Nevada & Las Alpujarras

Dominated by the Mulhacén (3479m), mainland Spain's highest peak, the Sierra Nevada (p310) makes a stunning backdrop to the warm city of Granada. Skiing in winter and hiking in summer can be mixed with exploration of the fascinating villages of Las Alpujarras, arguably Andalucía's most engaging collection of *pueblos blancos* (white villages). Appropriately, for one of the last outposts of Moorish settlement on Spanish soil, the hamlets of Las Alpujarras resemble North Africa, set oasis-like amid the woodlands and deep ravines for which the region is renowned. Capileira (p312), Las Alpujarras

## Córdoba's Mezquita

A church that became a mosque before reverting to a church, Córdoba's Mezquita (p258) charts the evolution of Western and Islamic architecture over a 1000-year trajectory. Its most innovative features include some early horseshoe arches, an intricate mihrab, and a veritable forest of 856 columns, many of them recycled from Roman ruins. The sheer scale of the Mezquita reflects Córdoba's erstwhile power as the most cultured city in 10th-century Europe. It was also inspiration for even greater buildings to come, most notably in Seville and Granada.

## La Rioja Wine Country

La Rioja is the sort of place where you could spend weeks meandering along quiet roads in search of the finest drop. Bodegas offering wine-tastings and picturesque villages that shelter excellent wine museums are the mainstay in this region. The Frank Gehry–designed Hotel Marqués de Riscal, close to Elciego, has been likened to Bilbao's Guggenheim in architectural scale and ambition, and has become the centre for wine tourism in the region.
Frank Gehry's Hotel Marqués de Riscal (p158), Elciego

# Toledo

Symbolic home to Spain's Catholic Church and the army, the medieval core of Toledo (p214) is an extraordinary piece of world heritage. Known as 'the city of the three cultures' (where Muslims, Jews and Christians once rubbed shoulders), it remains a fascinating labyrinth today with former mosques, synagogues and churches; the latter are still very much in use and the cathedral is one of Spain's most imposing. Given Toledo's proximity to Madrid, the city can get overrun with day-trippers. Stay overnight – that's when Toledo really comes into its own. Toledo's cathedral (p214)

## The Best... Islamic Splendour

**ALHAMBRA, GRANADA**
The priceless jewel in Andalucía's crown and the symbol of Al-Andalus. (p290)

**MEZQUITA, CÓRDOBA**
Perfection and harmony in this glorious early-Islamic mosque. (p258)

**ALCÁZAR, SEVILLE**
Pleasure palace with exquisite architecture and gardens. (p248)

**ALJAFERÍA, ZARAGOZA**
A rare, glittering outpost of Al-Andalus in the north. (p120)

# The Best...
## Art Galleries

**MUSEO DEL PRADO MADRID**
World-class gallery with Goya, Velázquez and the pick of European masters. (p192)

**CENTRO DE ARTE REINA SOFÍA, MADRID**
Stunning contemporary art gallery including Dalí, Miró and Picasso's *Guernica*. (p189)

**MUSEO PICASSO, MÁLAGA**
More than 200 Picasso works in a stunningly converted palace in the city of his birth. (p299)

**TEATRE-MUSEU DALÍ, FIGUERES**
Salvador Dalí's weird-and-wonderful legacy that's so much more than a museum. (p116)

## Madrid's Golden Art Triangle

Madrid may lack architectural landmarks, but it more than compensates with an extraordinary collection of art galleries. Housing works by Goya, Velázquez, El Greco and masters from across Europe, the showpiece is the Museo del Prado (p192), but also within a short stroll are the Centro de Arte Reina Sofía (p189), showcasing Picasso's *Guernica*, plus works by Dalí and Miró, and the Museo Thyssen-Bornemisza (p190), which carries all the big names spanning centuries.

Above: Centro de Arte Reina Sofía (p189), designed by architect Jean Nouvel

Left: Museo Thyssen-Bornemisza

## Flamenco in Andalucía

**16**

Who needs rock 'n' roll? Like all great anguished music, flamenco (p332) has the power to lift you out of the doldrums and stir your soul. It's as if by sharing in the pain of innumerable generations of dispossessed misfits you open a door to a secret world of musical ghosts and ancient Andalucian spirits. On the other side of the coin, flamenco culture can also be surprisingly jolly, jokey and tongue-in-cheek. There's only one real proviso: you have to hear it live, preferably in its Seville-Jerez-Cádiz heartland.

## Camino de Santiago

**17**

Every year, tens of thousands of pilgrims and walkers with all manner of motivations set out to walk across northern Spain. Their destination, Santiago de Compostela (p169), is a place of untold significance for Christians, but the appeal of this epic walk goes far beyond the religious. With numerous routes across the north, there is no finer way to get under Spain's skin and experience the pleasures and caprices of its natural world. Catedral de Santiago de Compostela (p172)

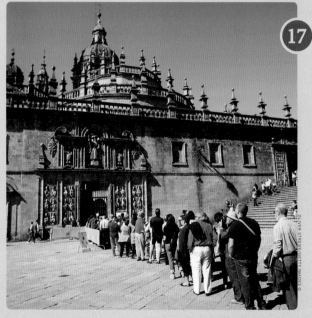

## León Catedral

With its soaring towers, flying buttresses and an interior that will simply take your breath away, León's fabulous cathedral (p168) is truly one of the Gothic masterpieces of Spain. Add to this a large student population who flood the streets with night-time revelry, an attractive old quarter and a flurry of other sights and monuments and it becomes clear that León is, above all else, a fantastic place to experience everyday life in the heart and soul of Spain.

18

## The Best...
## Most Authentic Flamenco

**PEÑA LA PERLA, CÁDIZ**
Upbeat *alegrías* performed by equally upbeat *gaditanos*. (p276)

**CASA DE LA MEMORIA, SEVILLE**
The most intimate of the many nightly flamenco shows. (p253)

**EL LAGÁ TIO PARRILLA, JEREZ**
In true Jerez fashion, shows end with a rousing, fast-paced *bulería* (flamenco song). (p273)

**PEÑA DE LA PLATERÍA, GRANADA**
Claims to be Spain's oldest flamenco afficionados' *peña* (club). (p298)

**CORRAL DE LA MORERÍA, MADRID**
The capital's best flamenco can be heard here. (p208)

# The Best...
## Village Escapes

**LAS ALPUJARRAS**
The villages of these valleys are an organic blend of man-made and natural beauty. (p310)

**AÍNSA**
Medieval stone village in the Pyrenean foothills. (p124)

**ARCOS DE LA FRONTERA**
The poster child for Andalucía's white hill villages. (p264)

**EL ROCÍO**
A guns-at-noon atmosphere, a spectacular festival and a wild hinterland. (p269)

## Paradores

Sleeping like a king has never been easier than in Spain's state-run chain of *paradores* (p348) – often palatial, always supremely comfortable former castles, palaces, monasteries and convents. There are (at last count) 94 of them scattered across the country. Ranking among Europe's most atmospheric sleeping experiences, many are sited on prime real estate (for example, inside the grounds of Granada's Alhambra) and prices are more reasonable than you might imagine, especially if you book online and far in advance. *Paradore in Sigüenza*

DAVID C TOMLINSON/GETTY IMAGES ©

## Jamón

**20**

*Jamón* (cured ham; p343) is Spain's culinary constant and one of the few things that unite the country. If there is a national dish, this is it, more so even than paella. Nearly every bar and restaurant in Spain has at least one *jamón* on the go at any one time, strapped into a cradle-like frame called a *jamonera*. Wafer-thin slices of the best *jamón* (known as *jamón ibérico de bellota*, although there are many different kinds) is simplicity itself and our idea of Spanish culinary heaven.

IAN CUMMING/DESIGN PICS/GETTY IMAGES ©

## Cádiz

Cádiz (p273) has a laid-back, live for the present feel. Locals party the sweltering summer nights away in the old town squares and waterfront bars, while Carnival celebrations are renowned throughout the country for their fun and fervour. The city itself has charm as well – fascinating historical monuments, snaking whitewashed lanes, panoramic viewpoints and a cathedral square as beautiful as any in Spain.

## Segovia

One of the most beautiful medium-sized towns in Spain, Segovia has the usual glittering array of Castilian churches and a fine location, strung out along a ridge against a backdrop of often snowcapped mountains. But two buildings of legend set Segovia apart. Its multi-turreted Alcázar (p226) provided the inspiration for Walt Disney's castle confection, while a gigantic but elegant Roman aqueduct (p226) of granite blocks has stood the test of time for almost 2000 years.

## Michelin-starred Restaurants

Spanish cuisine (p343) is quite simply fantastic. Few countries on Earth can offer such diversity, such innovative chefs and a general public who are so passionate about eating. You can eat phenomenally well almost anywhere, but at least once in your trip book a table (you'll need to do this quite some time in advance) at one of Spain's multi-Michelin-star gastronomic temples – some of which are considered amongst the best restaurants in the world. Dining at Mas Pau (p115), Figueres

23

### The Best...
## Places for Spanish Food

**OLD TOWN, SAN SEBASTIÁN**
Spain's culinary capital, with more Michelin stars than Paris(!). (p150)

**BARCELONA**
Home of Catalonia's legendary cuisine, blending the traditional with the innovative. (p60)

**LA LATINA, MADRID**
The best tapas from around Spain in one medieval, inner-city neighbourhood. (p206)

**VALENCIA**
The birthplace of paella and still the place to find the most authentic version. (p125)

**SEVILLE**
Andalucía's tapas obsession, heart and soul. (p240)

## Costa Brava

Easily accessible by air and land from the rest of Europe, and filled with villages and beaches of the kind that spawned northern Europe's summer obsession with the Spanish coast, the Costa Brava (p114) in Catalonia is one of our favourite corners of the Mediterranean. Beyond this, however, the spirit of Salvador Dalí lends personality and studied eccentricity to the Costa Brava experience, from his one-time home in Port Lligat near Cadaqués to Dalí-centric sites in Figueres and Castell de Púbol. Tossa de Mar (p107), Costa Brava

# The Best...
# Beaches

**COSTA BRAVA**
Cliffs, coves, forests and a turquoise sea combine to make pure oceanic poetry. (p114)

**PLAYA DE LA CONCHA, SAN SEBASTIÁN**
Arguably the most perfect city beach in Europe. (p150)

**CABO DE GATA**
The Mediterranean before the tourist invasion. (p315)

**TARIFA & THE COSTA DE LA LUZ**
World class windsurfing and miles of near-pristine beaches. (p305)

SHAUN EGAN/GETTY IMAGES ©

**(25)**

## Las Fallas

Spain's noisiest festival (p129) is also one of its most spectacular. Taking place every March in Valencia, Las Fallas is an explosive fiesta of fireworks, music and bonfires that light up the sky for almost a week. But this is more than just noise. A festival with deep cultural roots and great inventiveness, Las Fallas sees each Valencia neighbourhood try to outdo the others in elaborate wood and papier-mâché sculptures that go up in flames in an extraordinary climax.

# Spain's Top Itineraries

# Barcelona & Around
## Eastern Highlights

**5 DAYS**

*Spain's most exciting city delivers on all fronts. Once you're done with Barcelona, this itinerary whips you through Roman Spain in Tarragona, Islamic marvels in Zaragoza and ends with Girona's huddle of ancient streets.*

FRANCE

ANDORRA

GIRONA ④

③ ZARAGOZA

① BARCELONA

② TARRAGONA

*Golfo de Valencia*

MEDITERRANEAN SEA

## ① Barcelona (p51)

In a couple of rushed days you can just about tick off the main sites in Barcelona. Start your explorations of the city at **La Sagrada Família**, Gaudí's unfinished masterpiece. See more of his Modernista madness at the nearby **Casa Batilló**, **La Pedrera** and the **Park Güell**. On day two explore the medieval maze of the **Barri Gòtic** and Barcelona's most famous street, **La Rambla**. If time permits make a dash to the zany collection of art hanging in the **Museu Picasso**.

BARCELONA ⟶ TARRAGONA

🚗 **1¼ hours** Along AP7 🚆 **1½ hours** Around 16 per day

## ② Tarragona (p109)

Lorded over by a dominating **Catedral**, Tarragona is often bypassed by tourists, but its tangle of medieval streets hide more than just a house of God. At the bottom of the old town stand reminders of Roman Tarragona: a breathtaking **Amfiteatre Romà**, the fascinating **Pretori i Circ Romans** and **Fòrum Romà**, and the ever-rewarding **Museu Nacional Arqueològic de Tarragona**.

TARRAGONA ⟶ ZARAGOZA

🚗 **2½ hours** Along AP2 🚆 **1¼ hours** Numerous per day

## ③ Zaragoza (p118)

One of the most interesting yet overlooked cities in Spain, Zaragoza has a lot going for it. Wonderful Islamic palaces – tick; heavy hitting Christian shrines – tick; remarkable Roman ruins – tick; glut of great museums – tick; superb restaurants – tick. You visiting it on this tour – oh yes!

ZARAGOZA ⟶ GIRONA

🚗 **3½ hours** Along the AP2 & AP7 🚆 **3¼ hours** Two per day via Barcelona

## ④ Girona (p110)

The wobbly medieval streets of Girona are filled with gems, including the billowing baroque facade of the **Catedral**, a fascinating **Jewish quarter**, some beautiful gardens and delicious places to eat.

Basílica de Nuestra Señora del Pilar (p118), Zaragoza
HUGHES HERVÃO/GETTY IMAGES ©

**5 DAYS**

# Barcelona to Granada
## The Big Hitters

*Even in five days, you can get a taste of what makes Spain special. Spend a couple of days in Barcelona, take a high-speed train to Madrid for one night, then a train or car, via magnificent Toledo, to Granada for two more nights.*

BARCELONA ①

*Golfo de Valencia*

② MADRID

③ TOLEDO

④ GRANADA

MEDITERRANEAN SEA

## ① Barcelona (p51)

There's no better introduction to Spain than strolling along **La Rambla**, then branching out into the 15th-century **Barri Gòtic** with its fine monuments, lovely plazas and medieval streetscape. You could pause in the **Museu Picasso**, but make sure you leave time for the city's astonishing collection of works left by Antoni Gaudí: **La Sagrada Família** is one of Spain's most extraordinary buildings, followed closely by **Casa Batlló**, **La Pedrera** and **Park Güell**.

BARCELONA ◗ MADRID

🚗 **Six hours** Along the A2 via Zaragoza 🚆 **Three hours** From Barcelona's Estació Sants to Madrid's Puerta de Atocha

## ② Madrid (p177)

With just a day in the Spanish capital, head for the **Museo del Prado** with its masterpieces by Velázquez, Goya and a host of European masters, followed by a visit to the nearby **Centro de Arte Reina Sofía**. For some quiet downtime, immerse yourself in the oasis that is the **Parque del Buen Retiro**. After dark skip from bar to bar in **La Latina**, a *barrio* famous for its delicious tapas varieties.

MADRID ◗ TOLEDO

🚗 **One hour** Along AP41 🚆 **30 minutes** From Madrid's Puerta de Atocha

## ③ Toledo (p214)

The Rome of Spain, the labyrinth of narrow streets and plazas of Toledo are crammed with Christian, Jewish and Islamic monuments. Check out the dominating **Catedral**, the **Sinagoga del Tránsito** and the **Mezquita del Cristo de la Luz**.

TOLEDO ◗ GRANADA

🚗 **4¼ hours** Along the A4 and A44 🚆 **5½ hours** via Madrid

## ④ Granada (p279)

Explore the **Albayzín**, Granada's one-time Islamic quarter with its whitewashed tangle of laneways. Also don't miss the gilded **Capilla Real**, the city's extravagant Christian counterpoint to the dominant Islamic splendour. For food, Granada has some of Spain's most generous tapas and there are excellent places for flamenco. But it's the **Alhambra**, arguably Spain's most beautiful collection of buildings, that you came so far to see.

Tapas bar, Mercado de San Miguel (p199), Madrid
MATTES RENÁ/GETTY IMAGES ©

**10 DAYS**

# Madrid to Santiago de Compostela
## Spain's Beguiling North

*If your holiday extends to 10 days, you can (with your own wheels) range through Spain's Castilian heartland, visit San Sebastián, then follow the stunning northern coast to Galicia. Your starting point is the nation's capital, Madrid.*

ATLANTIC OCEAN

Bay of Biscay

SAN SEBASTIÁN 5

BILBAO 6

SANTIAGO DE COMPOSTELA 8

7

SANTILLANA DEL MAR

LEÓN 4

SEGOVIA 2

SALAMANCA 3

PORTUGAL

1 MADRID

# ① Madrid (p177)

Whip about the main sights, taking in the breathtaking art of the **Museo Thyssen-Bornemisza** and then continuing on to the **Museo del Prado**, one of the world's most renowned art galleries. Have an evening drink at **Plaza de Santa Ana**, followed by a tapas crawl around the bars of **La Latina**.

MADRID ⟶ SEGOVIA

🚗 **One hour** Along the A6 and AP 61 🚆 **30 minutes** From Madrid's Chamartín station

# ② Segovia (p226)

One of Spain's most engaging inland towns, Segovia has a splendid Roman-era **aqueduct** and the whimsical **Alcázar**. In between are delightful streets, fine restaurants, sweeping views and architectural highlights.

SEGOVIA ⟶ SALAMANCA

🚗 **Two hours** Along the AP6 and AP51 🚌 **2¾ hours** Two buses daily

# ③ Salamanca (p222)

Salamanca's exceptional architecture finds glorious expression in the **Plaza Mayor**, arguably Spain's most beautiful square. The city is at its floodlit best at night, with irresistible energy flowing through the streets.

SALAMANCA ⟶ LEÓN

🚗 **2½ hours** Along the A66 and the N630

# ④ León (p166)

Nothing can prepare you for the first time you step inside Leon's **Catedral**, where masses of stained-glass windows bathe the interior in ethereal light. The **Real Basílica de San Isidoro** is also splendid, as is the charming old quarter, **Barrio Húmedo**.

Bahía de la Concha (p150), San Sebastián
ANGUS OBORN/GETTY IMAGES ©

LEÓN ⟶ SAN SEBASTIÁN

🚗 **Four hours** On the A231 and AP1 🚆 **Five hours**

# ⑤ San Sebastián (p150)

Graceful architecture and the postcard-perfect **Playa de la Concha** are a stunning combination best viewed from atop **Monte Igueldo**. San Sebastián is also known for its mind-blowing tapas and Michelin-starred restaurants, such as **Arzak**.

SAN SEBASTIÁN ⟶ BILBAO

🚗 **One hour** Along AP8

# ⑥ Bilbao (p144)

Best known for the **Museo Guggenheim**, Bilbao has plenty more to offer, including the excellent **Museo de Bellas Artes**, the **Euskal Museoa**, fine riverside walks and superb food.

BILBAO ⟶ SANTILLANA DEL MAR

🚗 **1½ hours** Along the A8

# ⑦ Santillana del Mar

All along the coast of Cantabria and Asturias, isolated coves conceal picturesque fishing villages, but if you can linger in just one place, pass the night in **Santillana del Mar**, a timeless village with an idyllic setting.

SANTILLANA DEL MAR ⟶ SANTIAGO DE COMPOSTELA

🚗 **Five hours** On the E70 or **six hours** on the A6

# ⑧ Santiago de Compostela (p169)

Santiago de Compostela is a suitably epic last stop on your journey through northern Spain. Its **Catedral** is the city's soaring centrepiece, but the city radiating out from here is a microcosm of urban Spain.

## 10 DAYS

# Seville to Valencia
## Andalucía & the Mediterranean

*Ten days in Spain just about enables you to see the best of Andalucía, including magnificent cities and hilltop villages, as well as get a taste of the Spanish Mediterranean. You'll need a car for Andalucía. Consider flying from Granada to Valencia to save a long slog behind the wheel.*

VALENCIA ⑥

CÓRDOBA ④

SEVILLE ①

GRANADA ⑤

② ③ RONDA
ARCOS DE LA FRONTERA

MEDITERRANEAN SEA

MOROCCO

ALGERIA

# ① Seville (p231)

Seville is Andalucía in a nutshell. The **Barrio de Santa Cruz** is all dressed in white, there are exquisite Islamic monuments such as the **Alcázar**, and the **Catedral** and **Giralda** are superb. Throw in some of Spain's best tapas and a thriving flamenco scene, and you'll find two days here is barely enough.

SEVILLE ❯ ARCOS DE LA FRONTERA

🚗 **One hour** Along the AP4 and A382 🚌 **Two hours** Two per day

# ② Arcos de la Frontera (p264)

You've seen the pictures of brilliantly white villages clinging precariously to an Andalucian hilltop. There are many candidates throughout the region, but none surpasses Arcos de la Frontera. Breathtaking from a distance and enchanting within, this is one place where the reality is every bit as beautiful as you imagined.

ARCOS DE LA FRONTERA ❯ RONDA

🚗 **One hour** Along the A384 and A374 🚌 **Two hours** Three per day

# ③ Ronda (p267)

Clifftop Ronda is another dreamy Andalucian *pueblo blanco* (white village). The views from the **Puente Nuevo** are exceptional, but turn around to explore the town and you'll unearth Arab-era baths, fine churches, Spain's most beautiful bullring and ancient walls.

RONDA ❯ CÓRDOBA

🚗 **2¾ hours** Along the A45 🚌 **Two hours**

# ④ Córdoba (p255)

One of the most celebrated landmarks of world Islamic architecture, Córdoba's **Mezquita** should not be missed; its forest of striped horseshoe arches are aesthetic harmony wrought in stone. The **Judería**, gardens of the **Alcázar** and **Arab baths** are other highlights, as are Córdoba's restaurants and festivals.

CÓRDOBA ❯ GRANADA

🚗 **2¼ hours** Along the A45 and A92 🚌 **Four hours** Change in Bobadilla

# ⑤ Granada (p279)

If Córdoba represents Andalucía's early glories, Granada is its glittering highpoint. The **Alhambra**, arguably the most important cultural site in Spain, is blessed with the **Palacio Nazaríes** and **Generalife** gardens. There are fine views of the Alhambra and the Sierra Nevada from across the valley in the **Albayzín**.

GRANADA ❯ VALENCIA

🚗 **Five hours** Along the A7 🚌 **Seven hours**

# ⑥ Valencia (p125)

Valencia has many strings to its bow. Its most eye-catching attraction is the futuristic **Ciudad de las Artes y las Ciencias**, but the **Catedral**, **La Lonja** and beachside restaurants will more than fill your day here. The night belongs to the historic **Barrio del Carmen**.

Puente Nuevo (p267), Ronda
MICHELE FALZONE/GETTY IMAGES ©

# Barcelona to Cádiz
# The Best of Spain

*Two weeks will allow you to race around the main urban highlights of the country, taking in a little bit of everything from Barcelona style and tapas on the seashore in San Sebastián, to Madrid art galleries and flamenco in Seville. You can cover this route by car or train but be prepared for a couple of fairly long days of travel.*

## 1 Barcelona (p51)

Two days is the absolute minimum time to tick off the highlights of Barcelona. You should make a beeline straight for Gaudí's extraordinary **La Sagrada Família**, but also leave time for **Park Güell** as well as the **Museu Picasso**, the **Barri Gòtic** and the mouth-watering range of restaurants and bars.

BARCELONA ◆ PARC NACIONAL DE ORDESA Y MONTE PERDIDO

🚗 **Four hours** along the A2 and A22 to Torla

## 2 Parque Nacional de Ordesa y Monte Perdido (p122)

The magnificent Pyrenees mountains, which stand like soldiers between Spain and France, are full of beautiful, flower-filled valleys and bleak, rocky peaks and escarpments, but if we had to pick just one place in which to break the journey between Barcelona and San Sebastián it would be the **Parcque Nacional de Ordesa y Monte Perdido**. You should plan on a minimum of at least two nights in and around the park.

PARC NACIONAL DE ORDESA Y MONTE PERDIDO ◆ SAN SEBASTIÁN

🚗 **3½ hours** Along the N240 and A15

## 3 San Sebastián (p150)

San Sebastián offers one of the finest urban beaches in Europe, a hedonistic summer lifestyle and is, according to some of the world's top chefs, the culinary capital of the planet.

SAN SEBASTIÁN ◆ SEGOVIA

🚗 **4½ hours** Along the E5 via Burgos 🚆 **4¾ hours**

## 4 Segovia (p226)

Segovia might have the castle Sleeping Beauty dreamt about, as well as a Roman aqueduct that must have been created by someone who could dream big, but this Unesco-protected city remains somewhat off the standard Spanish tourist circuit, which makes a stop here all the more rewarding.

SEGOVIA ◆ MADRID

🚗 **1¼ hours** Along the AP6 🚆 **30 minutes to two hours** Arrives at Madrid Puerta de Atocha station

Catedral (p227), Segovia
CRAIG PERSHOUSE/GETTYIMAGES ©

GRANADA ➡ SEVILLE
🚗 2¾ hours Along the A92 🚃 Three hours

## ⑦ Seville (p231)

Put simply, Seville puts the exotic into Spain. This passionate city is the home of the soul-ripping sound of flamenco, the sombre and spectacular **Semana Santa** processions, the glory and gore of bull-fighting, and the jolly relief of the **Feria de Abril**. The divine **Alcázar** and near-perfect **Giralda** point to the majesty of Seville's Moorish past and the enormous **Catedral** will simply blow you away.

SEVILLE ➡ CÁDIZ
🚗 1½ hours Along the AP4 🚃 Two hours

## ⑤ Madrid (p177)

The capital of Spain has art galleries and museums to rival any European capital and a nightlife scene that the rest of the world can only stand back and stare at in awe. You should allow at least two days for Madrid.

MADRID ➡ GRANADA
🚗 4¼ hours Along the A15 🚃 4½ hours
Departs Madrid Chamartín station

## ⑥ Granada (p279)

The pinnacle of Islamic architecture in Europe is to be found in the beautiful city of Granada. The **Alhambra** might well be the most sublime sight in Spain but Granada is a city with more than one trick up its sleeve. The cobblestone streets of the **Albayzín**, or old town, are straight out of North Africa and the city's teashops and boutiques will keep you enthralled for hours. If time allows, tack on an extra couple of days for the nearby **Sierra Nevada** mountains and the snow-drop villages of **Las Alpujarras**.

## ⑧ Cádiz (p273)

Surrounded on three sides by water, Cádiz's lovely buildings have a languid waterfront atmosphere, while its tightly packed white-walled streets pulse with life. Highlights include the **Catedral** with stunning views from its tower and signposts to what may be Europe's oldest continuously inhabited city.

# Month by Month

## Top Events

 **Semana Santa (Holy Week)**, usually March or April

**Las Fallas**, March

**Bienal de Flamenco**, September

**Carnaval**, February or March

**Feria de Abril**, April

## January

### Three Kings
The Día de los Reyes Magos (Three Kings' Day), or simply Reyes, on 6 January, is the most important day on a Spanish kid's calendar. The evening before, three local politicians dress up as the three wise men and lead a sweet-distributing frenzy of Cabalgata de Reyes through the centre of most towns.

## February

### Life's a Carnaval
Riotously fun Carnaval, ending on the Tuesday 47 days before Easter Sunday, involves fancy-dress parades and festivities. It's wildest in Cádiz, Sitges and Ciudad Rodrigo.

### Return to the Middle Ages
In one of Spain's coldest corners, Teruel's inhabitants don their medieval finery and step back to the Middle Ages with markets, food stalls and a re-enactment of a local lovers' legend during the Fiesta Medieval.

### Contemporary Art Fair
One of Europe's biggest celebrations of contemporary art, Madrid's Feria Internacional de Arte Contemporánea (Arco) draws gallery reps and exhibitors from all over the world. It's a thrilling counterpoint to the old masters on display year-round in galleries across the capital.

## March

### Las Fallas
The extraordinary festival of Las Fallas consists of several days of all-night dancing and drinking, first-class fireworks and processions

**April** Feria de Abril
BRUCE YUANYUE BI/GETTY IMAGES ©

from 15 to 19 March. Its principal stage is Valencia city and the festivities culminate in the ritual burning of effigies in the streets.

## April

### ✨ Semana Santa (Holy Week)
Easter (the dates change each year) entails parades of *pasos* (holy figures), hooded penitents and huge crowds. It's extravagantly celebrated in Seville, as well as Málaga, Córdoba, Toledo and Ávila.

### ✨ Moros y Cristianos (Moors & Christians)
Colourful parades and mock battles between Christian and Muslim 'armies' in Alcoy, near Alicante, in late April make this one of the most spectacular of many such festivities staged in the Valencia and Alicante provinces.

### ✨ Feria de Abril (April Fair)
This week-long party, held in Seville in the second half of April, is the biggest of Andalucía's fairs. *Sevillanos* ride around on horseback and in elaborate horse-drawn carriages by day and, dressed up in their traditional finery, dance late into the night.

## May

### ✨ Feria del Caballo (Horse Fair)
A colourful equestrian fair in Andalucía's horse capital, Jerez de la Frontera, the Feria del Caballo is one of Andalucía's most festive and extravagant fiestas. It features parades, horse shows, bullfights and plenty of music and dance.

### ◉ Córdoba's Courtyards Open Up
Scores of beautiful private courtyards are opened to the public for two weeks in Córdoba for the Concurso de Patios Cordobeses. It's a rare chance to see an otherwise-hidden side of Córdoba, strewn with flowers and freshly painted.

### ✨ Fiesta de San Isidro
Madrid's major fiesta celebrates the city's patron saint with bullfights, parades, concerts and more. Locals dress up in traditional costumes and some of the events, such as the bullfighting season, last for a month.

## June

### ✨ Romería del Rocío
Focused on Pentecost weekend, the seventh after Easter, this festive pilgrimage is made by up to one million people to the shrine of the Virgin in El Rocío. This is Andalucía's Catholic tradition at its most curious and compelling.

### ✨ Feast of Corpus Christi
On the Thursday in the ninth week after Easter (sometimes May, sometimes June), religious processions and celebrations take place in Toledo and other cities.

### ✨ Bonfires & Fireworks
Midsummer bonfires, fireworks and roaming giants and other figures feature on the eve of the Fiesta de San Juan (24 June; Dia de Sant Joan), notably along the Mediterranean coast, including in Barcelona.

### ✪ Electronica Festival
Performers and spectators come from all over the world for Sónar, Barcelona's two-day celebration of electronic music and said to be Europe's biggest festival of its kind. Dates vary each year.

### ✨ Wine Battle
On 29 June, Haro, one of the premier wine towns of La Rioja, enjoys the Batalla del Vino, squirting wine all over the place in one of Spain's messiest playfights, pausing only to drink the good stuff.

ried into the sea or paraded on a flotilla of small boats.

### Feast of St James

The Día de Santiago marks the day of Spain's national saint and is spectacularly celebrated in Galicia at Santiago de Compostela. With so many pilgrims in town, it's the city's most festive two weeks of the year.

# August

### La Tomatina

Buñol's massive tomato-throwing festival, held in late August, must be one of the messiest get-togethers in the country. Thousands of people launch about 100 tonnes of tomatoes at one another in just an hour or so!

# September

### Bienal de Flamenco

There are flamenco festivals all over Spain throughout the year, but this is the most prestigious of them all. Held in Seville in even-numbered years (and Málaga every other year) it draws the biggest names in the genre.

### Feria de Pedro Romero

The honouring of Pedro Romero, one of the legends of bullfighting, is a good excuse for the people of Ronda to host weeks of partying. Highlights include a flamenco festival, an unusual program of bullfighting and much all-night partying.

### La Rioja's Grape Harvest

Logroño celebrates the feast day of St Matthew (Fiesta de San Mateo) and the year's

# July

### Festival Internacional de Guitarra

Córdoba's contribution to Spain's impressive calendar of musical events, this fine international guitar festival ranges from flamenco and classical to rock, blues and beyond. Headline performances take place in the Alcázar gardens at night.

### Running of the Bulls

The Fiesta de San Fermín (Sanfermines) is the week-long nonstop festival and party in Pamplona with the daily *encierro* (running of the bulls) as its centrepiece. Similar, smaller-scale events occur elsewhere through the summer.

### Día de la Virgen del Carmen

Around 16 July in most coastal towns, particularly in some parts of Andalucía, the image of the patron of fisherfolk is car-

grape harvest. There are grape-crushing ceremonies and endless opportunities to sample the fruit of the vine in liquid form.

### ✪ Barcelona's Big Party

Barcelona's Festes de la Mercè marks the end of summer with four days of parades, concerts, theatre, fire running and more. Barcelona's always fun, but this is a whole new level.

### ✪ San Sebastián Film Festival

It may not be Cannes, but San Sebastián's annual, two-week celebration of film is one of the most prestigious dates on Europe's film-festival circuit. It's held in the second half of the month and has been gathering plaudits since 1957.

### ✪ Romans & Carthaginians

In the second half of the month, locals dress up to re-enact ancient battles during the festival of Carthagineses y Romanos in Cartagena. It's among the more original mock battles staged around Spain.

# October

### ✪ Día de Nuestra Señora del Pilar

In Zaragoza on 12 October, the faithful mix with hedonists to celebrate this festival dedicated to Our Lady of the Pillar. The pillar in question is in the cathedral, but much of the fun happens in the bars nearby.

### ✪ Fiesta de Santa Teresa

The patron saint of Ávila is honoured with 10 days of processions, concerts and fireworks around her feast day.

# November

### ✪ Festival Jazz Madrid

One of two annual jazz festivals in the capital (the other is in the spring), this increasingly prestigious festival plays out in the famous jazz clubs and larger theatres across the city.

**Far left: April** Moros y Cristianos (p43)
**Left: August** La Tomatina

# What's New

*For this new edition of Discover Spain, our authors hunted down the fresh, the transformed, the hot and the happening. Here are a few of our favourites. For up-to-the-minute recommendations, see lonelyplanet.com/spain*

## 1 JEWISH ANDALUCIA

Andalucía's Jewish history finally emerges from the shadows at Seville's new Centro de Interpretación Judería de Sevilla (p241), at Granada's Palacio de los Olvidados (p289) and Toledo's Museo Sefardí (p215).

## 2 RISE & RISE OF FLAMENCO

New highlights of Andalucía's flamenco boom include Seville's relocated Casa de la Memoria (p253) and Casa de la Guitarra (p253), Córdoba's Centro Flamenco Fosforito (p257) and Granada's Casa del Arte Flamenco (p298).

## 3 MODERNISTA MASTERPIECES

Barcelona's magnificent Modernista heritage just got better with the reopening of Gaudí's Bellesguard. (p81), Puig i Cadafalch's Casa Amatller (p71) and Domènech i Montaner's Casa Lleó Morera (p70).

## 4 ARTISAN BEERS

Spain's love affair with beer has finally translated into a small but growing industry of microbrewers. Our pick of the newbies is Córdoba's Cervezas Califa (p263).

## 5 MADRID ROOFTOPS

The newly accessible roof terraces of Madrid – the Círculo de Bellas Artes (Map p188; La Azotea; Tartân Roof; www.circulobellas artes.com; Calle Marqués de Casa Riera 2; admission €3; ☺ roof terrace 9am-2am Mon-Thu, 9am-2.30am Fri, 11am-2.30am Sat & Sun; Ⓜ Sevilla, Plaza de España) and Mirador de Madrid (Map p188; www.centrocentro.org; 9th fl, Palacio de Comunicaciones, Plaza de la Cibeles; adult/child €2/0.50; ☺10.30am-1.30pm & 4-7pm Tue-Sun) – offer fabulous views out over central Madrid and beyond.

# Get Inspired

##  Books

o **The Ornament of the World** (2003) A fascinating look at Andalucía's Islamic centuries.

o **Ghosts of Spain** (2007) Giles Tremlett's take on contemporary Spain and its tumultuous past.

o **Getting to Mañana** (2004) Miranda Innes's terrific take on starting a new life in an Andalucian farmhouse.

o **A Late Dinner** (2007) Paul Richardson's beautifully written journey through Spanish food.

o **A Handbook for Travellers** (1845) Richard Ford's sometimes irascible, always enlightening window on 19th-century Spain.

o **Sacred Sierra: A Year on a Spanish Mountain** (2009) Jason Webster's excellent alternative to the expat-renovates-a-Spanish-farmhouse genre.

## Films

o **Broken Embraces** (2009) Pedro Almodóvar's film noir–inspired movie.

o **Mar Adentro** (2004) Alejandro Amenábar's

touching movie filmed in Galicia.

o **Jamón Jamón** (1992) Launched the careers of Javier Bardem and Penélope Cruz.

##  Music

o **Paco de Lucía Antología** (1995) Collected works by Spain's most celebrated flamenco guitarist.

o **Lagrimas Negras** (2003) Bebo Valdés and Diego El Cigala in stunning flamenco-Cuban fusion.

o **Sueña La Alhambra** (2005) Enrique Morente, one of flamenco's most enduring and creative voices.

o **La Luna en el Río** (2003) Carmen Linares, flamenco's foremost female voice in the second half of the 20th century.

## Websites

o **Lonely Planet** (www.lonelyplanet.com) Country information, build your own itinerary and the Thorn Tree Forum.

o **Paradores** (www.parador.es) Start planning that special night in Spain.

o **Via Verdes** (www.viasverdes.com) Fabulous website detailing Spain's 1800km of *vias verdes* (traffic-free greenways).

o **Spain Travel Guide** (www.spanish-fiestas.com) Detailed tourist information for most Spanish regions.

## Short on time?

This list will give you an instant insight into Spain.

**Read** *The New Spaniards* (2006) The updated version of John Hooper's classic portrait of contemporary Spain.

**Watch** *Todo sobre mi madre* (All About My Mother; 1999) Considered by many to be Almodóvar's masterpiece.

**Listen** *Una leyenda flamenca* (1993) Camarón de la Isla, flamenco's late, all-time singing legend.

**Log on** *Welcome to Spain* (www.spain.info) Useful official tourist office site.

Windmills, Consuegra (p227)
OLIVER STREWE/GETTY IMAGES ©

# Need to Know

**Currency**
Euro (€)

**Language**
Spanish (castellano). Also Catalan, Basque and Galician.

**Visas**
Generally not required for stays up to 90 days; some nationalities need a Schengen visa.

**Money**
ATMs widely available. Visa and Mastercard are widely accepted; American Express is less common.

**Mobile Phones**
Local SIM cards widely available and can be used in European and Australian mobile phones.

**Wi-Fi**
Widely available in hotels as well as many coffee shops and other public spaces.

**Internet Access**
Most large towns have one or two internet cafes.

**Tipping**
Small change, more if you wish.

For more information, see Survival Guide (p348).

## When to Go

Santiago de Compostela
**GO** May–Sep

Barcelona
**GO** year-round

Madrid
**GO** Mar–May, Sep & Oct

Valencia
**GO** year-round

Seville
**GO** Oct–Apr

Dry climate
Warm to hot summers, cold winters
Mild to hot summers, cold winters
Cold climate

### High Season
(Jun–Aug, Easter)

o Accommodation books out and prices increase by up to 50%.

o Low season in some inland places.

o Expect warm, dry, sunny weather; more humid in coastal areas.

### Shoulder
(Mar–May, Sep & Oct)

o A good time to travel with mild, clear weather and fewer crowds.

o Local festivals can send prices soaring.

### Low Season
(Nov–Feb)

o Cold in central Spain; rain in the north and northwest.

o Mild temperatures in Andalucía and the Mediterranean Coast.

o This is high season in ski resorts.

## Advance Planning

o **One month before** Reserve your entry ticket to Granada's Alhambra and book any long-distance train journeys. Reserve high-season accommodation.

o **Two weeks before** Book cookery courses in San Sebastián, Barcelona or elsewhere.

o **One week before** Book tour of Parque Nacional de Doñana. Reserve low-season accommodation.

# Daily Costs

## Budget
### Less than €75
o Dorm beds: €18 to €25

o Doubles in *hostales*: €55 to €65 (more in Madrid & Barcelona)

o Supermarkets and lunch *menú del día*

o Use museum and gallery 'free admission' afternoons

## Midrange
### €75–175
o Room in midrange hotel: €65 to €140

o Lunch and/or dinner in local restaurant

o Car rental: from €25 per day

## Top End
### More than €175
o Room in top-end hotel: €140 and up (€200 in Madrid and Barcelona)

o Fine dining for lunch and dinner

o Regularly stay in *paradores*

### Exchange Rates

| Australia | A$1 | €0.70 |
| --- | --- | --- |
| Canada | C$1 | €0.69 |
| Japan | ¥100 | €0.73 |
| New Zealand | NZ$1 | €0.63 |
| UK | UK£1 | €1.26 |
| US | US$1 | €0.76 |

For current exchange rates see www.xe.com.

# What to Bring
o **Passport or EU ID Card** You'll need it to enter the country and for credit card transactions.

o **Money belt** Petty theft is a small but significant risk in some cities and tourist areas.

o **National and/or International Driving Licence** Essential if you plan to rent a car.

o **Travel insurance**

# Arriving in Spain
o **Aeroport del Prat, Barcelona**

Buses €5.90; 30 to 40 minutes to the centre; every six to 15 minutes from 6.10am to 1.05am.

Trains €4.10; 35 minutes to the centre; from 5.42am to 11.38pm.

Taxis €25 to €30; 30 minutes to the centre.

o **Barajas airport, Madrid**

Metro & buses €4.50; 30 to 40 minutes to the centre; every five to 10 minutes from 6.05am to 1.30am.

Taxis €25 to €30; 20 minutes to the centre.

# Getting Around Spain
o **Air** Numerous internal flights, including with low-cost companies; some flights require a change in Madrid or Barcelona.

o **Bus** Private companies cover the whole country, more cheaply and more slowly than trains, often going where the rails don't.

o **Train** Extensive and extremely modern network with the high-speed AVE trains connecting Madrid with many cities in around two hours.

# Sleeping
o **Hostales** Budget accommodation, often with private bathroom.

o **Hotels** Wide range of midrange and top-end hotels.

o **Paradores** State-run hotels, usually in sumptuously converted historic buildings.

o **Casas Rurales** Charming and usually family-run rural accommodation.

# Be Forewarned
o **Museums** Most major museums close on Mondays.

o **Restaurants** Most restaurants open from 1.30pm to 4pm and from 9pm to 11.30pm.

o **Shops** Many smaller shops close from 2pm to 5pm.

# Barcelona

**Barcelona is a mix of sunny Mediterranean charm and European urban style.** From Gothic to Gaudí, the city bursts with art and architecture; Catalan cooking is among the country's best; summer sunseekers fill the beaches in and beyond the city; and the bars and clubs heave year-round.

From its origins as a middle-ranking Roman town, of which vestiges can be seen today, Barcelona became a medieval trade juggernaut. Its old centre constitutes one of the greatest concentrations of Gothic architecture in Europe. Beyond this core are some of the world's more bizarre buildings: surreal spectacles capped by Gaudí's church, La Sagrada Família.

Barcelona has been breaking ground in art, architecture and style since the late 19th century. From Picasso and Miró to the modern wonders of today, the racing heart of Barcelona has barely skipped a beat. Equally busy are the city's avant-garde chefs, who compete with old-time classics for the gourmet's attention.

Museu Nacional d'Art de Catalunya (MNAC), Montjuïc (p77)

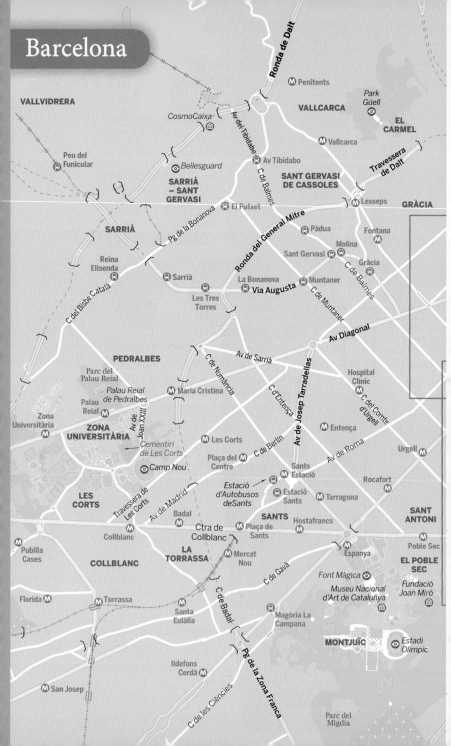

# Barcelona Highlights

## La Sagrada Família

The Sagrada Família (p72) is Antoni Gaudí's masterpiece, which he worked on for 43 years. It's a slender structure where everything is devoted to geometric perfection and sacred symbolism. It's also a work-in-progress spanning the generations but never losing Gaudí's modernity, originality and architectural synthesis of natural forms.

## ② Gaudí's Barcelona

Few architects have come to define a city quite like Antoni Gaudí in Barcelona. La Sagrada Família (p72) is the master architect's showpiece and is quite simply the most surprising, imaginative cathedral in the world. In the stately streets of L'Eixample, Casa Batlló (p70) is his most beautiful secular creation, closely followed by La Pedrera (p71).

Rooftop at Gaudí's La Pedrera (p71)

## La Rambla

La Rambla (p66) is Spain's most talked-about boulevard. It certainly packs a lot of colour into a short walk, with flower stands, historic buildings, a sensory-rich produce market, tourist tat and a ceaselessly changing parade of people from around the globe. Once a river and sewage ditch on the edge of medieval Barcelona, it still marks the southwest flank of the Barri Gòtic, the nucleus of old Barcelona.

## Barri Gòtic

You could easily spend several days or even a week exploring the Barri Gòtic (p60) without leaving the medieval streets. In addition to major sights, its tangle of narrow lanes and tranquil plazas conceal some of the city's most atmospheric shops, restaurants, cafes and bars. There are swarms of tourists afoot, but Barri Gòtic has plenty of local character as well, and it's full of rewards for the urban explorer.

## Nouveau Catalan Cuisine

The innovation and studied experimentation that has revolutionised Spanish cuisine and earned it world renown finds its true home in Barcelona. In the city's bars and restaurants, you'll find Catalonia's celebrated local staples alongside taste combinations that you never imagined in your wildest dreams. You can eat them as stand-up tapas or sit-down meals. Tapas, Quimet i Quimet (p89)

# Barcelona's Best...

## Places for Art

◦ **Museu Picasso** Picasso's early, pre-Cubist works. (p68)

◦ **Fundació Joan Miró** Showcases one of Spain's finest 20th-century artists. (p77)

◦ **Museu Nacional d'Art de Catalunya** Titian, Canaletto, Rubens and Gainsborough. (p77)

◦ **Museu d'Art Contemporani de Barcelona** Avant-garde contemporary art. (p67)

◦ **Fundació Antoni Tàpies** A homage to the elder statesman of contemporary Catalan art. (p76)

## Places for a View

◦ **La Sagrada Família** Stirring views from the cathedral's towers. (p72)

◦ **Mirador de Colom** Sweeping coastal and La Rambla views. (p61)

◦ **Casa Batlló** A swirling facade and a zany rooftop. (p70)

◦ **Camp Nou** When FC Barcelona are playing at home, this is the best view in town. (p81)

## Places for Innovative Catalan Cooking

◦ **Tickets** Gourmet tapas from Ferran Adrià's stable. (p89)

◦ **Tapas 24** A reputation for designer tapas. (p88)

◦ **Cal Pep** One of Barcelona's most celebrated and experimental tapas bars. (p86)

◦ **Cata 1.81** Delicately presented gourmet tapas served in a bar lined with quality wine. (p86)

◦ **Alkímia** Refined Catalan fare from a culinary alchemist. (p88)

## Plaças in the Ciutat Vella

o **Plaça Reial** Neoclassical square with Gaudí fountains. (p64)

o **Passeig del Born** Historic square with Barcelona's grandest Gothic church. (p69)

o **Plaça del Rei** Former royal courtyard within sight of the cathedral. (p64)

o **Plaça de Sant Josep Oriol** Small square, big impression and attractive backdrops. (p65)

# Need to Know

## VITAL STATISTICS
o **Area code** ☎93

o **Population** 1,621,000

o **Elevation** 12m

## ADVANCE PLANNING
o **Three months before** Book hotel and reserve a table at a top restaurant.

o **One month before** Check out reviews for theatre and live music and book tickets.

o **One week before** Browse the latest nightlife listings, art exhibitions and other events to attend while in town. Reserve spa visits and organised tours.

o **A few days before** Check the forecast on weather. com.

## RESOURCES
o **Barcelona** (www.bcn. cat/en) Town hall's official site with plenty of links.

o **Barcelona Turisme** (www.barcelonaturisme. com) City's official tourism website.

o **Lonely Planet** (www. lonelyplanet.com) Destination information, hotel bookings, traveller forum and more.

o **Porktie** (www.porktie. com) Recommendations of restaurants, bars and shops.

o **Spotted by Locals** (www.spottedbylocals. com) Insider tips.

## GETTING AROUND
o **Air** Barcelona's Aeroport del Prat (www.aena.es) has excellent connections with Europe and beyond.

o **Metro** The best way for getting around town, with six lines.

o **Train** Rail links with the rest of Spain and Europe.

o **Bus** Buses run along most city routes every few minutes between 5am and 6.30am to between around 10pm and 11pm.

## BE FOREWARNED
o **Museums and galleries** Most close on Monday (although most Gaudí sites open seven days).

o **Football** Tickets to Barcelona games must be booked 15 days before match day.

o **Crime** Violent crime is rare in Barcelona, but petty crime (bag-snatching, pickpocketing) is a major problem.

o **Areas to avoid** El Raval and the southern end of La Rambla late at night.

**Left:** Window of Casa Batlló (p70);
**Above:** Plaça Reial (p64)

(LEFT) MATT MUNRO/LONELY PLANET ©;
(ABOVE) MANFRED GOTTSCHALK/GETTY IMAGES ©

# Barcelona Walking Tour

*Barcelona: it might be cool, it might be fun, it might be relaxed, but that doesn't mean a visitor doesn't need a little helping hand in the form of a leisurely walking tour to get the most out of it.*

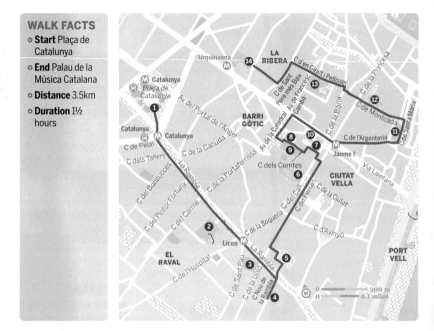

### 1 Plaça de Catalunya

There's nothing wrong with following the crowds to start off with, and this bustling square makes a good kick-off point for a leisurely wander down La Rambla (p66).

### 2 Mercat de la Boqueria

Seek out some breakfast in one of Europe's best-stocked and most colourful produce markets (p93).

### 3 Gran Teatre del Liceu

Barcelona's grand opera house (p60) was built in 1847, largely destroyed by fire in 1994, and reopened better than ever in 1999.

### 4 Palau Güell

Visit one of Gaudí's earlier efforts (p67). It may lack the playfulness of his later work but is still a fascinating blend of styles and materials.

### 5 Plaça Reial

Cross La Rambla via this shady square (p64). The lamp posts next to the central fountain are Gaudí's first known works.

### 6 Plaça de Sant Jaume

At the core of the Barri Gòtic, this square (p64) has been the political heart of the city for 2000 years.

### ⑦ Museu d'Història de Barcelona

You can examine the city's Roman origins in this nearby museum. This is one of Barcelona's most fascinating sights, so set aside at least an hour for the visit at some point during your stay in Barcelona.

### ⑧ Museu Frederic Marès

From the complex of buildings huddled around the museum and Plaça del Rei you'll pass the Museu Frederic Marès (p65), which houses an extensive collection from the 20th-century Catalan sculptor and collector.

### ⑨ Catedral

Barcelona's catedral (p61) is one of its most magnificent Gothic structures. The narrow old streets around the cathedral are traffic-free and occasionally dotted with very talented buskers.

### ⑩ Roman Walls

Make the loop down Via Laietana to admire what remains of the Roman walls.

### ⑪ Església de Santa Maria del Mar

Branch off down Carrer de l'Argenteria and circle Barcelona's finest Gothic church.

### ⑫ Museu Picasso

Head up Carrer de Montcada, home to several museums including the must-see Museu Picasso (p68). This collection focuses on his pre-Cubist years.

### ⑬ Mercat de Santa Caterina

Proceed north past the Mercat de Santa Caterina (p93), a daring 21st-century reincarnation of a grand 19th-century produce market, on the site of a medieval monastery.

### ⑭ Palau de la Música Catalana

Dogleg on to this Modernista high point and World Heritage Site.

## Barcelona in ...

### ONE DAY

Start your Barcelona adventure by taking a **walking tour** in the medieval warren of winding streets that is the **Barri Gòtic**. Allow plenty of time for admiring **La Catedral** (p61), the **Museu d'Història de Barcelon**a (p65) and the nearby **Museu Picasso** (p68).

### TWO DAYS

The following day, take a walk through Gaudí's unique **Park Güell** (p80), where the artificial can seem more natural than the natural. Next, head to **La Sagrada Família** (p72), Gaudí's breathtaking work in progress.

### FOUR DAYS

Start the third day with another round of Gaudí, visiting the extraordinary **Casa Batlló** (p70) and **La Pedrera** (p71). Follow this up with some beachside relaxation in **La Barceloneta**. Dedicate the fourth day to **Montjuïc**, with its museums, galleries, fortress, gardens and Olympic stadium.

Choir stalls in La Catedral (p61)
KRZYSZTOF DYDYNSKI/GETTY IMAGES ©

# Discover Barcelona

Gran Teatre del Liceu
DE AGOSTINI/S.VANNINI/GETTY IMAGES ©

## ◉ Sights

### LA RAMBLA & BARRI GÒTIC

Head to Spain's most famous street for that first taste of Barcelona's vibrant atmosphere.

Flanked by narrow traffic lanes and plane trees, the middle of La Rambla is a broad pedestrian boulevard, crowded every day until the wee hours with a cross-section of *barcelonins* and out-of-towners. Dotted with cafes, restaurants, kiosks and news-stands, and enlivened by buskers, pavement artists, mimes and living statues, La Rambla rarely allows a dull moment.

Barcelona's 'Gothic Quarter', east of La Rambla, is a medieval warren of narrow, winding streets, quaint plaças (plazas), and grand mansions and monuments from the city's golden age. Many of its buildings date from the 15th century or earlier.

#### Gran Teatre del Liceu   Architecture

(Map p62; ☎93 485 99 14; www. liceubarcelona.com; La Rambla dels Caputxins 51-59; tour 20/80min €5.50/11.50; ☺guided tour 10am, short tour 11.30am, noon, 12.30pm & 1pm; M Liceu) If you can't catch a night at the opera, you can still have a look around one of Europe's greatest opera houses, known to locals as the Liceu. Smaller than Milan's La Scala but bigger than Venice's La Fenice, it can seat up to 2300 people in its grand horseshoe auditorium.

Built in 1847, the Liceu launched such Catalan stars as Josep (aka José) Carreras and Montserrat Caballé. Fire virtually destroyed it in 1994, but city authorities were quick to get it back into operation. Carefully reconstructing the 19th-century auditorium and installing the latest in theatre technology, technicians finalised its restoration in October 1999. You can take a 20-minute guided tour around the main public areas of the theatre or join a longer guided tour.

On the 80-minute tour you are taken to the grand foyer, with its thick pillars and sumptuous chandeliers, and then up the marble staircase to the Saló dels Miralls (Hall of Mirrors). These both survived the 1994 fire and the latter was traditionally where theatregoers mingled during intermission. With mirrors, ceiling frescoes, fluted columns and high-and-mighty phrases in praise of the arts, it all exudes a typically neobaroque richness worthy of its 19th-century patrons. You are then led up to the 4th-floor stalls to admire the theatre itself.

The tour also takes in a collection of Modernista art, El Cercle del Liceu, which contains works by Ramon Casas. It is possible to book special tours, one that is similar to the guided tour described but including a half-hour music recital on the Saló dels Miralls, and another tour that penetrates the inner workings of the stage and backstage work areas.

## Mirador de Colom    Viewpoint

(Map p62; ☎93 302 52 24; Plaça del Portal de la Pau; lift adult/child €4.50/3; ⏰8.30am-8pm; ⓂDrassanes) High above the swirl of traffic on the roundabout below, Columbus keeps permanent watch, pointing vaguely out to the Mediterranean. Built for the Universal Exhibition in 1888, the monument allows you to zip up 60m in the lift for bird's-eye views back up La Rambla and across the ports of Barcelona.

## La Catedral    Church

(Map p62; ☎93 342 82 62; www.catedralbcn. org; Plaça de la Seu; admission free, special visit €6, choir admission €2.80; ⏰8am-12.45pm & 5.15-7.30pm Mon-Sat, special visit 1-5pm Mon-Sat, 2-5pm Sun & holidays; ⓂJaume I) Barcelona's central place of worship presents a magnificent image. The richly decorated main facade, laced with gargoyles and the stone intricacies you would expect of northern European Gothic, sets it quite apart from other churches in Barcelona. The facade was actually added in 1870, although the rest of the building was built between 1298 and 1460. The other facades are sparse in decoration, and the octagonal,

# The Modernistas' Mission

Antoni Gaudí (1852–1926), known above all for La Sagrada Família (p72), was just one, albeit the most imaginative, of a generation of inventive architects who left an indelible mark on Barcelona between 1880 and the 1920s. They were called the Modernistas.

The local offshoot of the Europe-wide phenomenon of art nouveau, Modernisme was characterised by its taste for sinuous, flowing lines and (for the time) adventurous combinations of materials such as tile, glass, brick, iron and steel. But Barcelona's Modernistas were also inspired by an astonishing variety of other styles too: Gothic and Islamic, Renaissance and Romanesque, Byzantine and baroque.

L'Eixample, where most of Barcelona's new building was happening at the time, is home to the bulk of the Modernistas' creations. Others in the city include Gaudí's Palau Güell (p67) and Park Güell (p80); Domènech i Montaner's Palau de la Música Catalana (p69), and the **Hotel España restaurant** (Map p62; ☎93 550 00 00; www.hotelespanya.com; Carrer de Sant Pau 9-11; r €164; ❄@⏰≈; ⓂLiceu).

# Central Barcelona

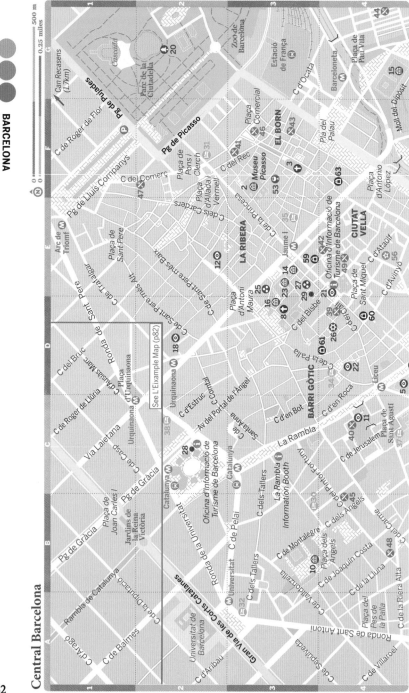

0   0.25 miles
0   500 m

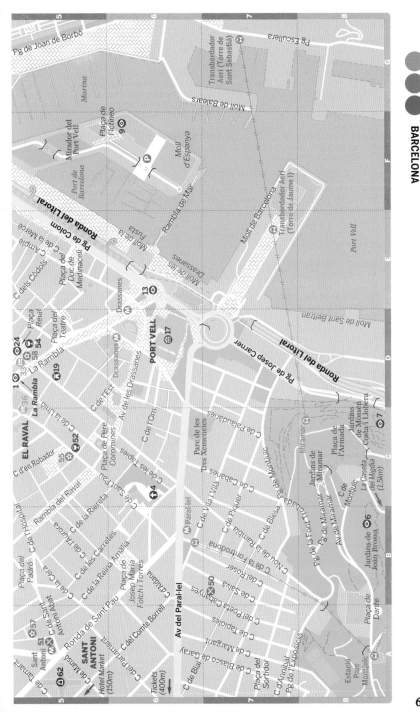

Pg de Joan de Borbó

Marina

Moll de Balears

Transbordador Aeri (Torre de Sant Sebastià)

Pg Escullera

Mirador del Port Vell

Plaça de Victineo **9**

Moll d'Espanya

Port de Barcelona

Transbordador Aeri (Torre de Jaume I)

Port Vell

Ronda del Litoral

Pg de Colom

Rambla de Mar

Moll de la Fusta

Moll de les Drassanes

Moll de Barcelona

Moll de Sant Beltran

C Ample

C de la Mercè

C dels Codols

Plaça del Duc de Medinaceli

**13**

Drassanes **M**

**PORT VELL**

**17**

Ronda del Litoral

Pg de Josep Carner

Plaça Reial

Plaça del Teatre

**1**

**36**

**33**

**24**

**58 54**

**19**

La Rambla

C de la Unió

**52**

**55**

C d'en Robador

C de l'Est

Drassanes **M**

Av de les Drassanes

C de l'Om

Plaça de Pere Coromines

C de les Tàpies

C de Sant Pau

**4**

C de Palaudàries

Parc de les Tres Xemeneies

C de Blai

C de Cabanes

Pg de Montjuïc

Miramar

Jardins de Miramar

Plaça de l'Armada

Jardins de Mossèn Costa i Llobera

**7**

EL RAVAL

Rambla del Raval

C de l'Hospital

C de la Riereta

Plaça del Padró

C de la Cera

C de l'Aurora

C de les Carretes

C de la Reina Amàlia

Plaça Maria Josep Maria Folch i Torres

C Catalana

Av del Paral·lel

Parallel **M**

C de Vila i Vila

C de la Rambla

Nou de la Rambla

C de Piquer

C de Blesa

C de la Font

Pg de Miramar

Av de Miralla

C de Montjuïc

La Caseta del Migdia (1.5km)

Jardins de Joan Brossa

**6**

Plaça de Dante

Estació Parc Montjuïc

Pg de l'Exposició

C d'Anníbal

Plaça del Sortidor

C de Blasco de Garay

C de Poeta Cabanyes

C de Margarit

C de Tapioles

C del Roser

C de Salvà

C del Rosal

**50**

SANT ANTONI

Ronda de Sant Pau

C del Comte Borrell

C Paral·lamí

Hotel Market (150m)

Tickets (400m)

C de Mansó

C del Parlament

C de Sant Antoni Abat

C de la Cera

**57**

**51**

**62**

C de Tamarit

C de Tamarit

Sant Antoni **M**

SANT ANTONI

63

# Central Barcelona

flat-roofed towers are a clear reminder that, even here, Catalan Gothic architectural principles prevailed.

## Plaça Reial  Square
(Map p62; M Liceu) One of the most photogenic squares in Barcelona, the Plaça Reial is a delightful retreat from the traffic and pedestrian mobs on the nearby Rambla. Numerous eateries, bars and nightspots lie beneath the arcades of 19th-century neoclassical buildings, with a buzz of activity at all hours.

## Plaça del Rei  Museum, Square
(Map p62) Plaça del Reia (King's Sq) is a picturesque plaza where Fernando and Isabel received Columbus following his first New World voyage. It is the courtyard of the former Palau Reial Major. The palace today houses a superb history museum, with significant Roman ruins underground.

## Plaça de Sant Jaume  Square
(Map p62; M Liceu or Jaume I) In the 2000 or so years since the Romans settled here, the area around this square (often remodelled), which started life as the forum, has

been the focus of Barcelona's civic life. This is still the central staging area for Barcelona's traditional festivals. Facing each other across the square are the Palau de la Generalitat (seat of Catalonia's regional government) on the north side and the *ajuntament* (town hall) to the south.

## Museu d'Història de Barcelona
Museum

(Map p62; ☎93 256 21 00; www.museuhistoria. bcn.cat; Plaça del Rei; adult/child €7/free, 1st Sun of month & 3-8pm Sun free; ☺10am-7pm Tue-Sat, 10am-8pm Sun; Ⓜ Jaume I) One of Barcelona's most fascinating museums takes you back through the centuries to the very foundations of Roman Barcino. You'll stroll over ruins of the old streets, sewers, laundries and wine- and fish-making factories that flourished here following the town's founding by Emperor Augustus around 10 BC. Equally impressive is the building itself, which was once part of the Palau Reial Major (Grand Royal Palace) on Plaça del Rei, among the key locations of medieval princely power in Barcelona.

## Museu Frederic Marès
Museum

(Map p62; ☎93 256 35 00; www.museumares. bcn.es; Plaça de Sant Iu 5; admission €4.20, after 3pm Sun & 1st Sun of month free; ☺10am-7pm Tue-Sat, 11am-8pm Sun; Ⓜ Jaume I) One of the wildest collections of historical curios lies inside this vast medieval complex, once part of the royal palace of the counts of Barcelona. A rather worn coat of arms on the wall indicates that it was also, for a while, the seat of the Spanish Inquisition in Barcelona. Frederic Marès i Deulovol (1893–1991) was a rich sculptor, traveller and obsessive collector, and displays of religious art and vast varieties of bric-a-brac litter the museum.

## Palau del Lloctinent
Historic Site

(Map p62; Carrer dels Comtes; ☺10am-7pm; Ⓜ Jaume I) **FREE** This converted 16th-century palace has a peaceful courtyard worth wandering through. Have a look upwards from the main staircase to admire the extraordinary timber *artesonado*, a sculpted ceiling made to seem like the

### If You Like...
### Roman Barcelona

If you like the signposts to Roman Barcelona in the Museu d'Història dela Ciutat, then journey back in time at these sites:

1 **ROMAN WALLS**
(Map p62) From Plaça del Rei it's worth a detour to see the two best surviving stretches of Barcelona's Roman walls, which once boasted 78 towers (as much a matter of prestige as of defence). One section is on the southeast side of Plaça de Ramon Berenguer el Gran, with the Capella Reial de Santa Àgata atop. The other is a little further south, by the northern end of Carrer del Sots-tinent Navarro. They date from the 3rd and 4th centuries, when the Romans rebuilt their walls after the first attacks by Germanic tribes from the north.

2 **TEMPLE ROMÀ D'AUGUST**
(Map p62; Carrer del Paradis 10; ☺10am-2pm Mon, to 7pm Tue-Sun; Ⓜ Jaume I) Opposite the southeast end of La Catedral, narrow Carrer del Paradis leads towards Plaça de Sant Jaume. Inside No 10, itself an intriguing building with Gothic and baroque touches, are four columns and the architrave of Barcelona's main Roman temple, dedicated to Caesar Augustus and built to worship his imperial highness in the 1st century AD.

upturned hull of a boat. Temporary exhibitions, usually related in some way to the archives, are often held here.

## Plaça de Sant Josep Oriol
Square

(Map p62; Ⓜ Liceu) This small plaza flanking the majestic Església de Santa Maria del Pi is one of the prettiest in the Barri Gòtic. Its bars and cafes attract buskers and artists and make it a lively place to hang out. It is surrounded by quaint streets, many dotted with appealing cafes, restaurants and shops.

## Sinagoga Major
Synagogue

(Map p62; ☎93 317 07 90; www.calldebarcelona.org; Carrer de Marlet 5; admission by suggested donation €2.50; ☺10.30am-6.30pm Mon-Fri, to 2.30pm Sat & Sun; Ⓜ Liceu) When

# ⭐ Don't Miss
# La Rambla

Barcelona's most famous street is both a tourist magnet and a window into Catalan culture, with cultural centres, theatres and architecturally intriguing buildings lining its sides. Set between narrow traffic lanes and flanked by plane trees, the middle of La Rambla is a broad pedestrian boulevard, crowded every day until the wee hours with a wide cross section of society. A stroll here is pure sensory overload, with souvenir hawkers, buskers, pavement artists, mimes and living statues all part of the ever-changing street scene.

It takes its name from a seasonal stream (*raml* in Arabic) that once ran here. From the early Middle Ages on, it was better known as the Cagalell (Stream of Shit) and lay outside the city walls until the 14th century. Monastic buildings were then built and, subsequently, mansions of the well-to-do from the 16th to the early 19th centuries. Unofficially, La Rambla is divided into five sections, which explains why many know it as Las Ramblas.

The initial stretch from Plaça de Catalunya is **La Rambla de Canaletes**, named after a turn-of-the-20th-century drinking fountain, the water of which supposedly emerges from what were once known as the springs of Canaletes. It used to be said that *barcelonins* 'drank the waters of Les Canaletes'. Nowadays people claim that anyone who drinks from the fountain will return to Barcelona, which is not such a bad prospect. This is the traditional meeting point for happy FC Barcelona fans when they win cups and competitions.

The second stretch, **La Rambla dels Estudis** (Carrer de la Canuda to Carrer de la Portaferrissa) is also called La Rambla dels Ocells (birds) because of its bird market.

## NEED TO KNOW

Map p62; Ⓜ Catalunya, Liceu or Drassanes

an Argentine investor bought a run-down electrician's store with an eye to converting it into central Barcelona's umpteenth bar, he could hardly have known he had stumbled onto the remains of what could be the city's main medieval synagogue (some historians cast doubt on the claim). A guide will explain what is thought to be the significance of the site in various languages.

## EL RAVAL

### MACBA
Museum

(Museu d'Art Contemporani de Barcelona; Map p62; ☎93 412 08 10; www.macba.cat; Plaça dels Àngels 1; adult/concession €10/8; ⏱11am-7.30pm Mon & Wed-Fri, 10am-9pm Sat, 10am-3pm Sun & holidays; ⓜUniversitat) Designed by Richard Meier and opened in 1995, MACBA has become the city's foremost contemporary art centre, with captivating exhibitions for the serious art lover. The permanent collection is on the ground floor and dedicates itself to Spanish and Catalan art from the second half of the 20th century, with works by Antoni Tàpies, Joan Brossa and Miquel Barceló, among others, though international artists, such as Paul Klee, Bruce Nauman and John Cage, are also represented.

### Palau Güell
Palace

(Map p62; ☎93 472 57 75; www.palau-guell.cat; Carrer Nou de la Rambla 3-5; adult/concession €12/8; ⏱10am-8pm Tue-Sun; ⓜDrassanes) Finally reopened in its entirety in May 2012 after several years of refurbishment, this is a magnificent example of the early days of Gaudí's fevered architectural imagination – the extraordinary neo-Gothic mansion, one of the few major buildings of that era raised in Ciutat Vella, gives an insight into its maker's prodigious genius.

Gaudí built the palace just off La Rambla in the late 1880s for his wealthy and faithful patron, the industrialist Eusebi Güell. Although a little sombre compared with some of his later whims, it is still a characteristic riot of styles (Gothic, Islamic, art nouveau) and materials. After the civil war the police occupied it and tortured political prisoners in the basement. The building was then abandoned, this leading to its long-term disrepair.

Up two floors are the main hall and its annexes; central to the structure is the magnificent music room with its rebuilt organ that is played during opening hours. The hall is a parabolic pyramid – each wall an arch stretching up three floors and coming together to form a dome. The family rooms are sometimes labyrinthine and dotted with piercings of light, or grand, stained-glass affairs. The roof is a mad tumult of tiled mosaics and fanciful design in the building's chimney pots. The audio guide, included in the entry price, is worth getting for its

Richard Meier's MACBA
MATT MUNRO/LONELY PLANET ©

JEAN-PIERRE LESCOURRET/GETTY IMAGES ©

## ★ Don't Miss
# Museu Picasso

Set in five contiguous medieval stone mansions, the celebrated Museu Picasso includes more than 3500 artworks from one of the giants of the art world. This collection is uniquely fascinating, concentrating on Picasso's formative years and several specific moments in his later life, but those interested primarily in cubism may not be satisfied.

A visit starts with sketches and oils from Picasso's earliest years in Málaga and A Coruña – around 1893–95.

The enormous *Ciència i Caritat* (Science and Charity) showcases his masterful academic techniques of portraiture.

His first consciously themed adventure, the Blue Period, is well covered. His nocturnal blue-tinted views of *Terrats de Barcelona* (Roofs of Barcelona) and *El Foll* (The Madman) are cold and cheerless, yet somehow spectrally alive.

Among the later works, done in Cannes in 1957, *Las Meninas* is a complex technical series of studies on Diego Velázquez' masterpiece of the same name (which hangs in the Prado in Madrid).

### NEED TO KNOW
Map p62; 📞93 256 30 00; www.museupicasso.bcn.cat; Carrer de Montcada 15-23; adult/child €14/free, temporary exhibitions adult/child €6.50/free, 3-8pm Sun & 1st Sun of month free; 🕘9am-7pm daily, until 9.30pm Thu; Ⓜ Jaume I

photo and music illustrations of Güell family life.

Picasso – who, incidentally, hated Gaudí's work – began his Blue Period in 1902 in a studio across the street at Carrer Nou de la Rambla 10. Begging to differ with Señor Picasso, Unesco declared the Palau, together with Gaudí's other main works (La Sagrada Família, Casa Batlló, La Pedrera, Park Güell, Casa Vicens and Colònia Güell crypt) a World Heritage site.

### Església de Sant Pau del Camp
Church

(Map p62; Carrer de Sant Pau 101; adult/concession €3/2; ⏱10am-1.30pm & 4-7.30pm Mon-Sat; MParal·lel) The best example of Romanesque architecture in the city is the dainty little cloister of this church. Set in a somewhat dusty garden, the 12th-century church also boasts some Visigothic sculptural detail on the main entrance.

## LA RIBERA

### Palau de la Música Catalana
Architecture

(Map p62; ✆93 295 72 00; www.palaumusica. org; Carrer de Sant Francesc de Paula 2; adult/child €17/free; ⏱guided tours 10am-3.30pm daily; MUrquinaona) This concert hall is a high point of Barcelona's Modernista architecture, a symphony in tile, brick, sculpted stone and stained glass. Built by Domènech i Montaner between 1905 and 1908 for the Orfeo Català musical society, it was conceived as a temple for the Catalan Renaixença (Renaissance).

### Basílica de Santa Maria del Mar
Church

(Map p62; ✆93 310 23 90; Plaça de Santa Maria del Mar; ⏱9am-1.30pm & 4.30-8.30pm, opens at 10.30am Sun; MJaume I) **FREE** At the southwest end of Passeig del Born stands the apse of Barcelona's finest Catalan Gothic church, Santa Maria del Mar (Our Lady of the Sea). Built in the 14th century with record-breaking alacrity for the time (it took just 54 years), the church is remarkable for its architectural harmony and simplicity.

### Parc de la Ciutadella
Park

(Map p62; Passeig de Picasso; MArc de Triomf) **FREE** Come for a stroll, a picnic, a visit to the zoo or to inspect Catalonia's regional parliament, but don't miss a visit to this, the most central green lung in the city. Parc de la Ciutadella is perfect for winding down.

## LA BARCELONETA & THE WATERFRONT

La Barceloneta, laid out in the 18th century and subsequently heavily over-developed, was once a factory workers' and fishermen's quarter. Today the smokestacks are gone (as are most of the fishing families), though an authentic, ungentrified air still permeates these narrow gridlike streets. You'll find some excellent seafood restaurants here and a few bohemianesque neighbourhood bars. Barceloneta meets the sea at the city's sparkling new waterfront, with a beachside promenade extending some 4.5km past artificial beaches, parks and new high-rises to El Fòrum.

On La Barceloneta's seaward side are the first of Barcelona's beaches, which are popular on summer weekends. The pleasant **Passeig Marítim de la Barceloneta** ( MBarceloneta or Ciutadella Vila Olímpica), a 1.25km promenade from La Barceloneta to Port Olímpic, is a haunt for strollers, runners and cyclists.

### Museu Marítim
Museum

(Map p62; ✆93 342 99 20; www.mmb.cat; Avinguda de les Drassanes; adult/child €5/2, 3-8pm Sun free; ⏱10am-8pm; MDrassanes) These mighty Gothic shipyards shelter the Museu Marítim, a remarkable relic from Barcelona's days as the seat of a seafaring empire. Highlights include a full-sized replica (made in the 1970s) of Don Juan of Austria's 16th-century flagship, fishing vessels, antique navigation charts and dioramas of the Barcelona waterfront.

### Museu d'Història de Catalunya
Museum

(Museum of Catalonian History; Map p62; ✆93 225 47 00; www.mhcat.net; Plaça de Pau Vila 3; adult/child €4.50/3.50, 1st Sun of month free; ⏱10am-7pm Tue & Thu-Sat, to 8pm Wed, to 2.30pm Sun; MBarceloneta) Inside the **Palau de Mar** (Map p62), this worthwhile museum takes you from the Stone Age through to the early 1980s. It is a busy hotchpotch of dioramas, artefacts, videos, models, documents and interactive bits: all up, an entertaining exploration of 2000 years of Catalan history.

# If You Like...
## Modernista Architecture

If you like Gaudí's Casa Batlló, you'll also like the following Modernista gems (including some by Gaudí):

### 1 COLÒNIA GÜELL

( ☎ 93 630 58 07; www.gaudicoloniaguell. org; Carrer de Claudi Güell; adult/student €7/5.50; ⊙10am-7pm Mon-Fri, to 3pm Sat & Sun; ☒FGC lines S4, S8 or S33) Apart from La Sagrada Família, Gaudí's last big project was the creation of a utopian textile workers' complex for his magnate patron Eusebi Güell outside Barcelona at Santa Coloma de Cervelló. Gaudí's main role was to erect the colony's church, Colònia Güell.

### 2 CASA LLEÓ MORERA

(Map p82; ☎ 93 676 27 33; www. casalleomorera.com; Passeig de Gràcia 35; adult/ concession/child under 12yr €15/€13.50/free; ⊙guided tour in English 10am Mon-Sat; ☒Passeig de Gràcia) Domènech i Montaner's 1905 contribution to the Manzana de la Discordia, with Modernista carving outside and a bright, tiled lobby in which floral motifs predominate, is perhaps the least odd-looking of the three main buildings on the block. In 2014 part of the building was opened to the public (by guided tour only), so you can appreciate the 1st floor, giddy with swirling sculptures, rich mosaics and whimsical decor.

### 3 COSMOCAIXA

(Museu de la Ciència; ☎ 93 212 60 50; www. fundacio.lacaixa.es; Carrer de Isaac Newton 26; adult/child €4/free; ⊙10am-8pm Tue-Sun; ☒60, ☒FGC Avinguda Tibidabo) Kids (and kids at heart) are fascinated by displays here and this science museum has become one of the city's most popular attractions. The single greatest highlight is the recreation over 1 sq km of a chunk of flooded Amazon rainforest (Bosc Inundat). More than 100 species of Amazon flora and fauna prosper in this unique, living diorama in which you can even experience a tropical downpour.

### L'Aquàrium                  Aquarium

(Map p62; ☎ 93 221 74 74; www.aquariumbcn. com; Moll d'Espanya; adult/child €20/15, dive €300; ⊙9.30am-11pm Jul & Aug, to 9pm Sep-Jun; ☒Drassanes) It is hard not to shudder at the sight of a shark gliding above you, displaying its toothy, wide-mouthed grin. But this, the 80m shark tunnel, is the highlight of one of Europe's largest aquariums. It has the world's best Mediterranean collection and plenty of colourful fish from as far off as the Red Sea, the Caribbean and the Great Barrier Reef. All up, some 11,000 fish (including a dozen sharks) of 450 species reside here.

### Torre Agbar              Architecture

(www.torreagbar.com; Avinguda Diagonal 225; ☒Glòries) Barcelona's very own cucumber-shaped tower, Jean Nouvel's luminous Torre Agbar, is among the most daring additions to the skyline since the first towers of La Sagrada Família went up. Completed in 2005, it shimmers at night in shades of midnight blue and lipstick red. At the time of publication, the Hyatt group was in negotiations to purchase the building and transform it into a luxury hotel.

## L'EIXAMPLE

Stretching north, east and west of Plaça de Catalunya, L'Eixample (the Extension) was Barcelona's 19th-century answer to overcrowding in the medieval city.

The development of L'Eixample coincided with the city's Modernisme period and so it's home to many Modernista creations. Apart from La Sagrada Família, the principal ones are clustered on or near L'Eixample's main avenue, Passeig de Gràcia.

### Casa Batlló              Architecture

(Map p82; ☎ 93 216 03 06; www.casabatllo.es; Passeig de Gràcia 43; adult/concession/child under 7yr €21.50/€18.50/free; ⊙9am-9pm daily; ☒Passeig de Gràcia) One of the strangest residential buildings in Europe, this is Gaudí at his hallucinogenic best. The facade, sprinkled with bits of blue, mauve and green tiles and studded with wave-shaped window frames and balconies, rises to an uneven blue-tiled roof with a solitary tower.

## Casa Amatller
Architecture

(Map p82; ☎93 487 72 17; www.amatller.org; Passeig de Gràcia 41; tour €10; ⏱tour Sat; Ⓜ Passeig de Gràcia) FREE One of Puig i Cadafalch's most striking bits of Modernista fantasy, Casa Amatller combines Gothic window frames with a stepped gable borrowed from Dutch urban architecture. But the busts and reliefs of dragons, knights and other characters dripping off the main facade are pure caprice.

The pillared foyer and staircase lit by stained glass are like the inside of some romantic castle.

The building was renovated in 1900 for the chocolate baron and philanthropist Antoni Amatller (1851–1910) and it will one day open partly to the public. Renovation – still continuing at the time of research – will see the 1st (main) floor converted into a museum with period pieces, while the 2nd floor will house the Institut Amatller d'Art Hispanic (Amatller Institute of Hispanic Art).

For now, you can wander into the foyer, admire the staircase and lift, and head through the shop to see the latest temporary exhibition out the back. Depending on the state of renovation, it is also possible to join a 1½-hour guided tour of the 1st floor, with its early-20th-century furniture and decor intact, and Amatller's photo studio. These are generally held on Saturdays; check the website for details.

Amatller was a keen traveller and photographer (his absorbing shots of turn-of-the-20th-century Morocco are occasionally on show). The tour also includes a tasting of Amatller chocolates in the original kitchen.

## La Pedrera
Architecture

(Casa Milà; Map p82; ☎93 484 59 00; www.lapedrera.com; Carrer de Provença 261-265; adult/student/child €16.50/14.85/8.25; ⏱9am-8pm Mar-Oct, to 6.30pm Nov-Feb; Ⓜ Diagonal) This undulating beast is another madcap Gaudí masterpiece, built in 1905–10 as a combined apartment and office block. Formally called Casa Milà, after the businessman who commissioned it, it is better known as La Pedrera (the Quarry) because of its

Jean Nouvel's Torre Agbar

# Don't Miss
# La Sagrada Família

If you have time for only one sight-seeing outing, this should be it. La Sagrada Família inspires awe by its sheer verticality, and in the manner of the medieval cathedrals it emulates, it's still under construction after more than 100 years. When completed, the highest tower will be more than half as high again as those that stand today.

Map p82

☎ 93 207 30 31

www.sagradafamilia.cat

Carrer de Mallorca 401

adult/senior & student/child under 11yr/ €14.80/12.80/free

⊘ 9am-8pm Apr-Sep, to 6pm Oct-Mar

Ⓜ Sagrada Família

## Nativity Facade

The Nativity Facade is the artistic pinnacle of the building, mostly created under Gaudí's personal supervision. You can climb high up inside some of the four towers by a combination of lifts and narrow spiral staircases – a vertiginous experience. Do not climb the stairs if you have cardiac or respiratory problems. The towers are destined to hold tubular bells capable of playing complex music at great volume. Their upper parts are decorated with mosaics spelling out 'Sanctus, Sanctus, Sanctus, Hosanna in Excelsis, Amen, Alleluia'.

## Passion Facade

The southwest Passion Facade, on the theme of Christ's last days and death, was built between 1954 and 1978 based on surviving drawings by Gaudí, with four towers and a large, sculpture-bedecked portal. The main series of sculptures, on three levels, are in an S-shaped sequence, starting with the Last Supper at the bottom left and ending with Christ's burial at the top right.

## Glory Facade

The Glory Facade is under construction and will, like the others, be crowned by four towers – the total of 12 representing the Twelve Apostles. Gaudí wanted it to be the most magnificent facade of the church. Inside will be the narthex, a kind of foyer made up of 16 'lanterns', a series of hyperboloid forms topped by cones.

## Museu Gaudí & Tours

Open the same times as the church, the Museu Gaudí, below ground level, includes interesting material on Gaudí's life and other works, as well as models and photos of La Sagrada Família. Although essentially a building site, the completed sections and museum may be explored at leisure. Fifty-minute guided tours (€4) are offered. Alternatively, pick up an audio tour (€4), for which you need ID.

**Local Knowledge**

# La Sagrada Família

*BY JORDI FAULÍ, DEPUTY ARCHITECTURAL DIRECTOR FOR LA SAGRADA FAMÍLIA*

1 **PASSION FACADE**
Among the Fachada de la Pasión's stand-out features are the angled columns, dramatic scenes from Jesus' last hours, an extraordinary rendering of the Last Supper and a bronze door that reads like a sculptured book. But the most surprising view is from inside the door on the extreme right.

2 **MAIN NAVE**
The majestic Nave Principal showcases Gaudí's use of tree motifs for columns to support the domes: he described this space as a forest. But it's the skylights that give the nave its luminous quality, even more so once the scaffolding is removed and light will flood down onto the apse and main altar.

3 **SIDE NAVE AND NATIVITY TRANSEPT**
Although beautiful in its own right, with windows that project light into the interior, this is the perfect place to view the sculpted tree-like columns and get an overall perspective of the main nave. Turn around and you're confronted with the inside of the Nativity Facade, an alternative view that most visitors miss; the stained-glass windows are superb.

4 **NATIVITY FACADE**
The Fachada del Nacimiento is Gaudí's grand hymn to Creation. Begin by viewing it front-on from a distance, then draw close enough (but to one side) to make out the details of its sculpted figures. The complement to the finely wrought detail is the majesty of the four parabolic towers that reach for the sky and are topped by Venetian stained glass.

5 **THE MODEL OF COLÒNIA GÜELL**
Among the many original models used by Gaudí in the Museu Gaudí, the most interesting is the church at Colònia Güell. From the side you can visualise the harmony and beauty of the interior, thanks to the model's ingenious use of rope and cloth.

# La Sagrada Família

## A TIMELINE

**1882** Francesc del Villar is commissioned to construct a neo-Gothic church.

**1883** Antoni Gaudí takes over as chief architect, and plans a far more ambitious church to hold 13,000 faithful.

**1926** Death of Gaudí; work continues under Domènec Sugrañes. Much of the **apse ❶** and **Nativity Facade ❷** is complete.

**1930** **Bell towers ❸** of the Nativity Facade completed.

**1936** Construction is interrupted by Spanish Civil War; anarchists destroy Gaudí's plans.

**1939-40** Architect Francesc de Paula Quintana i Vidal restores the crypt and meticulously reassembles many of Gaudí's lost models, some of which can be seen in the **museum ❹**.

**1976** Completion of **Passion Facade ❺**.

**1986-2006** Sculptor Josep Subirachs adds sculptural details to the Passion Facade including the panels telling the story of Christ's last days, amid much criticism for employing a style far removed from what was thought typical of Gaudí.

**2000** **Central nave vault ❻** completed.

**2010** Church completely roofed over; Pope Benedict XVI consecrates the church; work begins on a high-speed rail tunnel that will pass beneath the church's **Glory Facade ❼**.

**2026–28** Projected completion date.

## TOP TIPS

» **Light** The best light through the stained-glass windows of the Passion Facade bursts through into the heart of the church in the late afternoon.

» **Time** Visit at opening time on weekdays to avoid the worst of the crowds.

» **Views** Head up the Nativity Facade bell towers for the views, as long queues generally await at the Passion Facade towers.

KRZYSZTOF DYDYNSKI/GETTY IMAGES ©

**Spiral staircase**

**Nativity Facade**
Gaudí used plaster casts of local people and even of the occasional corpse from the local morgue as models for the portraits in the Nativity scene.

**Central nave vault**

**Apse**
Built just after the crypt in mostly neo-Gothic style, it is capped by pinnacles that show a hint of the genius that Gaudí would later deploy in the rest of the church.

CALLE MONTES/GETTY IMAGES ©

## Bell towers

The towers (eight completed) of the three facades represent the 12 Apostles. Lifts whisk visitors up one tower of the Nativity and Passion Facades (the latter gets longer queues) for fine views.

NIKADA/GETTY IMAGES ©

**③**

**②**

**⑥**

## Completed church

Along with the Glory Facade and its four towers, six other towers remain to be completed. They will represent the four Evangelists, the Virgin Mary and, soaring above them all over the transept, a 170m colossus symbolising Christ.

## Glory Facade

This will be the most fanciful facade of all, with a narthex boasting 16 hyperboloid lanterns topped by cones that will look something like an organ made of melting ice cream.

**⑦**

## Museu Gaudí

Jammed with old photos, drawings and restored plaster models that bring Gaudí's ambitions to life, the museum also houses an extraordinarily complex plumb-line device he used to calculate his constructions.

**⑤**

**④**

**Escoles de Gaudí**

## Crypt

The first completed part of the church, the crypt is in largely neo-Gothic style and lies under the transept. Gaudí's burial place here can be seen from the Museu Gaudí.

JEKATERINA NIKITINA/GETTY IMAGES ©

## Passion Facade

See the story of Christ's last days from Last Supper to burial in an S-shaped sequence from bottom to top of the facade. Check out the cryptogram in which the numbers always add up to 33, Christ's age at his death.

STEPHEN SAKS/GETTY IMAGES ©

uneven grey stone facade, which ripples around the corner of Carrer de Provença.

### Fundació Antoni Tàpies — Gallery

(Map p82; ☎ 93 487 03 15; www.fundaciotapies. org; Carrer d'Aragó 255; adult/concession €7/5.60; ☀10am-7pm Tue-Sun; Ⓜ Passeig de Gràcia) The Fundació Antoni Tàpies is both a pioneering Modernista building (completed in 1885) and the major collection of leading 20th-century Catalan artist Antoni Tàpies. A man known for his esoteric work, Tàpies died in February 2012, aged 88; he leaves behind a powerful range of paintings and a foundation intended to promote contemporary artists.

### Palau del Baró Quadras — Architecture

(Map p82; ☎ 93 467 80 00; Avinguda Diagonal 373; ☀8am-8pm Mon-Fri; Ⓜ Diagonal) FREE Puig i Cadafalch designed Palau del Baró Quadras (built 1902–06) in an exuberant Gothic-inspired style. The main facade is its most intriguing, with a soaring, glassed-in gallery. Take a closer look at the gargoyles and reliefs – the pair of toothy fish and the sword-wielding knight clearly have the same artistic signature as the architect behind Casa Amatller. Decor inside is eclectic, but dominated by Middle Eastern and East Asian themes.

### Recinte Modernista de Sant Pau — Architecture

(☎93 553 78 01; www.santpaubarcelona.org; Carrer de Cartagena 167; adult/concession/ child €8/5.60/free; ☀10am-6.30pm Mon-Sat, to 2.30pm Sun; Ⓜ Hospital de Sant Pau) Domènech i Montaner outdid himself as architect and philanthropist with the Modernista Hospital de la Santa Creu i de Sant Pau, redubbed in 2014 the 'Recinte Modernista'. It was long considered one of the city's most important hospitals, and only recently repurposed, its various spaces becoming cultural centres, offices and something of a monument. The complex, including 16 pavilions – together

with the Palau de la Música Catalana, a joint World Heritage site – is lavishly decorated and each pavilion is unique.

## MONTJUÏC

Montjuïc, the hill overlooking the city centre from the southwest, is dotted with museums, soothing gardens and the main group of 1992 Olympic sites, along with a handful of theatres and clubs.

### Museu Nacional d'Art de Catalunya (MNAC)    Museum

( 93 622 03 76; www.museunacional.cat; Mirador del Palau Nacional; adult/student/senior & child under 16yr €12/€8.40/free, 1st Sun of month free; 10am-8pm Tue-Sat, to 3pm Sun, library 10am-6pm Mon-Fri; Espanya) From across the city, the bombastic neobaroque silhouette of the **Palau Nacional** can be seen on the slopes of Montjuïc. Built for the 1929 World Exhibition and restored in 2005, it houses a vast collection of mostly Catalan art spanning the early Middle Ages to the early 20th century. The high point is the collection of extraordinary Romanesque frescoes.

### Fundació Joan Miró    Museum

( 93 443 94 70; www.fundaciomiro-bcn.org; Parc de Montjuïc; adult/child €11/free; 10am-8pm Tue-Sat, to 9.30pm Thu, to 2.30pm Sun & holidays; 55, 150, cable car Paral·lel) Joan Miró, the city's best-known 20th-century artistic progeny, bequeathed this art foundation to his hometown in 1971. Its light-filled buildings, designed by close friend and architect Josep Lluís Sert (who also built Miró's Mallorca studios), are crammed with seminal works, from Miró's earliest timid sketches to paintings from his last years.

### Font Màgica    Fountain

( 93 316 10 00; Avinguda de la Reina Maria Cristina; every 30min 7-9pm Fri & Sat Oct-Apr, 9.30-11pm Thu-Sun May-Sep; Espanya) A huge

# Montjuïc

## A ONE-DAY ITINERARY

Montjuïc, perhaps once the site of pre-Roman settlements, is today a hilltop green lung looking over city and sea. Interspersed across varied gardens are major art collections, a fortress, an Olympic stadium and more. A solid one-day itinerary can take in the key spots.

Alight at Espanya metro stop and make for **CaixaForum ❶**, always host to three or four free top-class exhibitions. The nearby **Pavelló Mies van der Rohe ❷** is an intriguing study in 1920s futurist housing by one of the 20th century's greatest architects. Uphill, the Romanesque art collection in the **Museu Nacional d'Art de Catalunya ❸** is a must, and its restaurant is a pleasant lunch stop. Escalators lead further up the hill towards the **Estadi Olímpic ❹**, scene of the 1992 Olympic Games. The road leads east to the **Fundació Joan Miró ❺**, a shrine to the master surrealist's creativity. Contemplate ancient relics in the **Museu d'Arqueologia de Catalunya ❻**, then have a break in the peaceful **Jardins de Mossèn Cinto Verdaguer ❼**, the prettiest on the hill, before taking the cable car to the **Castell de Montjuïc ❽**. If you pick the right day, you can round off with the gorgeously kitsch **La Font Màgica ❾** sound and light show, followed by drinks and dancing in an open-air nightspot in **Poble Espanyol ❿**.

**CaixaForum**
This former factory and barracks designed by Josep Puig i Cadafalch is an outstanding work of Modernista architecture; like a Lego fantasy in brick.

Olympic Needle

Piscines Bernat Picornell

**Poble Espanyol**
Amid the rich variety of traditional Spanish architecture created in replica for the 1929 Barcelona World Exhibition, browse the art on show in the Fundació Fran Daurel.

## TOP TIPS

» **Moving views** Ride the Transbordador Aeri from Barceloneta for a bird's eye approach to Montjuïc. Or take the Teleféric de Montjuïc cable car to the Castell for more aerial views.

» **Summer fun** The Castell de Montjuïc features outdoor summer cinema and concerts (see http://sala montjuic.org).

» **Beautiful bloomers** Bursting with colour and serenity, the Jardins de Mossèn Cinto Verdaguer are exquisitely laid out with bulbs, especially tulips, and aquatic flowers.

**Pavelló Mies van der Rohe**
Admire the inventiveness of the great German architect Ludwig Mies van der Rohe in this recreation of his avant garde German pavillion for the 1929 World Exhibition.

### La Font Màgica
Take a summer evening to behold the Magic Fountain come to life in a unique 15-minute sound and light performance, when the water glows like a cauldron of colour.

### Museu Nacional d'Art de Catalunya
Make a beeline for the Romanesque art selection and the 12th-century polychrome image of Christ in majesty, which was recovered from the apse of a country chapel in northwest Catalonia.

### Fundació Joan Miró
Take in some of Joan Miró's giant canvases, and discover little-known works from his early years in the Sala Joan Prats and Sala Pilar Juncosa.

**Museu Etnològic**

**Teatre Grec**

**Museu Olímpic i de l'Esport**

**Estadi Olímpic**

**Jardí Botànic**

**Jardins de Mossèn Cinto Verdaguer**

⑨ ③ ⑥ ⑤ ⑦ ④ ⑧

### Museu d'Arqueologia de Catalunya
Seek out the Roman mosaic depicting the Three Graces, one of the most beautiful items in this museum, which was dedicated to the ancient past of Catalonia and neighbouring parts of Spain.

### Castell de Montjuïc
Enjoy the sweeping views of the sea and city from atop this 17th-century fortress, once a political prison and long a symbol of oppression.

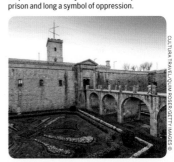

NIKADA/GETTY IMAGES ©

# ⭐ Don't Miss
## Park Güell

North of Gràcia and about 4km from Plaça de Catalunya, Park Güell is where Gaudí turned his hand to landscape gardening. It's a strange, enchanting place where his passion for natural forms really took flight – to the point where the artificial almost seems more natural than the natural.

Just inside the main entrance on Carrer d'Olot, immediately recognisable by the two Hansel-and-Gretel gatehouses, is the park's Centre d'Interpretaciò, in the Pavelló de Consergeria, which is a typically curvaceous former porter's home that hosts a display on Gaudí's building methods and the history of the park.

The spired house over to the right is the Casa-Museu Gaudí, where Gaudí lived for most of his last 20 years (1906–26). It contains furniture by him (including items that were once at home in La Pedrera, Casa Batlló and Casa Calvet) and other memorabilia. The house was built in 1904 by Francesc Berenguer i Mestres as a prototype for the 60 or so houses that were originally planned here.

The walk from metro stop Lesseps is signposted. From the Vallcarca stop, it is marginally shorter and the uphill trek eased by escalators. Bus 24 drops you at an entrance near the top of the park.

The park is extremely popular (it gets an estimated 4 million visitors a year, about 86% of them tourists) and in 2013 an entrance fee was imposed on the central area containing most of its attractions. Access is limited to a certain number of people every half-hour, and it's wise to book ahead online.

### NEED TO KNOW

☏ 93 409 18 31; www.parkguell.cat; Carrer d'Olot 7; admission to central area adult/child €7/€4.50; ☉ 8am-9.30pm daily; 🚌 24 or 32, Ⓜ Lesseps or Vallcarca

fountain that crowns the long sweep of the Avinguda de la Reina Maria Cristina to the grand facade of the Palau Nacional, Font Màgica is a unique performance in which the water can look like seething fireworks or a mystical cauldron of colour.

### Jardins
Gardens

**FREE** Towards the foot of the fortress, above the main road to Tarragona, the **Jardins de Mossèn Costa i Llobera** (Map p62; www.bcn.cat/parcsijardins; Carretera de Miramar 1; ⊙10am–sunset; cable car Transbordador Aeri, Miramar) **FREE** have a good collection of tropical and desert plants – including a veritable forest of cacti. Near the Estació Parc Montjuïc (cable car station) are the ornamental **Jardins de Mossèn Cinto Verdaguer** (www.bcn.cat/parcsijardins; ⊙10am–sunset; 🚌55, 150) **FREE**, full of beautiful bulbs and aquatic plants. East across the road are the landscaped **Jardins Joan Brossa** (Map p62; ⊙10am–sunset; cable car Telefèric de Montjuïc, Mirador) **FREE**, set on the site of a former amusement park. These gardens contain many Mediterranean species, from cypresses to pines and a few palms. From the **Jardins del Mirador**, opposite the Estació Mirador, you have fine views over the port of Barcelona.

## CAMP NOU, PEDRALBES & LA ZONA ALTA

### Camp Nou
Stadium

(🕿902 189900; www.fcbarcelona.com; Carrer d'Aristides Maillol; adult/child €23/17; ⊙10am–7.30pm Mon-Sat, to 2.30pm Sun; Ⓜ Palau Reial) Among Barcelona's most-visited sites is the massive stadium of Camp Nou (which means New Field in Catalan), home to the legendary Futbol Club Barcelona. Attending a game amid the roar of the crowds is an unforgettable experience. Football fans who aren't able to see a game can get a taste of all the excitement at the museum, with its multimedia exhibits, and a self-guided tour of the stadium.

### Bellesguard
Architecture

(🕿93 250 40 93; www.bellesguardgaudi.com; Carrer de Bellesguard 16; admission €7;

⊙10am–7pm Mon-Sat Apr–Oct, 10am–3pm Mon-Sat Nov–Mar; 🚈FGC Avinguda Tibidabo) This Gaudí masterpiece was recently rescued from obscurity, and opened to the public in 2013. Built between 1900 and 1909, this private residence (still owned by the original Guilera family) has a castle-like appearance with crenellated walls of stone and brick, narrow stained-glass windows, elaborate ironwork and a soaring turret mounted by a Gaudian cross. It's a fascinating work that combines both Gothic and Modernista elements.

## 🎓 Courses

### Cook and Taste
Cooking Course

(Map p62; 🕿93 302 13 20; www.cookandtaste.net; Carrer del Paradís 3; half-day workshop €65; Ⓜ Liceu) Learn to whip up a paella or stir a gazpacho in this Spanish cookery school.

## 🎏 Tours

### Barcelona Walking Tours
Walking Tour

(Map p62; 🕿93 285 38 34; www.barcelonaturisme.com; Plaça de Catalunya 17-S; Ⓜ Catalunya) The Oficina d'Informació de Turisme de Barcelona organises guided walking tours. One explores the **Barri Gòtic** (adult/child €15.50/free; ⊙in English 9.30am daily); another follows in the footsteps of **Picasso** (adult/child €21.50/7; ⊙in English 3pm Tue, Thu & Sat) and winds up at the Museu Picasso, entry to which is included in the price, and a third takes in the main jewels of **Modernisme** (adult/child €15.50/free; ⊙in English 4pm Fri). Also offered is a **gourmet tour** (adult/child €21.50/7; ⊙in English 10am Fri & Sat) of traditional purveyors of fine foodstuffs across the old city; it includes a couple of chances to taste some of the products.

### My Favourite Things
Tour

(🕿637 265405; www.myft.net; tours from €26) Offers tours (with no more than 10 participants) based on numerous themes: street art, shopping, culinary tours, musical journeys and forgotten neighbourhoods are among the offerings. Other activities include flamenco and

See Central Barcelona Map (p62)

salsa classes and bicycle rides in and out of Barcelona. Some of the more unusual activities cost more and times vary.

## 🛏 Sleeping

### LA RAMBLA & BARRI GÒTIC

#### El Jardí                                           Hotel €€
(Map p62; ☑ 93 301 59 00; www.eljardi-barcelona.com; Plaça de Sant Josep Oriol 1; d €90-120; ❄ 🛜; M Liceu) 'The Garden' has no garden but a handful of boxy doubles with balcony overlooking one of the prettiest squares in Barcelona. If you can snag one of them, it is well worth climbing up the stairs. If you can't get a room with a view, you are better off looking elsewhere.

#### DO                              Boutique Hotel €€€
(Map p62; ☑ 93 481 36 66; www.hoteldoreial.com; Plaça Reial 1; s/d from €230/280; ❄ 🛜 ☒; M Liceu) Overlooking the magnificent Plaça Reial, this 18-room property has handsomely designed rooms, set with beamed ceilings, wide plank floors and all-important soundproofing. The service

## L'Eixample

is excellent, and the facilities extensive, with roof terrace (with bar in summer), dipping pool, solarium and spa. Its excellent market-to-table restaurants draw in visiting foodies.

### EL RAVAL

**Hotel Sant Agustí**      Hotel €€
(Map p62; ☎93 318 16 58; www.hotelsa.com; Plaça de Sant Agustí 3; r from €125; ❄@☎; Ⓜ Liceu) This former 18th-century monastery opened as a hotel in 1840, making it the city's oldest. The location is perfect – a quick stroll off La Rambla on a curious square. Rooms sparkle, and are mostly spacious and light filled. Consider an attic double with sloping ceiling and bird's-eye views.

**Casa Camper**      Design Hotel €€€
(Map p62; ☎93 342 62 80; www.casacamper.com; Carrer d'Elisabets 11; s/d from €238/260; ☺❄@☎; Ⓜ Catalunya) The massive foyer looks like a contemporary-art museum, but the rooms are the real surprise. Decorated in red, black and white, each room has a sleeping and bathroom area, where you can put on your Camper slippers, enjoy the Vinçon furniture and contemplate the hanging gardens outside your window. Across the

corridor is a separate, private sitting room with balcony, TV and hammock. Get to the rooftop for sweeping cityscapes.

### LA RIBERA

**Chic & Basic**      Design Hotel €€
(Map p62; ☎93 295 46 52; www.chicandbasic.com; Carrer de la Princesa 50; s €81-87, d €103-150; ❄@☎; Ⓜ Jaume I) This is a very cool hotel indeed, with its 31 spotlessly white rooms and fairy-light curtains that change colour, adding an entirely new atmosphere to the space. The rooms are small, but the ceilings are high and the beds enormous. Many beautiful old features of the original building have been retained, such as the marble staircase. Chic & Basic also runs a *hostal* in **El Raval** (Map p62; ☎93 302 51 83; www.chicandbasic.com; Carrer dels Tallers 82; s/d from €71/84; ❄@; Ⓜ Universitat).

**Hotel Banys Orientals**      Boutique Hotel €€
(Map p62; ☎93 268 84 60; www.hotelbanysorientals.com; Carrer de l'Argenteria 37; s €96, d €115.50-143; ❄☎; Ⓜ Jaume I) Book well ahead to get into this magnetically popular designer haunt. Cool blues and aquamarines combine with dark-hued floors to lend this clean-lined, boutique hotel a quiet charm. All rooms, on the small side, look onto the street or back lanes. There are more spacious suites in two other nearby buildings.

### L'EIXAMPLE

**Hotel Market**      Boutique Hotel €
( ☎93 325 12 05; www.forkandpillow.com; Passatge de Sant Antoni Abad 10; s/d from €72/76; ❄@☎; Ⓜ Sant Antoni) Attractively located in a renovated building along a narrow lane just north of the grand old Sant Antoni market (now shut for renovation), this place has an air of simple chic. Room decor is a pleasing combination of white, dark nut browns, light wood and reds.

**Five Rooms**      Boutique Hotel €€
(Map p82; ☎93 342 78 80; www.thefiverooms.com; Carrer de Pau Claris 72; s/d from €155/165; ❄@☎; Ⓜ Urquinaona) Like they say, there are five rooms (standard rooms and

suites) in this 1st-floor flat virtually on the border between L'Eixample and the old centre of town. Each is different and features include broad, firm beds, stretches of exposed brick wall, restored mosaic tiles and minimalist decor. There are also two apartments.

### Room Mate Pau
Hotel €€

(Map p62; ☎93 343 63 00; pau.room-mate-hotels.com; Carrer de Fontanella 7; d €125-170; ❄️🛜; Ⓜ Urquinaona, Catalunya) Just a short stroll from Plaça de Catalunya, Room Mate Pau sits somewhere between upscale hostel and boutique hotel. The rooms are small and minimalist, but cleverly designed (with good mattresses, USB-connected flatscreen TVs). The enticing interior terrace with bar draws a young and hip crowd.

### Hotel Praktik
Boutique Hotel €€

(Map p82; ☎93 343 66 90; www.hotelprak-tikrambla.com; Rambla de Catalunya 27; r €119-129; ❄️🛜; Ⓜ Passeig de Gràcia) This Modernista gem hides a gorgeous little boutique number. While the high ceilings

and the bulk of the original tile floors have been maintained, the 43 rooms have daring ceramic touches, spot lighting and contemporary art. There is a chilled reading area and deck-style lounge terrace. The handy location on a tree-lined boulevard is an added plus.

### Hotel Constanza
Boutique Hotel €€

(Map p82; ☎93 270 19 10; www.hotelconstanza.com; Carrer del Bruc 33; s/d €80/100; ❄️@🛜; Ⓜ Girona, Urquinaona) This boutique beauty has stolen the hearts of many a visitor to Barcelona. Design touches abound, and details such as flowers in the bathroom add charm. Suites and studios are further options. The terrace is a nice spot to relax, looking over the rooftops of the L'Eixample.

## ❌ Eating

Barcelona is something of a foodies' paradise, combining rich Catalan cooking traditions with a new wave of culinary wizards by chefs at the vanguard of *nueva cocina española*.

### LA RAMBLA & BARRI GÒTIC

### Cafè de l'Acadèmia
Catalan €€

(Map p62; ☎93 319 82 53; Carrer dels Lledó 1; mains €13-19; ⏰1.30-4pm & 8.45-11.30pm Mon-Fri; Ⓜ Jaume I) Expect a mix of traditional dishes with the occasional creative twist. At lunchtime, local *ajuntament* (town hall) office workers pounce on the *menú del día*. In the evening it is rather more romantic, as low lighting emphasises the intimacy of the timber ceiling and wooden decor. On warm days, you can also dine on the pretty square at the front.

### La Vinateria del Call
Spanish €€

(Map p62; ☎93 302 60 92; www.lavinateriadelcall.com; Carrer de Sant Domènec del Call 9; small plates €7-12;

Decorative chimneys, Palau Güell (p67)
TRACY PACKER PHOTOGRAPHY/GETTY IMAGES ©

⏱7.30pm-1am; Ⓜ Jaume I) In a magical setting in the former Jewish quarter, this tiny jewelbox of a restaurant serves up tasty Iberian dishes including Galician octopus, cider-cooked chorizo and the Catalan *escalivada* (roasted peppers, aubergine and onions) with anchovies. Portions are small and made for sharing, and there's a good and affordable selection of wines.

### Allium                    Catalan, Fusion €€

(Map p62; ☎ 93 302 30 03; Carrer del Call 17; mains €8-16; ⏱ noon-4pm Mon-Tue, to 10.30pm Wed-Sat; Ⓜ Liceu) This inviting newcomer to Barri Gòtic serves beautifully prepared tapas dishes and changing specials (including seafood paella for one). The menu, which changes every two or three weeks, focuses on seasonal, organic cuisine. Its bright, modern interior sets it apart from other neighbourhood options; it's also open continuously, making it a good bet for those who don't want to wait until 9pm for a meal.

### Pla                                Fusion €€€

(Map p62; ☎ 93 412 65 52; www.elpla. cat; Carrer de la Bellafila 5; mains €18-25; ⏱ 7.30pm-midnight; 📷; Ⓜ Jaume I) One of Gòtic's long-standing favourites, Pla is a stylish, romantically lit medieval dining room where the cooks churn out such temptations as oxtail braised in red wine, seared tuna with oven-roasted peppers, and polenta with seasonal mushrooms. It has a tasting menu for €38 Sunday to Thursday.

## EL RAVAL

### Sésamo                        Vegetarian €

(Map p62; ☎ 93 441 64 11; Carrer de Sant Antoni Abat 52; tapas €6; ⏱ 8pm-midnight Tue-Sun; 📷; Ⓜ Sant Antoni) Widely held to be the best veggie restaurant in the city (admittedly not as great an accolade as it might be elsewhere), Sésamo is a cosy, fun place. The menu is mostly tapas, and most people go for the seven-course tapas menu (wine included; €25), but there are a few more substantial dishes.

# Eating Like a Local

*BY BEGO SANCHIS, OWNER OF COOK & TASTE COOKING SCHOOL*

### 1 BREAKFAST IN MERCAT DE LA BOQUERIA

Mercat de la Boqueria (p93) is the largest of Barcelona's 40 markets and is an obligatory stop for breakfast. Lose yourself in the passageways. Your visit is not complete until you've finished with *un desayuno de cuchara* (breakfast eaten with a spoon or fork).

### 2 PRE-LUNCH SNACK

Stop for a light lunch snack accompanied by a *cava* (sparkling wine) or *vermut* (vermouth) at a sunny outdoor table. Where else in the world can you see elegant señoras enjoying their *bocadillo* (filled roll) with a glass of sparkling wine before lunch?

### 3 LUNCH IN THE BARRIO OF FISHERMEN

Try a seafood rice dish in any bar in the Barrio de Pescadores (Barrio of Fishermen), otherwise known as La Barceloneta. Wander the streets, study the various options and, above all, chose a place where there are far more locals than tourists.

### 4 AFTERNOON TEA

Pause for one of Barcelona's three traditional pastries – a *chocolate con churros* (deep-fried donuts dipped in thick chocolate), *melindro* (a small baked cake) or *ensaimada* (another sweet, baked pastry). The best places are the chocolaterías along Carrer del Pi or, even better, Carrer dels Banys Nous, close to Plaça Sant Josep Oriol in the Barri Gòtic.

### 5 A TAPAS DINNER

The best way to sample so many different recipes is to base your dinner around tapas until your stomach says enough. You could stay the whole meal in one bar, but most locals hop from one bar to the next, trying the various house specialities in each one.

# If You Like…
## Tapas

If you like tapas, you find fantastic options all over the geographical and culinary map in Barcelona.

### 1 BAR PINOTXO
(Map p62; www.pinotxobar.com; Mercat de la Boqueria; mains €8-15; ⏰6am-4pm Mon-Sat; MLiceu) Bar Pinotxo is arguably La Boqueria's, and even Barcelona's, best tapas bar. It sits among the half-dozen or so informal eateries within the market, and the popular owner might serve up chickpeas with a sweet sauce of pine nuts and raisins, a fantastically soft mix of potato and spinach sprinkled with coarse salt, soft baby squid with cannellini beans, or a quivering cube of caramel-sweet pork belly.

### 2 CAL PEP
(Map p62; ☎93 310 79 61; www.calpep.com; Plaça de les Olles 8; mains €12-20; ⏰7.30-11.30pm Mon, 1-3.45pm & 7.30-11.30pm Tue-Fri, 1-3.45pm Sat, closed last 3 weeks Aug; MBarceloneta) It's getting a foot in the door here that's the problem – there can be queues out into the square with people trying to get in. Most people are happy elbowing their way to the bar for some of the tastiest gourmet seafood tapas in town.

### 3 CATA 1.81
(Map p82; ☎93 323 68 18; www.cata181.com; Carrer de València 181; tapas €6-8; ⏰7pm-midnight Mon-Sat; MPasseig de Gràcia) A beautifully designed venue, this is the place to come for fine wines and dainty gourmet dishes such as *raviolis amb bacallà* (salt-cod dumplings) or *truita de patates i tòfona negre* (thick potato tortilla with a delicate trace of black truffle).

Nice touches include the home-baked bread and cakes.

### Mam i Teca                    Catalan €€
(Map p62; ☎93 441 33 35; Carrer de la Lluna 4; mains €9-12; ⏰1-4pm & 8pm-midnight Mon, Wed-Fri & Sun, closed Sat lunch; MSant Antoni) A tiny place with half a dozen tables, Mam i Teca is as much a lifestyle choice

as a restaurant. Locals drop in and hang about at the bar, and diners are treated to Catalan dishes made with locally sourced products and adhering to Slow Food principles. Try, for example, cod fried in olive oil with garlic and red pepper, or pork ribs with chickpeas.

### Caravelle                    International €€
(Map p62; ☎93 317 98 92; Carrer del Pintor Fortuny 31; mains €10-13; ⏰8.30am-6.30pm Mon-Wed, 8.30am-1am Thu, 10.30am-1am Sat, 10.30am-6.30pm Sun; MLiceu) A bright little joint, beloved of the hipster element of the Raval and anyone with a discerning palate. Tacos as you've never tasted them (cod, lime aioli and radish; pulled pork with roast corn and avocado), a superior steak sandwich on homemade brioche with pickled celeriac and all manner of soul food. Drinks are every bit as inventive – try the homemade ginger beer or grapefruit soda.

## LA RIBERA

### Bormuth                    Tapas €
(Map p62; ☎93 310 21 86; Carrer del Rec 31; tapas from €3.50; ⏰5pm-midnight Mon & Tue, noon-1am Wed, Thu & Sun, noon-2.30am Fri & Sat; MJaume I) Opened on the pedestrian Carrer del Rec in 2013, Bormuth has tapped into the vogue for old-school tapas with modern-times service and decor, and serves all the old favourites – *patatas bravas*, *ensaladilla* (Russian salad), tortilla – along with some less predictable and superbly prepared numbers (try the chargrilled red pepper with black pudding). The split-level dining room is never less than animated, but there's a more peaceful space with a single long table if you can assemble a group.

### Casa Delfín                    Spanish €€
(Map p62; ☎93 319 50 88; www.tallerdetapas.com; Passeig del Born 36; mains €10-15; ⏰8am-midnight daily, until 1am Fri & Sat; MBarceloneta) One of Barcelona's culinary delights, Casa Delfín is everything you dream of when you think of Catalan (and Mediterranean) cooking. Start with the tangy and sweet *calçots* (a cross between a leek and

an onion; February and March only) or salt-strewn *padron* peppers, moving on to grilled sardines speckled with parsley, then tackle the meaty monkfish roasted in white wine and garlic.

### Comerç 24 International €€€

(Map p62; ☏ 93 319 21 02; www.carlesabellan.com; Carrer del Comerç 24; mains €24-32; ⏲ 1.30-3.30pm & 8.30-11pm Tue-Sat; Ⓜ Barceloneta) Michelin-starred chef Carles Abellán playfully reinterprets the traditional (suckling pig 'Hanoi style'), as well as more international classics, such as the bite-sized mini-pizza sashimi with tuna; *melón con jamón*, a *millefeuille* of layered caramelised Iberian ham and thinly sliced melon, or oxtail with cauliflower purée. If your budget will stretch to it, try a little of almost everything with the 'Menú del Gran Festival' (€116).

## LA BARCELONETA & THE WATERFRONT

### Can Recasens Catalan €€

( ☏ 93 300 81 23; Rambla del Poblenou 102; mains €6-14; ⏲ 9pm-1am Mon-Sat & 1-4pm Sat; Ⓜ Poblenou) One of Poblenou's most romantic settings, Can Recasens hides a warren of warmly lit rooms full of oil paintings, flickering candles, fairy lights and baskets of fruit. The food is outstanding, with a mix of salads, fondues, smoked meats, cheeses, and open-faced sandwiches piled high with delicacies such as wild mushrooms and brie, *escalivada* (grilled vegetables) and gruyere, and spicy chorizo.

### Can Majó Seafood €€€

(Map p62; ☏ 93 221 54 55; www.canmajo.es; Carrer del Almirall Aixada 23; mains €16-26; ⏲ 1-4pm Tue-Sun & 8-11.30pm Tue-Sat; ☒ 45, 57, 59, 64 or 157, Ⓜ Barceloneta) Virtually on the beach (with tables outside in summer), Can Majó has a long and steady reputation for fine seafood, particularly its rice dishes and bountiful *suquets* (fish stews). The bouillabaisse of fish and seafood is succulent. Sit outside (there are heat lamps in winter) and admire the beach goers.

## L'EIXAMPLE

### Fastvínic Cafe €

(Map p82; ☏ 93 487 32 41; www.fastvinic.com; Carrer de la Diputació 251; sandwiches €4.25-12; ⏲ noon-midnight Mon-Sat; Ⓜ Passeig de Gracia) ✿ A project in sustainability all

Tapas

round, this is Slow Food done fast, with ingredients, wine and building materials all sourced from Catalonia. Designed by Alfons Tost, there are air-purifying plants, energy-efficient LED lighting and a water and food recycling system.

### Tapas 24
Tapas €€

(Map p82; ☎ 93 488 09 77; www.carlesabellan. com; Carrer de la Diputació 269; tapas €4-9; ☉ 9am-midnight Mon-Sat; Ⓜ Passeig de Gràcia) Carles Abellan, master of Comerç 24 in La Ribera, runs this basement tapas haven known for its gourmet versions of old faves. Specials include the *bikini* (toasted ham and cheese sandwich – here the ham is cured and the truffle makes all the difference) and a thick black *arròs negre de sípia* (squid-ink black rice).

### Cinc Sentits
International €€€

(Map p82; ☎ 93 323 94 90; www.cincsentits. com; Carrer d'Aribau 58; tasting menus €65-109;

☉ 1.30-3pm & 8.30-10pm Tue-Sat; Ⓜ Passeig de Gràcia) Enter the realm of the 'Five Senses' to indulge in a jaw-dropping tasting menu (there is no à la carte, although dishes can be tweaked to suit diners' requests), consisting of a series of small, experimental dishes. The key is the use of fresh local produce, such as fish landed on the Costa Brava and top-quality suckling pig from Extremadura, along with the kind of creative genius that has earned chef Jordi Artal a Michelin star.

### Alkímia
Catalan €€€

(☎ 93 207 61 15; www.alkimia.cat; Carrer de l'Indústria 79; mains €18-29; ☉ 1.30-3.30pm & 8-11pm Mon-Fri; Ⓜ Sagrada Família) Jordi Vilà, a culinary alchemist, serves up refined Catalan dishes with a twist in this elegant, white-walled locale well off the tourist trail. Dishes such as his *arròs de nyora i safrà amb escamarlans de la costa* (saffron and sweet-chilli rice with crayfish) earned Vilà his first Michelin star. He presents a series of set menus from €68 to €130.

## MONTJUÏC

### Quimet i Quimet
Tapas €€

(Map p62; ☎93 442 31 42; Carrer del Poeta Cabanyes 25; tapas €4-11; ⏱noon-4pm & 7-10.30pm Mon-Fri, noon-4pm Sat & Sun; Ⓜ Paral·lel) Quimet i Quimet is a family-run business that has been passed down from generation to generation. There's barely space to swing a *calamar* in this bottle-lined, standing-room-only place, but it is a treat for the palate, with *montaditos* (tapas on a slice of bread) made to order. Let the folk behind the bar advise you, and order a drop of fine wine to accompany the food.

### Tickets
Modern Spanish €€€

(www.ticketsbar.es; Avinguda del Paral·lel 164; tapas €6-15; ⏱7-11.30pm Tue-Fri, 1.30-3.30pm & 7-11.30pm Sat, closed Aug; Ⓜ Paral·lel) This is one of the sizzling tickets in the restaurant world, a tapas bar opened by Ferran Adrià, of the legendary El Bulli, and his brother Albert. And unlike El Bulli, it's an affordable venture – if you can book a table, that is (you can only book online, and two months in advance).

## 🍷 Drinking

### Dry Martini
Bar

(☎93 217 50 72; www.javierdelasmuelas.com; Carrer d'Aribau 162-166; ⏱1pm-2.30am Mon-Thu, 6pm-3am Fri & Sat; Ⓜ Diagonal) Waiters with a discreetly knowing smile will attend to your cocktail needs here. The house drink, taken at the bar or in one of the plush green leather lounges, is a safe bet. The gin and tonic comes in an enormous mug-sized glass – a couple of these and you're well on the way. Out the back is a restaurant, **Speakeasy** (☎93 217 50 80; www.javierdelasmuelas.com; Carrer d'Aribau 162-166; mains €19-28; ⏱1-4pm & 8pm-midnight Mon-Fri, 8pm-midnight Sat, closed Aug; Ⓜ Diagonal).

### La Caseta del Migdia
Bar

(☎617 956572; www.lacaseta.org; Mirador del Migdia; ⏱8pm-1am Wed & Thu, 8pm-2am Fri, noon-2am Sat, noon-1am Sun, weekends only in winter; Ⓜ Paral·lel, funicular) The effort of getting to what is, for all intents and purposes, a simple *chiringuito* (makeshift cafe-bar) is well worth it. Stare out to sea over a beer or coffee by day. As sunset approaches the atmosphere changes, as lounge music (from samba to funk) wafts out over the hammocks. Walk below the walls of the Castell de Montjuïc along the dirt track or follow Passeig del Migdia – watch out for signs for the Mirador del Migdia.

### Ocaña Bar

(Map p62; ☏ 93 676 48 14; www.ocana.cat; Plaça Reial 13; ⏰5pm-2.30am Mon-Fri, from 11am Sat & Sun; Ⓜ Liceu) Named after a flamboyant artist who once lived on Plaça Reial, Ocaña is a beautifully designed space with fluted columns, stone walls, candlelit chandeliers and plush furnishings. Have a seat on the terrace and watch the passing people parade, or head downstairs to the Moorish-inspired Apotheke bar or the chic lounge a few steps away, where DJs spin for a mix of beauties and bohemians on weekend nights.

### Bar Marsella Bar

(Map p62; Carrer de Sant Pau 65; ⏰10pm-2.30am Mon-Wed, 10pm-3am Thu-Sat; Ⓜ Liceu) This bar has been in business since 1820, and has served the likes of Hemingway, who was known to be slumped here over an *absenta* (absinthe). The bar still specialises in absinthe, a drink to be treated with respect. Your glass comes with a lump of sugar, a fork and a little bottle of mineral water. Hold the sugar on the fork, over your glass, and drip the water onto the sugar so that it dissolves into the absinthe, which turns yellow. The result should give you a warm glow.

### El Xampanyet Wine Bar

(Map p62; ☏ 93 319 70 03; Carrer de Montcada 22; ⏰noon-3.30pm & 7-11pm Tue-Sat, noon-4pm Sun; Ⓜ Jaume I) Nothing has changed for decades in this, one of the city's best-known cava bars. Plant yourself at the bar or seek out a table against the decoratively tiled walls for a glass or three of the cheap house cava and an assortment of tapas, such as the tangy *boquerons en vinagre* (fresh anchovies in vinegar).

### Monvínic Wine Bar

(Map p82; ☏ 932 72 61 87; www.monvinic.com; Carrer de la Diputació 249; ⏰wine bar 1.30-11pm Mon-Sat; Ⓜ Passeig de Gracia) Proclaimed as 'possibly the best wine bar in the world' by the *Wall Street Journal,* and apparently considered unmissable by El Bulli's sommelier, Monvínic is an ode, a rhapsody even, to wine loving. The interactive wine list sits on the bar for you to browse on a digital tablet similar to an iPad and boasts more than 3000 varieties.

### La Fira Bar

( ☏ 682 323 714; Carrer de Provença 171; admission €5 (incl 1 drink); ⏰11pm-5am Fri & Sat; Ⓡ FGC Provença) A designer bar with a difference. Wander in past distorting mirrors and ancient fairground attractions from Germany. Put in coins and listen to hens squawk. Speaking of squawking, the music swings wildly from whiffs of house through '90s hits to Spanish pop classics. You can spend the earlier part of the night trying some of the bar's shots – it claims to have 500 varieties (but we haven't counted them up).

### Les Gens Que J'Aime Bar

(Map p82; ☏ 93 215 68 79; www.lesgensquejaime. com; Carrer de València 286; ⏰6pm-2.30am Sun-Thu, 7pm-3am Fri & Sat; Ⓜ Passeig de Gràcia) This intimate basement relic of the 1960s follows a deceptively simple formula: chilled jazz music in the background, minimal lighting from an assortment of flea-market lamps and a cosy, cramped scattering of red velvet-backed lounges around tiny dark tables.

## ⭐ Entertainment

### Palau de la Música Catalana Classical Music

(Map p62; ☏ 93 295 72 00; www.palaumusica. org; Carrer de Sant Francesc de Paula 2; ⏰box office 9.30am-9pm Mon-Sat; Ⓜ Urquinaona) A feast for the eyes, this Modernista confection is also the city's most traditional venue for classical and choral music, although it has a wide-ranging program, including flamenco, pop and – particularly – jazz. Just being here for a performance is an experience. Sip a

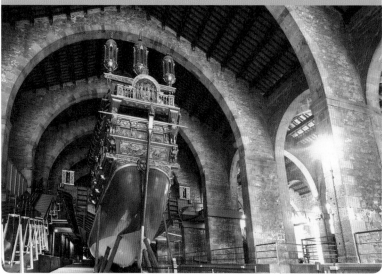

JEAN-PIERRE LESCOURRET/GETTY IMAGES ©

preconcert tipple in the foyer, its tiled pillars all a-glitter. Head up the grand stairway to the main auditorium, a whirlpool of Modernista whimsy.

### Filmoteca de Catalunya    Cinema
(Map p62; ☎93 567 10 70; www.filmoteca. cat; Plaça de Salvador Seguí 1-9; adult/concession €4/2 ; ⏰4-10pm Tue-Sun; Ⓜ Liceu) After almost a decade in the planning, the Filmoteca de Catalunya – Catalonia's national cinema – moved into this modern 6000-sq-metre building in 2012. It's a glass, metal and concrete beast that hulks in the midst of the most louche part of the Raval, but the building's interior shouts revival, with light and space, wall-to-wall windows, skylights and glass panels that let the sun in.

### Jazz Sí Club    Live Music
(Map p62; ☎93 329 00 20; www.tallerdemusics. com; Carrer de Requesens 2; admission €4-9, incl drink; ⏰8.30-11pm Tue-Sat, 6.30-10pm Sun; Ⓜ Sant Antoni) A cramped little bar run by the Taller de Músics (Musicians' Workshop) serves as the stage for a varied program of jazz jams through to some good flamenco (Friday nights). Thursday night is Cuban night, Tuesday and Sunday

are rock, and the rest are devoted to jazz and/or blues sessions. Concerts start around 9pm but the jam sessions can get going earlier.

### Sala Tarantos    Flamenco
(Map p62; ☎93 319 17 89; www.masimas.com/ tarantos; Plaça Reial 17; admission €10; ⏰shows 8.30pm, 9.30pm & 10.30pm; Ⓜ Liceu) Since 1963, this basement locale has been the stage for up-and-coming flamenco groups performing in Barcelona. These days Tarantos has become a mostly tourist-centric affair, with half-hour shows held three times a night. Still, it's a good introduction to flamenco, and not a bad setting for a drink.

### Harlem Jazz Club    Jazz
(Map p62; ☎93 310 07 55; www.harlemjazzclub. es; Carrer de la Comtessa de Sobradiel 8; admission around €7-8; ⏰8pm-5am Tue-Sat; Ⓜ Drassanes) This narrow, old-city dive is one of the best spots in town for jazz, as well as funk, Latin, blues and gypsy jazz. It attracts a mixed crowd who maintains a respectful silence during the acts. Most concerts start around 10pm. Get in early if you want a seat in front of the stage.

# 🛍️ Shopping

## Fires, Festes i Tradicions
Food, Drink

(Map p62; 📞93 269 12 61; Carrer de la Dagueria 13; ⏰4-8.30pm Mon, 10am-8.30pm Tue-Sat; M Jaume I) Whether assembling a picnic or hoping to bring home a few edible mementos, don't miss this little shop, which stocks a wide range of specialities from Catalonia, including jams, sweets, sausages and cheeses.

## L'Arca
Vintage, Clothing

(Map p62; 📞93 302 15 98; www.larca.es; Carrer dels Banys Nous 20; ⏰11am-2pm & 4.30-8.30pm; M Liceu) Step inside this enchanting shop for a glimpse of beautifully crafted apparel from the past, including 18th-century embroidered silk vests, elaborate silk kimonos, and wedding dresses and shawls from the 1920s. Owing to its incredible collection, it has provided clothing for films including *Titanic, Talk to Her* and *Perfume*.

## La Manual Alpargatera
Shoes

(Map p62; 📞93 301 01 72; lamanualalpargatera. es; Carrer d'Avinyó 7; ⏰9.30am-1.30pm & 4.30-8pm; M Liceu) Everyone from Salvador Dalí to Jean Paul Gaultier has ordered a pair of *espadrilles* (rope-soled canvas shoes or sandals) from this famous store, which is the birthplace of the iconic footwear. The shop was founded just after the Spanish Civil War, though the roots of the simple shoe design date back thousands of years.

## Vila Viniteca
Drink

(Map p62; 📞902 32 77 77; www.vilaviniteca.es; Carrer dels Agullers 7; ⏰8.30am-8.30pm Mon-Sat; M Jaume I) One of the best wine stores in Barcelona (and Lord knows, there are a few), this place has been searching out the best in local and imported wines since 1932. On a couple of November evenings it organises what has by now become an almost riotous wine-tasting event in Carrer dels Agullers and surrounding lanes, at which cellars from around Spain present their young new wines. At No 9 it has another store devoted to gourmet food products.

# ℹ️ Information

In addition to the following listed tourist offices, information booths operate at Estació Nord bus station, Plaça del Portal de la Pau and at the foot of the Mirador a Colom. At least three others are set up at various points around the city centre in summer.

Oficina d'Informació de Turisme de Barcelona has its main branch (Map p62; 📞93 285 38 34; www. barcelonaturisme.com; underground at Plaça de Catalunya 17-S; ⏰9.30am-9.30pm; M Catalunya) in Plaça de Catalunya. It concentrates on city information and can help book accommodation. The branch in the EU arrivals hall at Aeroport del Prat (Aeroport

Palau de la Música Catalana (p69)
MATT MUNRO/LONELY PLANET ©

del Prat, terminals 1, 2B & 2A; ⊙9am-9pm) has information on all of Catalonia; a smaller office at the international arrivals hall opens the same hours. The branch at Estació Sants (⊙8am-8pm; ⍰Estació Sants) has limited city information. There's also a helpful branch in the town hall (Map p62; ☑93 285 38 32; Carrer de la Ciutat 2; ⊙8.30am-8.30pm Mon-Fri, 9am-7pm Sat, 9am-2pm Sun & holidays; ⍰Jaume I).

La Rambla Information Booth (Map p62; www.barcelonaturisme.com; La Rambla dels Estudis 115; ⊙8.30am-8.30pm; ⍰Liceu)

Palau Robert Regional Tourist Office (Map p82; ☑93 238 80 91, from outside Catalonia 902 400012; www.gencat.net/probert; Passeig de Gràcia 107; ⊙10am-8pm Mon-Sat, to 2.30pm Sun; ⍰Diagonal) A host of material on Catalonia, audiovisual resources, a bookshop and a branch of Turisme Juvenil de Catalunya (for youth travel).

## ⓘ Getting There & Away

### Air

Aeroport del Prat (☑902 404704; www.aena.es) is 12km southwest of the centre at El Prat de Llobregat. Barcelona is a big international and domestic destination, with direct flights from North America, as well as many European cities.

Several budget airlines, including Ryanair, use Girona-Costa Brava airport, 11km south of Girona and about 80km north of Barcelona. Buses connect with Barcelona's Estació del Nord bus station.

### Bus

Long-distance buses leave from Estació del Nord. A plethora of companies operates to different parts of Spain, although many come under the umbrella of Alsa (☑902 422242; www.alsa.es). For other companies, ask at the bus station. There are frequent services to Madrid, Valencia and Zaragoza (20 or more a day) and several daily departures to distant destinations such as Burgos, Santiago de Compostela and Seville.

Eurolines (www.eurolines.es), in conjunction with local carriers all over Europe, is the main international carrier. Its website provides links to national operators; it runs services across Europe and to Morocco from Estació del Nord, and Estació d'Autobusos de Sants (Carrer de Viriat; ⍰Estació Sants), next to Estació Sants

## ♥ If You Like...
## Markets

If you like browsing markets for food, antiques or just pieces of old junk, check out the following.

### 1 MERCAT DE SANTA CATERINA
(Map p62; ☑93 319 17 40; www.mercatsantacaterina.com; Avinguda de Francesc Cambó 16; ⊙7.30am-2pm Mon, to 3.30pm Tue, Wed & Sat, to 8.30pm Thu & Fri, closed afternoons Jul & Aug; ⍰Jaume I) Come shopping for your tomatoes at this extraordinary-looking produce market, designed by Enric Miralles and Benedetta Tagliabue to replace its 19th-century predecessor. Finished in 2005, it is distinguished by its kaleidoscopic and undulating roof, held up above the bustling produce stands, restaurants, cafes and bars by twisting slender branches of what look like grey steel trees.

### 2 MERCAT DE LA BOQUERIA
(Map p62; ☑93 318 25 84; www.boqueria.info; La Rambla 91; ⊙8am-8.30pm Mon-Sat, closed Sun; ⍰Liceu) Mercat de la Boqueria is possibly La Rambla's most interesting building, not so much for its Modernista-influenced design (it was actually built over a long period, from 1840 to 1914, on the site of the former St Joseph monastery), but for the action of the food market within.

### 3 MERCAT DE SANT ANTONI
(Map p62; ☑93 209 31 58; www.mercatdesantantoni.com; Carrer de Comte d'Urgell 1; ⊙7am-2.30pm & 5-8.30pm Mon-Thu, 7am-8.30pm Fri & Sat; ⍰Sant Antoni) Just beyond the western edge of El Raval is Mercat de Sant Antoni, a glorious old iron and brick building that is currently undergoing renovation. In the meantime, a huge marquee has been erected alongside to house a food market. The second-hand book market still takes place alongside on Sunday mornings.

Barcelona. Another carrier is Linebús (www.linebus.com).

### Car & Motorcycle

The AP7 autopista (motorway) is the main toll road from France (via Girona and Figueres). It

Fundació Antoni Tàpies (p76)

DAMIEN SIMONIS/GETTY IMAGES ©

skirts inland around the city before proceeding south to Valencia and Alicante. About 40km southwest of Barcelona, the AP2, also a toll road, branches west off the AP7 towards Zaragoza. From there it links up with the A-2 dual carriageway for Madrid (no tolls). Several other shorter tollways fan out into the Catalan heartland from Barcelona.

## Train

The main train station in Barcelona is **Estació Sants** (Plaça dels Països Catalans; **M** Estació Sants), located 2.5km west of La Rambla. Direct overnight trains from Paris, Geneva, Milan and Zurich arrive here. From here it's a short metro ride to the Ciutat Vella or L'Eixample.

Estació Sants has a tourist office, a telephone and fax office, currency exchange booths open between 8am and 10pm, ATMs and left-luggage lockers.

Train is the most convenient overland option for reaching Barcelona from major Spanish centres such as Madrid and Valencia. It can be a long haul from other parts of Europe, where budget flights frequently offer a saving in time and money.

Eighteen high-speed Tren de Alta Velocidad Española (AVE) trains between Madrid and Barcelona run daily in each direction, nine of them in under three hours. A typical one-way price is

€114 but it comes down if you book a return or book well in advance on the website (which can bring the cost down to about €45).

## 🛈 Getting Around

Barcelona has abundant options for getting around town. The excellent metro can get you most places, with buses and trams filling in the gaps. Taxis are the best option late at night.

## To/From the Airport

**El Prat airport** Frequent aerobuses make the 35-minute run into town (€5.65) from 6am to 1am. Taxis cost around €25.

**Girona-Costa Brava airport** The 'Barcelona Bus' operated by Sagales (one way/return €16/25, 90 minutes) is timed with Ryanair flights and goes direct to Barcelona's Estació del Nord.

**Reus airport** Buses operated by Hispano-Igualdino (one way/return €16/25, 90 minutes) is timed with Ryanair flights and goes direct to Barcelona's Estació d'Autobuses de Sants.

## Car & Motorcycle

With the convenience of public transport and the high price of parking in the city, it's unwise to drive in Barcelona. However, if you're planning a road trip outside the city, a car is handy .

Avis, Europcar, National/Atesa and Hertz have desks at El Prat airport, Estació Sants and Estació del Nord.

## Public Transport

### Bus

The city transport authority, **Transports Metropolitans de Barcelona** (TMB; ☎010; www. tmb.net), runs buses along most city routes every few minutes from 5am or 6am to 10pm or 11pm. Many routes pass through Plaça de Catalunya and/or Plaça de la Universitat.

### Metro & FGC

The easy-to-use TMB Metro system has 11 numbered and colour-coded lines. It runs from 5am to midnight Sunday to Thursday and holidays, from 5am to 2am on Friday and days immediately preceding holidays, and 24 hours on Saturday.

Suburban trains run by the **Ferrocarrils de la Generalitat de Catalunya** (FGC; ☎93 205 15 15; www.fgc.net) include a couple of useful city lines. All lines heading north from Plaça de Catalunya stop at Carrer de Provença and Gràcia. One of these lines (L7) goes to Tibidabo and another (L6 to Reina Elisenda) has a stop near the Monestir de Pedralbes. Most trains from Plaça de Catalunya continue beyond Barcelona to Sant Cugat, Sabadell and Terrassa. Other FGC lines head west from Plaça d'Espanya, including one for Manresa that is handy for the trip to Montserrat.

## Tickets & Targetas

The metro, FGC trains, rodalies/*cercanías* (Renfe-run local trains) and buses come under one zoned-fare regime. Single-ride tickets on all standard transport within Zone 1 cost €2.15.

*Targetas* are multi-trip transport tickets. They are sold at all city-centre metro stations. The prices given here are for travel in Zone 1. Children under four years of age travel free.

**Targeta T-10** (€10.30) Ten rides (each valid for 1¼ hours) on the metro, buses and FGC trains. You can change between metro, FGC, *rodalies* and buses.

**Targeta T-DIA** (€7.60) Unlimited travel on all transport for one day.

**Two-/Three-/Four-/Five-Day Tickets** (€14/20/26/31) These provide unlimited travel on all transport except the Aerobús; buy them at metro stations and tourist offices.

## Taxi

Taxis charge €2.10 flag fall plus meter charges of €1.03 per kilometre (€1.30 from 8pm to 8am and all day on weekends). A further €3.10 is added for all trips to/from the airport, and €1 for luggage bigger than 55cm x 35cm x 35cm. The trip from Estació Sants to Plaça de Catalunya, about 3km, costs about €11. You can flag a taxi down in the streets or call a **taxi** (Fonotaxi ☎93 300 11 00, Radiotaxi ☎93 303 30 33, Radiotaxi BCN ☎93 225 00 00)

The call-out charge is €3.40 (€4.20 at night and on weekends).

# Catalonia & Eastern Spain

**From metropolitan Barcelona spreads a land of such diversity that you could spend weeks discovering it.** The stunning cove beaches of the Costa Brava are the jewel in the tourism crown, but for those who need more than a suntan, urban fun and Jewish history is to be found in the medieval city of Girona, while Figueres offers a shrine to Salvador Dalí in the form of its 'theatre-museum'. For something bigger and brasher, Valencia, way off to the south, is one of Spain's most engaging cities, filled with monuments spanning the centuries and an increasingly avant-garde spirit. Running across the north of the region, the Pyrenees rise to mighty 3000m peaks from a series of green and often remote valleys, dotted with villages that retain a palpable rural and even medieval air.

Add it all together and you get one of the most enticing areas of Spain.

Roses, Costa Brava

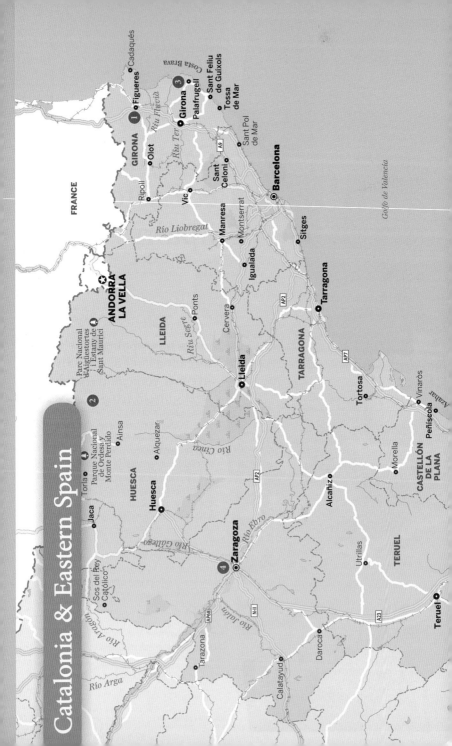
# Catalonia & Eastern Spain

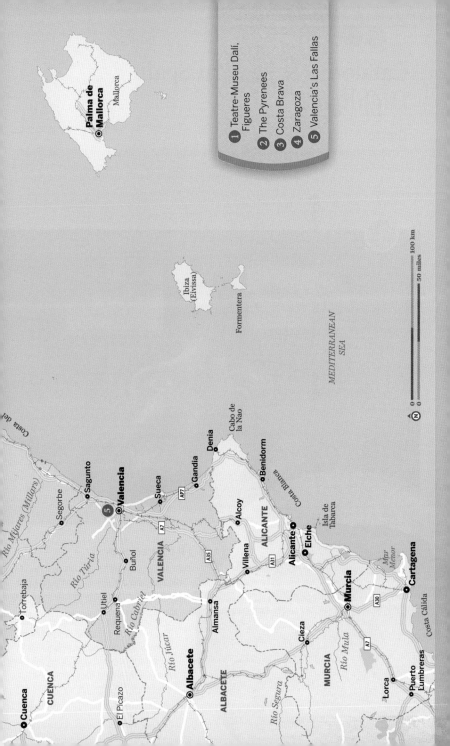

# Catalonia & Eastern Spain Highlights

## Teatre-Museu Dalí, Figueres

Dalí said: 'I want my museum to be like a single block, a labyrinth, a great surrealist object. The people who come to see it will leave with the sensation of having had a theatrical dream'. He also described the Teatre-Museu Dalí (p116) as a self-portrait, showing us his desires, enigmas, obsessions and passions. Face of Mae West Which Can Be Used as an Apartment, Teatre-Museu Dalí

### 2 The Pyrenees

The Pyrenees (p122) are Spain's most extensive and soul-stirring mountains. Although they unfold with similar drama across much of the range, if you had to choose just one mountain corner it would have to be the breathtaking Parque Nacional de Ordesa y Monte Perdido, where a dragon's back of limestone peaks skirts the French border.

Parque Nacional de Ordesa y Monte Perdido (p122)

## Costa Brava

**3**

Stretching north to the French border, the Costa Brava (p114), or 'rugged coast', is by far the prettiest and classiest of Spain's three principal holiday coasts. Though you'll find plenty of overdevelopment and English breakfasts, there are also unspoiled coves, charming seaside towns with quality restaurants, spectacular scenery and some of Spain's best diving around the protected Illes Medes. Scuba diving, Costa Brava

**4**

## Zaragoza

Every taste is catered for in Zaragoza (p118). For architecture enthusiasts there's a sacred cathedral beloved by pilgrims, as well as the gilded La Seo and the Aljafería, Spain's finest Islamic building outside of Andalucía. History buffs will love the signposts to Roman Caesaraugusta, while Zaragoza nights are the stuff of legend. Entrance of Aljafería (p120)

**5**

MIGUELANGEL MUÑOZ/GETTY IMAGES ©

## Valencia's Las Fallas

Though less well known than Barcelona, Madrid or Seville, Valencia is still one of Spain's most exciting cities. A magnificent cathedral, the lovely old quarter, fine beaches and outstanding restaurants are reason enough to visit. But Valencia is also home to the Ciudad de las Artes y las Ciencias (p128), an exceptional showpiece for the exciting new wave of innovative Spanish architecture. If you're visiting in mid-March you'll experience Las Fallas, an explosion of bonfires and all-night partying. Las Fallas de San José (p129)

# Catalonia & Eastern Spain's Best...

## Places for Roman and Romanesque

o **Tarragona** Spain's oldest and, arguably, finest set of Roman ruins was declared a World Heritage Site in 2000. (p109)

o **Zaragoza** Roman remains of Caesaraugusta. (p118)

o **Cartagena** Watch as archaeologists continue to uncover the city's Roman past. (p130)

o **Montserrat** Historic monastery under a towering mountain. (p106)

## Places to Recharge the Batteries

o **Cadaqués** Dalí's ghost and whitewashed Costa Brava charm. (p114)

o **Aínsa** Dreamy Aragonese hill town with panoramic views of the surrounding Pyrenees Mountains. (p124)

o **Valles de Echo & Ansó** The Aragonese Pyrenees' least-trammelled valleys. (p123)

o **Ochagavía** A charming stone village in the mist-shrouded western Pyrenees. (p123)

## Places to Get Active

o **Parque Nacional de Ordesa y Monte Perdido** Arguably the best hiking in Spain. (p122)

o **Serra del Cadí** A rock-climber's paradise in the Catalan Pyrenees. (p123)

o **Vall Ferrera** Great walking in Catalonia's largest nature reserve. (p123)

o **Val d'Aran** Skiing and hiking in this remote and peaceful mountain area. (p123)

## Places for a Great Meal

○ **El Celler de Can Roca, Girona** Rated the best restaurant in the world in 2013. (p113)

○ **Mas Pau, Figueres** Michelin-approved Catalan perfection. (p115)

○ **Casa Pascualillo, Zaragoza** Considered one of the best tapas bars in Spain. (p121)

○ **Delicat, Valencia City** Innovative tapas. (p129)

○ **Txalaka, Girona** Put a Basque chef in Catalonia and the results are bound to be exceptional. (p113)

**Left:** Cadaqués (p114);
**Above:** Monestir de Montserrat (p106)

# Need to Know

### ADVANCE PLANNING

○ **Three months before** Make sure you have your accommodation booked if you're arriving during the Las Fallas festival in Valencia.

○ **Two months before** Book your accommodation if you're planning to stay along the Costa Brava.

### RESOURCES

○ **Catalonia** (www.gencat. net/probert) Regional tourist office site for Catalonia.

○ **Aragón** (www. turismodearagon.com) good resource if you want to plan your trip around Aragón without having to make the bookings yourself.

○ **Valencia City** (www. turisvalencia.es) Everything you need to plan your visit to Valencia City.

○ **Beaches** (www. magrama.gob.es/ es/costas/servicios/ guia-playas) Guide to beaches; Spanish but self-explanatory.

### GETTING AROUND

○ **Air** International airports in Barcelona, Girona (Ryanair's Spanish hub), Valencia and Zaragoza.

○ **Bus** Intermittent services in the Pyrenees.

○ **Road** Coastal motorways and towards Madrid; small mountain roads in the Pyrenees.

○ **Train** Excellent network along the coast with good connections to the rest of Spain (often via Barcelona or Valencia).

○ **Train & Boat** In summer, a combination of rodalies (local trains) and boats connects the southern Costa Brava with Barcelona.

### BE FOREWARNED

○ **Dalí bookings** Book ahead for Teatre-Museu Dalí in Catalonia.

○ **Crowd avoidance** In summer the coast is packed. Head inland, where valleys and hill towns offer a more relaxed Spanish experience.

○ **Festivals** Big festivals such as Valencia's Las Fallas (March) and La Tomatino (August) equal full rooms and high prices. Plan well ahead.

# Catalonia & Eastern Spain Itineraries

*Catalonia and the Pyrenees encompass a huge variety of landscapes, sights and experiences. The following routes take you from sunny beaches to energetic cities and tranquil mountain passes, revealing the region's best.*

TORLA • • PARQUE NACIONAL  FRANCE
AÍNSA • DE ORDESA Y
MONTE PERDIDO
FIGUERES ❶ ❹ CADAQUÉS
GIRONA ❷ ❸ LA PERA
ZARAGOZA ❷
MEDITERRANEAN SEA
Golfo de Valencia
VALENCIA ❶

**3 DAYS**

### FIGUERES TO CADAQUÉS
## IN DALI'S FOOTSTEPS

Few artists have left such an enduring impression upon the territory they inhabited as Salvador Dalí. Your journey through Dalí's Catalonia begins, just as the great man's life did, in ❶**Figueres**, an unexciting town that may have inspired Salvador to seek refuge in a surreal world of his own making. It nonetheless hosts the mind-blowing Teatre-Museu Dalí, the single-most significant legacy to survive Dalí after his death. South of Figueres, charming ❷**Girona**, with its beautiful riverside setting, fascinating old quarter and enviable array of sights, is one of the urban highlights of northern Spain

and an ideal overnight base for the ❸**Castell de Púbol** in La Pera. This mansion's foundations may belong to the Gothic and Renaissance eras, but Dalí transformed it into a zany epitaph to his muse, Gala. Away to the northwest, close to mainland Spain's easternmost point, ❹**Cadaqués** is where Dalí spent much of his adult life. It is such a beautiful coastal village that you may feel tempted to do the same. If you can't stay forever then make do with a stroll through the blinding white old quarter and a hunt for the perfect nearby beach and restaurant.

**VALENCIA TO PARQUE NACIONAL DE ORDESA Y MONTE PERDIDO**
# LIFE IN THE INTERIOR

The underexplored province of Aragón may climb steeply up into the Pyrenees, but its central and southern heartland is the soul of inland Spain. Start in ❶ **Valencia**, a vibrant and utterly Mediterranean city. You'd need at least a day or two to soak up the buzz and explore the state-of-the-art museums and intriguing nooks and crannies of the old quarter. Move onto ❷ **Zaragoza**, one of Spain's most engaging cities. By day it's a living museum with weighty landmarks to Roman, Islamic and Christian Spain. But once night falls, Zaragoza has perfected the art of tapas, which is a precursor to frenetic nights that

are famous throughout the country. The quiet evenings of enchanted ❸ **Aínsa**, the quintessential Aragonese hill village, are within sight of the snow-speckled Pyrenees. Aínsa offers a radical change of pace and its central plaza is one of the most impressive small town squares in Spain. Continue the rural feel in ❹ **Torla**, gateway to the sublime ❺ **Parque Nacional de Ordesa y Monte Perdido**, which is home to some of the finest hiking trails in Spain and the country's most breathtaking high mountain scenery.

Río Onyar, Girona (p110)
STEFANO POLITI MARKOVINA/AWL IMAGES LTD/GETTY IMAGES ©

# Discover Catalonia & Eastern Spain

Tossa de Mar, Costa Brava
HIROSHI HIGUCHI/GETTY IMAGES ©

## AROUND BARCELONA

### Montserrat

Montserrat (Serrated Mountain), 50km northwest of Barcelona, is a 1236m-high mountain of strangely rounded rock pillars, shaped by wind, rain and frost from a conglomeration of limestone, pebbles and sand that once lay under the sea (or else by baby angels, depending on whom you talk to). With the historic Benedictine Monestir de Montserrat, one of Catalonia's most important shrines, cradled at 725m on its side, it's the most popular outing from Barcelona. From the mountain, on a clear day, you can see as far as the Pyrenees. Its caves and many mountain paths make for spectacular rambles, reachable by funiculars.

The *cremallera* (rack-and-pinion train) chugs up the mountainside, arriving just below the monastery, next to the cable car station.

### ◎ Sights & Activities

**Monestir de Montserrat**   Monastery
(www.abadiamontserrat.net) This monastery was founded in 1025 to commemorate numerous visions of the Virgin Mary. Today it houses a community of about 80 monks, and pilgrims come to venerate La Moreneta (the Black Virgin), a 12th-century Romanesque wooden sculpture of Mary with the baby Jesus; La Moreneta has been Catalonia's official patron since 1881.

**Museu de Montserrat**   Museum
(www.museudemontserrat.com; Plaça de Santa Maria; adult/student €7/6; ⊙10am-5.45pm,

**to 6.45pm Jul-Aug)** This museum has an excellent collection, ranging from an Egyptian mummy and Gothic altarpieces to fine canvases by Caravaggio, El Greco, Picasso and several Impressionists as well as a comprehensive collection of 20th-century classic Catalan art and some fantastic Orthodox icons.

## ⓘ Getting There & Away

Take the C16 from Barcelona, then the C58 shortly after Terrassa, followed by the C55 to Monistrol de Montserrat. Leave the car at the free car park at Monistrol Vila and take the *cremallera* up to the top.

The R5 line trains operated by **FGC** (www.fgc.net) run hourly from Plaça d'Espanya station, starting at 8.36am (52 to 56 minutes). They connect with the **cable car** (☏ 93 835 00 05; www.aeridemontserrat.com; one way/return €7/10; ☺ 9.40am-7pm, closed mid-Jan–Feb) at the Montserrat Aeri stop and the **cremallera** (☏ 902 312020; www.cremalleradmontserrat.com; one way/return €5.40/8.60) at the following stop, Monistrol de Montserrat.

····································

# Sitges

POP 28,620

Just 35km along the coast from Barcelona, this fishing-village-turned-pumping-beach-resort town has been a favourite with upper-class Barcelonians since the late 19th century, as well as a key location for the burgeoning Modernisme movement which paved the way for the likes of Picasso. A famous gay destination, in July and August Sitges turns into one big beach party with a nightlife to rival Ibiza; the beaches are long and sandy, the tapas bars prolific and the Carnaval bacchanalian.

## ◉ Sights & Activities

**Museu Romàntic**                    Museum
(www.museusdesitges.cat; Carrer de Sant Gaudenci 1; adult/student €3.50/2; ☺ 10am-2pm & 3.30-7pm Tue-Sat, 11am-3pm Sun) Housed in a late-18th-century Can Llopis mansion, this faded museum recreates with its furnishings and dioramas the lifestyle of a

19th-century Catalan landowning family, the likes of which would often have made their money in South America, and were commonly dubbed *indianos* on their return. Upstairs is an entertaining collection of several hundred antique dolls, some downright creepy. Hours vary seasonally.

### Fundació Stämpfli Art Contemporani
Gallery

(www.museusdesitges.cat; Plaça d'Ajuntament; adult/child €3.50/2; ☺3.30-7pm Fri, 10am-2pm & 3.30-7pm Sat, 11am-3pm Sun) This excellent gallery focuses on 20th-century art from the 1960s onwards. The striking paintings and sculptures by artists from all over the world, spread throughout the two renovated historical buildings, include works by Richard 'Buddy' di Rosa, Oliver Mosset and Takis. Extended hours in high season.

## 🍴 Eating

### El Pou
Tapas €€

(www.elpoudesitges.com; Carrer de Sant Pau 5; dishes €4-10; ☺noon-4pm & 8-11.30pm Wed-Mon; 🔊) The tiny Wagyu beef burgers at this friendly gourmet tapas place are an absolute delight, and the rest doesn't lag far behind; the traditional *patatas bravas* (potatoes in a spicy tomato sauce) sit alongside the likes of *mojama* (salted dried tuna) with almonds, fried aubergine and *xató* (a green salad with cod, tuna, anchovies and olives with a dressing containing garlic, almonds, hazelnuts, chilli pepper and more); the presentation delights the eye as much as the flavours delight the palate.

### eF & Gi
Fusion €€€

(www.efgirestaurant.com; Carrer Major 33; mains €18-25; ☺1-4pm & 7.30-11.30pm Wed-Mon Mar-Jan; 🔊) Fabio and Greg (eF & Gi) are not afraid to experiment and the results are startlingly good: the mostly Mediterranean menu, with touches of Asian inspiration, throws out such delights as chargrilled beef infused with lemongrass and kaffir lime, and tuna loin encrusted with peanuts and kalamata olives with mango chutney. Don't skip the dessert, either.

## ℹ️ Information

**Main Tourist Office** (📞938 94 42 51; www.sitgestur.cat; Plaça de E Maristany 2; ☺10am-2pm & 4-6.30pm or 8pm Mon-Sat, 10am-2pm Sun) By the train station.

**Left:** Museu Romàntic, Sitges (p107);
**Below:** Catedral facade, Tarragona (p110)

(LEFT) DEA/G.CIGOLINI/GETTY IMAGES ©; (BELOW) NICOLAS MOULIN PHOTOGRAPHY/GETTY IMAGES ©

## ⓘ Getting There & Away

From about 6am to 10pm four R2 rodalies trains an hour run to Barcelona's Passeig de Gràcia and Estació Sants (€4.10, 27 to 46 minutes). You can reach Barcelona airport (€3.40) by changing at El Prat de Llobregat. **Buses** (www.monbus.cat) also run to the airport from Passeig de Vilafranca (€6, 35 minutes).

## Tarragona

POP 140,180

The eternally sunny port city of Tarragona is a fascinating mix of Mediterranean beach life, Roman history and medieval alleyways. Easily Catalonia's most important Roman site, Tarragona's number-one attraction is its seaside-facing Roman amphitheatre. The town's medieval heart is one of the most beautifully designed in Spain, its maze of narrow cobbled streets encircled by steep walls and crowned with a splendid cathedral and its sandstone buildings seemingly suffused with golden light. Add into the mix plenty of tempting food options and an array of bars heaving into the wee hours and you get the most exciting urban centre in southern Catalonia.

## ◎ Sights & Activities

The tourist office dishes out three handy booklets detailing routes around the city taking in Roman, medieval and Modernista sites.

### Museu d'Història de Tarragona                    Ruins

(MHT; www.museutgn.com; adult/child per site €3.30/free, all sites €11.05/free; ⊙ sites 9am-9pm Tue-Sat, 10am-3pm Sun Easter-Sep, 10am-7pm Tue-Sat, 10am-3pm Sun Oct-Easter) The Museu d'Història de Tarragona consists of various separate Unesco World Heritage Roman sites, as well as some other historic buildings around town. Buy a combined ticket and get exploring!

**109**

### Museu Nacional Arqueològic de Tarragona
Museum

(www.mnat.cat; Plaça del Rei 5; adult/child €2.40/free; ⏱9.30am-6pm Tue-Sat, 10am-2pm Sun) This excellent museum does justice to the cultural and material wealth of Roman Tarraco. Well-laid-out exhibits include part of the Roman city walls, frescoes, sculpture and pottery. The mosaic collection traces the changing trends – from simple black-and-white designs to complex full-colour creations. A highlight is the large, almost complete *Mosaic de Peixos de la Pineda*, showing fish and sea creatures. It's open extended hours in high season.

### Catedral
Cathedral

(www.catedraldetarragona.com; Plaça de la Seu; adult/child €5/3; ⏱10am-7pm Mon-Sat mid-Mar–Oct, 10am-5pm Mon-Fri, 10am-7pm Sat Nov–mid-Mar) Sitting grandly atop town, Tarragona's cathedral has both Romanesque and Gothic features, as typified by the main facade. The cloister has Gothic vaulting and Romanesque carved capitals, one of which shows rats conducting a cat's funeral...until the cat comes back to life! It's a lesson about passions seemingly lying dormant until they reveal themselves. Chambers off the cloister house the **Museu Diocesà**, with an extensive collection extending from Roman hairpins to some lovely 12th- to 14th-century polychrome woodcarvings of a breastfeeding Virgin.

## ✖️ Eating

The quintessential Tarragona seafood experience can be had in **Serrallo**, the town's fishing port. About a dozen bars and restaurants here sell the day's catch, and on summer weekends in particular the place is packed.

### AQ
Catalan €€

(✆977 21 59 54; www.aq-restaurant.com; Carrer de les Coques 7; degustation €40-50; ⏱1.30-3.30pm & 8.30-11pm Tue-Sat) This is a bubbly designer haunt alongside the cathedral with stark colour contrasts (black, lemon and cream linen), slick lines and intriguing plays on traditional cooking. One of the

two degustation menus is the way to go here, or the weekday lunch *menú* for €18.

### Arcs Restaurant
Catalan €€€

(✆977 21 80 40; www.restaurantarcs.com; Carrer Misser Sitges 13; mains €18-22; ⏱1-4pm & 8.30-11pm Tue-Sat) Inside a medieval cavern with bright splashes of colour in the form of contemporary art, you are served some wonderful takes on Mediterranean dishes – with lots of delicious seafood carpaccios and tartars. Ingredients are of the highest quality – the fish of the day is always spectacular.

## ℹ️ Information

**Tourist Office** (✆977 25 07 95; www.tarragonaturisme.es; Carrer Major 39; ⏱10am-2pm & 3-5pm Mon-Fri, to 7pm Sat, 10am-2pm Sun) Good place for booking guided tours of the city. Opens extended hours in high season.

## ℹ️ Getting There & Away

The **bus station** (Plaça Imperial Tarraco) is 1.5km northwest of the old town along Rambla Nova. Destinations include Barcelona (€8.70, 1½ hours, 16 daily), Lleida (€10.70, 1¾ hours, five daily) and Valencia (€21.73, 3 to 4½ hours, seven daily).

The local train station is a 10-minute walk from the old town while fast AVE trains arrive at Camp de Tarragona station, a 15-minute taxi ride from the centre. Departures include Barcelona (both normal trains and rodalies on the R14, R15 and R16 lines, €7 to €38.20, 35 minutes to 1½ hours, every 30 minutes); Lleida (€8 to €24, 25 minutes to 1¾ hours, roughly half-hourly) and Valencia (€21.70 to €38, two to 3½ hours, 19 daily).

# GIRONA & THE DALÍ TRIANGLE

## Girona

POP 95,720

A tight huddle of ancient arcaded houses, grand churches, climbing cobbled streets and medieval baths, and Catalonia's most extensive and best-preserved Call (medieval Jewish quarter), all enclosed by defensive walls and the lazy Río Onyar,

MARTIN CHILD/GETTY IMAGES ©

constitute a powerful reason for visiting north Catalonia's largest city, Girona.

# ⊙ Sights

### Museu d'Història dels
### Jueus de Girona     Museum
(www.girona.cat/call; Carrer de la Força 8; adult/child €4/free; ⏰10am-8pm Mon-Sat, to 2pm Sun) Until 1492 Girona was home to Catalonia's second-most important medieval Jewish community (after Barcelona), and one of the finest Jewish quarters in the country. The Call (Catalan for 'ghetto'), was centred on the narrow Carrer de la Força for 600 years, until relentless persecution forced the Jews out of Spain. This excellent museum shows genuine pride in Girona's Jewish heritage without shying away from the less salubrious aspects, such as persecution by the Inquisition and forced conversions.

### Catedral     Cathedral
(www.catedraldegirona.org; Plaça de la Catedral; adult/student incl Basílica de Sant Feliu €7/5, Sun free; ⏰10am-7.30pm Apr-Oct, 10am-6.30pm Nov-Mar) The billowing baroque facade of the cathedral towers over a flight of 86 stairs rising from Plaça de la Catedral.

Though the beautiful double-columned Romanesque **cloister** dates to the 12th century, most of the building is Gothic, with the second-widest nave (23m) in Christendom. The 14th-century gilt-and-silver altarpiece and canopy are memorable, as are the bishop's throne and the museum, which holds the masterly Romanesque *Tapís de la creació* (Tapestry of the Creation) and a Mozarabic illuminated *Beatus* manuscript, dating from 975.

The *Creation* tapestry shows God at the epicentre and in the circle around him the creation of Adam, Eve, the animals, the sky, light and darkness.

### Passeig Arqueològic     Walls
(Passeig de la Muralla; ⏰10am-8pm) A walk along Girona's medieval walls is a wonderful way to appreciate the city landscape from above. There are several points of access, the most popular being across the street from the Banys Àrabs, where steps lead up into some heavenly gardens where town and plants merge into one organic masterpiece. The southernmost part of the wall ends right near Plaça de Catalunya.

**111**

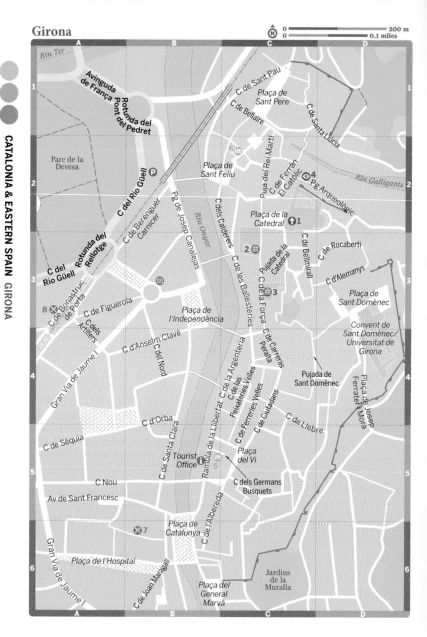

## Museu d'Història
## de Girona
Museum

(www.girona.cat/museuciutat; Carrer de la Força 27; adult/student/child €4/2/free; ⏰10.30am-5.30pm Tue-Sat, to 1.30pm Sun) The engaging and well-presented city history museum does Girona's long and impressive story justice, its displays covering everything from the city's Roman origins, through the siege of the city by Napoleonic troops

## Girona

to the *sardana* (Catalonia's national folk dance) tradition. A separate gallery houses cutting-edge temporary art and photography exhibits.

## 🛏 Sleeping

### Bells Oficis
B&B €€

( ☎972 22 81 70; www.bellsoficis.com; Carrer dels Germans Busquets 2; r incl breakfast €55-85; ❄ � ) A lovingly restored, 19th-century flat just by the Rambla in the heart of Girona makes a stylish and ultra-welcoming place to stop. Period details combine with modern styling most effectively: the whole package is immaculate. There are just five beautiful, light rooms: some share bathrooms – those with en suite have no bathroom door – while the largest (€105) has ample room for four people.

### Hotel Llegendes de Girona Catedral
Hotel €€€

( ☎972 22 09 05; www.llegendeshotel.com; Carrer Portal de la Barca 4; d €167-229; P ❄ � ) The rooms at this restored 18th-century building are supremely comfortable, with all manner of high-tech gadgets, and the all-glass bathrooms have huge rain showers. This incongruous but successful blend of modernity and antiquity includes, in the duplex 'Eros' rooms, a tantric sex sofa and instructional video. Some rooms have gorgeous cathedral views.

## ✗ Eating

### Txalaka
Basque €€

( ☎972 22 59 75; www.restaurant-txalaka.com; Carrer Bonastruc de Porta 4; mains €12-20, pintxos €2.50-4; ⏱1-4pm & 7.30-11.30pm; � ) For sensational Basque cooking and *pintxos* (tapas) washed down with *txakoli* (fizzy white wine from the Basque coast) poured from a great height, don't miss this popular local spot. Just load up your plate with bar-top snacks, make sure to order some hot ones from the kitchen too and pay according to the number of *montadito* (little sandwich) dishes.

### L'Alqueria
Rices €€

( ☎972 22 18 82; www.restaurantalqueria.com; Carrer de la Ginesta 8; mains €14-20; ⏱1-4pm & 9-11pm Wed-Sat, 1-4pm Tue & Sun) This smart minimalist *arrocería* serves the finest *arròs negre* (rice cooked in cuttlefish ink) and *arròs a la Catalan* in the city, as well as around 20 other superbly executed rice dishes, including paellas. Eat your heart out, Valencia! It's wise to book ahead for dinner.

### El Celler de Can Roca
Catalan €€€

( ☎972 22 21 57; www.cellercanroca.com; Carrer Can Sunyer 48; degustation menus €150-180; ⏱1-4pm & 8.30-11pm Tue-Sat Sep-Jul) Named best restaurant in the world in 2013 by the World's 50 Best Restaurants, this place, 2km west of central Girona in a refurbished country house, is run by three brothers. The focus is 'emotional cuisine' through ever-changing takes on Catalan dishes. The style is playful and a full range of molecular gastronomy techniques is employed. The voluminous wine list arrives on a trolley. Book online 11 months in advance; if you haven't, you can join a standby list.

## ℹ Information

**Tourist Office** ( ☎972 22 65 75; www.girona.cat/turisme; Rambla de la Llibertat 1; ⏱9am-8pm Mon-Fri, 9am-2pm & 4-8pm Sat, 9am-2pm Sun) Multilingual and helpful.

# ❶ Getting There & Away

**Girona-Costa Brava airport** (www.barcelona-girona-airport.com), a Ryanair hub, is located 11km south of the centre, with **Sagalés** (www.sagales.com) connecting it to Girona's main bus/train station (€2.75, 30 minutes, hourly), as well as Barcelona's Estació del Nord (€16/25 one way/return, 1¼ hours). A **taxi** (☑872 97 50 00) to central Girona costs around €27/35 day/night.

**Teisa** (www.teisa-bus.com) runs to Besalú (€4.10 to €4.70, one hour, four to eight daily) and Olot (€7.45 to €8.50, 1¼ hours, seven to 17 daily), while **Sarfa** (www.sarfa.com) serves Cadaqués (€10.80, 1¾ hours, one on weekdays) and other coastal destinations. The bus station is next to the train station.

Girona is on the train line between Barcelona (€8.40 to €15.90, 40 minutes to 1½ hours, up to 36 daily), Figueres (€4.10 to €5.45, 30 minutes), Portbou and the French border, with several through trains to France and beyond.

# Cadaqués & Around

POP 2900

If you have time for only one stop on the Costa Brava, make it Cadaqués. A white-washed village around a rocky bay, its narrow, hilly streets perfect for wandering, it and the surrounding area have a special magic – a fusion of wind, sea, light and rock – that isn't dissipated even by the throngs of summer visitors.

A portion of that magic owes itself to Salvador Dalí, who spent family holidays in Cadaqués during his youth, and lived much of his later life at nearby Port Lligat. Thanks to Dalí and other luminaries, such as his friend Federico García Lorca, Cadaqués pulled in a celebrity crowd for decades. One visit by the poet Paul Éluard and his Russian wife, Gala, in 1929 caused an earthquake in Dalí's life: he ran off to Paris with Gala (who was to become his lifelong obsession and, later, his wife) and joined the surrealist movement. In the 1950s the crowd he attracted was more jet-setting – Walt Disney, the Duke of Windsor and Greek shipowner Stavros Niarchos. In the 1970s Mick Jagger and Gabriel García Márquez popped by. Today the crowd is not quite as famous,

and leans heavily towards day-tripping French from across the border, but the enchantment of Cadaqués' atmosphere remains.

# ◉ Sights

### Museu de Cadaqués          Museum

(Carrer de Narcís Monturiol 15; adult/child €4/3; ⏱10.30am-1.30pm & 4-7pm Mon-Sat Apr-Jun & Oct, 10am-8pm daily Jul-Sep) Dalí often features strongly in the temporary exhibitions displayed here, as do his contemporaries, also connected to Cadaqués, such as Picasso. It opens roughly Easter to October, but this depends on the yearly exhibition.

#  Eating

### Es Baluard          Seafood €€

(☑972 25 81 83; www.esbaluard-cadaques.net; Riba Nemesi Llorens; mains €16-22; ⏱1-3.30pm & 8.30-11pm) The family that runs this old-school restaurant that's set into the old sea wall clearly worships at the throne of Poseidon, because the tastiest of his subjects wind up on your plate. Fish dishes drawing on local market produce, such as the *anchoas de Cadaqués* (anchovies from Cadaqués) and *gambitas de Roses* (prawns from Roses), dominate the menu and you shouldn't shy away from the *crema catalana*, either.

### Pilar          Catalan €€

(Carrer de la Miranda 4; mains €16-20; ⏱1-3.30pm & 8.30-10.30pm Mon-Sat, 1-4pm Sun) This compact, family-run place feels like you're eating in someone's flat. It's where locals come for some of the best rice dishes and *fideuà* (a paella-like dish made with vermicelli noodles) in town; the latter arrives crowned with rock lobster and other gifts of the sea.

# ❶ Information

**Tourist Office** (☑972 25 83 15; www.visitcadaques.org; Carrer del Cotxe 2; ⏱9am-1pm & 3-6pm Mon-Sat) Near where the main road meets the water; open longer hours in the high season.

## ℹ️ Getting There & Away

Sarfa buses connect Cadaqués to Barcelona (€23.70, 2¾ hours, two to five daily), Figueres (€5.30, one hour, three to seven daily) via Castelló d'Empúries, and Girona (€3.50, 1¾ hours, two to three daily).

# Figueres

POP 44,765

Twelve kilometres inland from the Golf de Roses, Figueres is a pleasant enough town with an unmissable attraction. Salvador Dalí was born in Figueres in 1904 and although his career took him to Madrid, Barcelona, Paris and the USA, he remained true to his roots. In the 1960s and '70s he created here the extraordinary Teatre-Museu Dalí – a monument to surrealism and a legacy that outshines any other Spanish artist, both in terms of popularity and sheer flamboyance. Whatever your feelings about the complex, egocentric Dalí, this museum is worth every cent and minute you can spare.

## 🔘 Sights

**Castell de Sant Ferran**  Fort

(www.lesfortalesescatalanes.info; adult/child €3/free; ⏰10.30am-6pm) This sturdy 18th-century fortress commands the surrounding plains from a low hill 1km northwest of the centre. Built in 1750 to repel any French invaders and large enough to house 16,000 men, it nevertheless fell to their Gallic neighbours – both in 1794 and 1808. Spain's Republican government held its final meeting of the civil war (on 8 February 1939) in the dungeons. It's a vast complex: the admission fee includes an audioguide; book

ahead for other guided tours (€10 to €15) involving jeeps and boats. Opening hours vary seasonally.

## 🍴 Eating

**Sidrería Txot's**  Basque €

(www.sidreriatxots.com; Avinguda Salvador Dalí 114; dishes €5-11; ⏰noon-midnight; 📶) Perch on a wooden seat and watch your Basque cider poured from on high from the barrel – the way it's supposed to be – before tucking into cold and hot *pintxos*, tasty burgers, cured meats, cheeses and salads, as well as dishes such as chorizo in cider and L'Escala anchovies on toast. The kitchen's open all afternoon – handy for a post-Dalí meal.

**Mas Pau**  Catalan €€€

(📞972 54 61 54; www.maspau.com; Avinyonet de Puigventós; degustation menu €72; ⏰1.30-3.30pm & 8.30-10.30pm Wed-Sat, 8.30-10.30pm Tue, 1.30-3.30pm Sun; 📶) Five kilometres along the road to Besalú, this enchanting 16th-century *masia* (farmhouse), made of rough-hewn stone offers a

Cadaqués
STUART BLACK/GETTY IMAGES ©

# Don't Miss
# Teatre-Museu Dalí

The first name that comes into your head when you lay your eyes on this red castle-like building, topped with giant eggs and stylised Oscar-like statues and studded with plaster-covered croissants, is Dalí. An entirely appropriate final resting place for the master of surrealism, its entrance watched over by medieval suits of armour balancing baguettes on their heads, it has assured his immortality.

www.salvador-dali.org

Plaça de Gala i Salvador Dalí 5

admission incl Dalí Joies & Museu de l'Empordà adult/child under 9 €12/free

⊘9am-8pm Jul-Sep, 9.30am-6pm Tue-Sun Mar-Jun & Oct, 10.30am-6pm Tue-Sun Nov-Feb

## Main Exhibits

Choice exhibits include **Taxi Plujós** (Rainy Taxi), composed of an early Cadillac, surmounted by statues. Put a coin in the slot and water washes all over the occupant of the car. The **Sala de Peixateries** (Fish Shop Room) holds a collection of Dalí oils, including the famous **Autoretrat Tou amb Tall de Bacon Fregit** (Soft Self-Portrait with Fried Bacon) and Retrat de Picasso (Portrait of Picasso). Beneath the former stage of the theatre is the crypt with Dalí's plain **tomb**, located at 'the spiritual centre of Europe' as Dalí modestly described it.

Gala – Dalí's wife and lifelong muse – is seen throughout – from the **Gala Mirando el Mar Mediterráneo** (Gala Looking at the Mediterranean Sea) on the 2nd level, which also appears to be a portrait of Abraham Lincoln from afar, to the classic **Leda Atómica** (Atomic Leda).

## Dalí Joies

A separate entrance (same ticket and opening times) leads into **Dalí Joies**, a collection of 37 jewels, designed by Dalí. He designed these on paper (his first commission was in 1941) and the jewellery was made by specialists in New York. Each piece, ranging from the disconcerting Ull del Temps (Eye of Time) through to the Cor Reial (Royal Heart), is unique.

## Exterior

Even outside, the building aims to surprise, from the collection of bizarre sculptures outside the entrance, on Plaça de Gala i Salvador Dalí, to the pink wall along Pujada del Castell. The **Torre Galatea**, added in 1983, is where Dalí spent his final years.

### Local Knowledge

# Teatre-Museu Dalí

*BY ANTONI PIXTOT, PAINTER AND DALÍ-APPOINTED DIRECTOR OF THE TEATRE-MUSEU DALÍ*

1 **TREASURE ROOM**
In this room, Dalí hung the paintings himself to impress visitors with their analogies or contrasts. It's filled with references to the Renaissance, the avant-garde and his obsessions with a scientific approach to form, Gala (his wife and muse) and sex. The star is Atomic Leda with Gala as the centrepiece, Dalí disguised as a swan, and numerous mythological echoes.

2 **THE WIND PALACE**
The ceiling in this old foyer of the theatre on the 1st floor is full of Dalí's imagery and iconography represented as a golden rain of money. We see Gala and Dalí flying up to the centre of this Wind Palace, their burial ceremony, and Dalí and Gala watching their own idyllic boat trip to a more spiritual dimension.

3 **MONSTERS**
Dalí's grotesque monsters are phantasmagoric beings that contemplate the theatre-museum from the courtyard. Made of everything from rocks and a whale skeleton from Cape Creus to Figueres plane trees and gargoyles, the monsters embody Dalí's dream to decorate by accumulating instead of selecting.

4 **POETRY OF AMERICA ROOM**
Apart from Dalí's 1943 masterpiece *Poetry of America* (also known as *The Cosmic Athletes*) in this room, the delicate green-pen drawing *The Argonauts* is worth a closer look to admire the almost imperceptible details of the foot of one of the Argonauts: there are wings in his shoe with gold, rubies and emeralds.

5 **MONUMENT TO FRANCESC PUJOLS**
Welcoming visitors to the museum at the entrance, this monument to the Catalan philosopher is based on a millenary olive tree and repository of the old feelings of the Catalan people. Everything in the installation links past and tradition to modern times. On top, an atom of hydrogen symbolises Dalí's trust in science.

dozen-course seasonal menu with an emphasis on fresh local ingredients; some dishes are truly inspired. They close early January to mid-March and open Sunday and Monday nights in summer. There are also comfortable rooms (double €102), relaxing gardens and a pool area.

### ⓘ Information

**Tourist Office** (📞972 50 31 55; www. visitfigueres.cat; Plaça del Sol; ⊙10am-2pm & 4-6pm Tue-Sat, 10am-3pm Sun & Mon) On the main road; open longer hours in high season.

### ⓘ Getting There & Away

Sarfa buses serve Cadaqués (€5.50, one hour, four weekdays) via Castelló d'Empúries.

There are hourly train connections to Girona (€4.10 to €5.45, 30 minutes) and Barcelona (€12 to €16, 1¾ hours) and to Portbou and into France and beyond.

## Castell de Púbol

Two kilometres away from the village of La Pera, just south of the C66 and 22km northwest of Palafrugell, the **Castell de Púbol** (www.salvador-dali.org; Plaça de Gala Dalí; adult/concession €8/6; ⊙10am-6pm Tue-Sun mid-Mar–early Jan) forms the southernmost point of northeast Catalonia's 'Salvador Dalí triangle', other elements of which include the Teatre-Museu Dalí in Figueres, and his home in Port Lligat.

Having promised to make his wife, Gala – his muse and the love of his life – 'queen of the castle', in 1969 Dalí finally found the ideal residence to turn into Gala's refuge, since at the age of 76, she no longer desired Dalí's hectic lifestyle. It's a semi-dilapidated Gothic and Renaissance stronghold which includes a 14th-century church in the quiet village of Púbol.

The sombre castle, its stone walls covered with creepers, is almost the antithesis of the flamboyance of the Teatre-Museu Dalí or Dalí's seaside home: Gala had it decorated exactly as she wished and received only whom she wished. Legend has it that Dalí himself

had to apply for written permission to visit her here.

The interior reflects her tastes: her bedroom is simple and almost unadorned; the 'everlasting' flowers that she was so fond of prevail everywhere and a gallery upstairs showcases a splendid collection of dresses designed for her by the likes of Pierre Cardin, Christian Dior and Elizabeth Arden. A slightly creepy mannequin, designed to look like Gala, sits with its back to the visitor.

Dalí touches nevertheless creep in: a radiator cover with radiators painted over the top, spindly-legged elephant statues in the exuberant garden, a see-through table with ostrich legs with a stuffed horse visible below, a melted clock on a coathanger in the guest room, and a stuffed giraffe staring at Gala's tomb in the crypt.

To get here, catch one of the frequent Palafrugell-bound buses from Girona (€3, 40 minutes), alight at the second La Pera stop along the C66 and walk the 2km to the castle, or else take a train from Girona to Flaça (€ 2.50, 12 minutes, hourly) and then catch a taxi for the last 4km.

# ZARAGOZA

POP 674,725

Zaragoza (Saragossa) rocks and rolls. The feisty citizens of this great city, on the banks of the mighty Río Ebro, make up over half of Aragón's population and they live a fairly hectic lifestyle with great tapas bars and raucous nightlife. But Zaragoza is so much more than just a city that loves to live the good life: it also has a host of historical sights spanning all the great civilisations (Roman, Islamic and Christian) that have left their indelible mark on the Spanish soul.

## ◎ Sights

### Basílica de Nuestra Señora del Pilar                    Church
(Plaza del Pilar; lift admission €3; ⊙7am-9.30pm, lift 10am-1.30pm & 4-6.30pm Tue-Sun) **FREE** Brace yourself for this great baroque cavern of Catholicism. The faithful

# Zaragoza

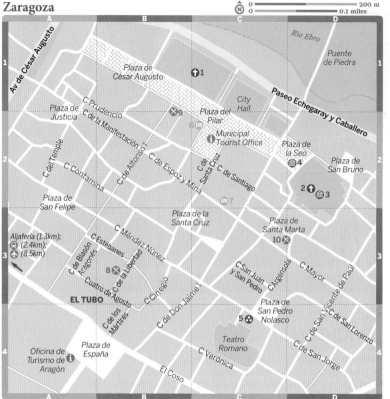

believe that it was here on 2 January AD 40 that Santiago saw the Virgin Mary descend atop a marble *pilar* (pillar). A chapel was built around the remaining pillar, followed by a series of ever-more-grandiose churches, culminating in the enormous basilica. A **lift** whisks you most of the way up the north tower from where you climb to a superb viewpoint over the domes and city.

## La Seo      Cathedral
(Catedral de San Salvador; Plaza de la Seo; adult/concession €4/3; ⊗10am-6pm Tue-Fri, 10am-noon & 3-6pm Sat, 10-11.30am & 2.30-6pm Sun Jun-Sep, shorter hours Oct-May) Dominating the eastern end of Plaza del Pilar, La Seo was built between the 12th and 17th centuries and displays a fabulous spread of architectural styles from Romanesque to baroque. The cathedral stands on the site of Islamic Zaragoza's main mosque (which in turn stood upon the temple of the Roman forum). The admission price

CESAR LUCAS ABREU/GETTY IMAGES ©

## Don't Miss
## Aljafería

The Aljafería is Spain's finest Islamic-era edifice outside Andalucía. Built as a pleasure palace for Zaragoza's Islamic rulers in the 11th century, it underwent its first alterations in 1118 when the city passed into Christian hands. In the 1490s the Catholic Monarchs, Fernando and Isabel, tacked on their own palace, whereafter the Aljafería fell into decay. Twentieth-century restorations brought the building back to life, and in 1987 Aragón's regional parliament was established here. Tours take place throughout the day (multilingual in July and August).

### NEED TO KNOW

Calle de los Diputados; admission €3, Sun free; ⊙10am-2pm Sat-Wed, plus 4.30-8pm Mon-Wed, Fri & Sat Jul & Aug

---

includes entry to La Seo's **Museo de Tapices** (Plaza de la Seo; ⊙10am-8.30pm Tue-Sun Jun-Sep, shorter hours Oct-May), an impressive collection of 14th- to 17th-century Flemish and French tapestries.

### Museo del Foro de Caesaraugusta          Museum
(Plaza de la Seo 2; adult/concession/child under 8 €3/2/free; ⊙9am-8.30pm Tue-Sat, 10am-2pm Sun Jun-Sep, shorter hours Oct-May; ♿) The trapezoidal building on Plaza de la Seo

is the entrance to an excellent reconstruction of part of Roman Caesaraugusta's forum, now well below ground level. The remains of porticoes, shops, a great *cloaca* (sewer) system, and a limited collection of artefacts from the 1st century AD are on display. An interesting multilingual 15-minute audiovisual show breathes life into it all and culminates with a clever 'talking head' of a statue which children, in particular, will enjoy.

## Museo del Teatro de Caesaraugusta    Ruin, Museum

(Calle de San Jorge 12; adult/concession/child under 8 €4/3/free; ⏰9am-8.30pm Tue-Sat, to 1.30pm Sun; 👪) Discovered during the excavation of a building site in 1972, the ruins of Zaragoza's Teatro Romano (Roman theatre) are the focus of this compelling museum. The theatre once seated 6000 spectators, and great efforts have been made to help visitors reconstruct the edifice's former splendour, including evening projections of a **virtual performance** (May–October) and an entertaining audiovisual production. The theatre is visible from the surrounding streets and the on-site (and excellent) cafe can be entered separately.

## 🛏 Sleeping

### Hotel Sauce    Boutique Hotel €€

(📞976 20 50 50; www.hotelsauce.com; Calle de Espoz y Mina 33; s €48, d €55-66; ❄🖥) This chic, small hotel has a great central location and overall light and airy look with white wicker, painted furniture, stripy fabrics and tasteful watercolours on the walls. The superior rooms are well worth the few euros extra. Breakfast (€8) includes homemade cakes and a much-lauded *tortilla de patatas* (potato omelette).

### Hotel Las Torres    Hotel €€

(📞976 39 42 50; www.hotellastorres.com; Plaza del Pilar 11; s/d incl breakfast from €75/85; ❄🖥) The rooms are seriously white at this central city hotel. So white they are almost clinical (although not many hospital rooms have chandeliers or hydromassage showers, it's true). The public spaces are decorated with whimsical illustrative art work and the views of the basilica are stunning. There's a small spa.

## 🍴 Eating

The tangle of lanes in El Tubo, immediately north of Plaza de España, is home to one of Spain's richest gatherings of tapas bars.

### Casa Pascualillo    Contemporary Tapas €

(Calle de la Libertad 5; tapas from €1.60, mains €5-14; ⏰noon-4pm & 7-11pm Tue-Sat, noon-4.30pm Sun) When *Metropoli*, the weekend magazine of *El Mundo* newspaper, sought out the best 50 tapas bars in Spain a few years back, it's no surprise that Casa Pascualillo made the final cut. The bar groans under the weight of enticing tapas such as El Pascualillo, a 'small' *bocadillo* (filled roll) of *jamón*, oyster mushrooms and onion. There's a more formal restaurant attached.

### El Ciclón    Contemporary Spanish €€

(Plaza del Pilar 10; raciones €7-8.50, set menus €15-20; ⏰11am-11.30pm) Opened in November 2013 by three acclaimed Spanish chefs (all with Michelin-star restaurant experience), the dishes here are superbly prepared. Choose between set menus and tapas and *raciones* (large-size tapas) such as the Canary Island favourite, *papas arrugadas* (new potatoes with a spicy coriander sauce), noodles with mussels, and artichokes with *migas* (fried breadcrumbs) and cauliflower cream.

### Tragantua    Tapas, Seafood €€

(Plaza Santa Marta; tapas from €1.50, mains €9.60-20; ⏰12.30-4pm & 8pm-12.30am) Locals flock here for reputedly the best *croquetas de jamón* (ham croquettes) in town; other popular mini bites include *bola de bacalau* (breadcrumbed cod) while more substantial tentacle-waving teasers include stewed baby octopus and the sizeable *langostino* (lobster) *de Vinaroz*. The ambience is comfortably traditional.

## ℹ Information

**Municipal Tourist Office** (📞976 20 12 00; www.zaragozaturismo.es; Plaza del Pilar; ⏰9am-9pm mid-Jun–mid-Oct, 10am-8pm mid-Oct–mid-Jun; 🖥) Has branch offices around town, including the train station.

**Oficina de Turismo de Aragón** (www.turismodearagon.com; Plaza de España; ⏰9am-2pm & 5-8pm Mon-Fri, from 10am Sat & Sun; 🖥) Has plenty of brochures on the province.

## Detour:
# Teruel

One of Spain's most attractive provincial cities, compact Teruel is an open-air museum of ornate Mudéjar monuments. But this is very much a living museum where the streets are filled with life – a reflection of a city reasserting itself with cultural attitude.

Teruel's **catedral** (Plaza de la Catedral; adult/child incl Museo de Arte Sacro €3/2; ⏰11am-2pm & 4-8pm) is a rich example of the Mudéjar imagination at work with its kaleidoscopic brickwork and colourful ceramic tiles. Inside, the astounding Mudéjar ceiling of the nave is covered with paintings that add up to a medieval cosmography – from musical instruments and hunting scenes to coats of arms and Christ's crucifixion.

The most impressive of Teruel's Mudéjar towers is the **Torre de El Salvador** (www.teruelmudejar.com; Calle El Salvador; adult/concession €2.50/1.80; ⏰11am-2pm & 4.30-7.30pm), an early-14th-century extravaganza of brick and ceramics built around an older Islamic minaret.

Teruel is on the highway and railway between Zaragoza and Valencia.

## 🛈 Getting There & Away

### Air

The **Zaragoza-Sanjurjo airport** (☎976 71 23 00; www.zaragoza-airport.com), 8.5km west of the city centre, has direct **Ryanair** (www.ryanair.com) flights to/from London (Stansted), Brussels (Charleroi), Paris (Beauvais), Milan (Bergamo) and Lanzarote (Canary Islands). **Iberia** (www.iberia.es) and **Air Europa** (www.aireuropa.com) also operate a small number of domestic and international routes.

### Bus

Dozens of bus lines fan out across Spain from the bus station attached to the Estación Intermodal Delicias train station. **ALSA** (☎902 422242; www.alsa.es) runs frequent daily buses to/from Madrid (from €16.50, 3¾ hours) and Barcelona (€15.50, 3¾ hours).

### Train

Zaragoza's futuristic **Estación Intermodal Delicias** (www.renfe.com; Calle Rioja 33) is connected by almost hourly high-speed AVE services to Madrid (€65.50, 1¼ hours) and Barcelona (€71, from 1½ hours). Other destinations include Huesca (from €7, one hour), Jaca (€14.55, 3½ hours) and Teruel (€19.70, 2¼ hours).

## 🛈 Getting Around

**Airport Buses** (☎902 360065; tickets €2) run to/from Paseo María Agustín 7 via the bus/train station every half-hour (hourly on Sunday).

Buses 34 and 51 travel between the city centre and the Estación Intermodal Delicias.

The C1 **tram** (www.urbandezaragoza.es; tickets €1.35) line opened in 2011 running through the centre of town from Plaza de España to Plaza de Bambola due south.

# THE PYRENEES

Leaving behind Zaragoza's parched flatlands, a hint of green tinges the landscape and there's a growing anticipation of very big mountains somewhere up ahead. And they are big. The Pyrenees boast several peaks well over the 3000m mark and they're among the most dramatic and rewarding on the Spanish side of the range.

## Parque Nacional de Ordesa y Monte Perdido

This is where the Spanish Pyrenees really take your breath away. At the heart of it all is a dragon's back of limestone peaks skirting the French border, with a south-eastward spur that includes Monte Perdido (3348m), the third-highest peak in the Pyrenees.

## Activities

For a range of walking options in the park, pick up a copy of the *Senderos* maps and route descriptions for the four sectors (Ordesa, Añisclo, Escuaín and Pineta) from any of the information offices. The Circo de Soaso is a classic day walk that follows the Valle de Ordesa to Circo de Soaso, a rocky balcony whose centrepiece is the Cola de Caballo (Horsetail) waterfall.

## Information

You can find information centres in the following villages. From November to March they are only open on weekends:

**Bielsa** (☏974 50 10 43; Bielsa; ◷9am-2pm & 3.15-6pm daily Apr-Oct, Sat & Sun Nov-Mar; 📶)

**Escalona** (☏974 50 51 31; Escalona; ◷9am-2pm & 3.15-6pm daily Apr-Oct, Sat & Sun Nov-Mar)

**Tella** (☏974 48 64 72; Tella; ◷9am-2pm & 3.15-6pm daily Apr-Oct, Sat & Sun Nov-Mar)

**Torla** (☏974 48 64 72; Torla; ◷9am-2pm & 4-7pm)

## Getting Around

The main entry point into the park is Torla, 3km south of the southwest corner of the national park. Private vehicles may not drive from Torla to Pradera de Ordesa during Easter week and from July to mid-September. During these periods a shuttle bus (one way/return €3/4.50) runs between Torla's Centro de Visitantes and Pradera de Ordesa. During the same periods, a one-way system is enforced on part of the Escalona–Sarvisé road. From the Puyarruego turn-off, 2km out of Escalona, to a point about 1km after the road diverges from the Bellos valley, only northwestward traffic is allowed. Southeastward traffic uses an alternative, more southerly road.

## If You Like...
# Mountains

If you like the Parque Nacional de Ordesa y Monte Perdido, we think you'll also like these stirring mountain areas:

**1 VAL D'ARAN**
A verdant valley, Catalonia's northernmost outpost, surrounded by spectacular 2000m-plus mountains and studded with ski resorts, including Baquiera.

**2 VALLES DE ECHO & ANSÓ**
Lush, little-visited valleys with old stone villages climbing deep into the Aragonese Pyrenees.

**3 VALL FERRERA**
At the heart of the Parc Natural de l'Alt Pirineu (Catalonia's biggest nature reserve), with pretty villages and good walking.

**4 SERRA DEL CADÍ**
Picturesque pre-Pyrenees range with ravines and peaks famous for rock climbing.

**5 VALLE DEL RONCAL**
Awash in greens and often concealed in mists, this is the most beautiful corner of the western Pyrenees.

**6 OCHAGAVÍA**
Grey slate, stone and cobblestone village in the lush, green western Pyrenees.

## Torla
POP 327

Torla is a lovely Alpine-style village of stone houses with slate roofs, although it does get overrun in July and August. Most people use Torla as a gateway to the national park, but the setting is also delightful, the houses clustered above Río Ara with a backdrop of the national park's mountains.

# If You Like…
## Aragón's Villages

If you like Aínsa, there are plenty more charming Aragón villages with interesting sights:

### 1 CASA PALACIO DE SEDA, SOS DEL REY CATÓLICO
(Plaza de la Hispanidad; adult/child €2.60/1.50, incl tour of village €4/2; ⏲10am-2pm & 4-8pm; ♿) Fernando is said to have been born in this building in 1452. It's an impressive noble mansion, which now contains an interpretative centre, with fine exhibits on the history of Sos and the life of the king. The tourist office, also housed here, runs guided tours of the building.

### 2 CASTLE, ALBARRACÍN
(Castillo; admission €2.50; ⏲guided tours 11am, noon, 1pm, 4.30pm & 5pm Sat-Mon, 1pm & 5.30pm Tue-Fri) Crowning the old town (with stunning views), this fascinating castle, with 11 towers and an area of 3600 sq metres, dates from the 9th century when Albarracín was an important Islamic military post. In private hands until 2005, the archaeological digs have revealed fascinating insights into the town's history. All is explained on the hour-long, Spanish-language tour (buy your tickets at the Museo de Albarracín); contact the Centro de Información to arrange English-language tours.

### 3 COLEGIATA DE SANTA MARÍA, ALQUÉZAR
(admission €2.50; ⏲11am-1.30pm & 4.30-7.30pm Wed-Mon) Alquézar is crowned by this large castle-monastery. Originally built as an *alcázar* (fortress) by the Arabs in the 9th century, it was subsequently conquered and replaced by an Augustinian monastery in 1099. Remnants are still visible. The columns within its delicate cloister are crowned by carved capitals depicting biblical scenes, and the walls are covered with spellbinding murals. On the upper level is a **museum** of sacred art.

## Eating

### Restaurante el Duende
Aragonese €€
(☎974 48 60 32; www.elduenderestaurante.com; Calle de la Iglesia; mains €15-22; ⏲1.30-3pm & 8-10pm, Sat & Sun Jan-Apr; ♿) Best restaurant in town with fine local cuisine, an extensive menu and eclectic decor in a lovely 19th-century building. Typical meaty dishes include wild boar with leeks and mushrooms.

## Aínsa
POP 2232

The beautiful hilltop village of medieval Aínsa (L'Aínsa in the local dialect), which stands above the modern town of the same name, is one of Aragón's gems, a stunning village hewn from uneven stone.

## ◉ Sights

### Iglesia de Santa María
Church
(belfry admission €1; ⏲belfry 11am-1.30pm & 4-7pm Sat & Sun) This restored Romanesque church lights up when you pop €1 into a box, with five minutes of Gregorian chants thrown in. The crypt and Gothic cloister are charming; you can also climb the **belfry** for glorious views of the mountains to the north and down over the terracotta rooftops of the old town.

### Castle
Castle
(ecomuseum admission €4; ⏲ecomuseum 11am-2pm Wed-Fri, 10am-2pm & 4-7pm Sat & Sun Easter-Oct) The castle and fortifications off the western end of the Plaza de San Salvador mostly date from the 1600s, though the main tower is 11th century; there are some reasonable views from the wall. It contains a fascinating **ecomuseum** on Pyrenean fauna (the focus is on the endangered lammergeier, with some caged birds of prey out the back) and the **Espacio del Geoparque de Sobrarbe** (www.geopar-

quepirineos.com; ⏱9.30am-2pm & 4-7pm daily) **FREE** with displays on the region's intriguing geology, as well as good views from the tower.

## ✕ Eating

**La Tea**                                    Italian €
(Plaza Mayor 21; pizza €6.50-8.50; ⏱noon-4pm & 7pm-midnight; 👪) Justifiably popular with a genuine pizza oven and crispy thin-based pizzas with vast choice of toppings. Alternate choices include a handful of superb pasta dishes, topped *tostadas* and vast salads. Head for the sprawl of tables and chairs on the plaza.

## ℹ Information

**Municipal Tourist Office** (📞974 50 07 67; www.ainsasobrarbe.net; Avenida Pirenáica 1; ⏱9am-9pm) Located in the new town down the hill.

**Regional Tourist Office** (📞974 50 05 12; www.turismosobrarbe.com; Plaza del Castillo 1, Torre Nordeste; ⏱10am-2pm & 4-7pm) Extremely helpful; within the castle walls.

## ℹ Getting There & Away

**Alosa** (📞902 21 07 00; www.alosa.es) runs daily buses to/from Barbastro (€5.80, one hour) and Torla (€4.30, one hour).

# VALENCIA
POP 815,000

Valencia, Spain's third-largest city, for ages languished in the long shadows cast by Madrid, Spain's political capital, and Barcelona, the country's cultural and economic powerhouse. No longer. Stunning public buildings have changed the city's skyline – Sir Norman Foster's **Palacio de Congresos**,

David Chipperfield's award-winning **Veles i Vents** structure beside the inner port, and, on the grandest scale of all, the Ciudad de las Artes y las Ciencias, designed in the main by Santiago Calatrava, local boy made good.

## ◎ Sights & Activities

### WESTERN VALENCIA

**Bioparc**                                    Zoo
(www.bioparcvalencia.es; Avenida Pio Baroja 3; adult/child €24/18; ⏱10am-dusk; 👪) ✦ 'Zoo' is far too old-fashioned and inept a term for this wonderful, innovative, ecofriendly and gently educational space. Wild animals apparently (fear not: only apparently) roam free as you wander from savannah to equatorial Africa and Madagascar, where large-eyed lemurs gambol around your ankles.

**Museo de Historia de Valencia**              Museum
(Calle Valencia 42; adult/child €2/1; ⏱10am-6pm or 7pm Tue-Sat, 10am-3pm Sun) This

Zebras in Bioparc
KRZYSZTOF DYDYNSKI/GETTY IMAGES ©

museum, very hands-on and with plenty of film and video, plots more than 2000 years of the city's history. Grab the informative folder in English.

# CENTRAL VALENCIA

**Catedral**            Cathedral

(Plaza de la Virgen; adult/child incl audioguide €5/3.50; ⏱10am-5.30pm or 6.30pm Mon-Sat, 2-5.30pm Sun, closed Sun Nov-Feb) Valencia's

## Valencia

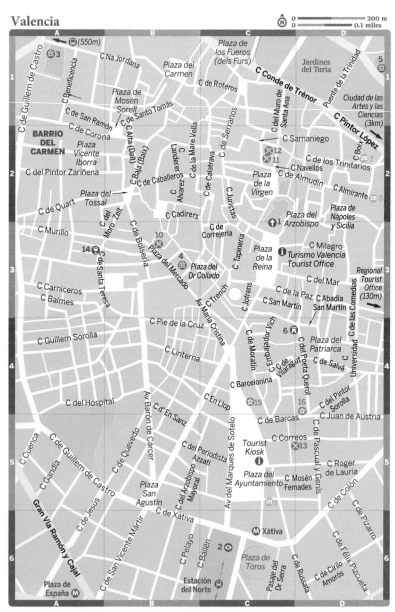

cathedral was built over the mosque after the 1238 reconquest. Its low, wide, brick-vaulted triple nave is mostly Gothic, with neoclassical side chapels. Highlights are rich Italianate frescoes above the altar-piece, a pair of Goyas in the **Chapel of San Francisco de Borja**, and in the flamboyant Gothic **Capilla del Santo Cáliz**, what's claimed to be the **Holy Grail**, the chalice from which Christ sipped during the Last Supper. It's a Roman-era agate cup, later modified, so at least the date is right.

### La Lonja                                    Historic Building
(Calle de la Lonja; adult/child €2/1; ⏰10am-6pm or 7pm Tue-Sat, to 3pm Sun) This splendid late-15th-century building, a Unesco World Heritage Site, was originally Valencia's silk and commodity exchange. Highlights are the colonnaded hall with its twisted Gothic pillars and the 1st-floor **Consulado del Mar** with its stunning coffered ceiling.

### Instituto Valenciano de Arte Moderno                          Gallery
(IVAM; www.ivam.es; Calle de Guillem de Castro 118; adult/child €2/1; ⏰10am-7pm Tue-Sun)

Hosts excellent temporary exhibitions and houses a small but impressive permanent collection of 20th-century Spanish art.

### Museo de Bellas Artes          Gallery
(San Pío V; www.museobellasartesvalencia.gva.es; Calle de San Pío V 9; ⏰10am-7pm Tue-Sun, 11am-5pm Mon) FREE Bright and spacious, the Museo de Bellas Artes ranks among Spain's best. Highlights include the grandiose Roman *Mosaic of the Nine Muses,* a collection of magnificent late-medieval altarpieces, and works by El Greco, Goya, Velázquez, Murillo and Ribalta, plus artists such as Sorolla and Pinazo of the Valencian Impressionist school.

### Palacio del Marqués de Dos Aguas                       Palace
(Calle del Poeta Querol 2) A pair of wonderfully extravagant rococo caryatids (columns in the shape of female figures) curl around the main entrance of this over-the-top palace. Inside, the **Museo Nacional de Cerámica (adult/child €3/free, Sat afternoon & Sun free; ⏰10am-2pm & 4-8pm Tue-Sat, 10am-2pm Sun)** displays ceramics from around the world – and especially from the renowned local production centres of Manises, Alcora and Paterna.

### Museo Fallero                          Museum
(Plaza Monteolivete 4; adult/child €2/1; ⏰10am-6pm or 7pm Tue-Sat, 10am-3pm Sun) Each Fallas festival (p129), only one of the thousands of *ninots,* the figurines that pose at the base of each *falla* (huge statues of papier mâché and polystyrene), is saved from the flames by popular vote. Those reprieved over the years are displayed here.

## 🕓 Tours

### Valencia Guías          Bicycle Tours
(📞963 85 17 40; www.valenciaguias.com; Paseo de la Pechina 32) Daily three-hour guided bicycle tours in English, Dutch and German (€25 including rental and snack; minimum two people).

TRAVELSTOCK44 - JUERGEN HELD/GETTY IMAGES © | ARCHITECTS SANTIAGO CALATRAVA AND FÉLIX CANDELA

## ★ Don't Miss
# Ciudad de las Artes y las Ciencias

The aesthetically stunning City of Arts & Sciences occupies a massive 350,000-sq-metre swathe of the old Turia riverbed. It's mostly the work of world-famous, locally born architect Santiago Calatrava. He's a controversial figure for many Valencians, who complain about the expense, and various design flaws that have necessitated major repairs. Nevertheless, if your taxes weren't involved, it's awe-inspiring stuff, and pleasingly family-oriented.

### NEED TO KNOW

City of Arts & Sciences; www.cac.es; combined ticket for Oceanogràfic, Hemisfèric & Museo de las Ciencias Príncipe Felipe adult/child €36.25/27.55

## 🛏 Sleeping

### Hotel Sorolla Centro    Hotel €€
(☎963 52 33 92; www.hotelsorollacentro.com; Calle Convento Santa Clara 5; s/d €66/77; ❄️ 🛜) Neat and contemporary but without design gimmicks, this offers solid value for comfortable, well-thought-out modern rooms with powerful showers and plenty of facilities. Staff are helpful and the location on a pedestrian street between the train station and main square is fab.

### Ad Hoc Monumental    Hotel €€
(☎963 91 91 40; www.adhochoteles.com; Calle Boix 4; s/d €72/84; ❄️ 🛜) Friendly Ad Hoc offers comfort and charm deep within the old quarter and also runs a splendid small restaurant (open for dinner Monday to Saturday). The late-19th-century building has been restored to its former splendour with great sensitivity, revealing original ceilings, mellow brickwork and solid wooden beams.

### Caro Hotel
Hotel €€€

(☎963 05 90 00; www.carohotel.com; Calle Almirante 14; r €143-214; P ❄ 🎧) Housed in a sumptuous 19th-century mansion, this sits atop some 2000 years of Valencian history, with restoration revealing a hefty hunk of the Arab wall, Roman column bases and Gothic arches. Each room is furnished in soothing dark shades, has a great king-sized bed, and varnished cement floors. Bathrooms are tops. For that very special occasion, reserve the 1st-floor grand suite, once the ballroom. Savour, too, its excellent restaurant Alma del Temple.

 **Eating**

#### CENTRAL VALENCIA

### Carosel
Valencian €

(☎961 13 28 73; www.carosel.es; Calle Taula de Canvis 6; mains €7-16, menu €15; ☺1-4pm & 9-11pm Tue-Sat, 1-4pm Sun) Jordi and his partner, Carol, run this delightful small restaurant with outdoor seating on a square. The freshest of produce from the nearby market is blended with Alicante and Valencia traditions to create salads, cocas, rices and other delicious titbits. Top value and warmly recommended.

### Delicat
Tapas, Fusion €€

(☎963 92 33 57; Calle Conde Almodóvar 4; mains €9-14; ☺1-4pm & 8.30-11.30pm Tue-Sat, 1-4pm Sun) At this particularly friendly, intimate option (there are only nine tables, plus the terrace in summer), Catina, up front, and her partner, Paco, on full view in the kitchen, offer an unbeatable-value, five-course menu of samplers for lunch and a range of truly innovative tapas anytime.

### Vuelve Carolina
Mediterranean €€

(☎963 21 86 86; www.vuelvecarolina.com; Calle Correos 8; mains €14-25; ☺1.30-4.30pm & 8.30-11.30pm Mon-Sat; 🎧) Overseen from a distance by three-star Michelin chef

# Las Fallas

The exuberant, anarchic swirl of **Las Fallas de San José** (www.fallas.es) – fireworks, music, festive bonfires and all-night partying – is a must if you're visiting Valencia in mid-March.

The *fallas* themselves are huge sculptures of papier mâché on wood (with, increasingly, environmentally damaging polystyrene), built by teams of local artists. Despite Spain's deep economic recession, in 2012 the combined cost of their construction was well over €8 million. Each neighbourhood sponsors its own *falla,* and when the town wakes after the *plantà* (overnight construction of the *fallas*) on the morning of 16 March, more than 350 have sprung up. Reaching up to 15m in height, with the most expensive costing in 2012 €400,000, these grotesque, colourful effigies satirise celebrities, current affairs and local customs.

Around-the-clock festivities include street parties, paella-cooking competitions, parades, open-air concerts, bullfights and free firework displays. Valencia considers itself the pyrotechnic capital of the world and each day at 2pm from 1 to 19 March a *mascletà* (more than five minutes of deafening thumps and explosions) shakes the window panes of Plaza del Ayuntamiento.

After midnight on the final day each *falla* goes up in flames – backed by yet more fireworks.

# Detour:
# Cartagena

Easy to slot into a journey between Valencia and Granada, Cartagena is a city that feels old. Stand on the battlements of the castle that overlooks this city and you can literally see layer upon layer of history spread below you.

As archaeologists continue to strip back more and more of the town's old quarter to reveal a long-buried – and fascinating – Roman and Carthaginian heritage, the city is finally starting to get the recognition it deserves as one of the most historically and culturally fascinating places on the east coast of Spain.

The **Museo del Teatro Romano** (www.teatroromanocartagena.org; Plaza del Ayuntamiento 9; adult/child €6/5; ☉10am-6pm or 8pm Tue-Sat, to 2pm Sun) is the city's finest museum. The tour transports visitors from the initial museum on Plaza del Ayuntamiento, via escalators and an underground passage beneath the ruined cathedral, to the magnificent, recently restored Roman theatre dating from the 1st century BC.

The **Bario del Foro Romano** (www.cartagenapuertodeculturas.com; Calle Honda; adult/child €5/4; ☉10am-5.30pm or 7pm Tue-Sun) has evocative remains of one of the town's main Roman streets linking the port with the forum, and including an arcade and thermal baths. The **Casa de la Fortuna** (Plaza Risueño; adult/child €2.50/2; ☉10am-2.30pm or 3pm Tue-Sun mid-Mar–mid-Dec, Sat & Sun mid-Dec–mid-Mar) consists of fascinating remains of an aristocratic Roman villa dating back to the 2nd and 3rd centuries, complete with murals and mosaics, and part of an excavated road. Finally, the **Muralla Púnica** (Calle de San Diego; adult/child €3.50/2.50; ☉10am-5.30pm or 7pm Tue-Sun, plus Mon Jul–mid-Sep), built around a section of the old Punic wall, concentrates on the town's Carthaginian and Roman legacy.

From Valencia you'll probably have to change bus or train in Alicante or Murcia in order to get to Cartagena.

---

Quique Dacosta, this trendy and upbeat bar-restaurant offers style – those clothes-horse bar stools could be more comfy though – and an inspiring selection of tapas and fuller plates. Service is solicitous.

**Seu Xerea**  Fusion €€€
(☎963 92 40 00; www.seuxerea.com; Calle Conde Almodóvar 4; mains €17-25; ☉1.30-3.30pm & 8.30-11pm Mon-Sat) Welcoming and popular, the creative, regularly changing, rock-reliable, à la carte menu features dishes both international and deep-rooted in Spain. Wines, selected by the owner, a qualified sommelier, are uniformly excellent. Degustation and tapas menus are on-hand for trying lots of morsels.

## LAS ARENAS

On weekends locals in their hundreds head for Las Arenas, just north of the port, where a long line of restaurants overlooking the beach all serve up authentic paella in a three-course meal costing around €20.

**La Pascuala**  Tapas €
(Calle de Eugenia Viñes 177; rolls €4-5; ☉9am-3.30pm Mon-Sat) A block back from the beach, this neighbourhood bar has barely changed since the '20s and is legendary for its *bocadillos* (filled rolls) that come absolutely stuffed with fillings. Half of Valencia seems to be in here around 11am for a mid-morning bite. It couldn't be more authentic. Try the super horse burger.

# 🍷 Drinking

The Barrio del Carmen has both the grungiest and grooviest collection of bars. On weekends, Calle de Caballeros, the main street, seethes with punters seeking *la marcha* (the action).

### Slaughterhouse     Cafe, Bar
(www.slaughterhouse.es; Calle de Denia 22; ⊘6pm-1.30am; 🛜) Once a butcher's shop (hence its title, also inspired by the Kurt Vonnegut novel of the same name), Slaughterhouse abounds in books (even in the toilets), new, old, for sale and simply for browsing. There's a limited menu of burgers, salads, cheeses, where every dish (€5 to €9) has a literary reference.

### Ubik Café     Cafe, Bar
(http://ubikcafe.blogspot.com.es; Calle Literato Azorín 13; ⊘5pm-1am Mon & Tue, noon-1am Wed-Sun; 🛜🍴) This child-friendly Russafa cafe, bar and bookshop is a comfy place to lounge and browse. It has a short, well-selected list of wines and serves cheese and cold-meat platters, salads and plenty of Italian specialities.

### Radio City     Club
(www.radiocityvalencia.es; Calle de Santa Teresa 19; ⊘10.30pm-3.30am Tue-Sun) Almost as much mini-cultural centre as club, Radio City, always seething, pulls in the punters with activities including cinema, flamenco and dancing to an eclectic mix. Pick up a flyer here for its younger sister, Music Box, also in the Centro Histórico, which stays open until dawn.

# ⭐ Entertainment

### Teatro Principal     Theatre
( 🎟tickets 902 48 84 88; www.teatres.gva.es; Calle de Barcas 15) One of Valencia's main venues for theatre.

### Filmoteca     Cinema
(www.ivac.gva.es; Plaza del Ayuntamiento; admission €2) This cinema, on the 4th floor of the Teatro Rialto building, screens undubbed classic and art-house films for a pittance.

### Black Note     Live Music
(www.blacknoteclub.com; Calle Polo y Peyrolón 15; ⊘9pm-3.30am Mon-Sat) Valencia's most active venue for jazz, boogaloo, funk and

Sierra del Cadí

CHRISTIAN KOBER/GETTY IMAGES ©

**Right:** Valencian tile panel at the Museo Nacional de Cerámica (p127);
**Below:** Las Fallas, Valencia (p129)
(BELOW) ALDO PAVAN/GETTY IMAGES ©; (RIGHT) GREG ELMS/GETTY IMAGES ©

soul, Black Note has live music around midnight most nights and good canned sounds. Admission, including first drink, ranges from free to €15, depending on who's grooving.

## ⓘ Information

Call ☏ 902 12 32 12 throughout the region for tourist information (at premium rates).

**Regional Tourist Office** ( ☏ 963 98 64 22; www.comunitatvalenciana.com; Calle de la Paz 48; ⏱ 10am-6pm Mon-Fri, to 2pm Sat) A fount of information about the Valencia region.

**Turismo Valencia Tourist Office** (VLC; ☏ 963 15 39 31; www.turisvalencia.es; Plaza de la Reina 19; ⏱ 9am-7pm Mon-Sat, 10am-2pm Sun) Has several other branches around town, including Plaza del Ayuntamiento **(Plaza del Ayuntamiento;** ⏱ 9am-7pm Mon-Sat, 10am-2pm Sun)**,** the AVE station and airport arrivals area.

## ⓘ Getting There & Away

### Air

Valencia's **airport** (VLC; ☏ 902 40 47 04) is 10km west of the city centre along the A3, towards Madrid. Budget flights serve major European destinations including London, Paris and Berlin.

### Bus

Valencia's **bus station** ( ☏ 96 346 62 66; Avenida Menéndez Pidal) is beside the riverbed. Bus 8 connects it to Plaza del Ayuntamiento.

**Avanza** (www.avanzabus.com) operates hourly bus services to/from Madrid (€29.40, four hours).

**ALSA** (www.alsa.es) has up to 10 daily buses to/from Barcelona (€29 to €35, four to five hours) and more than 10 to Alicante (€20.60 to €25, two to five hours), most via Benidorm.

### Train

From Valencia's **Estación del Norte** (Calle Xàtiva), major destinations include the following:

| DESTINATION | PRICE (€) | DURATION (HR) | FREQUENCY (PER DAY) |
| --- | --- | --- | --- |
| Alicante | 17-30 | 1½-2 | 11-13 |
| Barcelona | 40-44 | 3-4¼ | 14-18 |
| Madrid | 27-73 | 1¾-6½ | 13-20 |

## ❶ Getting Around

Valencia has an integrated bus, tram and metro network. Tourist offices sell the Valencia Tourist Card (www.valenciatouristcard.com; 24/48/72hr €15/20/25), entitling you to free urban travel and discounts at participating sights, shops and restaurants.

### To/From the Airport

Metro lines 3 and 5 connect the airport, central Valencia and the port. A taxi into the city centre costs around €18 (including a supplement for journeys originating at the airport).

### Car & Motorcycle

Street parking is a pain. Underground car parks are signposted throughout the centre. The cheapest central one is at the corner of Calles Barón de Cárcer and Hospital.

### Public Transport

Most buses run until about 10pm, with various night services continuing until around 1am. Buy a **Bonobús Plus** (€8 for 10 journeys) at major metro stations, most tobacconists and some newspaper kiosks or pay as you get on (€1.50).

The tram is a pleasant way to get to the beach and port. Pick it up at Pont de Fusta or where it intersects with the metro at Benimaclet.

Metro (www.metrovalencia.es) lines (five with a sixth on the way) cross town and serve the outer suburbs. The closest stations to the city centre are Ángel Guimerá, Xàtiva (for the train station), Colón and Pont de Fusta.

# Camino de Santiago & Basque Spain

**This is the Spain that most foreign visitors have yet to discover.** Spain's north coast and its hinterland are home to some of the most dramatic scenery in the country, from the Pyrenees of Navarra to wild coastline with picture-perfect villages.

The diversity and culinary innovation of the Basque Country finds expression in two cities: magnificent San Sebastián, one of the world's most beautiful seaside cities, and Bilbao, whose stirring Guggenheim Museum has become the symbol for the region. Away from the coast is the wine country of La Rioja and the stunning cathedral cities of Burgos and León. Above all else this is pilgrim territory: the Camino de Santiago, a medieval pilgrimage trail running from the French border right across north Spain, is undergoing a huge resurgence of interest. It all culminates in Santiago de Compostela, whose cathedral is as splendid as it is spiritually significant.

Vineyards, La Rioja (p157)
JESÚS I. BRAVO SOLER/GETTY IMAGES ©

Catedral, Burgos (p164)
JERONIMO ALBA/GETTY IMAGES ©

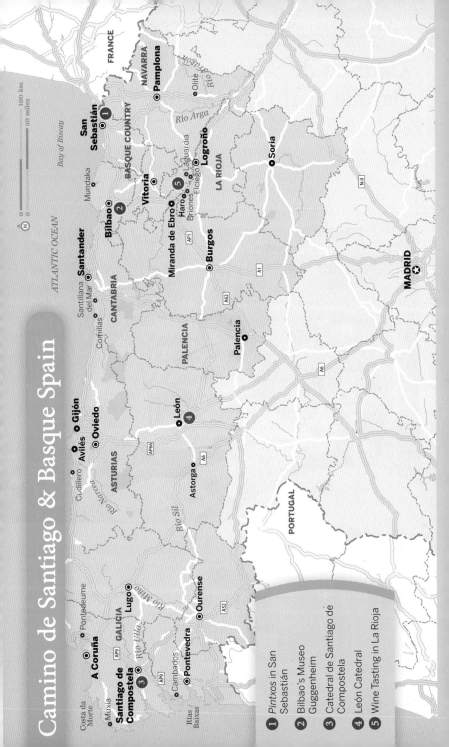

# Camino de Santiago & Basque Spain

1 *Pintxos* in San Sebastián
2 Bilbao's Museo Guggenheim
3 Catedral de Santiago de Compostela
4 León Catedral
5 Wine Tasting in La Rioja

# Camino de Santiago & Basque Spain Highlights

## *Pintxos* in San Sebastián

San Sebastián (p150) is a culinary Mecca: if you love food you must come here. The city holds 18 Michelin stars (and counting), more per capita than any other city in the world. It all owes a debt to the New Basque Cuisine Movement, which has lightened up traditional dishes and emphasised the remarkable local products.

## Bilbao's Museo Guggenheim

It wasn't so long ago that tourists gave industrial Bilbao a wide berth, but then along came the Museo Guggenheim (p148), a shimmering, titanium fish stuffed with cutting-edge modern art, and suddenly Bilbao was the place to be. But as well as Guggenheim art, Bilbao also has a clutch of other fantastic galleries and museums and a *pintxo* culture second only to San Sebastián's.

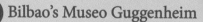

MARK MAWSON/GETTY IMAGES ©, ARCHITECT: FRANK GEHRY

## Catedral de Santiago de Compostela 3

The cathedral city of Santiago de Compostela is one of the most sacred cities in the Catholic world. This much-coveted destination for pilgrims along the Camino de Santiago is laden with spiritual significance, and its staggering cathedral (p172) cannot fail to leave you moved. Its artistic high point is the Pórtico de la Gloria featuring 200 masterly Romanesque sculptures.

KEN WELSH/GETTY IMAGES ©

CARLOS SANCHEZ PEREYRA/GETTY IMAGES ©

## 4

## León Catedral

Spain has some extraordinary cathedrals, but few combine delicacy and grandeur to such sublime effect as León's cathedral (p168). Prettily proportioned on the outside, and a kaleidoscope of colour within, the cathedral's 128 stained-glass windows will leave you breathless. The quiet slap of sandals on flagstones is also a reminder that this is an important staging post for pilgrims along the Camino de Santiago.

## 5

## Wine Tasting in La Rioja

Get out the *copas* (glasses) for La Rioja (p157) and for some of the best red wines produced in the country. Wine goes well with the region's ochre earth and vast blue skies. Under these skies lie space-age bodegas, vineyard tours (and tastings), fascinating museums charting the history of wine, great value hotels and some magnificently scenic countryside.

# Camino de Santiago & Basque Spain's Best...

## Places to Eat

● **Arzak** Three Michelin stars and the granddaddy of nueva cocina vasca. (p156)

● **La Cuchara de San Telmo** The king of San Sebastián *pintxo* bars. (p155)

● **Cervecería Morito** An old style bar with totally up-to-date tapas. (p165)

● **Mina Restaurante** The best in Basque cooking, according to some. (p146)

## Places for a Local Drop

● **Dinastía Vivanco** One of Spain's most interactive wine museums in Brione. (p160)

● **Laguardia** Charming hill-town in the heart of La Rioja wine country with plenty of wineries to visit nearby. (p159)

● **Museo de la Viña y el Vino de Navarra** Outstanding wine museum in a charming small town in Navarra. (p160)

● **Bodegas Ysios** The Rioja region's temple of wine. (p159)

## Daring Architecture

● **Museo Guggenheim** The building that changed the way we build. (p148)

● **Hotel Marqués de Riscal** Frank Gehry turns his hand to village improvements. (p158)

● **Bodegas Ysios** A wave-like structure rolling across the Riojan landscape. (p159)

● **León Catedral** The house of God on a huge scale. (p168)

● **Catedral de Santiago de Compostela** The magnificent reward at the end of the road. (p172)

# Need to Know

## Places for City Life

○ **San Sebastián** Gorgeous city, perfect beach and extraordinary food. (p150)

○ **Santiago de Compostela** Cathedral city beloved by pilgrims and aesthetes alike. (p169)

○ **León** Full of energy and with one of the finest cathedrals in Spain. (p166)

○ **Bilbao** Gritty city that's home to the iconic modern age Guggenheim. (p144)

○ **Burgos** Home of El Cid, a glittering cathedral and a pretty streetscape. (p164)

### ADVANCE PLANNING

○ **Six months before** Start planning your daily walking segments for the Camino de Santiago. Book summer accommodation in San Sebastián and Pamplona.

○ **Two months before** Book your table at Michelin-starred restaurant, Arzak in San Sebastián.

○ **One month before** Buy tickets online for Bilbao's Guggenheim museum.

### RESOURCES

○ **Basque Country** (www.basquecountry-tourism.com) Informative site for the Basque Country.

○ **Navarra** (www.turismo.navarra.es) Everything you need to know about Navarra.

○ **La Rioja** (www.lariojaturismo.com) Official tourist office site for La Rioja.

○ **Castilla y León** (www.turismocastillayleon.com) Informative site for northcentral Spain.

○ **Asturias Tourism** (www.turismoasturias.es) Excellent, comprehensive site of Asturias' regional tourism office.

○ **Galicia** (www.turgalicia.es) Excellent window on Galicia.

### GETTING AROUND

○ **Air** International airports in Bilbao, Santander, Oviedo, Santiago de Compostela, A Coruña and Vigo.

○ **Train** Renfe (www.renfe.es) trains connect to the rest of Spain, FEVE (V runs along the coast.

○ **Bus** Intermittent services where trains don't reach.

### BE FOREWARNED

○ **Accommodation** Can be hard to find in San Sebastián (May to September) and Santiago de Compostela (July).

○ **Arzak** The Basque Country's most celebrated restaurant closes the last two weeks in June and November.

○ **Bring an Umbrella** Swept by one rainy front after another blowing in from the Atlantic, Galicia has, overall, twice as much rain as the Spanish national average. June to August are the least rainy months.

○ **Summer** Book your coastal accommodation months in advance.

**Left:** Laguardia (p159), La Rioja; **bove:** Alameda Boulevard, San Sebastián (p150)

# Camino de Santiago & Basque Spain's Itineraries

*The two big hitters of Spain's little-trodden northern regions are the beaches, galleries and divine food of the great Basque cities of Bilbao and San Sebastián, and the Camino de Santiago pilgrimage route.*

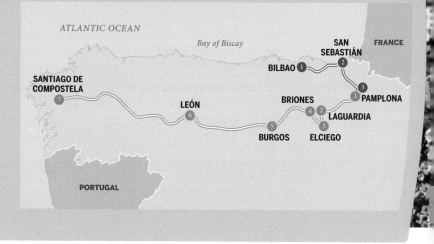

**3 DAYS**

**BILBAO TO PAMPLONA**
## BASQUE CITIES

Basque culture is one of the oldest in Europe, but ❶ **Bilbao** offers confirmation that a willingness to embrace the outrageously modern is central to the Basque psyche. This is a town of fiercely guarded Basque traditions, not least in the seven streets of the Parte Vieja (old town) where Bilbao was born. Not far away, the futuristic Museo Guggenheim is one of Europe's most extraordinary architectural innovations and deserves a full day of appreciation. For the remaining two days, lose yourself in ❷ **San Sebastián**, a gorgeous seaside city arrayed around a near-perfect beach. In the impossibly narrow lanes of the old town, bar tops groan under the weight of *pintxos* (Basque tapas), from basic Basque staples to the experimental high cuisine in miniature for which the region has become famous. Elsewhere in town, Michelin-starred restaurants provide a more formal but equally delicious dining experience. Finally, head an hour inland from San Sebastián to ❸ **Pamplona**, the capital of Navarra and a city renowned the world over for the legendary bull run held each morning during its annual Sanfermines festival.

**PAMPLONA TO SANTIAGO DE COMPOSTELA**

# CAMINO DE SANTIAGO

There are many different *caminos* (routes) to Santiago de Compostela. The most trodden route begins on the French-Spanish Basque country border, tumbles out of the Pyrenees and really gets into gear in ❶**Pamplona**, a city that hosts a crazy bull-running festival. Next, saunter through La Rioja, Spain's most prestigious wine-producing region. A good base for the area is ❷**Laguardia**, a medieval hilltop town surrounded by vineyards. One of the best bodegas, in the nearby village of ❸**Elciego**, is the Guggenheim-esque Bodegas Marqués de Riscal. Also along the Río Ebro, ❹**Briones** has the astonishing

Dinastía Vivanco, arguably La Rioja's best wine museum. Rising up from the plains of central Castilla y León is ❺**Burgos**, dominated by its cathedral – this is your next stop, followed by glorious ❻**León** and its sparkling cathedral windows. Moving ever westward, celebrate the completion of your journey with hundreds of foot-weary pilgrims in front of the great altar of the cathedral of ❼**Santiago de Compostela**, a sacred city whose golden granite buildings grow a jacket of moss in the seemingly constant drizzle.

Elciego (p158)
PABLOPHOTO/GETTY IMAGES ©

143

# Discover Camino de Santiago & Basque Spain

## At a Glance

- **Bilbao** (p144) Capital of the Basque Country.

- **San Sebastián** (p150) Attractive coastal city and culinary colossus.

- **La Rioja** (p157) Spain's premier wine country.

- **Camino de Santiago** (p160) The pilgrimage trail across northern Spain.

- **Santiago de Compostela** (p169) The goal of millions of pilgrims.

## BASQUE COUNTRY

........................................................

## Bilbao

POP 54,200

Bilbao (Bilbo in Basque) had a tough upbringing. Growing up in an environment of heavy industry and industrial wastelands, it was abused for years by those in power and had to work hard to get anywhere. But, like the kid from the estates who made it big, Bilbao's graft paid off when a few wise investments left it with a shimmering titanium fish called the Museo Guggenheim and a horde of arty groupies around the world.

### ◉ Sights

**Museo de Bellas Artes**          Art Gallery

(www.museobilbao.com; Plaza del Museo 2; adult/student/child €7/5/free, free Wed; ⊙10am-8pm Wed-Mon)
The Museo de Bellas Artes houses a compelling collection that includes everything from Gothic sculptures to 20th-century pop art. There are three main subcollections: classical art, with works by Murillo, Zurbarán, El Greco, Goya and van Dyck; contemporary art, featuring works by Gauguin, Francis Bacon and Anthony Caro; and Basque art, with works of the great sculptors Jorge de Oteiza and Eduardo Chillida, and strong paintings by the likes of Ignacio Zuloaga and Juan de Echevarria.

**Casco Viejo**          Old Town

The compact Casco Viejo, Bilbao's atmospheric old quarter, is full of charming streets, boisterous bars and plenty of

Casco Viejo
IZZET KERIBAR/GETTY IMAGES ©

quirky and independent shops. At the heart of the Casco are Bilbao's original seven streets, Las Siete Calles, which date from the 1400s.

### Euskal Museoa
Museum

(Museo Vasco; www.euskal-museoa.org/es/hasiera; Plaza Miguel Unamuno 4; adult/child €3/free, free Thu; ☉10am-7pm Tue-Fri, 10am-1.30pm & 4-7pm Sat, 10am-2pm Sun) This museum is probably the most complete museum of Basque culture and history in all of Spain. The story kicks off back in the days of prehistory and from this murky period the displays bound rapidly through to the modern age.

### Museo Marítimo Ría de Bilbao
Museum

(www.museomaritimobilbao.org; Muelle Ramón de la Sota 1; adult/student/child €6/3.50/free; ☉10am-8pm Tue-Sun, to 6pm Mon-Fri in winter) This space-age maritime museum, appropriately sited down on the waterfront, uses bright and well-thought-out displays to bring the watery depths of Bilbao and Basque maritime history to life. There's an outdoor section where children (and nautically inclined grown-ups) can clamber about a range of boats and pretend to be pirates and sailors.

## 🛌 Sleeping

### Pensión Iturrienea Ostatua
Boutique Hotel $$

(☎944 16 15 00; www.iturrieneaostatua.com; Calle de Santa María 14; r €50-70; 🛜) Easily the most eccentric hotel in Bilbao, it's part farmyard, part old-fashioned toyshop, and a work of art in its own right. The nine rooms here are so full of character that there'll be barely enough room for your own!

### Hostal Begoña
Boutique Hotel $$

(☎944 23 01 34; www.hostalbegona.com; Calle de la Amistad 2; s/d from €57/66; 🅿@🛜) The owners of this outstanding place don't need voguish labels for their very stylish and individual creation. Begoña speaks for itself with colourful rooms decorated with modern artworks, all with funky tiled bathrooms and wrought-iron beds.

## Artean Pass

The Artean Pass is a joint ticket for the Guggenheim (p148) and the Museo de Bellas Artes (p144), which, at €14 for adults, offers significant savings. It's available from either museum.

The common areas have mountains of books, traveller information and a rack of computers for internet usage.

### Gran Hotel Domine
Design Hotel $$$

(☎944 25 33 00; www.granhoteldominebilbao.com; Alameda Mazarredo 61; s/d from €170/190; 🅿❄@♨) Designer chic all the way, this stellar showpiece of the Silken chain has views of the Guggenheim from some of its pricier rooms, a giant column of rounded beach stones reaching for the heavens and a water feature filled with plates and glasses. Yes, it's a little different.

## 🍴 Eating

In the world of trade and commerce, the Basques are an outward-looking lot, but when it comes to food they refuse to believe that any other people could possibly match their culinary skills (and they may well have a point). This means that eating out in Bilbao is generally a choice of Basque, Basque or Basque food. Still, life could be worse and there are some terrific places to eat.

### Rio-Oja
Basque $

(☎944 15 08 71; Calle de Perro 4; mains €7-12; ☉9am-11pm) An institution that shouldn't be missed. It specialises in light Basque seafood and heavy inland fare, but to most foreigners the snails, sheep brains or squid floating in pools of its own ink are the makings of a culinary adventure story they'll be recounting for years. Don't worry, though: it really does taste much better than it sounds.

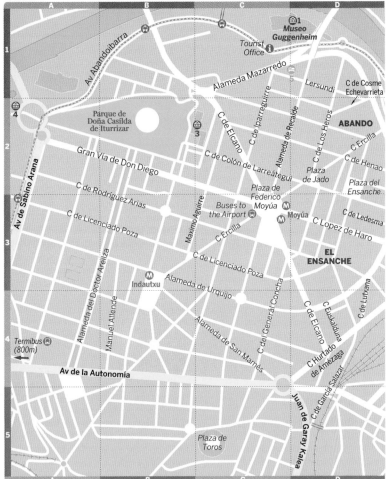

## Bascook
Contemporary Basque $$
(☎944 00 99 77; www.bascook.com; Calle de Barroeta Aldamar 8; menú del día €23; ☺lunch Mon-Sat, evenings Thu-Sat) The style of this unique place won't appeal to all. The lighting is more nightclub than restaurant and the menu is printed in the form of a newspaper, but even if the decor doesn't appeal the food probably will: an utterly modern and unusual take on Basque classics that's good enough to have locals battling for tables.

## Mina Restaurante
Contemporary Basque $$$
(☎944 79 59 38; www.restaurantemina.es; Muelle Marzana; tasting menu from €60; ☺closed Tue & Sun evening & Mon) Offering unexpected sophistication and fine dining in an otherwise fairly grimy neighbourhood, this riverside, and appropriately fish-based, restaurant has some critics citing it as the current *número uno* of Basque cooking. Reservations are essential.

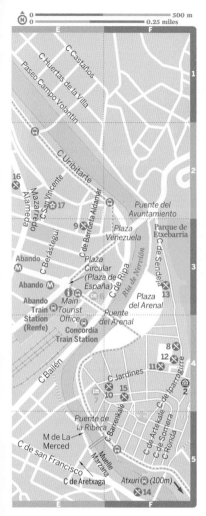

# Bilbao

## ⊚ Don't Miss Sights

## ⊚ Sights

## 🛌 Sleeping

## ⊗ Eating

## ⊕ Entertainment

## PINTXO BARS

Although it lacks San Sebastián's stellar reputation for *pintxos,* prices are generally slightly lower here (all charge from around €2.50 per *pintxo*) and the quality is about equal. There are literally hundreds of *pintxo* bars throughout Bilbao, but the Plaza Nueva on the edge of the Casco Viejo offers especially rich pickings, as do Calle de Perro and Calle Jardines. Some of the city's standouts, in no particular order:

**Bar Gure Toki**　　　　Pintxos **$$**
(Plaza Nueva 12; *pintxos* from €2.50) With a subtle but simple line in creative *pintxos* including some made with ostrich.

**Café-Bar Bilbao**　　　　Pintxos **$$**
(Plaza Nueva 6; *pintxos* from €2.50; ⊘7am-11pm Mon-Thu, 7am-11.30pm Fri, 9am-11.30pm Sat, 10am-3pm Sun) Cool blue southern tile work and warm northern atmosphere.

**Casa Victor Montes**　　Basque **$$**
(☏944 15 70 67; www.victormontesbilbao.com; Plaza Nueva 8; mains €15, *pintxos* from €2.50; ⊘10.30am-11pm Mon-Thu, 10.30am-midnight

## Zortziko Restaurante

Contemporary Basque **$$$**
(☏944 23 97 43; www.zortziko.es; Alameda Mazarredo 17; menus from €85, mains €26-38; ⊘Tue-Sat; 🍴) Michelin-starred chef Daniel García presents immaculate modern Basque cuisine in a formal 1920s-style French dining room. The highly inventive menu changes frequently but can include such delicacies as lamb sweetbreads stew with milk and thyme ice-cream.

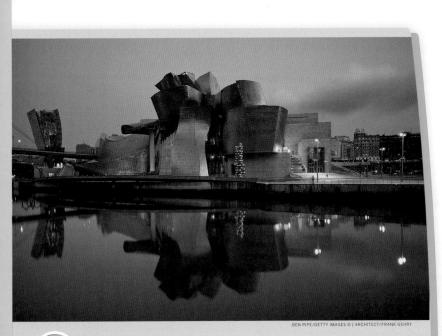

## ⭐ Don't Miss
# Museo Guggenheim

Opened in September 1997, Bilbao's Museo Guggenheim lifted modern architecture and Bilbao into the 21st century – with sensation. It boosted the city's already inspired regeneration, stimulated further development and placed Bilbao firmly in the world art and tourism spotlight.

Some might say, probably quite rightly, that structure overwhelms function here, and that the Guggenheim is more famous for its architecture than its content. But Canadian architect Frank Gehry's inspired use of flowing canopies, cliffs, promontories, ship shapes, towers and flying fins is irresistible.

Heading inside, the interior of the Guggenheim is purposely vast. The cathedral-like atrium is more than 45m high. Light pours in through the glass cliffs. Permanent exhibits fill the ground floor and include such wonders as mazes of metal and phrases of light reaching for the skies.

For most people, though, it is the temporary exhibitions that are the main attraction (check the website for upcoming shows).

Admission prices vary depending on special exhibitions and time of year. The prices we have quoted are the maximum (and most common); the last ticket sales are half an hour before closing. Free guided tours in Spanish take place at 11am and 5pm; sign up half an hour before at the information desk. Tours can be conducted in other languages but you must ask at the information desk beforehand. Groups are limited to 20, so get there early. Excellent self-guided audio tours in various languages are free with admission and there is a special children's audio guide.

## NEED TO KNOW

www.guggenheim-bilbao.es; Avenida Abandoibarra 2; adult/child €13/free; ⓧ10am-8pm, closed Mon Sep-Jun

**Fri-Sun)** As well known for its pintxos as its full meals.

### Sorginzulo
Pintxos $$

(Plaza Nueva 12; *pintxos* from €2.50; ☺9.30am-12.30am) A matchbox-sized bar with an exemplary spread of *pintxos*. The house special is calamari but it's only served on weekends.

### Berton Sasibil
Pintxos

(Calle Jardines 8; *pintxos* from €2.50; ☺8.30am-midnight Mon-Sat, 10am-4pm Sun) Here you can watch informative films on the crafting of the same superb *pintxos* that you're munching on.

### Claudio: La Feria del Jamón
Pintxos

(Calle Iparragirre 9-18; *pintxos* from €2.50) A creaky old place full of ancient furnishings. As you'll guess from the name and the dozens of legs of ham hanging from the ceiling, it's all about pigs. Opposite the bar, it has a shop selling hams to take away.

## ☆ Entertainment

### Kafe Antzokia
Live Music

( ☎944 24 61 07; www.kafeantzokia.com; Calle San Vicente 2) This is the vibrant heart of contemporary Basque Bilbao, featuring international rock bands, blues and reggae, but also the cream of Basque rock-pop. Weekend concerts run from 10pm to 1am, followed by DJs until 5am. Cover charge for concerts can range from €15 upwards. During the day it's a cafe, restaurant and cultural centre all rolled into one and has frequent exciting events on.

## ⓘ Information

**Tourist Office** (www.bilbaoturismo.net) main tourist office ( ☎944 79 57 60; www.bilbaoturismo.net; Plaza Circular 1; ☺9am-9pm; 🛜); airport ( ☎944 71 03 01; www.bilbaoturismo.net; ☺9am-9pm Mon-Sat, 9am-3pm Sun); Guggenheim (www.bilbaoturismo.net; Alameda Mazarredo 66; ☺10am-7pm daily, till 3pm Sun Sep-Jun); Bilbao's friendly tourist-office staffers are extremely helpful, well informed and, above all, enthusiastic about their city. At all offices ask for the free bimonthly *Bilbao Guía*, with its entertainment listings plus tips on restaurants, bars and nightlife. At the newly opened, state-of-the-art main tourist office there's free wi-fi access, a bank of touch-screen information computers and, best of all, some humans to help answer questions.

## ⓘ Getting There & Away

### Air

Bilbao's **airport** (BIO; ☎902 404704; www.aena.es) is near Sondika, to the northeast of the city. A number of European flag carriers serve the city and of the budget airlines **EasyJet** (www.easyjet.com) and **Vueling** (www.vueling.com) cover the widest range of destinations.

### Bus

Bilbao's main bus station, **Termibus** ( ☎944 39 50 77; Gurtubay 1, San Mamés), is west of the centre. There are regular services to the following destinations:

| DESTINATION | FARE (€) | DURATION (HR) |
| --- | --- | --- |
| Barcelona | 48 | 7-8 |
| Biarritz (France) | 198 | 3 |
| Logroño | 13 | 2¾ |
| Madrid | from 31 | 4¾ |
| Pamplona | 15 | 2¾ |
| San Sebastián | 6.47 | 1 |

### Train

The Abando train station is just across the river from Plaza Arriaga and the Casco Viejo. There are frequent trains to the following destinations:

| DESTINATION | FARE (€) | DURATION (HR) |
| --- | --- | --- |
| Barcelona | 65 | 6¾ |
| Burgos | 23 | 3 |
| Madrid | 64 | 5 |
| Valladolid | 26 | 4 |

## ⓘ Getting Around

### To/From the Airport

The **airport bus** (Bizkaibus A3247; ticket €1.40) departs from a stand on the extreme right as you leave arrivals. It runs through the northwestern section of the city, passing the Museo Guggenheim, stopping at Plaza de Federico Moyúa and terminating at the Termibus (bus station). It runs from the airport every 20 minutes in summer and every 30 minutes in winter from 6.20am to midnight. There is also a direct hourly bus from the airport to San Sebastián (€15.70, 1¼ hours). It runs from 7.45am to 11.45pm.

Taxis from the airport to the Casco Viejo cost about €21 to €26 depending on traffic.

........................................................

# San Sebastián

POP 183,300

It's said that nothing is impossible. This is wrong. It's impossible to lay eyes on San Sebastián (Basque: Donostia) and not fall madly in love. This stunning city is everything that grimy Bilbao is not: cool, svelte and flirtatious by night, charming and well mannered by day. Best of all is the summer fun on the beach. For its setting, form and attitude, Playa de la Concha is the equal of any city beach in Europe. Then there's Playa de Gros (also known as Playa de la Zurriola), with its surfers and sultry beach goers. As the sun falls on another sweltering summer's day, you'll sit back with a drink and an artistic *pintxo* and realise that, yes, you too are in love with sexy San Sebastián.

## ◉ Sights

**Playa de la Concha**  Beach

Fulfilling almost every idea of how a perfect city beach should be formed, Playa de la Concha and its westerly extension, **Playa de Ondarreta**, are easily among the best city beaches in Europe. Throughout the long summer months a fiesta atmosphere prevails, with thousands of tanned and toned bodies spread across the sands. The swimming is almost always safe.

**Monte Igueldo**  Viewpoint

The views from the summit of Monte Igueldo, just west of town, will make you feel like a circling hawk staring over the vast panorama of the Bahía de la Concha and the surrounding coastline and mountains. The best way to get there is via the old-world **funicular railway** (www. monteigueldo.es; return adult/child €3.10/2.30; ☉10am-9pm Jul, 10am-10pm Aug shorter hours rest of yr) to the **Parque de Atracciones** (www.monteigueldo.es; admission €2.20; ☉11.15am-2pm & 4-8pm Mon-Fri, until 8.30pm Sat & Sun Jul-Sep, shorter hours rest of yr), a slightly tacky mini theme park at the top of the hill. Individual rides (which include roller coasters, boat rides, carousels and pony rides) cost between €1 and €2.50 extra. Trains on the funicular railway depart every 15 minutes.

**Aquarium**  Aquarium

(www.aquariumss.com; Plaza Carlos Blasco de Imaz 1; adult/ child €13/6.50; ☉10am-9pm daily Jul-Aug, 10am-8pm Mon-Fri, 10am-9pm Sat & Sun Easter-Jun & Sep, shorter hours rest of yr) In the city's excellent aquarium you will fear for your life as huge sharks bear down on you, and you will get tripped-out by fancy

Waterfront, Playa de la Concha
WALTER BIBIKOW/GETTY IMAGES ©

# Detour:
## Guernica

Guernica (Basque: Gernika) is a state of mind. At a glance it seems no more than a modern and ugly country town. Apparently, prior to the morning of 26 April 1937, Guernica wasn't quite so ugly, but the horrifying events of that day meant that the town was later reconstructed as fast as possible with little regard for aesthetics. Franco, who'd been having some problems with the Basques, decided to teach them a lesson by calling in his buddy Hitler. On that fateful morning planes from Hitler's Condor Legion flew backwards and forwards over the town demonstrating their new found concept of saturation bombing. In the space of a few hours, the town was destroyed and many people were left dead or injured.

The tragedy of Guernica gained international resonance with Picasso's iconic painting *Guernica,* which has come to symbolise the violence of the 20th century. A copy of the painting now hangs in the entrance hall of the UN headquarters in New York, while the original hangs in the Centro de Arte Reina Sofía (p189) in Madrid.

Guernica's seminal experience is a visit to the **Museo de la Paz de Gernika** (Guernica Peace Museum; www.peacemuseumguernica.org; Plaza Foru 1; adult/child €5/3; 10am-7pm Tue-Sat, 10am-2pm Sun Mar-Sep, 10am-2pm & 4-6pm Tue-Sat, 10am-2pm Sun Oct-Feb), where audiovisual displays calmly reveal the horror of war and hatred, both in the Basque Country and around the world.

Guernica is an easy day trip from Bilbao by ET/FV train from Atxuri train station (€2.80, one hour). Trains run every half-hour.

fluoro jellyfish. The highlights of a visit are the cinema-screen-sized deep-ocean and coral-reef exhibits and the long tunnel, around which swim monsters of the deep. The aquarium also contains a maritime museum section. Allow at least 1½ hours for a visit.

### San Telmo Museoa    Museum
(www.santelmomuseoa.com; Plaza Zuloaga 1; adult/student/child €5/3/free, Tue free; 10am-8pm Tue-Sun) Both the oldest and one of the newest museums in the Basque Country, the San Telmo museum has existed since 1902 – sort of. It was actually closed for many years but after major renovation work it reopened in 2011 and is now a museum of Basque culture and society. The displays range from historical artefacts to the squiggly lines of modern art, and all the pieces reflect Basque culture and society.

## Tours

The tourist office runs a whole array of different city tours (including a running tour!) starting at €10.

### San Sebastián Food    Tour, Cooking Course
( 943 42 11 43; www.sansebastianfood.com; Hotel Maria Cristina, Paseo de la República Argentina 4) The highly recommended San Sebastián Food runs an array of *pintxo* tasting tours (from €95), self-guided foodie tours (€75) and cookery courses (from €145) in and around the city, as well as wine tastings (from €45) and day-long wine-tasting tours to La Rioja (€255).

### Sabores de San Sebastián    Tour
(Flavours of San Sebastián; 902 443442; www.sansebastianreservas.com; tour €18; 11.30am Tue & Thu Jul & Aug) The tourist office runs the Sabores de San Sebastián, a two-hour

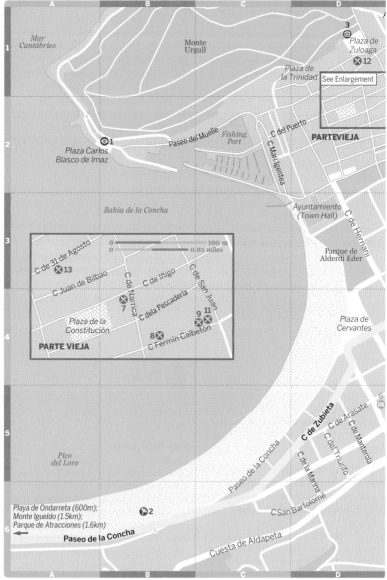

tour (in Spanish and English, French tours are available on request) of some of the city's *pintxo* haunts. Tours are also held with less frequency outside high season – contact the tourist office for dates.

## Sleeping

Accommodation standards in San Sebastián are generally good, but prices are high and availability in high season is very

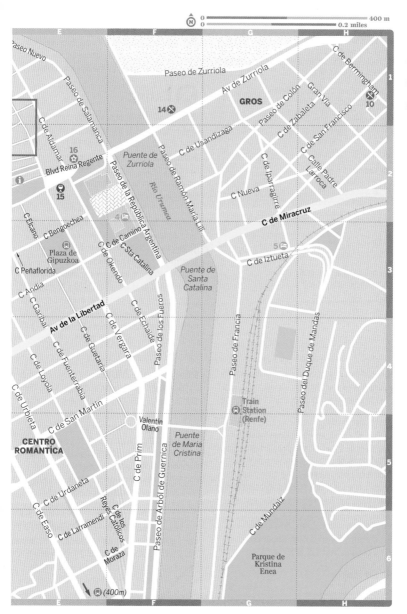

tight. In fact, with the city's increasing popularity, many of the better places are booked up for July and August months in advance. If you do turn up without a booking, head to the tourist office, which keeps a list of available rooms.

**Pensión Régil**     Pension $
( ☑ 943 42 71 43; www.pensionregil.com; Calle de Easo 9; s/d €53/59; 🛜) The furnishings might be cheap and the decor a bit pink and floral for our liking, but just look at that price! You really won't get a much

153

# San Sebastián

## ◎ Sights

## ✪ Activities, Courses & Tours

## ⊜ Sleeping

## ✗ Eating

## ⊙ Drinking & Nightlife

## ✪ Entertainment

better deal in San Sebastián in high season. Add in that all rooms have private bathrooms, it's very close to Playa de la Concha and the young owner, Inaki, is a bit of a charmer and you can't go wrong.

### Pensión Aida     Boutique Hotel $$
(🕿 943 32 78 00; www.pensionesconencanto. com; Calle de Iztueta 9; s €62, d €84-90, studios €132-152; ❄@🖙) The owners of this excellent *pensión* read the rule book on what makes a good hotel and have complied exactly. The rooms are bright and bold, full of exposed stone and everything smells fresh and clean. The communal area, stuffed with soft sofas and mountains of information, is a big plus.

### Hotel Maria Cristina     Historic Hotel $$$
(🕿 943 43 76 00; www.starwoodhotels.com; Paseo de la República Argentina 4; d from €335, ste from €620; P❄@🖙) In case you're wondering what sort of hotels Lonely Planet authors normally stay in, the absolutely impeccable Maria Cristina, with its huge and luxurious rooms, is not one of them. However, don't be downhearted, because

instead of hanging out with us you'll get to mix with royalty and Hollywood stars, who feel right at home in this palace-like hotel, which dominates the centre of the city. Yes, we know, you're still disappointed.

# ✗ Eating

With 16 Michelin stars (including three restaurants with the coveted three stars) and a population of 183,000, San Sebastián stands atop a pedestal as one of the culinary capitals of the planet. As if that alone weren't enough, the city is overflowing with bars – almost all of which have bar tops weighed down under a mountain of *pintxos* that almost every Spaniard will (sometimes grudgingly) tell you are the best in country. These statistics alone make San Sebastián's CV look pretty impressive. But it's not just us who thinks this: a raft of the world's best chefs, including such luminaries as Catalan super-chef Ferran Adriá, have said that San Sebastián is quite possibly the best place on the entire planet to eat.

### Restaurante Alberto     Seafood $
(🕿 943 42 88 84; Calle de 31 de Agosto 19; mains €12-15, menus €15; ⊙noon-4pm and 7pm-midnight Thu-Tue) A charming old seafood restaurant with a fishmonger-style window display of the day's catch. It's small and friendly and the pocket-sized dining room feels like it was once someone's living room. The food is earthy (well, OK, salty) and good, and the service swift.

### Bodegón Alejandro     Seafood $$
(🕿 943 42 71 58; Calle de Fermín Calbetón 4; menú del día from €16, mains €15-18; ⊙1-3.30pm Tue & Sun, 1-3.30pm & 8.30-10.30pm Wed-Sat) This highly regarded restaurant, which has a pleasant, casual style, has a menu from which you can select such succulent treats as tripe with veal cheeks, baby tomatoes stuffed with squid or just plain-old baked lobster. Oh, what choices!

### Restaurante Ni Neu     Contemporary Basque $$$
(🕿 943 00 31 62; www.restaurantenineu.com; Avenida de Zurriola 1; menus €18-38; ⊙10am-

8.30pm Sun & Tue-Wed, 10am-11.30pm Thu-Sat)
The light, fluffy and utterly modern dishes
of the Restaurante Ni Neu will leave you
hoping never to eat boring old-fashioned
meat and two veg again! Throw in a spectacular setting, inside the Kursaal Centre,
with a view straight over Playa de Gros
and bargain-priced meals, and you get a
place that's hard to beat.

## PINTXO BARS

No other city in Spain has made such
a culture out of the creation, and
consumption of *pintxos* and for many
people the overriding memory of their
stay in San Sebastián will be that of
late nights in the *pintxo* bars.

The following *pintxo* bars all charge
between €2.50 to €3.50 for one *pintxo*.

### La Cuchara de San
**Telmo**  Contemporary Basque **$$**
(www.lacucharadesantelmo.com; Calle de 31
de Agosto 28; pintxos from €2.50; ⏱7.30pm-
11pm Tue, noon-3.30pm & 7.30-11pm
Wed-Sun) This unfussy, hidden-away
(and hard to find) bar offers miniature
*nueva cocina vasca* (Basque nouvelle
cuisine) from a supremely creative
kitchen. Unlike many San Sebastián
bars this one doesn't have any *pintxos*
laid out on the bar top; instead you
must order from the blackboard menu
behind the counter.

### Bergara Bar  Pintxos **$$**
(General Artetxe 8; pintxos from €2.50;
⏱9am-11pm) The **Bergara Bar** is one of
the most highly regarded *pintxo* bars
in Gros, a growing powerhouse in the
*pintxo* bar stakes, and has a mouth-
watering array of delights piled onto the
bar counter as well as others chalked up
onto the board.

### Bar Borda Berri  Pintxos **$$**
(Calle Fermín Calbetón 12; ⏱noon-midnight)
Bar Borda Berri is a *pintxos* bar that really
stands out. The house special is pigs
ears (and they're much better than they
sound!).

# Pintxos in San Sebastián

*BY GABRIELLA RANELLI, COOKING
SCHOOL TEACHER AND GASTRONOMIC TOUR LEADER*

### 1  THE PINTXO CRAWL
The *pintxos* tradition is to go from bar to bar
trying one *pintxo* and a drink in each spot. The idea
is to try the house speciality in each one. Don't
count on sitting down.

### 2  CALLE DE FERMÍN CALBETÓN &
### CALLE DE 31 DE AGOSTO
If you only have one day, you can't miss Calle de
Fermín Calbetón or Calle de 31 de Agosto in the
Parte Vieja (Old Town). Any place with a lot of people
is probably a good bet, but if you come at any time
other than before lunch and before dinner, an empty
bar might just mean that you are off schedule.

### 3  GROS
The other great area for *pintxos* is in Gros, east
of the Parte Vieja across the Río Urumea. Gros is
where you will find more wine bars and sophisticated
contemporary *pintxos*. The pace is slower here
and people might linger longer in some of the bars
because the wine lists are especially tempting.

### 4  GILDA
The most emblematic *pintxo* in San
Sebastian is the Gilda. Its base always consists
of pickled guindilla peppers (a mild green chilli),
anchovies and olives and is traditionally served
piled on a plate and doused in extra-virgin olive
oil. But this being San Sebastián, some bars do
creative variations on the theme.

### 5  TXAKOLI DE GETARIA
The perfect (and most traditional)
accompaniment to many *pintxos* is a glass of
*txakoli*, the tart local white wine, which is often
poured into your glass from a great height. And
not just any *txakoli*: it really should be Txakoli de
Getaria, which is produced west of San Sebastián.
It goes especially well with a shrimp brochette.

# Three Shining Stars

The Basque Country seems to be engaged in an eternal battle with Catalonia for the title of the best foodie region in Spain and, just like in Catalonia, the Basque Country is home to an impressive number of restaurants that have been awarded a coveted three Michelin stars, as well as many more with one or two stars. Of the three star places all are in and around San Sebastián.

**Arzak** ( ☏ 943 27 84 65; www.arzak.info; Avenida Alcalde Jose Elosegui 273; meals €189; ⏰ closed Sun-Mon & Nov & late Jun) Acclaimed chef Juan Mari Arzak takes some beating when it comes to *nueva cocina vasca* (Basque nouvelle cuisine) and his restaurant is, not surprisingly, considered one of the best places to eat in Spain. Arzak is now assisted by his daughter Elena and they never cease to innovate. Reservations, well in advance, are obligatory. The restaurant is about 1.5km east of San Sebastián.

**Martín Berasategui Restaurant** ( ☏ 943 36 64 71; www.martinberasategui.com; Calle Loidi 4, Lasarte-Oria; tasting menu €195; ⏰ closed Sun dinner, Mon-Tue & Dec–mid-Jan) This superlative restaurant, about 9km southwest of San Sebastián, is considered by foodies to be one of the best restaurants in the world. The chef, Martín Berasategui, doesn't approach cooking in the same way as the rest of us. He approaches it as a science and the results are tastes you never knew existed. Reserve well ahead.

**Akelañe** ( ☏ 943 31 12 09; www.akelarre.net; Paseo Padre Orcolaga 56; tasting menu €170; ⏰ closed Sun & Mon yr-round, & Tue from Jan-Jun) This is where chef Pedro Subijana creates cuisine that is a feast to all five senses (and possibly a few senses we haven't yet named!). As with most of the region's top *nueva cocina vasca* restaurants, the emphasis here is on using fresh, local produce and turning it into something totally unexpected. It's in the suburb of Igeldo just west of the city.

## Astelena
Basque **$$**

(Calle de Iñigo 1; *pintxos* from €2.50; ⏰ 1-4.30pm & 8-11pm Tue & Thu-Sat, 1-4.30pm Wed) The *pintxos* draped across the counter in this bar, tucked into the corner of Plaza de la Constitución, stand out. Many of them are a fusion of Basque and Asian inspirations, but the best of all are perhaps the foie-gras-based treats. The great positioning means that prices are slightly elevated.

## Bar Goiz-Argi
Seafood **$$**

(Calle de Fermín Calbetón 4; *pintxos* from €2.50) *Gambas a la plancha* (prawns cooked on a hotplate) are the house speciality. Sounds simple, we know, but never have we tasted prawns cooked quite as perfectly as this.

# 🍷 Drinking & Entertainment

## Museo del Whisky
Bar

(Alameda Boulevard 5; ⏰ 3.30pm-3.30am) Appropriately named, this Irish/Scottish-style bar is full of bottles of Scotland's finest (3000 bottles to be exact) as well as a museum's worth of whisky-related knick-knacks – old bottles, tacky mugs and glasses and a nice, dusty, museum-like atmosphere.

## Altxerri Jazz Bar
Live Music

(www.altxerri.com; Blvd Reina Regente 2; ⏰ 4pm-3am) This jazz and blues temple has regular live gigs by local and international stars. Jamming sessions take over on nights with no gig, and there's an in-house art gallery.

## ℹ️ Information

**Oficina de Turismo** (📞943 48 11 66; www.
sansebastianturismo.com; Alameda del
Boulevard 8; 🕐9am-8pm Mon-Sat, 10am-7pm
Sun) This friendly office offers comprehensive
information on the city and the Basque
Country in general.

## ℹ️ Getting There & Away

### Air

The city's **airport** (📞902 404704; www.aena.
es) is 22km out of town, near Hondarribia. There
are regular flights to Madrid and Barcelona and
occasional charters to other major European
cities. Biarritz, just over the border in France, is
served by Ryanair and EasyJet, among various
other budget airlines, and is generally much
cheaper to fly into.

### Bus

The main bus station is a 20-minute walk south
of the Parte Vieja, between Plaza de Pío XII and
the river. Local buses 28 and 26 connects the bus
station with Alameda del Boulevard (€1.40, 10
minutes).

There are daily bus services to the following:

| DESTINATION | FARE (€) | DURATION (HR) |
|---|---|---|
| Biarritz (France) | 6.75 | 1¼ |
| Bilbao | 6.74-11.50 | 1 |
| Bilbao airport | 16.50 | 1¼ |
| Madrid | from 36 | 5-6 |
| Pamplona | 7.68 | 1 |

### Train

The main **Renfe train station** (Paseo de Francia)
is just across Río Urumea, on a line linking Paris to
Madrid. There are several services daily to Madrid
(from €47, five hours) and two to Barcelona (from
€64, six hours).

## LA RIOJA

Some of the best red wines in the country
are produced in La Rioja, whose ochre
earth and vast blue skies seem far more
Mediterranean than the Basque greens
further north. In fact, it's hard not to
feel as if you're in a different country
altogether.

View of Bahía de la Concha from Monte Igueldo, San Sebastián (p150)

# Logroño

POP 153,000

Logroño doesn't feel the need to be loud and brash. Instead it's a stately town with a heart of tree-studded squares, narrow streets and hidden corners. There are few monuments here, but there is a monumentally good selection of *pintxos* bars. In fact, Logroño is quickly gaining a culinary reputation to rival anywhere in Spain.

##  Sights

### Catedral de Santa María de la Redonda
Cathedral

(Calle de Portales; 8am-1pm & 6-8.45pm Mon-Sat, 9am-2pm & 6.30-8.45pm Sun) The Catedral de Santa María de la Redonda started life as a Gothic church before maturing into a full-blown cathedral in the 16th century.

### Museo de la Rioja
Museum

(Plaza San Agustin 23; 10am-2pm & 4-9pm Tue-Sat, 10am-2pm Sun) FREE After being closed for renovations for many years, this superb museum is now back in business and, in both Spanish and English, takes you on a wild romp through Riojan history and culture – from the days when our ancestors killed dinner with arrows to recreations of the kitchens your Spanish granny likes to pretend she grew up using.

## Eating

Make no mistake about it: Logroño is a foodie's delight. There are a number of very good restaurants and then there are the *pintxos* – few cities have such a dense concentration of excellent *pintxo* bars. Most of the action takes place on Calle Laurel and Calle de San Juan.

# The New Guggenheim

'If Bilbao has one, we want one too,' scream the villages of rural La Rioja. Impressed by the effect El Goog had on Bilbao's international standing and apparently unconcerned by the size and wealth difference between the big industrial city and their small farming communities, two villages have got themselves a Guggenheim lookalike.

When the owner of the Bodegas Marqués de Riscal, in the village of **Elciego**, decided he wanted to create something special, he certainly didn't hold back. The result is the spectacular Frank Gehry–designed **Hotel Marqués de Riscal** ( 945 18 08 80; www.starwoodhotels.com/luxury; Calle Torrea 1; r from €304; P ✳ 🛜). Costing around €85 million to construct and now managed by the Starwood chain, the building is a flamboyant wave of multicoloured titanium sheets that stands in utter contrast to the creaky old village behind it. If you want a closer look, you have three options. The easiest is to join one of the bodega's **wine tours** ( 945 18 08 88; www.marquesderiscal.com; tour €11) – it's necessary to book in advance. You won't get inside the building, but you will get to see its exterior from some distance. A much closer look can be obtained by reserving a table at one of the two superb in-house restaurants; the Michelin approved **Restaurante Marqués de Riscal** ( 945 18 08 80; Hotel Marqués de Riscal, Calle Torrea 1; menu from €70) or the **Bistró 1860** ( 945 18 08 80; Hotel Marqués de Riscal, Calle Torrea 1; menu from €49). For the most intimate look at the building, you'll need to reserve a room for the night, though be prepared to part with some serious cash!

# Detour:
# Altamira

Spain's finest prehistoric art, the wonderful paintings of bison, horses and other animals in the Cueva de Altamira, 2km southwest of Santillana del Mar, was discovered in 1879 by Cantabrian historian and scientist Marcelino Sanz de Sautuola and his eight-year-old daughter María Justina. By 2002 Altamira had attracted so many visitors that the cave was closed to prevent deterioration of the art, but a replica cave in the **Museo de Altamira** (museodealtamira.mcu.es; adult/EU senior or student/child €3/1.50/free, Sun & from 2pm Sat free; ⊘9.30am-8pm Tue-Sat, to 3pm Sun & holidays; [P]) now enables everyone to appreciate the inspired, 14,500-year-old paintings. Excellent other displays, in English and Spanish, cover prehistoric humanity and cave art around the world, from Altamira to Australia.

**Bar Soriano**　　　　Pintxos **$**
(Travesía de Laurel 2; *pintxos* from €2) The smell of frying food will suck you into this bar, which has been serving up the same delicious mushroom tapa, topped with a shrimp, for more than 30 years.

**La Cocina de Ramon**　Spanish **$$$**
(☎941 28 98 08; www.lacocinaderamon.es; Calle de Portales 30; menus €28-37; ⊘1-4pm & 8-11pm Tue-Sat, 1-4pm Sun) It looks unassuming from the outside, but Ramon's mixture of high-quality, largely locally grown market-fresh produce and tried-and-tested family recipes gives this place a lot of fans. But it's not just the food that makes it so popular: the service is outstanding, and Ramon likes to come and explain the dishes to each and every guest.

## ⓘ Getting There & Away

Buses bounce off to the following:

| DESTINATION | FARE (€) | DURATION (HR) |
|---|---|---|
| Bilbao | 13 | 2¾ |
| Burgos | 6 | 2¼ |
| Haro | 3.26 | 1 |
| Pamplona | 8.95 | 1¾ |
| Santo Domingo de la Calzada | 3.05 | ¾ |

By train, Logroño is regularly connected to the following:

| DESTINATION | FARE (€) | DURATION (HR) |
|---|---|---|
| Bilbao | from 16 | 2½ |
| Burgos | from 13 | 1¾ |
| Madrid | from 29 | 3¼ |
| Zaragoza | from 13 | 2½ |

## Laguardia
POP 1490 / ELEV 557M

It's easy to spin back the wheels of time in the medieval fortress town of Laguardia, or the 'Guard of Navarra' as it was once appropriately known, sitting proudly on its rocky hilltop. The walled old quarter, which makes up most of the town, is virtually traffic-free and is a sheer joy to wander around.

## ◎ Sights

**Bodegas Ysios**　　　　Winery
(www.ysios.com; Camino de la Hoya, Laguardia) Just a couple of kilometres to the north of Laguardia is the Bodegas Ysios. Designed by Santiago Calatrava as a 'temple dedicated to wine', it's wave-like roof made of aluminium and cedar wood matches the flow of the rocky mountains behind it. However, it looks its best at night when pools of light flow out of it.

# If You Like...
## Wine

If you like Bodegas Ysios near Laguardia, you may also like these other wine events and attractions:

### 1 DINASTÍA VIVANCO
(Museo de la Cultura del Vino; www.dinastiavivanco.com; adult/child €8/free; ☺10am-8pm Tue-Sat, 11am-6pm Sun Jul-Sep, shorter hours Oct-Jun) This space-age museum in Briones is the creation of Pedro Vivanco Paracuello. As he relates in the introductory film, he wanted to leave a legacy to the land that has provided for his family for generations. This museum is that legacy and it truly is an incredible one. Over several floors and numerous rooms, you will learn all about the history and culture of wine and the various processes that go into its production.

### 2 BODEGAS PALACIO
( ✆945 60 01 51; www.bodegaspalacio.com; Carretera de Elciego; tour €5; ☺tours 11am & 1pm Mon, 4.30pm Tue-Fri, 11.30am & 1pm Sat, 1.30pm Sun, closed afternoons Jul & Aug) Bodegas Palacio, only 1km from Laguardia on the Elciego road, is a wine cellar most receptive to visitors. Its tours run several times daily Monday to Saturday in Spanish, English and German. Reservations on the above number are not essential but are a good idea (especially out of season). The same bodega also runs excellent wine courses.

### 3 MUSEO DE LA VIÑA Y EL VINO DE NAVARRA
(www.guiartenavarra.com; Plaza de los Teobaldos 10; adult/child €3.50/2; ☺10am-2pm & 4-7pm Mon-Sat, 10am-2pm Sun Mar-Oct, shorter hours Nov-Feb) Don't miss this Olite museum, which is a fascinating journey through wine and wine culture. Everything is well labelled and laid out and some fascinating facts are revealed. It's in the same building as the tourist office.

## 🍴 Eating

**Restaurante Amelibia** Spanish $$
( ✆945 62 12 07; Barbacana 14; menú del día €17;

☺1-3.30pm Sun-Mon & Wed-Thu, 1-3.30pm & 9-10.30pm Fri-Sat) There are few things we like doing more in Laguardia than sitting back in this classy restaurant, staring out the windows at a view over the scorched plains and distant mountain ridges and dining on sublime traditional Spanish dishes – the meat dishes in particular are of exquisitely high quality.

## 🛈 Information

**Tourist Office** ( ✆945 60 08 45; www.laguardia-alava.com; Calle Mayor 52; ☺10am-2pm & 4-7pm Mon-Fri, 10am-2pm & 5-7pm Sat, 10.45am-2pm Sun) Has a list of local bodegas that can be visited.

## 🛈 Getting There & Away

Several slow daily buses connecting Vitoria and Logroño pass through Laguardia.

# CAMINO DE SANTIAGO

## Pamplona

POP 195,800 / ELEV 456M

Senses are heightened in Pamplona (Basque: Iruña), capital of the fiercely independent Kingdom of Navarra, alert constantly to the fearful sound of thundering bulls clattering like tanks down cobbled streets and causing mayhem and bloodshed all the way. Of course, visit outside the eight days in July when the legendary festival of Sanfermines takes over the minds and souls of a million people and the closest you'll come to a bloodthirsty bull is in a photograph. For those who do dare venture here outside fiesta time, despite the overriding feeling that you're the only one who missed the party, you will find Pamplona a fascinating place. And for those of you who come during fiesta week? Welcome to one of the biggest and most famous festivals in the world – if you hadn't drunk so much, it would have been a week you would remember forever!

# The Running of the Bulls

Liberated, obsessive or plain mad is how you might describe aficionados (and there are many) who regularly take part in Pamplona's **Sanfermines** (Fiesta de San Fermín), a nonstop cacophony of music, dance, fireworks and processions – and the small matter of running alongside a handful of agitated, horn-tossing *toros* (bulls) – that takes place from 6 to 14 July each year.

*El encierro,* the running of the bulls from their corrals to the bullring for the afternoon bullfight, takes place in Pamplona every morning during Sanfermines. Six bulls are let loose from the Coralillos de Santo Domingo to charge across the square of the same name. They continue up the street, veering onto Calle de los Mercaderes from Plaza Consistorial, then sweep right onto Calle de la Estafeta for the final charge to the ring. Devotees, known as *mozos* (the brave or foolish, depending on your point of view), race madly with the bulls, aiming to keep close – but not too close. The total course is some 825m long and lasts little more than three minutes.

Those who prefer to be spectators rather than action men (and we use the word 'men' on purpose here as, technically, women are forbidden from running, although an increasing number are doing it anyway) bag their spot along the route early. Some people rent a space on one of the house balconies overlooking the course. Whichever the vantage point, it's all over in a few blurred seconds.

Each evening a traditional bullfight is held. Sanfermines winds up at midnight on 14 July with a candlelit procession, known as the **Pobre de Mí** (Poor Me), which starts from Plaza Consistorial.

Concern has grown about the high numbers of people taking part in recent *encierros*. Since records began in 1924, 16 people have died during Pamplona's bullrun. Many of those who run are full of bravado (and/or drink) and have little idea of what they're doing. For dedicated *encierro* news, check out www.sanfermin.com.

Animal rights groups oppose bullrunning as a cruel tradition, and the participating bulls will almost certainly all be killed in the afternoon bullfight. The PETA-organised anti-bullfighting demonstration, the **Running of the Nudes**, takes place two days before the first bullrun.

# Sights

## Catedral
Cathedral

(www.catedraldepamplona.com; Calle Dormitalería; guided tour per adult/child €5/free; ◷10.30am-7pm Tue-Sat & 10.30am-2pm Sun) Pamplona's main cathedral stands on a rise just inside the city ramparts amid a dark thicket of narrow streets. The cathedral is a late-medieval Gothic gem spoiled only by its rather dull neoclassical facade, an 18th-century appendage. The vast interior reveals some fine artefacts, including a silver-plated Virgin and the splendid 15th-century tomb of Carlos III of Navarra and his wife Doña Leonor. The real joy is the Gothic **cloister**, where there is marvellous delicacy in the stonework.

## Museo de Navarra
Museum

(www.cfnavarra.es/cultura/museo; Calle Cuesta de Santo Domingo 47; adult/student/child €2/1/free, Sat afternoon & Sun free; ◷9.30am-2pm & 5-7pm Tue-Sat, 11am-2pm Sun) Housed in a former medieval hospital, this superb museum has an eclectic collection of archaeological finds (including a number of fantastic Roman mosaics unearthed

mainly in southern Navarra), as well as a selection of art, including Goya's *Marqués de San Adrián*. Labelling is in Spanish only, but foreign translation leaflets are available.

 ## Sleeping

During Sanfermines, hotels raise their rates mercilessly – all quadruple their normal rack rates and many increase them fivefold – and it can be near impossible to get a room without reserving between six months and a year in advance.

### Hotel Puerta del Camino
Boutique Hotel $$
( ☎ 948 22 66 88; www.hotelpuertadelcamino. com; Calle Dos de Mayo 4; s/d from €72/85; P ❄ 🛜) A very stylish hotel inside a converted convent (clearly the nuns appreciated the finer things in life!) beside the northern gates to the old city. The rooms are filled with unexpected touches such as bulbous lamps and huge leather bedheads. Some rooms have views

across the intricate city walls and beyond to the soaring Pyrenees.

### Palacio Guendulain
Historic Hotel $$$
( ☎ 948 22 55 22; www.palacioguendulain. com; Calle Zapatería 53; s/d incl breakfast from €132/143; P ❄ 🛜) To call this stunning hotel, inside the converted former home of the viceroy of New Granada, sumptuous is an understatement. On arrival, you're greeted by a museum-piece 17th-century carriage and a collection of classic cars being guarded by the viceroy's private chapel. The rooms contain *Princess and the Pea*–soft beds, enormous showers and regal armchairs.

 ## Eating

### Bar-Restaurante Gaucho
Pintxos $
(Travesía Espóz y Mina 7; *pintxos* €2-3; ⏱7am-3pm & 6.30-11pm) This bustling bar serves multi-award-winning *pintxos* that, despite some serious competition, many a local

**Left:** Catedral, Pamplona (p161);
**Below:** Replica of cave paintings, Museo de Altamira (p159)
(LEFT) MARTIN ZALBA/GETTY IMAGES ©; (BELOW) GONZALO AZUMENDI/GETTY IMAGES ©

will tell you are the finest in the city – and we tend to agree with them! Try the ones made of sea urchins or the crispy spinach and prawn caramel ones.

### Baserri
Basque $

( ☏ 948 22 20 21; Calle de San Nicolás 32; menú del día €14; ☺ 9.30am-midnight Mon-Thu, 9.30am-1.30am Fri, 11am-4am Sat, 11.30am-midnight Sun) This place has won so many awards for its *pintxos* that we could fill this entire book listing them. In fact, it's staggering to know that so many food awards actually exist! You can taste a selection of *pintxos* by opting for the €24 tasting menu.

### Casa Otaño
Basque $$

( ☏ 948 22 50 95; Calle de San Nicolás 5; menú del día €18, mains €15-18; ☺ 1-4pm & 9-11pm Mon-Sat) A little pricier than many on this street but worth the extra. Its formal atmosphere is eased by the dazzling array of pink and red flowers spilling off the balcony. Great dishes range from the locally caught trout to heavenly duck.

## ⓘ Information

**Tourist Office** ( ☏ 848 42 04 20; www.turismo.navarra.es; Avenida da Roncesvalles 4; ☺ Mon-Fri 9am-7pm, Sat 10am-2pm & 4-7pm, Sun 10am-2pm) This extremely well-organised office, just opposite the statue of the bulls in the new town, has plenty of information about the city and Navarra. There are a couple of summer-only tourist info booths scattered throughout the city.

## ⓘ Getting There & Away

### Air

Pamplona's **airport** ( ☏ 902 40 47 04), about 7km south of the city, has regular flights to Madrid, Barcelona and one or two other Spanish cities. **Bus 16** (tickets €1.35) travels between the city (from the bus station and Calle de las Navas de Tolosa) and the suburb of Noáia, from where it's about a 200m walk to the airport. A taxi costs about €15.

## Bus

From the **main bus station** (☎902 02 36 51; www.estaciondeautobusesdepamplona.com; Ave de Yanguas y Miranda 2), buses leave for most towns throughout Navarra, although service is restricted on Sunday.

Regular bus services travel to the following:

| DESTINATION | FARE (€) | DURATION (HR) |
| --- | --- | --- |
| Bilbao | 15 | 2¾ |
| Logroño | 8.95 | 1¾ |
| San Sebastián | 7.68 | 1 |

## Train

Pamplona's train station is linked to the city centre by **bus 9** from Paseo de Sarasate every 15 minutes. Tickets are also sold at the **Renfe agency** (Calle de Estella 8; ⊙9am-1.30pm & 4.30-7.30pm Mon-Fri, 9am-1pm Sat).

Trains run to/from the following:

| DESTINATION | FARE (€) | DURATION (HR) | FREQUENCY (DAILY) |
| --- | --- | --- | --- |
| Madrid | from 29 | 3 | 4 |
| San Sebastián | from 15 | 2 | 2 |

# Burgos

POP 179,250 / ELEV 861M

The extraordinary Gothic cathedral of Burgos is one of Spain's glittering jewels of religious architecture and it looms large over the city and skyline. On the surface, conservative Burgos seems to embody all the stereotypes of a north-central Spanish town, with sombre grey-stone architecture, the fortifying cuisine of the high *meseta* (plateau) and a climate of extremes. But this is a city that rewards deeper exploration: below the surface lie good restaurants and, when the sun's shining, pretty streetscapes that extend far beyond the landmark cathedral.

## ◉ Sights

**Catedral**     Cathedral

(Plaza del Rey Fernando; adult/child under 14yr incl multilingual audioguide €6/1.50; ⊙10am-6pm) This Unesco World Heritage–listed cathedral is a masterpiece. A former modest Romanesque church, work began on a grander scale in 1221. Remarkably, within 40 years most of the French Gothic structure had been completed. You can

Picos de Europa

MATT MUNRO/LONELY PLANET ©

# Detour:
## Picos de Europa

These jagged, deeply fissured mountains straddling southeast Asturias, southwest Cantabria and northern Castilla y León amount to some of the finest walking country, and some of the most exciting country of any kind, in Spain.

A star attraction of the Picos' central massif is the gorge that divides it from the western Macizo El Cornión. The popular Garganta del Cares (Cares Gorge) trail can be busy in summer, but the walk is always an exciting experience. This part of the Picos also has plenty of less heavily tramped paths and climbing challenges. Arenas de Cabrales is a popular base with a lot of accommodation, but Poncebos, Sotres, Bulnes and Caín also have sleeping options.

enter the cathedral from Plaza de Santa María for free, and have access to the **Capilla del Santísimo Cristo**, with its much-revered 13th-century crucifix, and the **Capilla de Santa Tecla**, with its extraordinary ceiling. However, we recommend that you visit the cathedral in its entirety.

## 🛏 Sleeping

### Hotel Norte y Londres
Historic Hotel **$$**

(☎947 26 41 25; www.hotelnorteylondres. com; Plaza de Alonso Martínez 10; s/d €66/100; **P @ 🛜**) Set in a former 16th-century palace and with understated period charm, this fine hotel promises spacious rooms with antique furnishings, polished wooden floors and pretty balconies; those on the 4th floor are more modern. The bathrooms are exceptionally large, the service exceptionally efficient.

### Hotel La Puebla
Boutique Hotel **$$**

(☎947 20 00 11; www.hotellapuebla.com; Calle de la Puebla 20; s/d €45/66; **❄ @ 🛜**) This boutique hotel adds a touch of style to the Burgos hotel scene. The rooms aren't huge and most don't have views, but they're softly lit, beautifully designed and supremely comfortable. Extra perks include bikes and a pillow menu, while, on the downside, some readers have complained about the level of street noise.

## 🍴 Eating

### Cervecería Morito
Tapas **$**

(Calle Sombrerería 27; tapas €3, raciones €5-7; ⏱12.30-3.30pm & 7-11.30pm) Cervecería Morito is the undisputed king of Burgos tapas bars and it's always crowded, deservedly so. A typical order is *alpargata* (lashings of cured ham with bread, tomato and olive oil) or the *pincho de morcilla* (small tapa of local blood sausage). The presentation is surprising nouvelle, especially the visual feast of salads.

### El Huerto de Roque
Contemporary Castilian **$$**

(www.elhuertoderoque.com; Calle de Santa Águeda 10; mains €10-12, menú del día €15; ⏱restaurant 1-4pm Tue-Sat, gastrobar 8pm-2am Thu-Sat; 🍴) 🌿 Come here for an inexpensive lunch with plenty of choice of dishes. The emphasis is on fresh market and ecological produce including typical plates including vegetable spring rolls with a sweet and sour sauce, and crab in a Thai green curry sauce. The atmosphere throughout is boho-rustic with original tiles, wooden furniture and edgy artwork.

## ℹ Information

**Municipal Tourist office** (☎947 28 88 74; www. aytoburgos.es; Plaza de Santa María; ⏱10am-8pm) Pick up its 24-hour, 48-hour and 72-hour guides to Burgos; they can also be downloaded as PDFs online.

# If You Like…
## Cathedrals

If you like the cathedrals in León and Burgos, the cathedrals in the following towns should also appeal:

### PALENCIA
(Calle Mayor Antigua 29; cathedral & crypt €2, incl museum €3; ⏱10am-1.30pm & 4.30-7.30pm Mon-Fri, 10am-2pm & 4-5.30pm Sat, 4.30-8pm Sun) The **Puerta del Obispo** (Bishop's Door) is the highlight of the facade of the imposing cathedral, among the largest in Castilla. One of the most stunning chapels is the **Capilla El Sagrario**: its ceiling-high altarpiece tells the story of Christ in dozens of exquisitely carved and painted panels. The stone screen behind the choir stalls is a masterpiece of bas-relief attributed to Gil de Siloé.

### PLASENCIA
(Plaza de la Catedral; Catedral Nueva free, Catedral Vieja €2; ⏱9am-1pm & 5-7pm Mon-Sat, 9am-1pm Sun) Plasencia's cathedral is actually two-in-one. The 16th-century **Catedral Nueva** is a Gothic-Renaissance blend with a handsome plateresque facade, soaring *retablo* (altarpiece) and intricately carved choir stalls. Within the Romanesque **Catedral Vieja** are classic 13th-century cloisters surrounding a trickling fountain and lemon trees. Also on view is the soaring octagonal **Capilla de San Pablo** with a dramatic 1569 Caravaggio painting of John the Baptist.

### ASTORGA
(Plaza de la Catedral; cathedral free, museum €3, incl Palacio Episcopal €5; ⏱church 9-10.30am Mon-Sat,11am-1pm Sun, museum 10am-2pm & 4-8pm Tue-Sun) The cathedral's striking plateresque southern facade is created from caramel-coloured sandstone with elaborate sculptural detail. Work began in 1471 and continued over three centuries, resulting in a mix of styles. The mainly Gothic interior has soaring ceilings and a superb 16th-century altarpiece by Gaspar Becerra.

**Regional Tourist Office** (www.turismocastillayleon.com; Plaza de Alonso Martínez 7; ⏱9am-8pm Sun-Thu, 9am-9pm Fri & Sat)

## ⓘ Getting There & Away

The **bus station** (Calle de Miranda 4) is south of the river, in the newer part of town. The train station is a considerable hike northeast of the town centre – bus 2 (tickets €1.10) connects the train station with Plaza de España. **Renfe** (☏947 20 91 31; Calle de la Moneda 21; ⏱9.30am-1.30pm & 4.30-7.30pm Mon-Fri), the national rail network, has a convenient sales office in the centre of town.

**Bus** Regular buses run to Madrid (€18.50, three hours, up to 20 daily), Bilbao (€13.20, two hours, eight daily) and León (€15.30, two hours, three daily).

**Train** Destinations include Madrid (from €35.80, 2½ to 4½ hours, seven daily), Bilbao (from €22.90, three hours, four daily), León (from €21.10, two hours) and Salamanca (from €16.20, 2½ hours, three daily).

## León

POP 132,740 / ELEV 527M

León is a wonderful city, combining stunning historical architecture with an irresistible energy. Its standout attraction is the cathedral, one of the most beautiful in all of Spain. By day you'll encounter a city with its roots firmly planted in the soil of northern Castile, with its grand monuments, loyal Catholic heritage and role as an important staging post along the Camino de Santiago. By night León is taken over by its large student population, who provide it with a deep-into-the-night soundtrack of revelry that floods the narrow streets and plazas of the picturesque old quarter, the Barrio Húmedo.

## ◉ Sights

**Real Basílica de San Isidoro** Church (⏱7.30am-11pm) FREE Even older than León's cathedral, the Real Basílica de San Isidoro provides a stunning Romanesque counterpoint to the former's Gothic strains, with extraordinary frescoes in the attached Panteón the main highlight.

Fernando I and Doña Sancha founded the church in 1063 to house

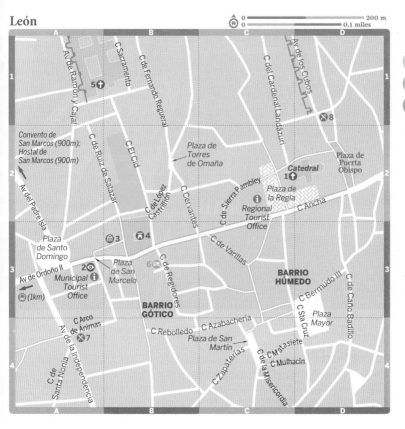

## León

the remains of the saint, as well as the remains of themselves and 21 other early Leónese and Castilian monarchs. Sadly, Napoleon's troops sacked San Isidoro in the early 19th century, although there's still plenty to catch the eye.

**Barrio Gótico**    Historic Quarter
Stately Plaza de San Marcelo is home to the **ayuntamiento** (town hall), which occupies a charmingly compact Renaissance-era palace. The Renaissance theme continues in the form of the splendid **Palacio de los Guzmanes** (1560), where the facade and patio stand out; the latter is accessible only on a free guided tour that leaves at regular intervals from 11.30am to 4.30pm. Next door is Antoni Gaudí's contribution to León's skyline, the castle-like, neo-Gothic **Casa de Botines** (1893), now a bank.

## 🛏 Sleeping

**La Posada Regia**    Historic Hotel $$
(☏ 987 21 31 73; www.regialeon.com; Calle de Regidores 9-11; s/d incl breakfast €55/90; ❄ 🛜)

**167**

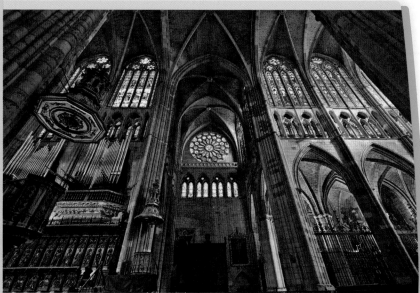
ANDREA PISTOLESI/GETTY IMAGES ©

# ★ Don't Miss
# Catedral

León's 13th-century cathedral, with its soaring towers, flying buttresses and breathtaking interior, is the city's spiritual heart. Whether spotlit by night or bathed in glorious sunshine, the cathedral, arguably Spain's premier Gothic masterpiece, exudes a glorious, almost luminous quality. The show-stopping facade has a radiant rose window, three richly sculpted doorways and two muscular towers. After going through the main entrance, lorded over by the scene of the Last Supper, an extraordinary gallery of *vidrieras* (stained-glass windows) awaits.

French in inspiration and mostly executed from the 13th to the 16th centuries, the windows' kaleidoscope of coloured light is offset by the otherwise gloomy interior. There seems to be more glass than brick – 128 windows with a surface of 1800 sq metres in all – but numbers cannot convey the ethereal quality of light permeating this cathedral.

Other treasures include a silver urn on the altar, by Enrique de Arfe, containing the remains of San Froilán, León's patron saint. Also note the magnificent choir stalls and the peaceful, light-filled claustro, its 15th-century frescoes providing a perfect complement to the main sanctuary. The **Museo Catedralicio-Diocesano**, off the cloisters, has an impressive collection encompassing works by Juní and Gaspar Becerra alongside an assemblage of early-Romanesque carved statues of the Virgin Mary.

Part of the cathedral is under restoration, but this has been turned cleverly to its advantage, by allowing you to climb up to one of the platforms high in the main sanctuary. from where there are stunning views. Guided visits leave on the hour (€3) and are accessed from outside the cathedral next to its northern wall.

## NEED TO KNOW

www.catedraldeleon.org; adult/concession/child under 12yr €5/4/free; ☺8.30am-1.30pm & 4-8pm Mon-Sat, 8.30am-2.30pm & 5-8pm Sun

This place has the feel of a *casa rural* despite being in the city centre. The secret is a 14th-century building, magnificently restored (wooden beams, exposed brick and understated antique furniture), with individually styled rooms and supremely comfortable beds and bathrooms. As with anywhere in the Barri Gòtic, weekend nights can be noisy.

### Hostal de San Marcos
Historic Hotel $$$

(✆987 23 73 00; www.parador.es; Plaza de San Marcos 7; d incl breakfast from €198; ❄@☞) Despite the confusing '*hostal*' in the name, León's sumptuous *parador* is one of the finest hotels in Spain. With palatial rooms fit for royalty and filled with old-world luxury and decor, this is one of the Parador chain's flagship properties, and as you'd expect, the service and attention to detail are faultless. It also houses the **Convento de San Marcos** (Plaza de San Marcos) FREE.

## Eating

### Delirios
Contemporary Castilian $$

(✆987 23 76 99; www.restaurantedelirios.com; Calle Ave Maria 2; mains €15-18; ☺1.30-3.30pm & 9pm-11.30 Tue-Sat, 1.30-3.30pm Sun) One of the city's more adventurous dining options where innovative combinations such as tuna tataki with orange and ginger, and brie and foie gras with coconut hit the mark virtually every time. More staid tastebuds can opt for dishes such as steak with parsnip chips, while the chocolate mousse with passionfruit is designed to put a satisfied waddle in every diner's step. Reservations recommended.

### Alfonso Valderas
Seafood $$

(✆987 20 05 05; Calle Arco de Ánimas 1; mains €13.65-18.90; ☺1.30-4pm & 9-11.30pm Mon-Sat, 1.30-4pm Sun) The city's most famous restaurant for *bacalao* (salt cod), prepared around 25 different ways. If this is your first encounter with this versatile fish, order it *al pil-pil* (with a mild chilli sauce). Otherwise, you might want to try the pig's trotters filled with cod. The dining room

is grandly elegant, with a magnificent grandfather clock and a baffling display cabinet of antique shoes. Reservations recommended.

## ℹ Information

**Municipal Tourist Office** (✆987 87 83 27; Plaza de San Marcelo; ☺9.30am-2pm & 5-7.30pm)

**Regional Tourist Office** (✆987 23 70 82; www.turismocastillayleon.com; Calle el Cid 2; ☺9am-8pm)

## ℹ Getting There & Away

The train and bus stations lie on the western bank of Río Bernesga, off the western end of Avenida de Ordoño II.

**Bus** Departing from the bus station (Paseo del Ingeniero Sáez de Miera) to Madrid (€24.95, 3½ hours, eight daily), Astorga (€3.80, one hour, 17 daily), Burgos (€15.30, two hours, three daily), and Valladolid (€10.20, two hours, nine daily).

**Car & Motorcycle** Parking bays (€12 to €16 for 12 hours) are found in the streets surrounding Plaza de Santo Domingo.

**Train** Regular daily trains travel to Valladolid (from €13.90, two hours), Burgos (from €21.10, two hours), and Madrid (from €27.25, 4¼ hours).

## Santiago de Compostela
POP 79,000 / ELEV 260M

Locals say the arcaded, stone streets of Santiago de Compostela are at their most beautiful in the rain, when the old city glistens. Most would agree, however, that it's hard to catch the Galician capital in a bad pose. Whether you're wandering the medieval streets of the old city, nibbling on tapas in the taverns, or gazing down at the rooftops from atop the cathedral, Santiago seduces.

The faithful believe that Santiago Apóstol (St James the Apostle) preached in Galicia and, after his death in Palestine, was brought back by stone boat and buried here. The tomb was supposedly rediscovered in about 814 by a religious hermit following a guiding star

# Santiago de Compostela

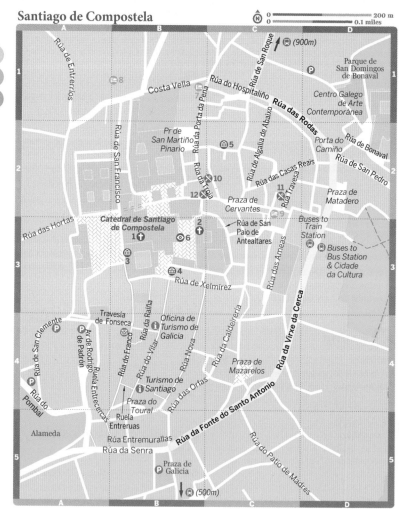

(hence, the name 'Compostela' derives from the Latin *campus stellae*, field of the star). The Asturian king Alfonso II had a church erected above the holy remains, pilgrims began flocking to it and by the 11th century the pilgrimage was becoming a major European phenomenon, bringing a flood of funds into the city.

Today an average of 150,000 pilgrims and countless thousands of other visitors make the journey here each year.

## ⊙ Sights

### Museo da Catedral — Museum

(Colección Permanente; www.catedraldesantiago.es; Praza do Obradoiro; adult/senior, pilgrim, unemployed & student/child €6/4/free; ☉9am-8pm Apr-Oct, 10am-8pm Nov-Mar) The Cathedral Museum spreads over four floors and includes the cathedral's large, 16th-century, Gothic/plateresque cloister. You'll see a sizeable section of Maestro Mateo's original carved stone choir (destroyed in 1604 but recently pieced

## Santiago de Compostela

back together), an impressive collection of religious art (including the *botafumeiros,* in the 2nd-floor library), the lavishly decorated 18th-century *sala capitular* (chapter house) and, off the cloister, the Panteón de Reyes, with tombs of kings of medieval León.

### Mosteiro de San Paio de Antealtares
Convent

(Praza da Quintana) Across the plaza from the Puerta Santa is the long, stark wall of the Mosteiro de San Paio de Antealtares, founded by Alfonso II for Benedictine monks to look after St James' relics, and converted to a nunnery in 1499.

### Museo das Peregrinacións e de Santiago
Museum

(www.mdperegrinacions.com; Praza das Praterías; adult/senior, pilgrim & student/child €2.50/1.50/free; ⊙10am-2pm & 5-8pm Tue-Sat, 11am-2pm Sun) The recently converted building on Praza das Praterías stages changing exhibitions on the themes of pilgrimage and Santiago (man and city), and affords close-up views of some of the cathedral's towers from its 3rd-floor windows. The museum's permanent collection – an extensive and interesting assemblage of art, artefacts,

models and memorabilia – resides in its **original building** (www.mdperegrinacions.com; Rúa de San Miguel 4; ⊙10am-8pm Tue-Fri, 10.30am-1.30pm & 5-8pm Sat, 10.30am-1.30pm Sun) FREE 300m away, though there are plans eventually to move it to the new site.

## 🖝 Tours

Turismo de Santiago (p175) offers a range of two-hour walking tours in English and/or Spanish that give a fascinating glimpse into the stories behind Santiago's old stone walls. From April to September, a general Old-Town tour in English (€10) starts from Praza das Praterías at 4pm Thursday to Saturday and noon on Sunday.

## 🛏 Sleeping

### Hotel Costa Vella
Boutique Hotel $$

(☏981 56 95 30; www.costavella.com; Rúa da Porta da Pena 17; s €59, d €81-97; ❄🛜) Tranquil, thoughtfully designed rooms – some with typically Galician *galerías* (glassed-in balconies) – a friendly welcome and a lovely garden cafe make this old stone house a wonderful option, and the €6 breakfast is substantial. Even if you don't stay, it's an ideal spot for breakfast or coffee. Book ahead from May to September.

### Smart Hotel Boutique Literario San Bieito
Boutique Hotel $$

(☏981 57 28 90; www.hotelsanbieito.com; Cantón de San Bieito 1; s/d incl breakfast €80/95; ❄@🛜) An excellent conversion of a 16th-century building with 20 bright, comfortable and reasonably spacious rooms in fashionable greys and whites, all with exterior windows and individually controlled air-con.

### San Francisco Hotel Monumento
Historic Hotel $$

(☏981 58 16 34; www.sanfranciscohm.com; Campillo San Francisco 3; s €110, d €137-165; ℗❄@🛜🏊) The courtyards and the low-lit hallways with their stone door frames recall the hotel's former life as a

**Don't Miss**
# Catedral de Santiago de Compostela

The grand heart of Santiago, the cathedral soars above the city centre in a splendid jumble of moss-covered spires and statues. Built piecemeal over several centuries, its beauty is a mix of the original Romanesque structure and later Gothic and baroque flourishes. The tomb of Santiago beneath the main altar is a magnet for all who come to the cathedral.

www.catedraldesantiago.es

Praza do Obradoiro

🕐7am-8.30pm

## Facade

What we see today is actually the fourth church to stand on this spot. It has a traditional Latin-cross layout and three naves. The lavish baroque facade facing Praza do Obradoiro was erected in the 18th century, replacing the weather-damaged Romanesque one. This is the cathedral's main entrance, but owing to repair work on the towers and interior, it's likely to be closed until about 2021. In the meantime, most people enter through the south door on Praza das Praterías.

## Pórtico de la Gloria

The artistically unparalleled **Pórtico de la Gloria** (Galician: Porta da Gloria), just inside the Obradoiro entrance, features 200 Romanesque sculptures by Maestro Mateo, who was placed in charge of the cathedral-building program in the late 12th century. The restoration work means, unfortunately, that you may well find the Pórtico partly shrouded in scaffolding.

## Altar Mayor

Towards the far (west) end of the cathedral's main nave, to the right of the fantastically elaborate, Churrigueresque **Altar Mayor** (Main Altar), a small staircase leads up to a 13th-century statue of Santiago, which the faithful queue up to kiss or embrace. From here you emerge on the left side, then descend some steps to contemplate the Cripta Apostólica, which we are assured is Santiago's tomb. Behind the Altar Mayor is the **Puerta Santa (Holy Door; Praza das Praterías)**, which opens onto Praza da Quintana and is cracked open only in holy years (next in 2021).

A special pilgrims' Mass is usually celebrated at noon daily, with other Masses usually at 9.30am or 10am daily, 1.15pm Sunday, 6pm Saturday and Sunday, and 7.30pm daily. Touristic visits are not allowed during these services.

**Local Knowledge**

# Catedral de Santiago de Compostela

BY IÑAKI GAZTELUMENDI, SANTIAGO TOURISM GURU

### 1 OBRADOIRO FACADE

I've lived in Santiago all my life, but it's still a privilege to see the overwhelmingly baroque Fachada del Obradoiro every day. Study it closely, but also step back into the middle of the plaza where the 360-degree views are a journey through the evolution of art, from the Middle Ages to the 18th century.

### 2 MAIN ENTRANCE

I'm always surprised how many people rush inside. Pause instead to contemplate the splendour of the El Pórtico de la Gloria, where I have a special weakness for the 24 elders of the apocalypse with musical instruments. Inside, near the Altar Mayor, the figure of Maestro Mateo moves me with its simplicity amid the extravagant beauty elsewhere.

### 3 PLAZA DE LA QUINTANA

Of the four plazas that connect the cathedral to the rest of the old town, Plaza de la Quintana is the most enigmatic, divided as it is between Quintana of the Dead and Quintana of the Living. Seek out the subtly beautiful granite panel on the monastery facade of the Mosteiro de San Paio de Antealtares.

### 4 THE CATHEDRAL'S ROOF

As you climb through the labyrinth of staircases, you'll see the great eras of the cathedral's architectural history. But the cathedral was built not just through the genius of its architects, but rather through the labour of local people, and from the summit the panoramic views are a reminder that the cathedral is the centrepiece of a living, breathing city.

### 5 EL PALACIO GELMÍREZ

Don't miss the interior of this palace, an annex to the cathedral, with its numerous Romanesque gems. I particularly like the kitchen and dining room with their scenes of Galician banquets. It's rare to find two main pillars of Santiago life (gastronomy and the social life that grew up around the cathedral) in one place.

Franciscan monastery. But the rooms, minimalist, modern and spacious, are all about contemporary comfort, and there's a great indoor pool. This is luxury in historic surroundings at prices much lower than Santiago's more famous *parador*.

## 🍴 Eating

### O Curro da Parra
Contemporary Galician **$$**

(www.ocurrodaparra.com; Rúa do Curro da Parra 7; mains €17-23, tapas €4-8; ☙1.30-3.30pm & 8.30-11.30pm Tue-Sat, 1.30-3.30pm Sun) With a neat little stone-walled dining room upstairs and a narrow tapas and wine bar below, O Curro da Parra serves up a broad range of thoughtfully created, market-fresh fare. You might go for pork cheeks with apple purée and spinach – or just ask what the fish and seafood of the day are. On weekday lunchtimes there's a good-value €12 *menú mercado* (market menu).

### O Filandón
Tapas, Raciones **$$**

(Rúa Acibechería 6; raciones €14-20, medias-raciones €10-12; ☙12.30-4pm & 8.30pm-1am) Squeeze past the cheese-shop counter into the thin, cellar-like bar area behind, where you'll receive exceedingly generous free *pinchos* (snacks) with drinks, and can order plates of ham, sausage, cured meats, cheese or peppers. Thousands of notes and words of wisdom scribbled by past clients dangle from the walls.

### Bierzo de Enxebre
Leonese **$$**

(www.bierzoenxebre.es; Rúa da Troia 10; raciones €9-17; ☙1-4pm & 8-11.30pm) The cuisine at this busy spot is that of El Bierzo, a rural area of northwest Castilla y León, meaning excellent grilled and cured meats, but also cheeses, pies and vegetables. There are two small, stone-walled, wood-beamed dining rooms and a few prized outside tables.

## ❶ Information

**Oficina de Turismo de Galicia** (www.turgalicia.
es; Rúa do Vilar 30-32; ⏱10am-8pm Mon-Fri,
11am-2pm & 5-7pm Sat, 11am-2pm Sun) The
scoop on all things Galicia.

**Turismo de Santiago** (📞981 55 51 29; www.
santiagoturismo.com; Rúa do Vilar 63; ⏱9am-
9pm, to 7pm approx Nov-Mar) The efficient main
municipal tourist office.

## ❶ Getting There & Away

### Air

Santiago's **Lavacolla airport** (📞981 54 75 00;
www.aena-aeropuertos.es) is 11km east of the city.

### Bus

The **bus station** (📞981 54 24 16; Praza de
Camilo Díaz Baliño; 📶) is about a 20-minute walk
northeast of the city centre. **Castromil-Monbus**
(📞902 292900; www.monbus.es) runs to many
places in Galicia; **ALSA** (📞902 422242; www.
alsa.es) operates further afield, including Madrid
(eight to ten hours, €47 to €68, five daily).

### Train

The **train station** (📞981 59 18 59; Rúa do
Hórreo) is about a 15-minute walk south from
the Old Town. All trains are run by **Renfe** (📞902
320320; www.renfe.com). Trains run to Madrid
(5½ to 9½ hours, €34 to €54) four times daily.

## ❶ Getting Around

Santiago is walkable, although it's a bit of a hike
from the train and bus stations to the city centre.
Private vehicles are barred from the Old Town
from about 10am to dusk for most of the summer.
Underground car parks around its fringes
generally charge about €16 per 24 hours.

Up to 37 Empresa Freire buses (€3, 35
minutes) run daily between Lavacolla airport and
Rúa do Doutor Teixeiro, in the new town southwest
of Praza de Galicia, via the bus station. Taxis
charge around €20.

# Madrid & Around

**No city on earth is more alive than Madrid.** This beguiling place has a sheer energy that carries a simple message: this city knows how to live. In recent years Madrid has transformed itself into Spain's premier style centre and its calling cards are many: astonishing art galleries, relentless nightlife, an exceptional live music scene, a feast of fine restaurants and tapas bars, and a population that's mastered the art of the good life. Away from the capital, the endless horizons of Central Spain's thinly populated high *meseta* (plateau) are where you'll find some of Spain's most engaging towns. Renaissance Salamanca, lovely little Segovia, and Toledo are places where history seems written on every stone. These areas will give you a real insight into the soul of Spain.

Metrópolis building, Gran Vía (p185)

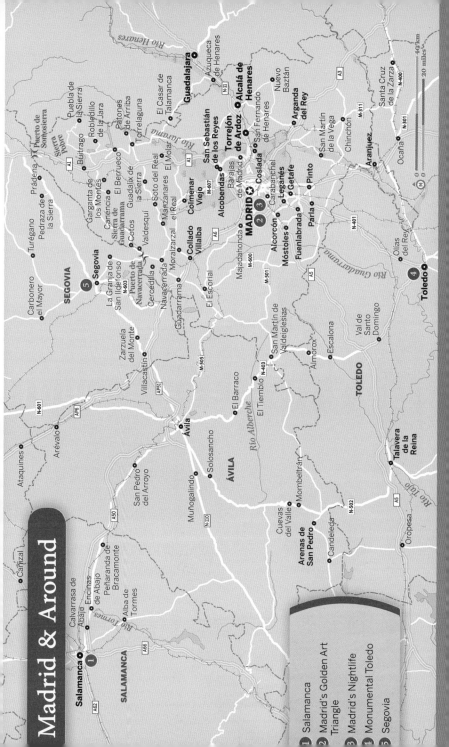

# Madrid & Around

1 Salamanca
2 Madrid's Golden Art Triangle
3 Madrid's Nightlife
4 Monumental Toledo
5 Segovia

# Madrid & Around Highlights

## Salamanca

The university city of Salamanca (p222) in Castilla y León is monumental (as recognised by Unesco) and very cultural (it was Europe's Capital of Culture in 2002), but the full Salamanca experience requires a little local knowledge. Behind the grand facades, it's all about discovering secret corners and learning new ways to look at its well-known sights. Plaza Mayor (p224)

**1**

**2** Madrid's Golden Art Triangle

Within a mile of each other, Madrid's three world-class art galleries – the Museo del Prado (p193), Museo Thyssen-Bornemisza (p190) and Centro de Arte Reina Sofía (p189) – have made the city one of Europe's most important artistic capitals. Spanish icons share wall space with a host of European masters, but you'll find little-known artistic gems all across Madrid. Statue of Velázquez, Museo del Prado (p192)

/GETTY IMAGES ©

## Madrid's Nightlife

**3**

Nights in the Spanish capital (p205) are the stuff of legend. They're invariably long and loud most nights of the week, rising to a deafening crescendo as the weekend nears.

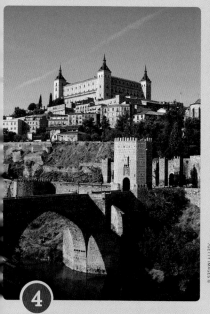

**4**

## Monumental Toledo

On a hilltop southwest of Madrid, picturesque Toledo (p214) is like a window on the Spanish soul. There are so many monuments to the city's polyglot Christian, Jewish and Muslim past across the city that it has the quality of a living museum: this is one place where comparisons to the great cities of North Africa and the Middle East are not misplaced. Río Tajo and Alcázar (p214)

**5**

## Segovia

The old town of Segovia (p226) has monuments that span Spanish history. At one end stands one of Europe's best-preserved Roman aqueducts, while at the other is the fairy-tale (yet fortresslike) Alcázar, which inspired the designers of Disneyland's famous castle. In between, stunning religious buildings and fine restaurants stand watch over the lively streets. Plaza del Azoguejo and El Acueducto (p226)

# Madrid & Around's Best...

## Galleries for Art-Lovers

○ **Museo del Prado** Goya, Velázquez and much more in an unrivaled world-class collection. (p193)

○ **Museo Thyssen-Bornemisza** Stunning showpiece of European masters. (p190)

○ **Centro de Arte Reina Sofía** Picasso's *Guernica*, plus Miró and Dalí. (p189)

○ **Real Academia de Bellas Artes de San Fernando** Little-known gallery with big-name masterpieces. (p198)

## Tapas Bars

○ **Almendro 13** Traditional tapas in La Latina. (p200)

○ **Casa Alberto** One of Madrid's longest-standing and most traditional *tabernas* (taverns). (p201)

○ **La Cocina de Toño** Creative tapas that rule the roost in the city of Salamanca. (p225)

○ **Mercado de San Miguel** Billing itself as a 'culinary cultural centre' and who are we to argue? (p199)

○ **Alfileritos 24** Innovative dishes served in 14th-century surrounds. (p218)

## Places with a View

○ **Toledo** Cross the Puente de Alcántara for a fairy-tale view of Toledo. (p214)

○ **Plaza Mayor, Salamanca** One of Spain's most beautiful squares, especially at night. (p224)

○ **Segovia** Head 2km north of town for the photo opportunity to impress the folks back home. (p226)

○ **Windmills of Consuegra** Don Quixote's famous windmills in all their glory. (p227)

## Signposts to the Past

○ **Old Madrid** Plaza Mayor sits in the heart of the oldest quarter of Madrid. (p186)

○ **Toledo** Churches, synagogues and mosques reflect a history of religious intermingling. (p214)

○ **Acueducto**, **Segovia** An astonishing feat of Roman engineering. (p226)

○ **Ávila** Magnificent 12th-century defensive walls still guard this erstwhile bastion of medieval glory. (p219)

# Need to Know

## ADVANCE PLANNING

○ **Three months before** Reserve your hotel as early as you can.

○ **One month before** Book a table at the popular high-end restaurants.

○ **One week before** Book online entry to the Museo del Prado to avoid queues on arrival.

## RESOUCES

○ **Centro de Turismo Madrid** (www.esmadrid.com) Tourist information for Madrid, with branches across the city.

○ **Le Cool** (www.madrid.lecool.com) Weekly updates on upcoming events in Madrid with an emphasis on the alternative, off-beat and avant-garde.

○ **Castilla y León** (www.turismocastillayleon.com) Informative site for northcentral Spain.

○ **Castilla-La Mancha** (www.turismocastillalamancha.com) Castilla-La Mancha's tourism portal.

## GETTING AROUND

○ **Air** Madrid's Barajas Airport (www.aena.es) has excellent connections with Europe and beyond.

○ **Train** An extensive rail system connects most of Central Spain.

○ **Bus** Wherever trains don't go.

○ **Road** Good network of motorways, with smaller connecting roads.

○ **Metro** Best for getting anywhere in Madrid, including the airport.

○ **Taxis** Some of the cheapest in Europe.

## BE FOREWARNED

○ **Museums and galleries** Most close on Monday.

○ **Centro de Arte Reina Sofía** Opens Monday, closes Tuesday.

○ **Madrid restaurants** Many close during August and on Mondays the rest of the year.

○ **Crime** Madrid is a generally safe city, although you should, as in most European cities, be wary of pickpockets on transport and around major tourist sights.

**Left:** Mercado de San Miguel (p199);
**Above:** Windmills of Don Quixote (p227)
(LEFT) /GETTY IMAGES ©; (ABOVE) /GETTY IMAGES ©

# Madrid Walking Tour

*Madrid has world-class art galleries and other sights, but as much as anything this is a city to savour, taste, smell and enjoy by simply exploring its streets, plazas and parks. This walking tour will help you get the most out of Madrid.*

**WALK FACTS**
- **Start** Plaza de la Puerta del Sol
- **Finish** Plaza de la Cibeles
- **Distance** 5km
- **Duration** Three to four hours

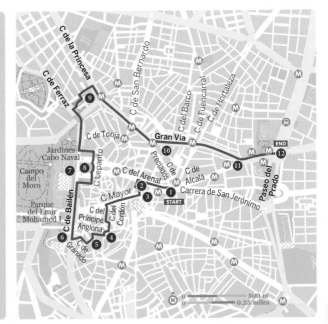

### ① Plaza de la Puerta del Sol

Start in the pulsating, geographic centre of Spain, the Plaza de la Puerta del Sol, and head northwest along Calle del Arenal.

### ② Iglesia de San Ginés

This is one of Madrid's oldest places of Christian worship and houses some fine paintings.

### ③ Chocolatería de San Ginés

Down a narrow lane just behind the church, Chocolatería de San Ginés (p205) is justifiably famous for its *chocolate con churros* (deep-fried Spanish donuts with chocolate), the ideal Madrid indulgence at any hour of the day.

### ④ Iglesia de San Pedro El Viejo

With it's clearly Mudéjar bell tower, this 15th-century church is one of the few remaining windows onto the world of medieval Madrid.

### ⑤ Plaza de la Paja

Linger for awhile in the charming Plaza de la Paja and then twist down through lanes of La Morería to Calle de Bailén.

### ⑥ Jardines de las Vistillas

Have a soothing *cerveza* (beer) at one of the wonderful *terrazas* (cafes with outdoor tables) that fringe the Jardines de las Vistillas and enjoy the view towards the Sierra de Guadarrama.

### ⑦ Palacio Real

Overlooking the Plaza de Oriente, the Palacio Real (p187) was Spain's seat of royal power for centuries.

### ⑧ Plaza de Oriente

Plaza de Oriente (p187) is a splendid arc of greenery and graceful architecture which could be Madrid's most agreeable plaza. You'll find yourself surrounded by gardens, the Palacio Real and the Teatro Real, and peopled by an ever-changing cast of *madrileños* at play.

### ⑨ Plaza de España

Follow the walkway extension of Calle de Bailén, which leads into Plaza de España, surrounded by monumental towers. The western flank of the square marks the start of the Gran Vía.

### ⑩ Gran Vía

It's difficult to imagine Madrid without the Gran Vía, a Haussmannesque boulevard that was slammed through tumble down slums in the 1910s and 1920s and is now known for its chi-chi shops.

### ⑪ Metrópolis Building

At the southern end of Gran Vía the stunning French-designed Metrópolis building has a winged statue of victory sitting atop its dome.

### ⑫ Plaza de la Cibeles

Head downhill to Plaza de la Cibeles, a place that evokes the splendour of imperial Madrid.

# Madrid in...

### ONE DAY

So many Madrid days begin in the Plaza Mayor, or perhaps nearby with a breakfast of *chocolate con churros* (chocolate with deep-fried doughnuts). Drop by the **Plaza de la Villa** (p204) and visit the **Palacio Real** (p187) and spend the afternoon at the **Museo del Prado** (p192). To kick off the night, take in a flamenco show at **Las Tablas** (p208), followed by a leisurely drink at **Café del Real** (p205).

### TWO DAYS

Visit the **Centro de Arte Reina Sofía** (p189) early to beat the crowds, then climb up through sedate streets to soak up the calm of the **Parque del Buen Retiro** (p191). Catch the metro across town to admire the Goya frescoes in the **Ermita de San Antonio de la Florida** (p191).

### THREE DAYS

Head out east to take a tour of the **Plaza de Toros** (p209) bullring, before dipping into the **Museo Lázaro Galdiano** (p191). Spend time shopping along Calle de Serrano, Calle de José Ortega y Gasset and surrounding streets before exploring the laneways of Malasaña.

Plaza de la Puerta del Sol (p204)

DRIENDL GROUP/GETTY IMAGES ©

# Discover Madrid & Around

## MADRID

POP 3.2 MILLION / ELEV 667M

### Sights

Madrid has three of the finest art galleries in the world: if ever there existed a golden mile of fine art, it would have to be the combined charms of the Museo del Prado, the Centro de Arte Reina Sofía and the Museo Thyssen-Bornemisza. Beyond the museums' walls, the combination of stately architecture and feel-good living has never been easier to access than in the beautiful plazas, where *terrazas* (cafes with outdoor tables) provide a front-row seat for Madrid's fine cityscape and endlessly energetic street life. Throw in some outstanding city parks (the Parque del Buen Retiro, in particular) and areas like Chueca, Malasaña and Salamanca, which each have their own identity, and you'll quickly end up wondering why you decided to spend so little time here.

### PLAZA MAYOR & ROYAL MADRID

These *barrios* (districts) are where the story of Madrid began. As the seat of royal power, this is where the splendour of imperial Spain was at its most ostentatious and where Spain's overarching Catholicism was at its most devout – think expansive palaces, elaborate private mansions, ancient churches and imposing convents amid the clamour of modern Madrid.

**Plaza Mayor**　　　　　　　　Square
**(Map p188; Plaza Mayor; Ⓜ Sol)** Madrid's grand central square, a rare but expansive open-

Plaza Mayor
JOSIE ELIAS/GETTY IMAGES ©

ing in the tightly packed streets of central Madrid, is one of the prettiest open spaces in Spain, a winning combination of imposing architecture, picaresque historical tales and vibrant street life coursing across its cobblestones. At once beautiful in its own right and a reference point for so many Madrid days, it also hosts the city's main tourist office (p211), a Christmas market in December and arches leading to many laneways that lead out into the labyrinth of Madrid.

### Palacio Real                                 Palace
(Map p188; 📞91 454 88 00; www.patrimonionacional.es; Calle de Bailén; adult/concession €10/5, guide/audioguide/pamphlet €7/4/1, EU citizens free last 3 hours Mon-Thu; ⏰10am-8pm Apr-Sep, to 6pm Oct-Mar; 🚇Ópera) Spain's lavish Palacio Real is a jewel box of a palace, although it's used only occasionally for royal ceremonies; the royal family moved to the modest Palacio de la Zarzuela years ago.

When the Alcázar burned down on Christmas Day 1734, Felipe V, the first of the Bourbon kings, decided to build a palace that would dwarf all its European counterparts. Felipe died before the palace was finished, which is perhaps why the Italianate baroque colossus has a mere 2800 rooms, just one-quarter of the original plan.

### Plaza de Oriente                             Square
(Map p188; Plaza de Oriente; 🚇Ópera) A royal palace that once had aspirations to be the Spanish Versailles; sophisticated cafes watched over by apartments that cost the equivalent of a royal salary; the **Teatro Real** (Map p188; 📞902 24 48 48; www.teatro-real.com; Plaza de Oriente; 🚇Ópera), Madrid's opera house and one of Spain's temples to high culture; some of the finest sunset views in Madrid... Welcome to Plaza de Oriente, a living, breathing monument to imperial Madrid.

### Campo del Moro & Jardines de Sabatini        Gardens
In proper palace style, lush gardens surround the Palacio Real. To the north are the

formal French-style **Jardines de Sabatini** (Map p188; ⏰9am-10pm May-Sep, 9am-9pm Oct-Apr; 🚇Ópera). Directly behind the palace are the fountains of the **Campo del Moro** (Map p188; 📞91 454 88 00; www.patrimonionacional.es; Paseo de la Virgen del Puerto; ⏰10am-8pm Mon-Sat, 9am-8pm Sun & holidays Apr-Sep, 10am-6pm Mon-Sat, 9am-6pm Sun & holidays Oct-Mar; 🚇Príncipe Pío), so named because this is where the Muslim army camped before a 12th-century attack on the Alcázar. Now, shady paths, a thatch-roofed pagoda and palace views are the main attractions.

### Convento de las Descalzas Reales            Convent
(Convent of the Barefoot Royals; Map p188; www.patrimonionacional.es; Plaza de las Descalzas 3; adult/child €7/4, incl Convento de la Encarnación €10/5, EU citizens free Wed & Thu afternoon; ⏰10am-2pm & 4-6.30pm Tue-Sat, 10am-3pm

# Central Madrid

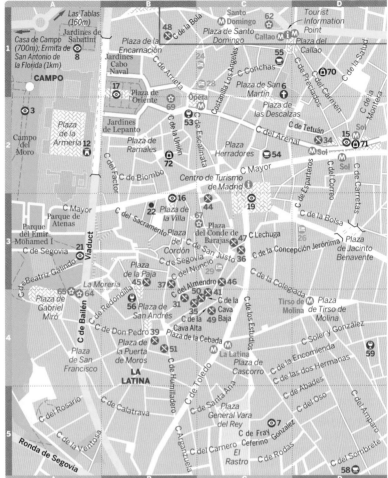

Sun; MÓpera, Sol) The grim plateresque walls of the Convento de las Descalzas Reales offer no hint that behind the facade lies a sumptuous stronghold of the faith. On the obligatory guided tour you'll see a gaudily frescoed Renaissance stairway, a number of extraordinary tapestries based on works by Rubens, and a wonderful painting entitled *The Voyage of the 11,000 Virgins*. Some 33 nuns still live here and there are 33 chapels dotted around the convent.

## LA LATINA & LAVAPIÉS

### El Rastro
Market

(Map p188; Ribera de Curtidores; ☉8am-3pm Sun; MLa Latina) A Sunday morning at El Rastro is a Madrid institution. You could easily spend an entire morning inching your way down the Calle de la Ribera de Curtidores and through the maze of streets that hosts El Rastro flea market every Sunday morning. Cheap clothes, luggage, old flamenco records, even older photos of Madrid, faux designer purses,

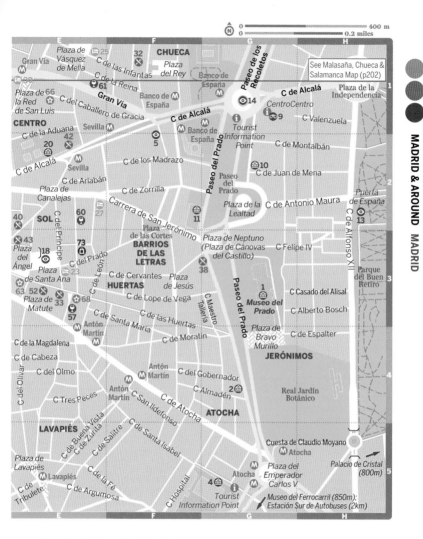

grungy T-shirts, household goods and electronics are the main fare. For every 10 pieces of junk, there's a real gem (a lost masterpiece, an Underwood typewriter) waiting to be found.

## EL RETIRO & THE ART MUSEUMS

### Centro de Arte Reina Sofía    Museum

(Map p188; ☑ 91 774 10 00; www.museoreinaso-fia.es; Calle de Santa Isabel 52; adult/concession €8/free, Sun free, 7-9pm Mon & Wed-Sat free; ☺10am-9pm Mon, Wed, Thu & Sat, 10am-7pm Sun, closed Tue; Ⓜ Atocha) Home to Picasso's *Guernica,* arguably Spain's single most famous artwork, the Centro de Arte Reina Sofía is Madrid's premier collection of contemporary art. In addition to plenty of paintings by Picasso, other major drawcards are works by Salvador Dalí (1904–1989) and Joan Miró (1893–1983). The collection principally spans the 20th century up to the 1980s.

# Central Madrid

The occasional non-Spaniard artist makes an appearance (including Francis Bacon's *Lying Figure;* 1966), but most of the collection is strictly peninsular.

## Museo Thyssen-Bornemisza    Museum
(Map p188; ☏ 902 760 511; www.museothyssen. org; Paseo del Prado 8; adult/concession/child €10/free, Mon free; ◷ 10am-7pm Tue-Sun, noon-4pm Mon; Ⓜ Banco de España) The Thyssen is one of the most extraordinary private collections of predominantly European art in the world. Where the Prado or Reina Sofía enable you to study the body of work of a particular artist in depth, the Thyssen is the place to immerse yourself in a breathtaking breadth of artistic styles. Most of the big names are here, sometimes with just a single painting, but the Thyssen's gift to Madrid and the art-loving public is to have them all under one roof.

## Parque del Buen Retiro
Gardens

**(Map p188;** ⏰ **6am-midnight May-Sep, to 11pm Oct-Apr;** Ⓜ **Retiro, Príncipe de Vergara, Ibiza, Atocha)** The glorious gardens of El Retiro are as beautiful as any you'll find in a European city. Littered with marble monuments, landscaped lawns, the occasional elegant building (the Palacio de Cristal is especially worth seeking out) and abundant greenery, it's quiet and contemplative during the week but comes to life on weekends. Put simply, this is one of our favourite places in Madrid.

## SALAMANCA

### Museo Arqueológico Nacional
Museum

**(Map p202; man.mcu.es; Calle de Serrano 13; admission €3, 5-8pm Sat & 9.30am-noon Sun free;** ⏰ **9.30am-8pm Tue-Sat, 9.30am-3pm Sun;** Ⓜ **Serrano)** Reopened after a massive overhaul of the building, the showpiece National Archaeology Museum contains a sweeping accumulation of artefacts behind its towering facade. The large collection includes stunning mosaics taken from Roman villas across Spain, intricate Muslim-era and Mudéjar handiwork, sculpted figures such as the *Dama de Ibiza* and *Dama de Elche,* examples of Romanesque and Gothic architectural styles and a partial copy of the prehistoric cave paintings of Altamira (Cantabria).

### Museo Lázaro Galdiano
Museum

**(**☏ **91 561 60 84; www.flg.es; Calle de Serrano 122; adult/concession €6/3, last hour free;** ⏰ **10am-4.30pm Mon & Wed-Sat, to 3pm Sun;** Ⓜ **Gregorio Marañón)** In an imposing early-20th-century Italianate stone mansion, the Museo Lázaro Galdiano has some 13,000 works of art and objets d'art. Apart from works by Bosch, Zurbarán, Goya, Claudio Coello, El Greco and Constable, this is a rather oddball assembly of all sorts of collectables. In room 14 copies of some of Goya's more famous works are hung together to make a collage, including *La maja* and the frescoes of the Ermita de San Antonio de la Florida.

## Paintings in the Centro de Arte Reina Sofía

- *Guernica* (Pablo Picasso; room 206)
- *Naturaleza muerta* (Pablo Picasso; 1912)
- *El gran masturbador* (Salvador Dalí; 1929)
- *Muchacha en la ventana* (Salvador Dalí; 1925)
- *Monumento imperial a la mujer niña* (Salvador Dalí; 1929)
- *Pastorale* (Joan Miró; 1923–24)
- *Danseuse espagnole* (Joan Miró; 1928)
- *L'atelier aux sculptures* (Miquel Barceló; 1993)
- *Los cuatro dictadores* (Eduardo Arroyo; 1963)
- *Retrato de Josette* (Juan Gris; 1916)
- *Cartes et dés* (Georges Braque; 1914)
- *El peine del viento I* (Eduardo Chillida; 1962)
- *Homenaje a Mallarmé* (Jorge Oteiza; 1958)
- *Pintura* (Antoni Tàpies; 1955)
- *Otoños* (Pablo Palazuelo; 1952)

## PARQUE DEL OESTE & NORTHERN MADRID

### Ermita de San Antonio de la Florida
Gallery

**(Glorieta de San Antonio de la Florida 5;** ⏰ **9.30am-8pm Tue-Sun, hours vary Jul & Aug;** Ⓜ **Príncipe Pío)** `FREE` The frescoed ceilings of the Ermita de San Antonio de la Florida are one of Madrid's most surprising secrets. Recently restored and also known as the **Panteón de Goya**, the

# Don't Miss
# Museo del Prado

Welcome to one of the world's premier art galleries. The more than 7000 paintings held in the Museo del Prado's collection are like a window onto the historical vagaries of the Spanish soul, at once grand and imperious in the royal paintings of Velázquez, darkly tumultuous in the 'Black Paintings' of Goya, and outward-looking with works from all across Europe.

Map p188

www.museodelprado.es

Paseo del Prado

adult/child €14/free, 6-8pm Mon-Sat & 5-7pm Sun free, audioguides €3.50, admission plus official guidebook €23

🕐10am-8pm Mon-Sat, 10am-7pm Sun

Ⓜ Banco de España

## Goya

Francisco José de Goya y Lucientes (Goya) is found on all three floors of the Prado, but we recommend starting at the southern end of the ground or lower level. In room 89, Goya's *El dos de mayo* and *El tres de mayo* rank among Madrid's most emblematic paintings; they bring to life the 1808 anti-French revolt and subsequent execution of insurgents in Madrid. Alongside, in rooms 87 and 88, are some of his darkest and most disturbing works, *Las pinturas negras* (Black Paintings), so called because of the dark browns and black that dominate, but also for the distorted animalesque appearance of their characters. There are more Goyas on the 1st floor in rooms 69 to 73. Among them are two more of Goya's best-known and most intriguing oils: *La maja vestida* and *La maja desnuda*.

## Velázquez

Diego Rodriguez de Silva y Velázquez (Velázquez) is another of the grand masters of Spanish art who brings so much distinction to the Prado. Of all his works, *Las meninas* (room 50) is what most people come to see. Completed in 1656, it is more properly known as La Família de Felipe IV (The Family of Felipe IV). The rooms surrounding *Las meninas* (rooms 14 and 15) contain more fine works by Velázquez.

## The Rest

Having experienced the essence of the Prado, you're now free to select from the astonishingly diverse works that remain. If Spanish painters have piqued your curiosity, Bartolomé Esteban Murillo, José de Ribera and the stark figures of Francisco de Zurbarán should be on your itinerary. Another alternative is the Prado's outstanding collection of Flemish art.

---

**Local Knowledge**

## Museo del Prado

*BY LEONARDO HERNÁNDEZ, MEMBER OF FRIENDS OF THE PRADO AND REGULAR PRADO VISITOR*

### 1 EDIFICIO JERÓNIMOS

The museum's extension, designed by Spanish architect Rafael Moneo, is worth visiting on its own. Highlights include the Sala de las Musas (Room of the Muses), the giant doors by Cristina Iglesias, the upper garden and El Claustro de los Jerónimos (Jerónimos' Cloister).

### 2 LA RENDICIÓN DE BREDA (LAS LANZAS), BY DIEGO VELÁZQUEZ

Velázquez's masterpiece shows the moment in 1625 in which Ambrosio Spinola, a Spanish general, accepted the surrender of the Dutch town of Breda after a siege. The Spanish novelist Arturo Pérez-Reverte mixed fantasy and reality in his novel *The Sun over Breda,* claiming that his character Captain Alatriste appeared in the painting but was later mysteriously erased by Velázquez.

### 3 LA FAMÍLIA DE CARLOS IV, BY FRANCISCO DE GOYA

This painting is a small fragment of Spanish history transferred to canvas. It shows the royal family in 1800 with Fernando (later Fernando VII) dressed in blue on the left. His fiancée has not yet been chosen, which may be why Goya depicts her with no facial definition.

### 4 EL DESCENDIMIENTO, BY ROGER VAN DER WEYDEN

This 1435 painting is unusual, both for its size and for the recurring crossbow shapes in the painting's upper corners, which are echoed in the bodies of Mary and Christ. Once the central part of a triptych, the painting is filled with drama and luminous colours.

### 5 LA CONDESA DE VILCHES, BY FEDERICO MADRAZO

The painter was a friend of the model, which may be why he is able to transmit all her grace and sensuality. The light blue dress, the tone of her skin, the brightness in her eyes, and the slightly pointed smile suggest a timeless sympathy that endures through the centuries.

# Museo del Prado

## PLAN OF ATTACK

Begin on the 1st floor with **Las meninas** ❶ by Velázquez. Although it alone is worth the entry price, it's a fine introduction to the 17th-century golden age of Spanish art; nearby are more of Velázquez' royal paintings and works by Zurbarán and Murillo. While on the 1st floor, seek out Goya's **La maja vestida and La maja desnuda** ❷ with more of Goya's early works in neighbouring rooms. Downstairs at the southern end of the Prado, Goya's anger is evident in the searing **El dos de mayo and El tres de mayo** ❸, and the torment of Goya's later years finds expression in the adjacent rooms with his **Las pinturas negras** ❹, or Black Paintings. Also on the lower floor, Hieronymus Bosch's weird and wonderful **The Garden of Earthly Delights** ❺ is one of the Prado's signature masterpieces. Returning to the 1st floor, El Greco's **Adoration of the Shepherds** ❻ is an extraordinary work, as is Peter Paul Rubens' **Las tres gracias** ❼ which forms the centrepiece of the Prado's gathering of Flemish masters. (Note: this painting may be moved to the 2nd floor.) A detour to the 2nd floor takes in some lesser-known Goyas, but finish in the **Edificio Jerónimos** ❽ with a visit to the cloisters and the outstanding bookshop.

## ALSO VISIT:

Nearby are Museo Thyssen-Bornemisza and Centro de Arte Reina Sofía. They form an extraordinary trio of galleries.

### TOP TIPS

» **Book online** Purchase your ticket online (www.museodelprado.es) and avoid the queues.

» **Best time to visit** As soon after opening time as possible.

» **Free tours** The website (www.museo delprado.es/coleccion/que-ver/) has self-guided tours for one- to three-hour visits.

**Las meninas (Velázquez)**
This masterpiece depicts Velázquez and the Infanta Margarita, with the king and queen whose images appear, according to some experts, in mirrors behind Velázquez.

IMAGNO/GETTY IMAGES ©

**Goya Entrance**

**Main Ticket Office**

**Edificio Jerónimos**
Opened in 2007, this state-of-the-art extension has rotating exhibitions of Prado masterpieces held in storage for decades for lack of wall space, and stunning 2nd-floor granite cloisters that date back to 1672.

**Adoration of the Shepherds (El Greco)**
There's an ecstatic quality to this intense painting. El Greco's distorted rendering of bodily forms came to characterise much of his later work.

## Las tres gracias (Rubens)

A late Rubens masterpiece, *The Three Graces* is a classical and masterly expression of Rubens' preoccupation with sensuality, here portraying Aglaia, Euphrosyne and Thalia, the daughters of Zeus.

## La maja vestida & La maja desnuda (Goya)

These enigmatic works scandalised early 19th-century Madrid society, fuelling the rumour mill as to the woman's identity and drawing the ire of the Spanish Inquisition.

## El dos de mayo & El tres de mayo (Goya)

Few paintings evoke a city's sense of self quite like Goya's portrayal of Madrid's valiant but ultimately unsuccessful uprising against French rule in 1808.

## Las pinturas negras (Goya)

*Las pinturas negras* are Goya's darkest works. *Saturno devorando a su hijo* evokes a writhing mass of tortured humanity, while *La romería de San Isidro* and *El aquelarre* are profoundly unsettling.

**Edificio Villanueva**

① ⑦ ②

**Information Counter & Audioguides**

**Jerónimos Entrance (Main Entrance)**

**Gift Shop**

**Cafeteria**

**Murillo Entrance**

⑤ ③ ④

**Velázquez Entrance**

## The Garden of Earthly Delights (Bosch)

A fantastical painting in triptych form, this overwhelming work depicts the Garden of Eden and what the Prado describes as 'the lugubrious precincts of Hell' in exquisitely bizarre detail.

## Paintings in the Museo del Prado

- *Las meninas* (Velázquez)
- *La rendición de Breda* (Velázquez)
- *La maja desnuda* & *La maja vestida* (Goya)
- *El tres de mayo* (Goya)
- *Las pinturas negras* (*Black Paintings;* Goya)
- *El jardín de las delicias* (*The Garden of Earthly Delights;* Hieronymus Bosch)
- *Adán y Eva* (Adam & Eve Dürer)
- *El lavatorio* (Tintoretto)
- *La trinidad* (El Greco)
- *David vencedor de Goliath* (Caravaggio)
- *El sueño de Jacob* (Ribera)
- *Las tres gracias* (*The Three Graces,* Rubens)
- *Artemisa* (Rembrandt)

southern of the two small chapels is one of the few places to see Goya's work in its original setting, as painted by the master in 1798 on the request of Carlos IV. Simply breathtaking.

##  Tours

### Visitas Guiadas Oficiales
Guided Tour

(Official Guided Tours; Map p188; ☎902 221 424; www.esmadrid.com/guidedtours; Plaza Mayor 27; adult/child €5.90/free, cycling & roller-blade tours adult €6.90; MSol) Over 40 highly recommended walking, cycling and roller-blade tours conducted in Spanish and English. Organised by the Centro de Turismo de Madrid (p211). Stop by the office and pick up its *M – Visitas Guiadas/ Guided Tours* catalogue.

### Wellington Society
Walking Tour

(☎609 143 203; www.wellsoc.org; tours €65-90) A handful of quirky historical tours laced with anecdotes and led by the inimitable Stephen Drake-Jones. Membership costs €65 and includes a day or evening walking tour.

### Insider's Madrid
Walking Tour

(☎91 447 38 66; www.insidersmadrid.com; tours from €60) An impressive range of tailor-made tours, including walking, tapas, flamenco and bullfighting tours.

### Madrid Bike Tours
Cycling

(☎680 581 782; www.madridbiketours.com; 4hr tours €55) Londoner Mike Chandler offers a guided two-wheel tour of Madrid as well as tours further afield.

### Adventurous Appetites
Walking Tour

(☎639 331073; www.adventurousappetites. com; 4hr tours €50; ☺8pm-midnight Mon-Sat) English-language tapas tours through central Madrid. Prices include the first drink but exclude food.

##  Sleeping

### PLAZA MAYOR & ROYAL MADRID

### Hotel Meninas
Boutique Hotel €€

(Map p188; ☎91 541 28 05; www.hotelmeninas. com; Calle de Campomanes 7; s/d from €89/109; ✳@⊛; MÓpera) This is a classy, cool choice. The colour scheme is blacks, whites and greys, with dark-wood floors and splashes of fuchsia and lime green. Flat-screen TVs in every room, modern bathroom fittings, internet access points, and even a laptop in some rooms, round out the clean lines and latest innovations. Past guests include Viggo Mortensen and Natalie Portman.

### Mario Room Mate
Boutique Hotel €€

(Map p188; ☎91 548 85 48; www.room-mate-hotels.com; Calle de Campomanes 4; s €80-125, d €100-150; ✳⊛; MÓpera) Entering this swanky boutique hotel is like crossing the threshold of Madrid's latest nightclub: staff dressed all in black, black walls and swirls of red lighting in the lobby. Rooms can be small, but have high ceilings, simple furniture and light tones contrasting smoothly with muted colours and dark surfaces. Some rooms are pristine white; others have splashes of colour with zany murals.

## LA LATINA & LAVAPIÉS

### Posada del Dragón
Boutique Hotel €€

(Map p188; ✆91 119 14 24; www.posadadel-dragon.com; Calle de la Cava Baja 14; r from €91; ❄️🛜; M La Latina) At last, a boutique hotel in the heart of La Latina. This restored 19th-century inn sits on one of our favourite Madrid streets, and rooms either look out over the street or over the pretty internal patio. The rooms? Some are on the small side, but they've extremely comfortable beds, and bold, brassy colour schemes and designer everything. There's a terrific bar-restaurant downstairs.

## SOL, SANTA ANA & HUERTAS

### Hotel Alicia
Boutique Hotel €€

(Map p188; ✆91 389 60 95; www.room-matehoteles.com; Calle del Prado 2; d €100-175, ste from €200; ❄️🛜; M Sol, Sevilla, Antón Martín) One of the landmark properties of the designer

Room Mate chain of hotels, Hotel Alicia overlooks Plaza de Santa Ana with beautiful, spacious rooms. The style (the work of designer Pascua Ortega) is a touch more muted than in other Room Mate hotels, but the supermodern look remains intact, the downstairs bar is oh-so-cool, and the service is young and switched on.

### Praktik Metropol
Boutique Hotel €€

(Map p188; ✆91 521 29 35; www.hotelpraktik-metropol.com; Calle de la Montera 47; s/d from €65/79; ❄️🛜; M Gran Vía) You'd be hard-pressed to find better value anywhere in Europe than here in this recently overhauled hotel. The rooms have a fresh, contemporary look with white wood furnishings, and some (especially the corner rooms) have brilliant views down to Gran Vía and out over the city. It's spread over six floors and there's a roof terrace if you don't have a room with a view.

### Hotel Plaza Mayor
Hotel €€

(Map p188; ✆91 360 06 06; www.h-plazamayor.com; Calle de Atocha 2; s/d from €55/70; ❄️🛜; M Sol, Tirso de Molina) We love this place. Sitting just across from the Plaza Mayor, here you'll find stylish decor, helpful

Palacio Real (p187)

## If You Like...
## Spanish Art

If you can't get enough of world-renowned ground-breaking art, you've come to the right city.

### 1 MUSEO AL AIRE LIBRE
(Map p202; www.munimadrid.es/ museoairelibre; cnr Paseo de la Castellana & Paseo de Eduardo Dato; ⏰24hr; Ⓜ Rubén Darío) This fascinating open-air collection of 17 abstract sculptures includes works by the renowned Basque artist Eduardo Chillida, the Catalan master Joan Miró, Eusebio Sempere and Alberto Sánchez, one of Spain's foremost sculptors of the 20th century.

### 2 CAIXA FORUM
(Map p188; www.fundacio.lacaixa.es; Paseo del Prado 36; ⏰10am-8pm; Ⓜ Atocha) This extraordinary structure is one of Madrid's most eye-catching landmarks. Seeming to hover above the ground, this brick edifice is topped by an intriguing summit of rusted iron. On an adjacent wall is the *jardín colgante* (hanging garden), a lush vertical wall of greenery almost four storeys high.

### 3 REAL ACADEMIA DE BELLAS ARTES DE SAN FERNANDO
(Map p188; ☏91 524 08 64; http://rabasf.insde. es; Calle de Alcalá 13; adult/child €6/free, Wed free; ⏰10am-3pm Tue-Sun Sep-Jun, hours vary Jul & Aug; Ⓜ Sol, Sevilla) In any other city, this gallery would be a stand-out attraction, but in Madrid it often gets forgotten in the rush to the Prado, Thyssen or Reina Sofía.

### 4 MUSEO SOROLLA
(museosorolla.mcu.es; Paseo del General Martínez Campos 37; adult/child €3/free, Sun & 2-8pm Sat free; ⏰9.30am-8pm Tue-Sat, 10am-3pm Sun; Ⓜ Iglesia, Gregorio Marañón) The Valencian artist Joaquín Sorolla immortalised the clear Mediterranean light of the Valencian coast. His Madrid house, a quiet mansion surrounded by lush gardens that he designed himself, was inspired by what he had seen in Andalucía and now contains the most complete collection of the artist's works.

staff and charming original elements of this 150-year-old building. The rooms are attractive, some with a light colour scheme and wrought-iron furniture. The pricier attic rooms boast dark wood and designer lamps, and have lovely little terraces with wonderful rooftop views of central Madrid.

**Hotel Urban**  Luxury Hotel €€€
(Map p188; ☏91 787 77 70; www.derbyhotels. com; Carrera de San Jerónimo 34; r from €225; ❄ ⓢ ♿; Ⓜ Sevilla) This towering glass edifice is the epitome of art-inspired designer cool. It boasts original artworks from Africa and Asia, and dark-wood floors and dark walls are offset by plenty of light, while the dazzling bathrooms have wonderful designer fittings – the washbasins are sublime. The rooftop swimming pool is one of Madrid's best and the gorgeous terrace is heaven on a candlelit summer's evening.

## MALASAÑA & CHUECA

**Hotel Óscar**  Boutique Hotel €€
(Map p188; ☏91 701 11 73; www.room-matehoteles.com; Plaza de Vázquez de Mella 12; d €90-200, ste €150-280; ❄ ⓢ ♿; Ⓜ Gran Vía) Outstanding. Hotel Óscar belongs to the highly original Room Mate chain of hotels, and the designer rooms ooze style and sophistication. Some have floor-to-ceiling murals, the lighting is always funky, and the colour scheme is asplash with pinks, lime greens, oranges or more-minimalist black and white.

**Hotel Abalú**  Boutique Hotel €€
(Map p202; ☏91 531 47 44; www.hotelabalu. com; Calle del Pez 19; d/apt from €80/110; ❄ ⓢ; Ⓜ Noviciado) Malasaña's very own boutique hotel is an oasis of style amid the *barrio's* time-worn feel. Suitably located on cool Calle del Pez, each room here has its own design drawn from the imagination of Luis Delgado, from retro chintz to Zen, baroque and pure white (and most aesthetics in between). You're close to Gran Vía, but away from the tourist scrum.

# ✘ Eating

## PLAZA MAYOR & ROYAL MADRID

**Mercado de San Miguel**  Tapas €€
(Map p188; www.mercadodesanmiguel.es; Plaza
de San Miguel; tapas from €1; ☉10am-midnight
Sun-Wed, 10am-2am Thu-Sat; Ⓜ Sol) One
of Madrid's oldest and most beautiful
markets, the Mercado de San Miguel has
undergone a stunning major renovation.
Within the early-20th-century glass walls,
the market has become an inviting space
strewn with tables. You can order tapas
and sometimes more substantial plates
at most of the counter-bars, and everything here (from caviar to chocolate) is as
tempting as the market is alive.

**Taberna La Bola**  Madrileño €€
(Map p188; ☎91 547 69 30; www.labola.es; Calle
de la Bola 5; mains €16-24; ☉1.30-4.30pm &
8.30-11pm Mon-Sat, 1.30-4.30pm Sun, closed
Aug; Ⓜ Santo Domingo) Taberna La Bola (going strong since 1870 and run by the sixth
generation of the Verdasco family) is a
much-loved bastion of traditional Madrid
cuisine. If you're going to try *cocido a
la madrileña* (meat-and-chickpea stew;
€20) while in Madrid, this is a good place
to do so. It's busy and noisy and very
Madrid.

**Restaurante Sobrino
de Botín**  Castilian €€€
(Map p188; ☎91 366 42 17; www.
botin.es; Calle de los Cuchilleros
17; mains €19-27; Ⓜ La Latina,
Sol) It's not every day
that you can eat in the
oldest restaurant in the
world (the *Guinness
Book of Records* has
recognised it as the
oldest – established
in 1725). And it has
also appeared in many
novels about Madrid,
from Ernest Hemingway

to Frederick Forsyth. Roasted meats are
the specialty.

## TAPAS

Many *madrileños* wouldn't eat *bacalao*
(salted cod) anywhere except **Casa
Revuelta** (Map p188; ☎91 366 33 32; Calle de
Latoneros 3; tapas from €2.60; ☉10.30am-4pm
& 7-11pm Tue-Sat, 10.30am-4pm Sun, closed Aug;
Ⓜ Sol, La Latina), clinched by the fact that
the owner painstakingly extracts every
fish bone in the morning.

## LA LATINA & LAVAPIÉS

**Naïa Bistro**  Modern Spanish €€
(Map p188; ☎91 366 27 83; www.naiabistro.com;
Plaza de la Paja 3; mains €12-20; set menus €30-
45; ☉1.30-4.30pm & 8.30-11.30pm Tue-Sun;
Ⓜ La Latina) On the lovely Plaza de la Paja,
Naïa has a real buzz about it, with modern Spanish cuisine, a chill-out lounge
downstairs and outdoor tables on lovely
Plaza de la Paja. The emphasis throughout is on natural ingredients, healthy food
and exciting tastes.

Teatro Real, Plaza de Oriente (p187)
HISHAM IBRAHIM/GETTY IMAGES ©

KRZYSZTOF DYDYNSKI/GETTY IMAGES ©

### Ene Restaurante    Fusion €€

(Map p188; ☏ 91 366 25 91; www.enerestaurante.com; Calle del Nuncio 19; mains €11-22, brunch €22; ⏱1-4pm & 8.30pm-midnight daily, brunch 12.30-4.30pm Sat & Sun; Ⓜ La Latina) Just across from Iglesia de San Pedro El Viejo, one of Madrid's oldest churches, Ene is anything but old world. The design is cutting edge and awash with reds and purples, while the young and friendly waiters circulate to the tune of lounge music. The food is Spanish-Asian fusion and there are also plenty of *pintxos* (Basque tapas) to choose from.

### Posada de la Villa    Madrileño €€€

(Map p188; ☏ 91 366 18 80; www.posadadelavilla.com; Calle de la Cava Baja 9; mains €19-28; ⏱1-4pm & 8pm-midnight Mon-Sat, 1-4pm Sun, closed Aug; Ⓜ La Latina) This wonderfully restored 17th-century *posada* (inn) is something of a local landmark. The atmosphere is formal, the decoration sombre and traditional (heavy timber and brickwork), and the cuisine decidedly local – roast meats, *cocido* (meat-and-chickpea stew), *callos* (tripe) and *sopa de ajo* (garlic soup).

### TAPAS

Madrid's home of tapas is La Latina, especially along Calle de la Cava Baja and the surrounding streets. **Almendro 13** (Map p188; ☏ 91 365 42 52; Calle del Almendro 13; mains €7-15; ⏱12.30-4pm & 7.30pm-midnight Sun-Thu, 12.30-5pm & 8pm-1am Fri & Sat; Ⓜ La Latina) is famous for quality rather than frilly elaborations, with cured meats, cheeses, tortillas and *huevos rotos* (literally, 'broken eggs') the house specialties. Down on Calle de la Cava Baja, **Txacolina** (Map p188; ☏ 91 366 48 77; Calle de la Cava Baja 26; tapas from €3.50; ⏱8pm-midnight Mon & Tue, 1-4pm & 8pm-midnight Wed-Sat, 1-4pm Sun; Ⓜ La Latina) does Basque 'high cuisine in miniature', although these are some of the biggest *pintxos* (Basque tapas) you'll find; wash it all down with a *txacoli*, a sharp Basque white. On the same street, **Casa Lucas** (Map p188; ☏ 91 365 08 04; www.casalucas.es; Calle de la Cava Baja 30; tapas/raciones from €5/12; ⏱1-3.30pm & 8pm-midnight Thu-Tue, 1-3.30pm Wed; Ⓜ La Latina) and **La Chata** (Map p188; ☏ 91 366 14 58; Calle de la Cava Baja 24; mains €12-21, tapas selection for 2 people €20; ⏱1-4pm & 8.30pm-midnight Thu-Mon, 8.30pm-midnight Tue & Wed; Ⓜ La Latina) are also hugely popular. Not far away, **Juana**

**La Loca** (Map p188; ☎91 364 05 25; Plaza de la Puerta de Moros 4; tapas from €4.50, mains €8-19; ⏰noon-1am Tue-Sun, 8pm-1am Mon; Ⓜ La Latina) does a magnificent *tortilla de patatas* (potato and onion omelette), as does **Txirimiri** (Map p188; ☎91 364 11 96; www.txirimiri.es; Calle del Humilladero 6; tapas from €4; ⏰noon-4.30pm & 8.30pm-midnight, closed Aug; Ⓜ La Latina). **Taberna Matritum** (Map p188; ☎91 365 82 37; Calle de la Cava Alta 17; mains €13-18; ⏰1.30-4pm & 8.30pm-midnight Wed-Sun, 8.30pm-midnight Mon & Tue; Ⓜ La Latina) serves great tapas and desserts by the master chocolatier Oriol Balaguer.

## SOL, SANTA ANA & HUERTAS

**Casa Alberto**  Spanish, Tapas €€
(Map p188; ☎91 429 93 56; www.casaalberto.es; Calle de las Huertas 18; tapas from €3.25, raciones €8.50-16, mains €14-21; ⏰1.30-4pm & 8pm-midnight Tue-Sat, 1.30-4pm Sun; Ⓜ Antón Martín) One of the most atmospheric old *tabernas* of Madrid, Casa Alberto has been around since 1827. The secret to its staying power is vermouth on tap, excellent tapas at the bar and fine sit-down meals; Casa Alberto's *rabo de toro* (bull's tail) is famous among aficionados.

**La Terraza del Casino**  Contemporary Spanish €€€
(Map p188; ☎91 521 87 00; www.casinodemadrid.es; Calle de Alcalá 15; mains €32-65, set menus from €69-135; ⏰1.30-3.30pm & 9-11pm Mon-Sat; Ⓜ Sevilla) Perched atop the lavish Casino de Madrid building, this temple of haute cuisine is presided over by celebrity chef Paco Roncero and is the proud

# Madrid for Children

Madrid has plenty to keep the little ones entertained. A good place to start is **Casa de Campo** (Ⓜ Batán), where there are swimming pools, the **Zoo Aquarium de Madrid** (☎902 34 50 14; www.zoomadrid.com; Casa de Campo; adult/child €23/19; ⏰10.30am-8.30pm Jul & Aug, reduced hours Sep-Jun; 🚌37 from Intercambiador de Príncipe Pío, Ⓜ Casa de Campo) and the **Parque de Atracciones** (☎91 463 29 00; www.parquedeatracciones.es; Casa de Campo; adult/child €30/free; ⏰noon-midnight Sun-Fri, to 1am Sat Jul & Aug, reduced hours Sep-Jun; 🚌37 from Intercambiador de Príncipe Pío, Ⓜ Batán) amusement park, which has a 'Zona Infantil' with sedate rides for the really young. To get to Casa de Campo, take the **Teleférico** (☎91 541 11 18; www.teleferico.com; 1-way/return €4/5.75; ⏰noon-9pm Mon-Fri, to 9.30pm Sat & Sun Jun-Aug, reduced hours Sep-May; Ⓜ Argüelles), one of the world's most horizontal cable cars, which putters for 2.5km out from the slopes of La Rosaleda.

The **Museo del Ferrocarril** (☎902 22 88 22; www.museodelferrocarril.org; Paseo de las Delicias 61; adult/child €6/4; ⏰9.30am-3pm Tue-Fri, 10am-8pm Sat, 10am-3pm Sun, closed Aug; Ⓜ Delicias) is home to old railway cars, train engines and more. The **Museo Naval** (Map p188; ☎91 523 87 89; www.armada.mde.es/museonaval; Paseo del Prado 5; ⏰10am-7pm Tue-Sun; Ⓜ Banco de España) FREE will appeal to those fascinated by ships.

The **Museo de Cera** (Map p202; ☎91 319 26 49; www.museoceramadrid.com; Paseo de los Recoletos 41; adult/child €17/12; ⏰10am-2.30pm & 4.30-8.30pm Mon-Fri, 10am-8.30pm Sat & Sun; Ⓜ Colón) is Madrid's modest answer to Madame Tussaud's, with more than 450 wax characters.

Other possibilities include seeing Real Madrid play at the Estadio Santiago Bernabéu (p210), wandering through the soothing greenery of the Parque del Buen Retiro (p191), where in summer there are puppet shows and boat rides, or skiing at **Madrid Xanadú** (☎902 36 13 09; www.madridsnowzone.com; Calle Puerto de Navacerrada; per hour adult/child €22/19, day pass €36/33, equipment rental €18; ⏰10am-midnight; 🚌528, 534).

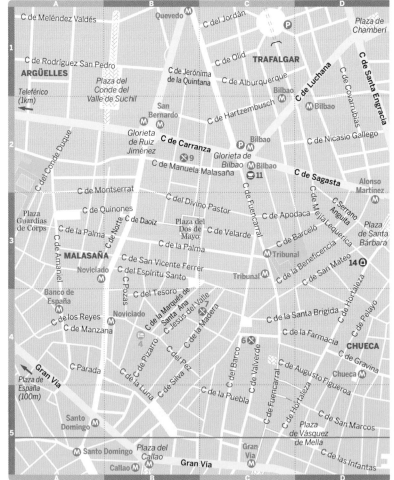

# Malasaña, Chueca & Salamanca

### ⊙ Sights
1 Museo al Aire Libre ...................................... G1
2 Museo Arqueológico Nacional ............... F4
3 Museo de Cera .............................................. F4

### ⊜ Sleeping
4 Hotel Abalú ..................................................... B4

### ⊗ Eating
5 Biotza .............................................................. G4
6 Bodega de la Ardosa ................................ C4
7 Casa Julio ...................................................... C4

8 La Colonial de Goya .................................. H4
9 La Musa .......................................................... B2
10 Sergi Arola Gastro .................................... E1

### ⊜ Drinking & Nightlife
11 Café Comercial .......................................... C2
12 Gran Café de Gijón .................................... E5

### ⊜ Shopping
13 Agatha Ruiz de la Prada ........................ G3
14 Patrimonio Comunal Olivarero ............. D3

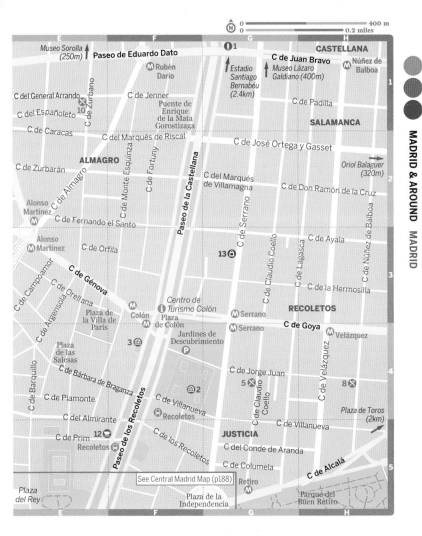

bearer of two Michelin stars. It's all about culinary experimentation, with a menu that changes as each new idea emerges from the laboratory and moves into the kitchen. The *menu degustación* (€135) is a fabulous avalanche of tastes.

**Vi Cool** Contemporary Spanish €€
(Map p188; ☑91 429 49 13; www.vi-cool.com; Calle de las Huertas 12; mains €8-19; ⏰1.30-4.15pm & 8.30pm-midnight Tue-Sun; Ⓜ Antón Martín) Catalan master chef Sergi Arola is one of the most restless and relentlessly

creative culinary talents in the country. Aside from his showpiece **Sergi Arola Gastro** (Map p202; ☑91 310 21 69; www.sergiarola.es; Calle de Zurbano 31; mains €50-58, set menus €105-135; ⏰2-3.30pm & 9-11.30pm Tue-Sat; Ⓜ Alonso Martínez), he has dabbled in numerous new restaurants around the capital and in Barcelona, but this is one of his most interesting yet – a modern bar-style space with prices that enable the average mortal to sample his formidable gastronomic skills.

# If You Like…
## Plazas

If you like the Plaza Mayor, we think you'll easily fall in love with these other central Madrid plazas:

### 1 PLAZA DE LA VILLA
(Map p188; Plaza de la Villa; MÓpera) The intimate Plaza de la Villa is one of Madrid's prettiest. It's enclosed on three sides by wonderfully preserved examples of 17th-century *barroco madrileño* (Madrid-style baroque architecture).

### 2 PLAZA DE SANTA ANA
(Map p188; Plaza de Santa Ana; MSevilla, Sol, Antón Martín) Plaza de Santa Ana is a delightful confluence of elegant architecture and irresistible energy, and is the starting point for many a long Huertas night.

### 3 PLAZA DE LA PUERTA DEL SOL
(Map p188; Plaza de la Puerta del Sol; MSol) The official centre point of Spain is a gracious hemisphere of elegant facades that's often very crowded. It is, above all, a crossroads. People here are forever heading somewhere else, on foot, by metro (three lines cross here) or by bus (many lines terminate and start nearby).

## TAPAS

In Huertas, **La Casa del Abuelo** (Map p188; ☏91 000 01 33; www.lacasadelabuelo.es; Calle de la Victoria 12; raciones from €9.60; ☉noon-midnight Sun-Thu, noon-1am Fri & Sat; MSol) is famous for *gambas a la plancha* (grilled prawns) or *gambas al ajillo* (prawns sizzling in garlic on little ceramic plates) and a *chato* (small glass) of the heavy, sweet El Abuelo red wine; they cook over 200kg of prawns here on a good day. For *patatas bravas* (fried potatoes lathered in a spicy tomato sauce), **Las Bravas** (Map p188; ☏91 522 85 81; www.lasbravas.com; Callejón de Álvarez Gato 3; raciones €3.55-10; ☉12.30-4.30pm & 7.30pm-12.30am; MSol, Sevilla) is the place. For *bacalao*, **Casa Labra** (Map p188; ☏91 532 14 05; www.casalabra.es; Calle de Tetuán 11;

tapas from €0.90; ☉9.30am-3.30pm & 5.30-11pm; MSol) has been around since 1860 and was a favourite of the poet Federico García Lorca.

## SALAMANCA
### TAPAS

In Salamanca, **Biotza** (Map p202; www.biotzarestaurante.com; Calle de Claudio Coello 27; cold/hot pintxos €2.80/3.40, raciones from €6, set menus from €18; ☉9am-2am Mon-Sat; MSerrano) offers creative Basque *pintxos* in stylish surrounds, while **La Colonial de Goya** (Map p202; ☏91 435 76 08; www.restauranterincondegoya.es; Calle de Jorge Juan 34; tapas €3-4.50, mains €11-18; ☉1-4pm & 8pm-midnight; MVelázquez) serves up a staggering choice of *pintxos*, including 63 varieties of canapés. Further south, aong the Paseo del Prado, there's only one choice for tapas and it's one of Madrid's best: **Estado Puro** (Map p188; ☏91 330 24 00; www.tapasenestadopuro.com; Plaza Neptuno/Plaza de Cánovas del Castillo 4; tapas €2-13; ☉noon-midnight Mon-Sat, to 4pm Sun; MBanco de España, Atocha).

## MALASAÑA & CHUECA
**La Musa**    Spanish, Fusion €€
(Map p202; ☏91 448 75 58; www.grupolamusa.com; Calle de Manuela Malasaña 18; tapas from €3.75, mains €7-15; ☉9am-midnight Mon-Wed, 9am-1am Fri, 1pm-2am Sat, 1pm-midnight Sun; MSan Bernardo) Snug yet loud, a favourite of Madrid's hip young crowd yet utterly unpretentious, La Musa is all about designer decor, lounge music on the sound system and memorably fun food (breakfast, lunch and dinner). The menu is divided into three types of tapas – hot, cold and BBQ.

### TAPAS

Chueca is another stellar tapas *barrio*. Don't miss **Bocaito** (Map p188; ☏91 532 12 19; www.bocaito.com; Calle de la Libertad 4-6; tapas from €3.50, mains €10-29; ☉1-4pm & 8.30pm-midnight Mon-Fri, 8.30pm-midnight Sat; MChueca, Sevilla), a purveyor of Andalucian *jamón* (ham) and seafood and a favourite haunt of filmmaker Pedro Almodóvar.

**Bodega de La Ardosa** (Map p202; ☎91 521 49 79; Calle de Colón 13; tapas & raciones €3.50-11; ⊙8.30am-2am Mon-Fri, 12.45pm-2.30am Sat & Sun; ⓂTribunal) is extremely popular for its *salmorejo* (cold, tomato-based soup), *croquetas, patatas bravas* and *tortilla de patatas*, while **Casa Julio** (Map p202; ☎91 522 72 74; Calle de la Madera 37; 6/12 croquetas €5/10; ⊙9.30am-3.30pm & 6.30pm-midnight Mon-Sat, closed Aug; ⓂTribunal) is widely touted as the home of Madrid's best *croquetas*.

# 🍷 Drinking

## PLAZA MAYOR & ROYAL MADRID

### Chocolatería de San Ginés          Cafe

(Map p188; Pasadizo de San Ginés 5; ⊙24hr; ⓂSol) One of the grand icons of the Madrid night, this *chocolate con churros* (Spanish donuts with chocolate) cafe sees a sprinkling of tourists throughout the day, but locals pack it out in their search for sustenance on their way home from a nightclub sometime close to dawn. Only in Madrid…

### Café del Real          Bar, Cafe

(Map p188; Plaza de Isabel II 2; ⊙8am-1am Mon-Thu, 8am-2:30am Fri, 9am-2:30am Sat, 10am-11:30pm Sun; ⓂÓpera) A cafe and cocktail bar in equal parts, this intimate little place serves up creative coffees and a few cocktails to the soundtrack of chill-out music. The best seats are upstairs, where the low ceilings, wooden beams and leather chairs are a great place to pass an afternoon with friends.

### Chocolatería Valor          Cafe

(Map p188; www.chocolateriasvalor.es; Postigo de San Martín; ⊙9am-10.30pm Sun, 8am-10.30pm Mon-Thu, 8am-1am Fri, 9am-1am Sat; ⓂCallao) It may be Madrid tradition to indulge in *chocolate con churros* around sunrise on your way home from a nightclub, but for everyone else who prefers a more reasonable hour, this is possibly the best *chocolatería* in town. Our favourite chocolate variety among many has to be *cuatro sentidos de chocolate* (four senses of chocolate; €7.95), but we'd happily try everything on the menu to make sure.

Museo Arqueológico Nacional (p191)

## LA LATINA & LAVAPIÉS

### Gau&Café  Cafe
(Map p188; www.gaucafe.com; Calle de Tribulete
14, 4th fl; ⏰11am-midnight Mon-Fri, 1.30pm-
midnight Sat; MLavapiés) Decoration that's
light and airy, with pop-art posters of
Audrey Hepburn and James Bond. A
large terrace with views over the Lavapiés
rooftops. A stunning backdrop of a ruined
church atop which the cafe sits. With so
much else going for it, it almost seems
incidental that it also serves great teas,
coffees and snacks (and meals). The cafe
is around 300m southwest of Plaza de
Lavapiés along Calle de Tribulete; look for
the glass doors.

### Delic  Bar, Cafe
(Map p188; www.delic.es; Costanilla de San
Andrés 14; ⏰11.30am-midnight Mon-Fri, 1.30pm-
midnight Sat; MLa Latina) We could go on for
hours about this long-standing cafe-bar,
but we'll reduce it to its most basic elements: nursing an exceptionally good
mojito (€8) or three on a warm summer's
evening at Delic's outdoor tables on one

of Madrid's prettiest plazas is one of life's
great pleasures. Bliss.

### La Escalera de Jacob  Cocktail Bar
(Map p188; www.laescaleradejacob.es; Calle de
Lavapiés 9; concerts from €6; ⏰7pm-2am Mon-
Fri, 10am-2am Sat & Sun; MAntón Martín, Tirso
de Molina) As much a cocktail bar as a live-
music venue or theatre, 'Jacob's Ladder' is
one of Madrid's most original stages. Ma-
gicians, storytellers, children's theatre, live
jazz and other genres are all part of the
mix. This alternative slant on life makes
for some terrific live performances.

## SOL, SANTA ANA & HUERTAS

### La Venencia  Bar
(Map p188; ☎91 429 73 13; Calle de Echegaray
7; ⏰1-3.30pm & 7.30pm-1.30am; MSol, Sevilla)
La Venencia is a *barrio* classic, with fine
sherry from Sanlúcar and manzanilla
from Jeréz poured straight from the
dusty wooden barrels, accompanied by a
small selection of tapas with an Andalucian bent. Otherwise, there's no music,
no flashy decorations; it's all about you,

**Left:** Palacio de Cristal, Parque del Buen Retiro (p191);
**Below:** Catedral Nueva, Salamanca (p222)

(LEFT) SYLVAIN SONNET/GETTY IMAGES ©; (BELOW) DESIGN PICS/KEN WELSH/GETTY IMAGES ©

your *fino* (sherry) and your friends.

### El Imperfecto
Cocktail Bar

(Map p188; Plaza de Matute 2; ☺3pm-2am Mon-Thu, to 2.30am Fri & Sat; Ⓜ Antón Martín) Its name notwithstanding, the 'Imperfect One' is our ideal Huertas bar, with live jazz most Tuesdays at 9pm and a drinks menu as long as a saxophone, ranging from cocktails (€7, or two mojitos for €10) and spirits to milkshakes, teas and creative coffees. Its pina colada is one of the best we've tasted and the atmosphere is agreeably buzzy yet chilled.

## MALASAÑA & CHUECA

### Museo Chicote
Cocktail Bar

(Map p188; www.museo-chicote.com; Gran Vía 12; ☺5pm-3am Mon-Thu, to 3.30am Fri & Sat; Ⓜ Gran Vía) The founder of this Madrid landmark (complete with 1930s-era interior) is said to have invented more than 100 cocktails, which the likes of Hemingway, Ava Gardner, Grace Kelly, Sophia Loren and Frank Sinatra have all enjoyed at one time or another. It's at its best after midnight, when a lounge atmosphere takes over, couples cuddle on the curved benches and some of the city's best DJs do their stuff.

### Café Comercial
Cafe

(Map p202; Glorieta de Bilbao 7; ☺7.30am-midnight Mon-Thu, 7.30am-2am Fri, 8.30am-2am Sat, 9am-midnight Sun; 🛜; Ⓜ Bilbao) This glorious old Madrid cafe proudly fights a rearguard action against progress with heavy leather seats, abundant marble and old-style waiters. It dates back to 1887 and has changed little since those days, although the clientele has broadened to include just about anyone, from writers and their laptops to old men playing chess.

### Gran Café de Gijón
Cafe

(Map p202; www.cafegijon.com; Paseo de los Recoletos 21; ☺7am-1.30am; Ⓜ Chueca, Banco de España) This graceful old cafe has been serving coffee and meals since

1888 and has long been a favourite with Madrid's literati for a drink or a meal – *all* of Spain's great 20th-century literary figures came here for coffee and *tertulias* (literary discussions). You'll find yourself among intellectuals, conservative Franco diehards and young *madrileños* looking for a quiet drink.

## ☆ Entertainment

All of the following publications and websites provide comprehensive, updated listings of showings at Madrid's theatres, cinemas and concert halls:

**EsMadrid Magazine** (www.esmadrid.com) Monthly tourist-office listings for concerts and other performances; available at tourist offices, some hotels and online.

**In Madrid** (www.in-madrid.com) Monthly English-language expat publication given out free (check the website for locations) with lots of information about what to see and do in town.

**La Netro** (www.lanetro.com/madrid) Comprehensive online guide to Madrid events.

### LIVE MUSIC & FLAMENCO

Madrid may not be the spiritual home of flamenco, and its big names may feel more at home in the atmospheric flamenco taverns of Andalucía, but Madrid remains one of Spain's premier flamenco stages.

**Corral de la Morería**                    Flamenco
(Map p188; ☎91 365 84 46; www.corralde-lamoreria.com; Calle de la Morería 17; admission incl drink €50, mains from €21, set menus €38; ⏰7pm-12.15am, shows 9pm & 10.55pm; MÓpera) This is one of the most prestigious flamenco stages in Madrid, with 50 years' experience as a leading flamenco venue and top performers most nights. The stage area has a rustic feel, and tables are pushed up close. The performances have a far better price-to-quality ratio than the meals.

**Las Carboneras**                    Flamenco
(Map p188; ☎91 542 86 77; www.tablaolas-carboneras.com; Plaza del Conde de Miranda 1; admission incl drink €33; ⏰shows 8.30pm & 10.30pm Mon-Thu, 8.30pm & 11pm Fri & Sat; MÓpera, Sol, La Latina) Like most of the *tablaos* (flamenco venues) around town, this place sees far more tourists than locals, but the quality is nonetheless unimpeachable. It's not the place for gritty, soul-moving spontaneity, but it's still an excellent introduction and one of the few places that flamenco aficionados seem to have no complaints about.

**Las Tablas**    Flamenco
(☎91 542 05 20; www.lastablasmadrid.com; Plaza de España 9; admission incl drink €27; ⏰shows 8pm & 10pm; MPlaza de España) Las Tablas has a reputation for quality flamenco and reasonable prices; it could just be the best choice in town. Most nights you'll

Alcázar, Segovia (p226)
RUTH TOMLINSON/GETTY IMAGES ©

see a classic flamenco show, with plenty of throaty singing and soul-baring dancing. Antonia Moya and Marisol Navarro, leading lights in the flamenco world, are regular performers here.

### Café Central                                    Jazz
(Map p188; 📞 91 369 41 43; www.cafecentralmadrid.com; Plaza del Ángel 10; admission €12-18; 🕐 12.30pm-2.30am Sun-Thu, 12.30pm-3.30am Fri & Sat; Ⓜ Antón Martín, Sol) In 2011, the respected jazz magazine *Down Beat* included this art-deco bar on the list of the world's best jazz clubs, the only place in Spain to earn the prestigious accolade (said by some to be the jazz equivalent of earning a Michelin star) and with well over 9000 gigs under its belt, it rarely misses a beat.

### Populart                                         Jazz
(Map p188; 📞 91 429 84 07; www.populart.es; Calle de las Huertas 22; 🕐 6pm-2.30am Sun-Thu, to 3.30am Fri & Sat; Ⓜ Antón Martín, Sol) FREE One of Madrid's classic jazz clubs, this place offers a low-key atmosphere and top-quality music, which is mostly jazz with occasional blues, swing and even flamenco thrown into the mix. Compay Segundo, Sonny Fortune and the Canal Street Jazz Band have all played here. Shows start at 10.45pm but, if you want a seat, get here early.

### Café Berlin                                      Jazz
(Map p188; 📞 91 521 57 52; berlincafe.es; Calle de Jacometrezo 4; admission €5-12; 🕐 10pm-5.30am Tue-Sun Sep-Jul; Ⓜ Callao, Santo Domingo) El Berlín has been something of a Madrid jazz stalwart since the 1950s, although a recent makeover has brought flamenco, R&B, soul, funk and fusion. The art-deco interior adds to the charm. Headline acts play at 11.30pm on Fridays and Saturdays, with other performances sprinkled throughout the week.

### Costello Café
### & Niteclub                                  Live Music
(Map p188; www.costelloclub.com; Calle del Caballero de Gracia 10; admission €5-10; 🕐 8pm-3am Sun-Wed, 6pm-3.30am Thu-Sat; Ⓜ Gran Vía) Very cool. Costello Café & Niteclub weds

## Bullfighting

Love it or loath it, bullfighting is still a big part of Madrid life, and from the **Fiesta de San Isidro** (www.esmadrid.com) in mid-May until the end of October, Spain's top bullfighters come to swing their capes at **Plaza de Toros Monumental de Las Ventas** ( 📞 91 725 18 57; Calle de Alcalá 237; admission free, tour adult/child €10/7; 🕐 10am-6pm; Ⓜ Las Ventas) FREE. Las Ventas, as it is commonly known, is the most important bullring in the bullfighting world and the circle of sand enclosed by four storeys, which can seat up to 25,000 spectators, evokes more a sense of a theatre than a sports stadium. Guided visits (conducted in English and Spanish) take you out onto the sand and into the royal box; tours last 40 minutes and start on the hour. For a more in-depth discussion of bullfighting, turn to p341.

smooth-as-silk ambience to an innovative mix of pop, rock and fusion in Warhol-esque surrounds. There's live music at 9.30pm every night except Sundays, with resident and visiting DJs keeping you on your feet until closing time from Thursday to Saturday.

### ContraClub                                   Live Music
(Map p188; 📞 91 365 55 45; www.contraclub.es; Calle de Bailén 16; admission €6-12; 🕐 10pm-6am Wed-Sat; Ⓜ La Latina) ContraClub is a crossover live-music venue and nightclub, with live flamenco on Wednesday and an eclectic mix of other live music (jazz, blues, world music and rock) from Thursday to Saturday. After the live acts (which start at 10.30pm), the resident DJs serve up equally eclectic beats (indie, pop, funk and soul) to make sure you don't move elsewhere.

## FOOTBALL

### Estadio Santiago Bernabéu    Football

(☎91 398 43 00, 902 291 709; www.realmadrid.com; Avenida de Concha Espina 1; tour adult/child €19/13; ⏰10am-7pm Mon-Sat, 10.30am-6.30pm Sun, except match days; Ⓜ Santiago Bernabéu) The home of **Real Madrid**, Estadio Santiago Bernabéu is a temple to football and is one of the world's great sporting arenas. For a self-guided **tour** of the stadium, buy your ticket at ticket window 10 (next to gate 7). Tickets for matches start at around €40 and can be bought online at www.realmadrid.com, while the all-important telephone number for booking tickets (which you later pick up at gate 42) is ☎902 324 324, which only works if you're calling from within Spain.

The stadium is north of the city, along the Paseo de la Castellana, around 3.5km north of the Plaza de la Cibeles.

## 🛍 Shopping

On a Sunday morning, don't forget El Rastro (p188), Madrid's epic flea market.

### El Flamenco Vive    Flamenco

(Map p188; www.elflamencovive.es; Calle Conde de Lemos 7; ⏰10.30am-2pm & 5-9pm Mon-Sat; Ⓜ Ópera) This temple to flamenco has it all, from guitars and songbooks to well-priced CDs, polka-dotted dancing costumes, shoes, colourful plastic jewellery and literature about flamenco. It's the sort of place that will appeal as much to curious first timers as to serious students of the art. It also organises classes in flamenco guitar.

### María Cabello    Wine

(Map p188; Calle de Echegaray 19; ⏰9.30am-2.30pm & 5.30-9pm Mon-Fri, 10am-2.30pm & 6.30-9.30pm Sat; Ⓜ Sevilla, Antón Martín) All wine shops should be like this. This family-run corner shop really knows its wines and the interior has scarcely changed since 1913, with wooden shelves and even a faded ceiling fresco. There are fine wines in abundance (mostly Spanish, and a few foreign bottles), with some 500 labels on show or tucked away out the back.

### Agatha Ruiz de la Prada    Fashion

(Map p202; www.agatharuizdelaprada.com; Calle de Serrano 27; ⏰10am-8.30pm Mon-Sat; Ⓜ Serrano) This boutique has to be seen to be believed, with pinks, yellows and oranges everywhere you turn. It's fun and exuberant, but not just for kids. It also has serious and highly original fashion. Agatha Ruiz de la Prada is one of the enduring icons of la movida, Madrid's 1980s outpouring of creativity.

### Oriol Balaguer    Food

(www.oriolbalaguer.com; Calle de José Ortega y Gasset 44; ⏰9am-8pm Mon-Fri, 10am-8pm Sat, 10am-2.30pm Sun; Ⓜ Nuñez de Balboa) Catalan pastry chef Oriol Balaguer has a formidable CV – he worked in the kitchens of Ferran Adrià in Catalonia and won the prize for the World's Best Dessert (the 'Seven Textures of Chocolate') in 2001. His chocolate boutique is presented like a small art gallery, except that it's dedicated to exquisite finely crafted chocolate collections and cakes. You'll never be able to buy ordinary chocolate again.

### Patrimonio Comunal Olivarero    Food

(Map p202; www.pco.es; Calle de Mejía Lequerica 1; ⏰10am-2pm & 5-8pm Mon-Fri, 10am-2pm Sat; Ⓜ Alonso Martínez) To pick some of the country's olive-oil varieties (Spain is the world's largest producer), Patrimonio Comunal Olivarero is perfect. With examples of the extra-virgin variety (and nothing else) from all over Spain, you could spend ages agonising over the choices. The staff know their oil and are happy to help out if you speak a little Spanish.

### Casa de Diego    Accessories

(Map p188; perso.ya.com/jlleran; Plaza de la Puerta del Sol 12; ⏰9.30am-8pm Mon-Sat; Ⓜ Sol) This classic shop has been around since 1858, making, selling and repairing Spanish fans, shawls, umbrellas and canes. Service is old style and occasionally grumpy, but the fans are works of antique art. There's another **branch** (Map p188; ☎91 531 02 23; Calle del los Mesoneros Romanos 4; ⏰9.30am-1.30pm & 4.45-8pm Mon-Sat; Ⓜ Callao, Sol) nearby.

# ℹ️ Information

**Centro de Turismo de Madrid** (Map p188; 📞91 588 16 36; www.esmadrid.com; Plaza Mayor 27; ⏰9.30am-8.30pm; Ⓜ️Sol) is an excellent city tourist office with a smaller office underneath.

Other branches include **Plaza de Colón** (Map p202; www.esmadrid.com; Plaza de Colón; ⏰9.30am-8.30pm; Ⓜ️Colón) and the **Palacio de Cibeles** (Map p188; Plaza de Cibeles 1; ⏰10am-8pm Tue-Sun; Ⓜ️Plaza de España), as well as information points at **Plaza de la Cibeles** (Map p188; Plaza de la Cibeles; ⏰9.30am-8.30pm; Ⓜ️Banco de España), **Plaza del Callao** (Map p188; Plaza del Callao; Ⓜ️Callao), closed for renovations at the time of writing, outside the **Centro de Arte Reina Sofía** (Map p188; cnr Calle de Santa Isabel & Plaza del Emperador Carlos V; ⏰9.30am-8.30pm; Ⓜ️Atocha) and at the T2 and T4 terminals at Barajas airport.

# ℹ️ Getting There & Away

## Air

Madrid's **Barajas Airport** (📞902 404 704; www.aena.es; Ⓜ️Aeropuerto T1, T2 & T3; Aeropuerto T4) is one of Europe's busiest and is served by almost 100 airlines. Direct flights – whether with low-cost carriers or other airlines – connect the city with destinations across Europe. A smaller but nonetheless significant number of airlines also fly into Madrid direct from the Americas, Asia and Africa, and there are plenty of domestic flights to Madrid from other Spanish cities.

## Bus

**Estación Sur de Autobuses** (📞91 468 42 00; www.estaciondeautobuses.com; Calle de Méndez Álvaro 83; Ⓜ️Méndez Álvaro), just south of the M30 ring road, is the city's principal bus station. It serves most destinations to the south and many in other parts of the country. Most bus companies have a ticket office here, even if their buses depart from elsewhere.

## Car & Motorcycle

Madrid is surrounded by two main ring roads, the outermost M40 and the inner M30; there are also two partial ring roads, the M45 and the more-distant M50. The R5 and R3 are part of a series of toll roads built to ease traffic jams.

## Train

Madrid is served by two main train stations. The bigger of the two is **Puerta de Atocha** (Ⓜ️Atocha Renfe), at the southern end of the city centre, while **Chamartín** (Ⓜ️Chamartín) lies in the north of the city. The bulk of trains for Spanish destinations depart from Atocha, especially those going south. International services arrive at and

Catedral, Toledo (p214)

CARLOS MUINA/GETTY IMAGES ©

leave from Chamartín. For bookings, contact Renfe (☏ 902 240 202; www.renfe.es) at either train station.

High-speed **Tren de Alta Velocidad Española** (AVE) services connect Madrid with Seville (via Córdoba), Valladolid (via Segovia), Toledo, Valencia (via Cuenca), Málaga and Barcelona (via Zaragoza and Huesca or Tarragona). Most high-speed services operate from Madrid's Puerta de Atocha station. The Madrid–Segovia/Valladolid service leaves from the Chamartín station.

## ❶ Getting Around

### To/From the Airport

**Barajas Airport** Metro (6.05am-2am), bus (24hr) and minibus to central Madrid; taxis are a flat rate €30.

**Exprés Aeropuerto** (Airport Express; www.emtmadrid.es; per person €5; ☉24hr; 🛜) The Exprés Aeropuerto runs between Puerta de Atocha train station and the airport. Buses run every 13 to 23 minutes from 6am to 11.30pm, and every 35 minutes throughout the rest of the night. The trip takes 40 minutes. From 11.55pm until 5.35am, departures are from the Plaza de la Cibeles, not the train station.

**Metro** (www.metromadrid.es) Line 8 of the metro runs from the airport to the Nuevos Ministerios transport interchange on Paseo de la Castella, where it connects with lines 10 and 6. It operates from 6.05am to 2am. A one-way ticket to/from the airport costs €4.50 (10-trip Metrobús ticket €12.20). Even if you have a 10-trip ticket, you'll need to buy the airport supplement from machines at any metro station. The journey to Nuevos Ministerios takes around 15 minutes, around 25 minutes from T4.

### Bus

Buses operated by **Empresa Municipal de Transportes de Madrid** (EMT; ☏ 902 507 850; www.emtmadrid.es) travel along most city routes regularly between about 6.30am and 11.30pm. There are 26 night-bus *búhos* (owls) routes operating from midnight to 6am, with all routes originating in Plaza de la Cibeles.

### Metro

Madrid's modern metro (www.metromadrid.es), Europe's second-largest, is a fast, efficient and safe way to navigate Madrid, and generally easier than getting to grips with bus routes. There are 11 colour-coded lines in central Madrid, in addition to the modern southern suburban MetroSur system as well as lines heading east to the major population centres of Pozuelo and Boadilla del Monte. Colour maps showing the metro system are available from any metro station or online. The metro operates from 6.05am to 2am.

### Taxi

You can pick up a taxi at ranks throughout town or simply flag one down. Flag fall is €2.40 from 6am to 9pm daily, €2.90 the rest of the time. You pay between €1 and €1.20 per kilometre depending on the hour. Several supplementary charges, usually posted inside the taxi, may apply. There's no charge for luggage.

**Radio-Teléfono Taxi** (☏ 91 547 82 00; www.radiotelefono-taxi.com)

San Lorenzo de El Escorial
LUIS DAVILLA/GETTY IMAGES ©

## San Lorenzo de El Escorial

POP 18,447 / ELEV 1032M

The imposing palace and monastery complex of San Lorenzo de El Escorial is an impressive place, rising up from the foothills of the mountains that shelter Madrid from the north and west. The one-time royal getaway is now a prim little town overflowing with quaint shops, restaurants and hotels catering primarily to throngs of weekending *madrileños*. The fresh, cool air here has been drawing city dwellers since the complex was first ordered to be built by Felipe II in the 16th century. Most visitors come on a day trip from Madrid.

## ◉ Sights

The main entrance to the **Real Monasterio de San Lorenzo** (☎91 890 78 18; www.patrimonionacional.es; adult/concession €10/5, guide/audioguide €7/4, EU citizens last 3 hours Wed & Thu free; ⊙10am-8pm Apr-Sep, 10am-6pm Oct-Mar, closed Mon) is on its western facade. Above the gateway a statue of St Lawrence stands guard, holding a symbolic gridiron, the instrument of his martyrdom (he was roasted alive on one). From here you'll first enter the **Patio de los Reyes**, which houses the statues of the six kings of Judah.

Directly ahead lies the sombre **basilica**. As you enter, look up at the unusual flat vaulting by the choir stalls. Once inside the church proper, turn left to view Benvenuto Cellini's white Carrara marble statue of Christ crucified (1576).

The remainder of the ground floor contains various treasures, including some tapestries and an El Greco painting – impressive as it is, it's a far cry from El Greco's dream of decorating the whole complex. Continue downstairs to the northeastern corner of the complex. You pass through the **Museo de Arquitectura** and the **Museo de Pintura**. The former tells (in Spanish) the story of how the complex was built; the

## Detour: Alcalá de Henares

East of Madrid, Alcalá de Henares is full of surprises with historical sandstone buildings seemingly at every turn. Throw in some sunny squares and a legendary university, and it's a terrific place to escape the capital for a few hours.

The town is dear to Spaniards because it's the birthplace of literary figurehead Miguel de Cervantes Saavedra. The site believed by many to be Cervantes' birthplace is re-created in the illuminating **Museo Casa Natal de Miguel de Cervantes** (☎91 889 96 54; www.museo-casa-natal-cervantes.org; Calle Mayor 48; ⊙10am-6pm Tue-Sun) FREE, which lies along the beautiful, colonnaded Calle Mayor.

Alcalá de Henares is just 35km east of Madrid, heading towards Zaragoza along the A2.

There are regular bus departures (every five to 15 minutes) from Madrid's Intercambiador de Avenida de América. The trip takes about one hour (€2.99).

latter contains a range of 16th- and 17th-century Italian, Spanish and Flemish art.

Head upstairs into a gallery around the eastern part of the complex known as the **Palacio de Felipe II** or **Palacio de los Austrias**. You'll then descend to the 17th-century **Panteón de los Reyes** (Crypt of the Kings), where almost all Spain's monarchs since Carlos I are interred.

## ℹ Information

**Tourist office** (☎91 890 53 13; www.sanlorenzoturismo.org; Calle de Grimaldi 4, El Escorial; ⊙10am-2pm & 3-6pm Tue-Sat, 10am-2pm Sun)

MADRID & AROUND TOLEDO

ABUELA PINOCHO/GETTY IMAGES ©

## ℹ️ Getting There & Away

Every 15 minutes (every 30 minutes on weekends) buses 661 and 664 run to El Escorial (€4.20, one hour) from platform 30 at the Intercambiador de Autobuses de Moncloa in Madrid.

San Lorenzo de El Escorial is 59km northwest of Madrid and it takes 40 minutes to drive there. Take the A6 highway to the M600, then follow the signs to El Escorial.

A few dozen Renfe (📞902 24 02 02; www. renfe.es) C8 *cercanías* (local-area trains) make the trip daily from Madrid's Atocha or Chamartín train station to El Escorial (€5.40, one hour).

## Toledo

POP 83,110 / ELEV 655M

Though one of the smaller of Spain's provincial capitals, Toledo looms large in the nation's history and consciousness as a religious centre, bulwark of the Spanish church, and once-flourishing symbol of a multicultural medieval society. The Old Town today is a treasure chest of churches, museums, synagogues and mosques set in a labyrinth of narrow streets, plazas and inner patios in a lofty setting high above Río Tajo.

## 👁️ Sights

### Catedral                        Cathedral
**(Plaza del Ayuntamiento; adult/child €8/free;** 🕐**10.30am-6.30pm Mon-Sat, 2-6.30pm Sun)**
Toledo's cathedral reflects the city's historical significance as the heart of Catholic Spain and it's one of the most extravagant cathedrals in the country. The heavy interior, with sturdy columns dividing the space into five naves, is on a monumental scale. Every one of the numerous side chapels has artistic treasures, with the other main highlights being the *coro* (choir), Capilla Mayor, Transparente, *sacristia* (sacristy) and bell tower (for €3 extra).

### Alcázar                   Fortress, Museum
**(Museo del Ejército; Calle Alféreces Provision-ales; adult/child €5/free;** 🕐**11am-5pm)** At the highest point in the city looms the foreboding Alcázar. Rebuilt under Franco, it has been reopened as a vast military museum. The usual displays of uniforms and medals are here, but the best part is the exhaustive historical section, with an in-depth overview of the nation's history in Spanish and English.

### Sinagoga del Tránsito   Synagogue

(museosefardi.mcu.es; Calle Samuel Leví; adult/child €3/1.50, Sat after 2pm & all day Sun free, combined ticket with Museo del Greco €5; ⊘9.30am-8pm Tue-Sat Apr-Sep, to 6.30pm Tue-Sat Oct-Mar, 10am-3pm Sun) This magnificent synagogue was built in 1355 by special permission of Pedro I. The synagogue now houses the **Museo Sefardí**. The vast main prayer hall has been expertly restored and the Mudéjar decoration and intricately carved pine ceiling are striking. Exhibits provide an insight into the history of Jewish culture in Spain, and include archaeological finds, a memorial garden, costumes and ceremonial artefacts.

### Museo del Greco   Museum, Gallery

(☑925 22 44 05; museodelgreco.mcu.es; Paseo del Tránsito; adult/child €3/1.50, after 2pm Sat & all day Sun free, combined ticket with Sinagoga del Tránsito €5; ⊘9.30am-8pm Tue-Sat Apr-Sep, to 6.30pm Oct-Mar, 10am-3pm Sun) In the early 20th century, an aristocrat bought what he thought was El Greco's house and did a stunning job of returning it to period style. He was wrong, but the museum remains worthwhile. As well as the house itself, with its lovely patio and good information on the painter's life, there are excavated cellars from a Jewish-quarter palace and a good selection of paintings, including a set of the apostles by El Greco, a Zurbarán, and works by El Greco's son and followers.

### Mezquita del Cristo de la Luz   Mosque

(Calle Cristo de la Luz; admission €2.50; ⊘10am-2pm & 3.30-6.45pm Mon-Fri, 10am-6.45pm Sat & Sun) On the northern slopes of town you'll find a modest, yet beautiful, mosque (the only one remaining of Toledo's 10) where architectural traces of Toledo's medieval Muslim conquerors are

# Toledo Top Tips

### TAKE THE ESCALATOR

A **remonte peatonal** (⊘7am-11pm Mon-Fri, 8am-2am Sat, 8am-10pm Sun), which starts near the Puerta de Alfonso VI and ends near the Monasterio de Santo Domingo El Antiguo, is a good way to avoid the steep uphill climb to reach the historic quarter of town.

### PULSERA TURÍSTICA

The Pulsera Turística is a bracelet (€8) that gets you into six key Toledo sights, all of which cost €2.50 on their own. There's no time limit, but make sure it doesn't fall off! Buy the bracelet at any of the sights covered, which are Monasterio San Juan de los Reyes, Sinagoga de Santa María la Blanca, Iglesia de Santo Tomé, Iglesia del Salvador, Iglesia San Ildefonso and Mezquita Cristo de la Luz.

### TOP VISTAS

For superb city views, head over the Puente de Alcántara to the other side of Río Tajo and head along the road that rises to your right, where the vista becomes more marvellous with every step. If you're staying overnight, along this road, the **Parador Conde de Orgaz** (☑925 22 18 50; www.parador.es; Cerro del Emperador; r €105-207; ⓟ❈⊛✿) has superlative views, as does the restaurant known as **La Ermita** (www.laermitarestaurante.com; Carretera de Circunvalación; mains €18-22, degustation menu €48; ⊘1.30-4pm & 8.45-11pm), which has a short, quality menu of elaborate Spanish cuisine.

# Toledo

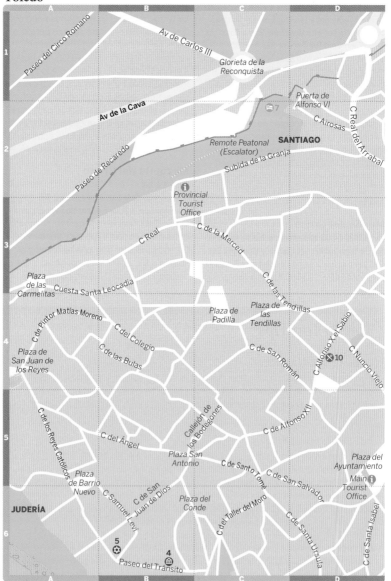

still in evidence. Built around AD 1000, it suffered the usual fate of being converted into a church (hence the religious frescoes), but the original vaulting and arches survived.

## Sleeping

**Casa de Cisneros**  Boutique Hotel €€
( 925 22 88 28; www.hostal-casa-de-cisneros. com; Calle del Cardenal Cisneros; s/d €40/66;

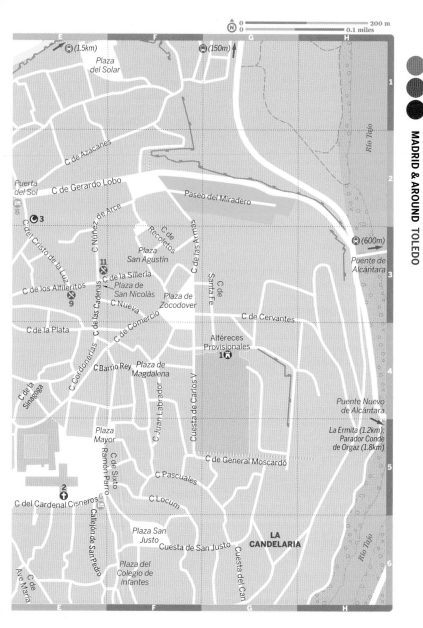

Right by the cathedral, this lovely 16th-century house was once the home of the cardinal and Grand Inquisitor Cisneros (often known as Ximénes). It's a top choice, with cosy, seductive rooms with original wooden beams and walls and voguish bathrooms. Archaeological works have revealed the remains of Roman baths and part of an 11th-century Moorish palace in the basement.

# Toledo

## Hacienda del Cardenal
Historic Hotel €€

(☏925 22 49 00; www.hostaldelcardenal.com; Paseo de Recaredo 24; r incl breakfast €55-120; ❋🛜) This wonderful 18th-century mansion has soft ochre-coloured walls, arches and columns. Some rooms are grand, others are spartan, and all come with dark furniture, plush fabrics and parquet floors. Several overlook the glorious terraced gardens.

## Hotel Abad
Hotel €€

(☏925 28 35 00; www.hotelabad.com; Calle Real del Arrabal 1; r/apt from €58/120; 🅿❋🛜) Compact, pretty and pleasing, this hotel sits on the lower slopes of the old town and offers good value. Rooms blend modern comfort with exposed old brick very successfully; some have small balconies, but those at the back are notably quieter. There are also apartments available next door.

# ⊗ Eating

## Kumera
Modern Spanish €

(☏925 25 75 53; www.restaurantekumera.com; Calle Alfonso X El Sabio 2; meals €9-10, set menus €20-35; ⊗8am-2.30am Mon-Fri, 11am-2.30am Sat & Sun) With arguably the best price-to-quality ratio in town, this place serves up innovative takes on local traditional dishes such as *cochinito* (suckling pig), *rabo de toro* (bull's tail) or *croquetas* (croquettes, filled with *jamón*, squid, cod or wild mushrooms), along-

side gigantic toasts and other creatively conceived dishes. The dishes with foie gras as the centrepiece are especially memorable.

## Alfileritos 24
Modern Spanish €€

(www.alfileritos24.com; Calle de los Alfileritos 24; mains €15-20, bar food €4.50-12; ⊗9.30am-midnight, to 1am Fri & Sat) The 14th-century surroundings of columns, beams and barrel-vault ceilings are snazzily coupled with modern artwork and bright dining rooms in an atrium space spread over four floors. The menu demonstrates an innovative flourish in the kitchen, with dishes like green rice with quail or loins of venison with baked-in-the-bag Reineta apple.

## La Abadía
Castilian, Tapas €€

(www.abadiatoledo.com; Plaza de San Nicolás 3; raciones €4-15) In a former 16th-century palace, this atmospheric bar and restaurant has arches, niches and subtle lighting and is spread over a warren of brick-and-stone-clad rooms. The menu includes lightweight dishes and tapas, but the 'Menú de Montes de Toledo' (€19) is a fabulous collection of tastes from the nearby mountains.

# ⓘ Information

**Main tourist office** (☏925 25 40 30; www.toledo-turismo.com; Plaza del Ayuntamiento; ⊗10am-6pm) Within sight of the cathedral.

**Provincial tourist office** (www.diputoledo.es; Subida de la Granja; ⊗8am-6pm Mon-Fri, 10am-5pm Sat, 10am-3pm Sun) At the top of the escalator.

**Tourist office** (Estación de Renfe; ⊗10am-3pm) At the train station.

# ⓘ Getting There & Away

For most major destinations, you'll need to backtrack to Madrid.

From Toledo's **bus station** (Avenida de Castilla La Mancha), buses depart for Madrid's Plaza Eliptica roughly every half hour (from €5.35, one hour to 1¾ hrs), some direct, some via villages. There are also services to Cuenca (€14, 2¼ hours).

From the pretty **train station** (☏902 240 202; Paseo de la Rosa) high-speed AVE (Alta Velocidad Española; high-speed services) trains run every hour or so to Madrid (one way/return €13/20, 30 minutes).

## ℹ️ Getting Around

Buses (€1.50) run between Plaza de Zocodover and the bus station (bus 5) and train station (buses 61 and 62). Bus 12 does a circuit within the old town.

Driving in the old town is a nightmare. There are several underground car parks throughout the area. Zones blocked off by bollards can be accessed if you have a hotel reservation. At the base of the old town are several large free car parks.

........................................................

# Ávila

POP 59,010 / ELEV 1130M

Ávila's old city, surrounded by imposing city walls comprising eight monumental gates, 88 watchtowers and more than 2500 turrets, is one of the best-preserved medieval bastions in all Spain. In winter, when an icy wind whistles in off the plains, the old city huddles behind the high stone walls as if seeking protection from the harsh Castilian climate. At night, when the walls are illuminated to magical effect, you'll wonder if you've stumbled into a fairy tale. Within the walls, Ávila can appear caught in a time warp. It's a deeply religious city that, for centuries, has drawn pilgrims to the cult of Santa Teresa de Ávila, with many churches, convents and high-walled palaces. As such, Ávila is the essence of Castilla, the epitome of old Spain.

## ◎ Sights

### Murallas                                    Walls

(adult/child under 12yr €5/free; ⏱10am-8pm Tue-Sun; 👪) Ávila's splendid 12th-century walls stretch for 2.5km atop the remains of earlier Roman and Muslim battlements and rank among the world's best-preserved medieval defensive perimeters. Two sections of the walls can be climbed – a 300m stretch that can be accessed from just inside the **Puerta del Alcázar**, and a longer 1300m stretch that runs the length of the old city's northern perimeter. The admission price includes a multilingual audioguide.

Raised to a height of 12m between the 11th and 12th centuries, the walls have been much restored and modified, with various Gothic and Renaissance touches, and even some Roman stones reused in the construction. At dusk they attract swirls of swooping and diving swallows.

# Who Was Santa Teresa?

Teresa de Cepeda y Ahumada, probably the most important woman in the history of the Spanish Catholic Church, was born in Ávila on 28 March 1515, one of 10 children of a merchant family. Raised by Augustinian nuns after her mother's death, she joined the Carmelite order at age 20. After her early, undistinguished years as a nun, she was shaken by a vision of hell in 1560, which crystallised her true vocation: she would reform the Carmelites.

In stark contrast to the opulence of the church in 16th-century Spain, her reforms called for the church to return to its roots, taking on the suffering and simple lifestyle of Jesus Christ. The Carmelites demanded the strictest of piety and even employed flagellation to atone for their sins. Not surprisingly, all this proved extremely unpopular with the mainstream Catholic Church.

With the help of many supporters, Teresa founded convents all over Spain and her writings proved enormously popular. She died in 1582 and was canonised by Pope Gregory XV in 1622.

**Right:** Acueducto, Segovia (p226);
**Below:** Puerta del Alcázar, Ávila (p219);

(BELOW) DANITA DELIMONT/GETTY IMAGES ©; (RIGHT) LOURDES ORTEGA POZA/GETTY IMAGES ©

## Convento de Santa Teresa          Museum

(Plaza de la Santa; ⏰8.45am-1.30pm & 3.30-9pm Tue-Sun) FREE Built in 1636 around the room where the saint was born in 1515, this is the epicentre of the cult surrounding Teresa. There are three attractions in one here: the church, a relics room and a museum. Highlights include the gold-adorned chapel (built over the room she was born), the baroque altar and the, albeit macabre, relic of the saint's ring finger (complete with ring). Apparently Franco kept it beside his bedside throughout his rule.

## Catedral del Salvador          Cathedral

(Plaza de la Catedral; admission €4; ⏰10am-7.30pm Mon-Fri, 10am-8pm Sat, noon-6.30pm Sun) Ávila's 12th-century cathedral is both a house of worship and an ingenious fortress: its stout granite apse forms the central bulwark in the historic city walls.

The sombre Gothic-style facade conceals a magnificent interior with an exquisite early-16th-century altar frieze showing the life of Jesus, plus Renaissance-era carved choir stalls and a museum with an El Greco painting and a splendid silver monstrance by Juan de Arfe. Push the buttons to illuminate the altar and the choir stalls.

## Monasterio de la Encarnación          Monastery

(Calle de la Encarnación; admission €2; ⏰9.30am-1.30pm & 3.30-6pm Mon-Fri, 10am-1pm & 4-6pm Sat & Sun) North of the city walls, this unadorned Renaissance monastery is where Santa Teresa fully took on the monastic life and lived for 27 years. One of the three main rooms open to the public is where the saint is said to have had a vision of the baby Jesus. Also on display are relics like the piece of wood used by Teresa as a pillow (ouch!) and the chair upon which St John of the Cross made his confessions.

## 🛏️ Sleeping

### Hotel El Rastro
Historic Hotel €

( 🕿 920 35 22 25; www.elrastroavila.com; Calle Cepedas; s/d €35/55; ❄ 🛜) This atmospheric hotel occupies a former 16th-century palace with original stone, exposed brickwork and a natural earth-toned colour scheme exuding a calm understated elegance. Each room has a different form, but most have high ceilings and plenty of space. Note that the owners also run a marginally cheaper, same-name *hostal* (budget hotel) around the corner.

### Hotel Las Leyendas
Historic Hotel €€

( 🕿 920 35 20 42; www.lasleyendas.es; Calle de Francisco Gallego 3; s/d incl breakfast €56/79; ❄ 🛜) Occupying the house of 16th-century Ávila nobility, this intimate hotel overflows with period touches wedded to modern amenities. Some rooms have views out across the plains, others look onto an internal garden. The decor varies between original wooden beams, exposed brick and stonework and more modern rooms with walls washed in muted earth tones. Breakfast is a little sparse.

## 🍴 Eating

### Soul Kitchen
Contemporary Castilian €€

(www.soulkitchen.es; Calle de Caballeros 13; mains €9-€19; ⏰10am-midnight Mon-Fri, 11am-2am Sat, 11am-midnight Sun; 🎵 👪) Opened in 2013, this restaurant has the kind of contemporary energy that can seem lacking in Avila's staider restaurants. The eclectic menu changes regularly and ranges from salads, with dressings like chestnut and fig, to hamburgers with cream of *setas* (oyster mushrooms). Lighter eats include bruschetta with tasty toppings. Live music, poetry readings (and similar) take place in summer.

### Hostería Las Cancelas
Castilian €€

( 🕿 920 21 22 49; www.lascancelas.com; Calle de la Cruz Vieja 6; mains €16-25; ⏰1-4pm &

221

7.30-11pm) This courtyard restaurant occupies a delightful interior patio dating back to the 15th century. Renowned for being a mainstay of Ávila cuisine, traditional meals are prepared with a salutary attention to detail; the *solomillo con salsa al ron y nueces* (sirloin in a rum and walnut sauce) is a rare deviation from tradition. Reservations recommended.

**Mesón del Rastro**  Castilian €€
(www.elrastroavila.com; Plaza del Rastro 1; mains €12-21; ⊙1-4pm & 9-11pm) The dark-wood beamed interior announces immediately that this is a bastion of robust Castilian cooking and has been since 1881. Expect delicious mainstays such as *judías del barco de Ávila* (beans) and *cordero asado* (roast lamb), mercifully light salads and, regrettably, the occasional coach tour. The *menú degustacón,* priced for two people (€30), comes warmly recommended, but only if you're *really* hungry.

## 🍷 Drinking

**La Bodeguita de San Segundo**  Wine Bar
(www.vinoavila.com; Calle de San Segundo 19; ⊙11am-midnight Thu-Tue) Situated in the 16th-century Casa de la Misericordia, this superb wine bar is standing-room only most nights and more tranquil in the quieter afternoon hours. Its wine list is renowned throughout Spain with more than 1000 wines to choose from, with tapas-sized servings of cheeses and cured meats the perfect accompaniment.

## Salamanca Card

Visitors should consider the **Salamanca Card** (www.salamancacard. com), which offers free entry to most museums, an MP3 audio guide to the city, and discounts at some restaurants, hotels and shops. It can be purchased online or from tourist offices, and costs €19/23 for 24/48 hours.

## ℹ Information

**Centro de Recepción de Visitantes** (📞920 35 40 00, ext 790; www.avilaturismo.com; Avenida de Madrid 39; ⊙9am-8pm) Municipal tourist office.

**Regional tourist office** (📞920 21 13 87; www. turismocastillayleon.com; Casa de las Carnicerías, Calle de San Segundo 17; ⊙9am-2pm & 5-8pm Mon-Sat, 9.30am-5pm Sun)

## ℹ Getting There & Away

### Bus
Frequent services to Segovia (€5.85, one hour), Salamanca (€7.60, 1½ hours) and Madrid (€9.45, 1½ hours); a couple of daily buses also head for the main towns in the Sierra de Gredos.

### Car & Motorcycle
From Madrid the driving time is around one hour; the toll costs €9.70.

### Train
There are services to Madrid (from €8.75, 1¼ to two hours), Salamanca (from €12,1¼ hours, eight daily) and León (from €22, three hours, three daily).

........................................................

# Salamanca
POP 153,470

Whether floodlit by night or bathed in the light of sunset, there's something magical about Salamanca. This is a city of rare beauty, awash with golden sandstone overlaid with ochre-tinted Latin inscriptions, an extraordinary virtuosity of plateresque and Renaissance styles. The monumental highlights are many, with the exceptional Plaza Mayor (illuminated to stunning effect at night) an unforgettable highlight. But this is also Castilla's liveliest city; home to a massive Spanish and international student population that throngs the streets at night and provides the city with so much youth and vitality.

## ◎ Sights & Activities

**Catedral Nueva**  Cathedral
(Plaza de Anaya; ⊙9am-8pm) FREE The tower of this late-Gothic cathedral lords over the city centre, its compelling churrigueresque (ornate style of baroque)

ATLANTIDE PHOTOTRAVEL/CORBIS ©

# ⭐ Don't Miss
# Universidad Civil

The visual feast of the entrance facade is a tapestry in sandstone, bursting with images of mythical heroes, religious scenes and coats of arms. It's dominated by busts of Fernando and Isabel. Founded initially as the Estudio Generál in 1218, the university reached the peak of its renown in the 15th and 16th centuries. Behind the facade, the highlight of an otherwise modest collection of rooms lies upstairs: the extraordinary **university library**, the oldest university library in Europe.

Containing some 2800 manuscripts gathering dust, the library is a real cemetery of forgotten books. Note the fine late-Gothic features and beautiful *techumbre* (carved wooden ceiling).

Among the small lecture rooms arranged around the courtyard downstairs, the **Aula de Fray Luis de León** was named after the celebrated 16th-century theologian and writer whose statue adorns the Patio de las Escuelas Menores outside. Arrested by the Inquisition for having translated the Song of Solomon into Spanish, the sardonic theologian returned to his class after five years in jail and resumed lecturing with the words, 'As I was saying yesterday...'. It was here, too, that the famous Spanish philosopher and essayist, Miguel de Unamuno, claimed the Nationalist rising was 'necessary to save Western Civilization', and was saved from the fury of the crowd by Franco's wife.

The **Escalera de la Universidad** (University Staircase) that connects the two floors has symbols carved into the balustrade, seemingly of giant insects having a frolic with several bishops – to decode them was seen as symbolic of the quest for knowledge.

## NEED TO KNOW

Calle de los Libreros; adult/concession €4/2, Mon morning free; 🕒9.30am-1.30pm & 4-6.30pm Mon-Sat, 10am-1.30pm Sun

# Frog-Spotting

Arguably a lot more interesting than trainspotting (and you don't have to drink tea from a thermos flask), a compulsory task facing all visitors to Salamanca is to search out the frog sculpted into the facade of the Universidad Civil. Once pointed out, it's easily enough seen, but the uninitiated can spend considerable time searching. Why bother? Well, they say that those who detect it without help can be assured of good luck and even marriage within a year. Some hopeful students see a guaranteed examination's victory in it. If you believe all this, stop reading now: if you need help, look at the busts of Fernando and Isabel. From there, turn your gaze to the largest column on the extreme right of the front. Slightly above the level of the busts is a series of skulls, atop the leftmost of which sits our little amphibious friend (or what's left of his eroded self).

dome visible from almost every angle. The interior is similarly impressive, with elaborate choir stalls, main chapel and retrochoir all courtesy of the prolific José Churriguera. The ceilings are also exceptional, along with the Renaissance doorways, particularly the **Puerta del Nacimiento** on the western face, that stands out as one of several miracles worked in the city's native sandstone.

### Catedral Vieja — Cathedral

(Plaza de Anaya; admission €4.75; ⏱10am-7.30pm) The Catedral Nueva's largely Romanesque predecessor, the Catedral Vieja is adorned with an exquisite 15th-century **altarpiece**, one of the finest outside Italy, with 53 panels depicting scenes from the lives of Christ and Mary, topped by a representation of the Final Judgment. The cloister was largely ruined in an earthquake in 1755, but the Capilla de Anaya houses an extravagant alabaster sepulchre and one of Europe's oldest organs, a Mudéjar work of art dating from the 16th century.

### Plaza Mayor — Square

Built between 1729 and 1755, Salamanca's exceptional square is widely considered to be Spain's most beautiful central plaza. The square is particularly memorable at night when illuminated (until midnight) to magical effect. Designed by Alberto Churriguera, it's a

remarkably harmonious and controlled baroque display. The medallions placed around the square bear the busts of famous figures.

## 🏃 Tours

The municipal tourist office organises two-hour guided tours of the city. These depart at 2pm on weekdays from in front of the tourist office in Plaza Mayor and cost €20 per person. They are held in Spanish, French or English and include admission to the Catedral Vieja. Reservations essential.

## 🛏 Sleeping

### Hostal Concejo — Hostal €

( ☎923 21 47 37; www.hconcejo.com; Plaza de la Libertad 1; s/d €45/60; P ❄ 🛜) A cut above the average *hostal,* the stylish Concejo has polished-wood floors, tasteful furnishings, light-filled rooms and a superb central location. Try and snag one of the corner rooms (like number 104) with its traditional glassed-in balcony, complete with a table, chairs and people-watching views.

### Microtel Placentinos — Boutique Hotel €€

( ☎923 28 15 31; www.microtelplacentinos.com; Calle de Placentinos 9; s/d incl breakfast Sun-Thu €57/73, Fri & Sat €88/100; ❄ 🛜) One of Salamanca's most charming boutique hotels,

Microtel Placentinos is tucked away on a quiet street and has rooms with exposed stone walls and wooden beams. The service is faultless, and the overall atmosphere is one of intimacy and discretion. All rooms have a hydromassage shower or tub and there's a summer-only outside whirlpool spa.

#  Eating

**La Cocina de Toño**     Tapas €€
(www.lacocinadetoño.es; Calle Gran Via 20; tapas €1.30-3.80, mains €7-20; ⏱2-4pm & 8-10pm Tue-Sat, 2-5pm Sun) This place owes its loyal following to its creative *pinchos* (snacks) and half-servings of dishes such as escalope of foie gras with roast apple and passionfruit gelatin. The restaurant serves more traditional fare as befits the decor, but the bar is one of Salamanca's gastronomic stars. Slightly removed from the old city, it draws a predominantly Spanish crowd.

**Mesón Las Conchas**     Castilian €€
(Rúa Mayor 16; mains €10-21; ⏱bar 8am-midnight, restaurant 1-4pm & 8pm-midnight; 🛗) Enjoy a choice of outdoor tables, an atmospheric bar or the upstairs, wood-beamed dining area. The bar caters mainly to locals who know their *embutidos* (cured meats). For sit-down meals, there's a good mix of roasts, *platos combinados* (meat-and-three-veg dishes) and *raciones* (full-plate-size tapas). It serves a couple of cured meat platters (€35 for two people), and a highly rated oven-baked turbot.

# 🛈 Information

Municipal & regional tourist office (☎923 21 83 42; www.turismodesalamanca.com; Plaza Mayor 14; ⏱9am-2pm & 4.30-8pm Mon-Fri, 10am-8pm Sat, 10am-2pm Sun) The regional tourist office shares an office with the municipal office on Plaza Mayor. An audio city barcode guide (www.audioguiasalamanca.es) is available with the appropriate app.

## Local Knowledge

# Salamanca

*BY BEATRIZ CASTAÑO & JUAN OLAZABAL, ADOPTED CHARROS (SALAMANCA NATIVES)*

### 1 LA PLAZA MAYOR
By all means admire the plaza's 88 arches adorned with busts of the great and good, and the way the sun turns the plaza's local sandstone to gold. But the essence of Salamanca is to take up residence at one of the outdoor tables and watch all the life of Salamanca flow through the plaza.

### 2 THE CATHEDRALS & PLAZA ANAYA
Apart from the cathedrals' landmark architectural features, look for the astronaut mischievously carved into the Catedral Nueva's northern door during restorations, and the cracks and broken stained-glass windows from the 1755 earthquake. Right outside, students pass the afternoon – sometimes in song – in Plaza Anaya, one of Salamanca's most charming corners.

### 3 THE UNIVERSITY FACADE
The facade of Salamanca's prestigious university is a plateresque masterpiece. But the devil lies in the detail. Trying to find the famous frog of Salamanca is a local rite of passage: according to local legend, the student who fails to find it will fail in their studies. But its origins probably lie in lust – it's actually a symbol of female sexuality…

### 4 TAPAS ALONG CALLE VAN DYCK
Tapas is a Salamanca passion and Calle de Van Dyck, north of the old town, is the most emblematic tapas street, where it's all about Salamanca's famous pork products, especially *embutidos* (cured meats). Hop from bar to bar and try the *pincho moruno* (marinated kebab), *lomo* (cured pork sausage), *jamón* and *chanfaina* (a paella accompanied with various pork cuts).

### 5 STAYING OUT LATE
When the Plaza Mayor clock announces the onset of night, the party begins. A quarter of people in Salamanca are students, which means that the city never sleeps. The most famous drink is *el garrafón* (any alcohol of low quality), but be warned – the hangovers can last for days.

## ℹ️ Getting There & Away

### Bus

The bus station is a 10-minute walk, from Plaza Mayor. Buses include the following destinations: Madrid (regular/express €16/24, 2½ to three hours, hourly), Ávila (€8, 1½ hours, five daily), Segovia (€14, 2½ hours, four daily) and Valladolid (€10, 1½ hours, eight daily).

### Train

The train station is a 15-minute walk from Plaza Major. There are regular departures to Madrid's Chamartín station (€23, 2½ hours), Ávila (€12, 1¼ hour) and Valladolid (from €12, 1½ hours).

## ℹ️ Getting Around

Bus 4 runs past the bus station and around the old-city perimeter to Calle Gran Vía. From the train station, the best bet is bus 1, which heads into the centre along Calle de Azafranal.

## Segovia

POP 55,220 / ELEV 1002M

Unesco World Heritage–listed Segovia has always had a whiff of legend about it, not least in the myths that Segovia was founded by Hercules or by the son of Noah. It may also have something to do with the fact that nowhere else in Spain has such a stunning monument to Roman grandeur (the soaring aqueduct) survived in the heart of a vibrant modern city. Or maybe it's because art really has imitated life Segovia-style – Walt Disney is said to have modelled Sleeping Beauty's castle in California's Disneyland on Segovia's Alcázar. Whatever it is, the effect is stunning: a city of warm terracotta and sandstone hues set amid the rolling hills of Castilla and against the backdrop of the Sierra de Guadarrama.

## ◎ Sights

### Acueducto
Aqueduct

Segovia's most recognisable symbol is El Acueducto (Roman Aqueduct), an 894m-long engineering wonder that looks like an enormous comb plunged into Segovia. First raised here by the Romans in the 1st century AD, the aqueduct was built with not a drop of mortar to hold the more than 20,000 uneven granite blocks together. It's made up of 163 arches and, at its highest point in Plaza del Azoguejo, rises 28m high.

The aquaduct was originally part of a complex system of aqueducts and underground canals that brought water from the mountains more than 15km away. Its pristine condition is attributable to a major restoration project in the 1990s. For a different perspective, climb the stairs next to the aqueduct that begin behind the tourist office.

### Alcázar
Castle

(www.alcazardesegovia.com; Plaza de la Reina Victoria Eugenia; adult/concession/child under 6yr €5/3/free, tower €2, EU citizens 3rd Tue of month free; ⊙10am-7pm; ♿) Rapunzel towers, turrets topped with slate witches' hats and a *deep* moat at its base make the Alcázar a prototype fairy-tale castle, so much so that its design inspired Walt Disney's vision of Sleeping Beauty's castle. Fortified since Roman days, the site takes its name from the Arabic *al-qasr* (fortress). It was rebuilt in the 13th and 14th centuries, but the whole lot burned down in 1862. What you see today is an evocative, over-the-top reconstruction of the original.

---

## Best Views of Town

For *the* shot of Segovia to impress the folks back home, head out of town due north (towards Cuéllar) for around 2km. The view of the city unfolds in all its movie-style magic, with the aqueduct taking a star role – as well it should. Other fine views are to be had from the Convento de los Carmelitas Descalzos and from the car park next to the Alcázar.

# Detour:
# The Windmills of Don Quixote

Part of the charm of a visit to central Spain is the chance to track down the real life locations in which Miguel de Cervantes placed his picaresque hero, Don Quixote. These days it requires less puzzling over maps as, to celebrate the fourth centenary of this epic tale in 2007, the 250km route of Don Quixote was created with sign posts that direct you along paths, cattle ways and historic routes throughout the region.

Of all the places and sights you can ponder along the way the *molinos de vientos* (windmills) are the most obvious, for it was these 'monstrous giants' that so haunted El Quixote and with which he tried to battle. Although **Consuegra's** are the most attractive, those that are specifically mentioned in Cervantes novel are the windmills of **Campo de Criptana** and **Mota del Cuervo**. Other highlights on the trail include the castle of **Belmonte** and **El Toboso**, where the knight discovered the lovely Dulcinea.

---

Highlights include the **Sala de las Piñas**, with its ceiling of 392 pineapple-shaped 'stalactites', and the **Sala de Reyes**, featuring a three-dimensional frieze of 52 sculptures of kings who fought during the Reconquista. The views from the summit of the Torre de Juan II are truly exceptional.

### Iglesia de Vera Cruz                    Church
(Carretera de Zamarramala; admission €1.75; ⏱10.30am-1.30pm & 4-7pm Tue-Sun Dec-Oct) This 12-sided church is one of the best-preserved of its kind in Europe. Built in the early 13th century by the Knights Templar and based on Jerusalem's Church of the Holy Sepulchre, it once housed a piece of the *Vera Cruz* (True Cross), now in the nearby village church of Zamarramala (on view only at Easter).

### Catedral                    Cathedral
(Plaza Mayor; adult/concession €3/2, Sun morning free; ⏱9.30am-6.30pm) Started in 1525 on the site of a former chapel, Segovia's cathedral is a powerful expression of Gothic architecture that took almost 200 years to complete. The austere three-nave interior is anchored by an imposing choir stall and enlivened by 20-odd chapels, including the **Capilla del Cristo del Consuelo**, which houses a magnificent

Romanesque doorway, and the **Capilla de la Piedad**, containing an important altarpiece by Juan de Juni.

## 🛏 Sleeping

### Hospedería La Gran
### Casa Mudéjar          Historic Hotel €€
(☎921 46 62 50; www.lacasamudejar.com; Calle de Isabel la Católica 8; r €80; ❇@🛜) Spread over two buildings, this place has been magnificently renovated, blending genuine, 15th-century Mudéjar carved wooden ceilings in some rooms with modern amenities. In the newer wing, the rooms on the top floors have fine mountain views out over the roof-tops of Segovia's old Jewish quarter. Adding to the appeal, there's a small spa and the **restaurant** comes highly recommended.

### Hotel Infanta Isabel          Hotel €€
(☎921 46 13 00; www.hotelinfantaisabel.com; Plaza Mayor 12; r €55-95; P❇🛜) The colon-naded building fits well with the hotel's interior of period furnishings in most of the spacious rooms. The style may be classic in orientation, but there's a lovely sense of light and space here and the bathrooms are being gradually updated. Some rooms overlook Plaza Mayor.

# If You Like...
## Castles

While Segovia's Disneyesque Alcázar may get all the attention, lonely hilltop castles are something of a regional specialty. Our favourites include the following:

### 1 CASTILLO DE PEDRAZA
(Pedraza de la Sierra; admission €5; ⏰11am-2pm & 5-8pm Wed-Sun) At the far end of town stands the lonely Castillo de Pedraza, unusual for its intact outer wall.

### 2 COCA CASTLE
(www.castillodecoca.com; Coca; guided tours €2.70; ⏰tours 10.30am-1pm & 4.30-6pm Mon-Fri, 11am-1pm & 4-7pm Sat & Sun) A typically dusty, inward-looking Castilian village, 50km northwest of Segovia, Coca is presided over by a stunning all-brick castle, a virtuoso piece of Gothic-Mudéjar architecture.

### 3 CASTILLO TEMPLARIO
(Ponferrada; adult/concession €4/2, Wed free; ⏰10am-2pm & 4.30-8.30pm Tue-Sun) Built by the Knights Templar in the 13th century, the walls of the fortress-monastery Castillo Templario rise high over Río Sil, and the square, crenulated towers ooze romance and history. The castle has a lonely and impregnable air, and is a striking landmark in Ponferrada's otherwise bleak urban landscape. Houses the Templars' Library with some 1,400 books.

### 4 CASTILLO DE PEÑAFIEL
(Peñafiel; castle €3, incl museum €7, audioguides €2; ⏰11am-2.30pm & 4.30-8.30pm Tue-Sun) Dramatically watching over Peñafiel, this castle houses the state-of-the-art **Museo Provincial del Vino**. Telling a comprehensive story of the region's wines, this wonderful museum is informative and entertaining with interactive displays, dioramas, backlit panels and computer terminals. The pleasures of the end product are not neglected: wine tasting costs €7 if you do it solo, €10 with an expert to explain it all. The castle itself is one of the longest and narrowest in Spain, and also worth exploring.

## Eating

**La Almuzara**    Italian, Vegetarian €
(Calle Marqués del Arco 3; mains €7.50-10; ⏰noon-4pm & 8pm-midnight Wed-Sun, 8pm-midnight Tue; ☀️👶) If you're a vegetarian, you don't need to feel like an outcast in this resolutely carnivorous city. La Almuzara offers a dedicated vegetarian menu, as well as pizzas, pastas and close to 18 innovative salads. They are not too pious to scrimp on desserts either with some decadent daily-changing choices. The ambience is warm and artsy.

**Restaurante El Fogón Sefardí**    Jewish €€
(📞921 46 62 50; www.lacasamudejar.com; Calle de Isabel la Católica 8; mains €20-25, tapas from €2.50; ⏰1.30-4.30pm & 5.30-11.30pm) Located within the Hospedería La Gran Casa Mudéjar, this is one of the most original places in town. Sephardic and Jewish cuisine is served either on the intimate patio or in the splendid dining hall with original, 15th-century Mudéjar flourishes. The theme in the bar is equally diverse. Stop here for a taste of the award-winning tapas. Reservations recommended.

**Casa Duque**    Grill €€
(📞921 46 24 87; www.restauranteduque.es; Calle de Cervantes 12; mains €9-20; ⏰12.30-4.30pm & 8.30-11.30pm) Cochinillo asado (roast suckling pig) has been served at this atmospheric mesón (tavern) since the 1890s. For the uninitiated, try the menú segoviano (€32), which includes cochinillo, or the menú gastronómico (€39). Downstairs is the informal cueva (cave), where you can get tapas and full-bodied cazuelas (stews). Reservations recommended.

## Information

Centro de Recepción de Visitantes (tourist office; 📞921 46 67 20; www.turismodesegovia.com; Plaza del Azoguejo 1; ⏰10am-7pm Sun-Fri, 10am-8pm Sat) Segovia's main tourist office runs two-hour guided tours, departing daily at

Coca Castle

KEN WELSH/GETTY IMAGES ©

11.15am for a minimum of four people (€14 per person). Reserve ahead.

**Regional tourist office** (www.segoviaturismo. es; Plaza Mayor 10; ⊙9am-8pm Sun-Thu, 9am-9pm Fri & Sat)

## ℹ Getting There & Away

### Bus

The bus station is just off Paseo de Ezequiel González. Buses run half-hourly to Segovia from Madrid's Paseo de la Florida bus stop (€8, 1½ hours). Buses also depart to Ávila (€6, one hour, eight daily) and Salamanca (€14, 2½ hours, four daily), among other destinations.

### Car & Motorcycle

Of the two main roads down to the AP6, which links Madrid and Galicia, the N603 is the prettier.

The nearest underground car park to the historic centre is in Plaza de la Artillería near the aqueduct.

### Train

There are a couple of options by train: just two normal trains run daily from Madrid to Segovia (€8, two hours), leaving you at the main train station 2.5km from the aqueduct. The faster option is the high-speed Avant (€13, 28 minutes), which deposits you at the newer Segovia-Guiomar station, 5km from the aqueduct.

## ℹ Getting Around

Bus 9 does a circuit through the historic centre, bus 8 goes to Segovia train station and bus 11 goes to Segovia-Guiomar station. All services cost €1.10 and leave from just outside the aqueduct.

# Seville & Andalucía's Hill Towns

**A parched region fertile with culture, a conquered land that went on to conquer, a fiercely traditional place that has accepted rapid modernisation: western Andalucía has multiple faces.** Here, in the cradle of quintessential Spain, the questions are often as intriguing as the answers. Who first concocted flamenco? How did tapas become a national obsession? Could Cádiz be Europe's oldest settlement? Are those really Christopher Columbus' bones inside Seville cathedral? And, where on earth did the audacious builders of Córdoba's Mezquita get their divine inspiration from? Putting together the missing pieces of the puzzle is what makes travel in the region the glorious adventure that it is.

Seville is western Andaucia's Holy Grail, Córdoba is its former Roman and Moorish capital, while the White Towns will lure you into quieter rural areas and perhaps inspire you to visit the region's only national park amid the bird-rich wetlands of Doñana.

Flamenco performance, Tablao El Arenal (p253)
YADID LEVY/LONELY PLANET ©

Puerta del Perdón, Catedral (p245)

# Seville & Andalucía's Hill Towns

PORTUGAL

Peñarroya-Pueblonuevo

Río Guadiato

CÓRDOBA

Aracena

Cazalla de la Sierra

Constantina

Parque Natural Sierra de Hornachuelos

**1**

Parque Natural Sierra de Aracena y Picos de Aroche

**Córdoba**

Nerva

HUELVA

Río Odiel

Río Tinto

SEVILLA

Río Huéznar

Lora del Río

Palma del Río

Pradollano

Valverde del Camino

Carmona

Río Corbones

ANDALUCÍA

Écija

Aguilar de la Frontera

Bollullos Par del Condado

**2 3**

**Seville**

Alcalá de Guadaira

Puente Genil

Ayamonte

**Huelva**

Lepe

Moguer

Almonte

Río Guadalquivir

Dos Hermanas

Río Guadaira

Marchena

Osuna

Isla Cristina

Punta Umbría

El Arahal

Parque Nacional de Doñana

Los Palacios y Villafranca

Utrera

Morón de la Frontera

Embalse del Conde del Guadalhorce

Lucio de los Ansares

Lebrija

Villamartín

Olvera

Lucio del Membrillo

Sanlúcar de Barrameda

Chipiona

El Puerto de Santa María

Rota

**Arcos de la Frontera**

Embalse de Bornos

Parque Natural Sierra de Grazalema

**MÁLAGA**

Álora

Ronda

Cártama

**5**

Puerto Real

**Cádiz**

Jerez de la Frontera

Ubrique

Parque Natural Sierra de las Nieves

Coín

San Fernando

Medina Sidonia

**CÁDIZ**

Río Guadiaro

San Pedro de Alcántara

Mijas

Marbella

Bahía de Cádiz

**4**

Embalse de Barbate

Vejer de la Frontera

Parque Natural Los Alcornocales

Río Genal

Estepona

ATLANTIC OCEAN

Barbate

La Línea de la Concepción

Costa del Sol

Algeciras

**Gibraltar**

Tarifa

Strait of Gibraltar

Mediterranean Sea

Tangier

MOROCCO

**1** Córdoba's Mezquita

**2** Flamenco

**3** Seville Cathedral

**4** Cádiz

**5** White Towns

N

0 — 50 km
0 — 25 miles

# Seville & Andalucía's Hill Towns' Highlights

## Córdoba's Mezquita

Córdoba's great Mezquita (p258) is a one-off. Using ancient Roman columns and an old Visigothic floor plan, its ambitious Moorish builders fashioned one of the world's largest mosques which, since the 1236 Reconquest, has served as a Christian church. Filled with arches, columns, crosses, choirs, calligraphy and unusual beauty, it pays glorious homage to just about every architectural style since the birth of Christ.

## Flamenco

The intensity and spontaneity of flamenco (p25) has never translated well onto CDs or studio recordings. Instead, to ignite the goose-bumps and inspire the powerful emotional spirit known to aficionados as '*duende*', you have to be there at a performance, stamping your feet and passionately yelling '*óle*'. The best place to see flamenco is in its historical heartland in and around the cities of Seville, Cádiz and Jerez de la Frontera.

## Seville Cathedral

**3**

The 13th-century builders of Seville's cathedral (p245) wanted to construct a church so big that future generations would think they were mad. They gloriously succeeded. Only a bunch of loco architectural geniuses could have built a Gothic masterpiece this humongous. Throw in Columbus' tomb, golden-age art, a part-Moorish belltower and Spain's most ostentatious altarpiece, and you've done half a day's sightseeing before you've even left the building. Giralda

## Cádiz

**4**

In a settlement over 3000 years old, it isn't always easy to nail down the underlying allure. Welcome to Cádiz (p273), a city of heady atmosphere and foggy legends that is generally considered to be the oldest continuously inhabited settlement in Europe. Equally legendary are the *gaditanos*, an upfront and gregarious populace whose Carnaval is an exercise in ironic humour and whose upbeat flamenco songs will bring warmth to your heart.

## White Towns

**5**

Andalucía's *Ruta de Pueblos Blancos* links 20 quintessential *pueblos blancos* (white towns; p265) splayed across a rugged stretch of land between Arcos de la Frontera and Ronda. Yet, these aren't the only bleached white citadels to punctuate this hilly and historic landscape. Andalucía contains scores more White Towns, all similar in their outward appearance, but each, on closer inspection, hiding distinctly different cultures and personalities. Vejer de la Frontera (p265)

# Seville & Andulucía's Hill Towns' Best…

## Tapas Bars

○ **La Brunilda, Seville** Creative *nuevo* tapas dispatched from one of the best tapas bars in Seville. (p252)

○ **Los Coloniales, Seville** Quality tapas line up like catwalk models. (p251)

○ **El Aljibe, Cádiz** The super-cool tapas here are almost enough reason alone to visit Cádiz. (p276)

○ **Taberna San Miguel El Pisto, Córdoba** Brimming with local character and delicious tapas. (p263)

## Rural Bliss

○ **Grazalema** Few *pueblos blancos* (white towns) are as generically perfect as this one. (p266)

○ **Zahara de la Sierra** Set around a vertiginous crag and humming with Moorish mystery. (p265)

○ **El Rocío** Overlooking misty marshes and dominated by a shimmering white church. (p269)

○ **Parque Nacional Doñana** Vitally important wetlands and delicate ecosystems. (p269)

## Journeys Back in Time

○ **Itálica** A 2nd-century Roman town with a massive amphitheatre. (p253)

○ **Medina Azahara** The ghosts of Moorish Al-Andalus live on in this abandoned city. (p262)

○ **Cádiz** The oldest settlement in Europe that became an Identikit for Spanish colonial architectue. (p273)

○ **Córdoba** The perfect melding of Islamic and Christian houses of worship. (p255)

## Party Time

○ **Feria de Abril (April)**
Andalucía's biggest feria is a joyful celebration of the arrival of spring. (p43)

○ **Semana Santa (Easter)**
Large, life-size religious sculptures are paraded through Seville. (p240)

○ **Bienal de Flamenco (September)** Spain's biggest flamenco festival, held in Seville every second year. (p44)

○ **Romeria del Rocio (Pentecost)** Thousands of pilgrims pay their respects to the Virgin. (p43)

### ADVANCE PLANNING

○ **Three months before**
Book your hotel for Seville's Feria de Abril or Carnaval in Cádiz.

○ **Two weeks before**
Reserve your high-speed AVE ticket (www.renfe.es) from Madrid to Seville.

### RESOURCES

○ **Andalucía Te Quiere** (www.andalucia.org) Terrific tourist-office site for the entire region.

○ **Andalucia.com** (www.andalucia.com) Excellent privately run site on Andalucía.

○ **La Guía de Flamenco** (www.guiadeflamenco.com) The best source of upcoming flamenco concerts.

○ **Flamenco Tickets** (www.flamencotickets.com) Secure online site for pre-buying flamenco tickets.

### GETTING AROUND

○ **Air** International airports with intra-Spain connections in Seville. Seasonal connections to Jerez de la Frontera.

○ **Train** Renfe has good connections between Seville, Córdoba, Cádiz and Jerez de la Frontera.

○ **Bus** Alsa buses link the main cities, Damas buses serve Huelva province, Comes and Amarillos tackle the smaller White Towns of Cádiz and Málaga provinces.

○ **Car** Excellent network of roads. Avoid driving in central Seville.

### BE FOREWARNED

○ **Winter closures**
January and February are the cheapest months for accommodation, but many hotels and restaurants temporarily close.

○ **Spring bookings** With so many spring festivals, Andalucía gets incredibly busy from late March to early June. Book ahead.

○ **Late hours** Andalucía eats and goes out late (dinner is rarely before 9pm). Adjust your habits so you don't miss out on the fun.

○ **Pickpockets** Beware of pickpockets in Seville, particularly around the Cathedral and the Plaza de España.

**Left:** Semana Santa procession, Seville (p240);
**Above:** Medina Azahara (p262)
(LEFT) KEN GILLHAM/GETTY IMAGES ©;
(ABOVE) RAMON RUTI/GETTY IMAGES ©

**237**

# Seville & Andalucía's Hill Towns Itineraries

*Western Andalucía is classic Spain. This vast region could fill many weeks of travel but it's still possible to get bewitched by it in a short time.*

**3 DAYS**

### CÁDIZ TO RONDA
## THE WHITE TOWNS

Atlantic waves crash against sea walls and narrow streets echo to the sound of cawing gulls and frying fish. Ah, the romance of **❶ Cádiz**, where this tour begins. Stroll the Malecón (sea wall), lap up the huge beach and enjoy some gritty flamenco. Looming moodily atop a rocky hill an hour southeast of Cádiz is **❷ Vejer de la Frontera**. With a cool labyrinth of twisting streets heavy in the scent of the exotic and some fabulous nearby beaches, Vejer might well end up being your favourite White Town. Squiggle your way northeast along country roads into increasingly wild terrain until you hit gorgeous **❸ Grazalema**; a village of spotless whitewash houses topped in a wig of redtiled roofs and surrounded by the pillar-like rocks of the Sierra de Grazalema. A short but breathtaking drive away is miniscule **❹ Zahara de la Sierra** which positively hums in Moorish mystery and contains all the elements of a classic White Town. From here it's a stunning drive to **❺ Ronda**, the largest and liveliest of the White Towns and a place famous for its gorge-spanning bridge.

**Top Left:** Zahara de la Sierra (p265); **Top Right:** Feria del Caballo, Jerez (p43)
(TOP LEFT) DESEO/GETTY IMAGES ©; (TOP RIGHT) JON ARNOLD IMAGES/GETTY IMAGES ©

**5**
DAYS

**SEVILLE TO CÓRDOBA**

# FLAMENCO & SHERRY

Flamenco was born in western Andalucía, and it's in the intimate tiled courtyards of
❶**Seville**, the genre's reputed birthplace, where you can still hear flamenco in its purest
form. With hundreds of tapas bars and monuments to visit, Seville deserves at least two
days. An hour south of Seville by regular train, or just off the AP4, ❷**Jerez de la Frontera**
shares many of the same passions – it's a hotbed of authentic flamenco (ask at the Centro
Andaluz de Flamenco for the latest performances), fantastic places to eat, and is famous
for its Andalucian horses. Jerez also has world-renowned sherry bodegas, most of which
run tours. A short distance away, the burning White Town of ❸**Arcos de la Frontera** is one
of the signature images of sultry southern Spain and is the *pueblo blanco* par excellence. If
time allows, drive through pretty hills and golden fields of crops northeast to ❹**Córdoba**.
This isn't a city renowned for its flamenco scene (though there is still some action) but it
excels at art of another kind: flower sprinkled, whitewash patios and a melding of Islamic
and Christian architectural styles.

# r Seville & ía's Hill Towns

## At a Glance

- **Seville** (p240) The definition of Andalucía.
- **Córdoba** (p255) The past glories of Roman and Moorish Spain's former capital.
- **White Towns** (p264) Green hills, long views and searing whitewashed villages.
- **Jerez de la Frontera** (p269) Sherry, flamenco and horse culture.
- **Cádiz** (p273) Spain's ancient coastal city with its beaches and fortifications.

Flamenco dancer
ANDREA PISTOLESI/GETTY IMAGES ©

## SEVILLE & AROUND

POP 703,000

Some cities have looks. Others have personality. The *sevillanos* – lucky devils – get both, courtesy of their flamboyant, charismatic, ever-evolving Andalucian metropolis founded, according to mythology, 3000-years ago by the Greek God Hercules. Doused in never-ending sunlight, Seville's beauty is relatively easy to uncover: watch pretty girls in polka-dot dresses ride in carriages to the Feria de Abril. Its soul is a darker and more complex force. Flamenco was partially born here in the dusty taverns of Triana, and greedy conquistadors once roamed the sinuous streets of El Arenal counting their colonial gold. Tugged by the pull of both forces, it is Seville's capriciousness that leaves the heaviest impression. Come here in April and watch as haunting **Semana Santa** (www.semana-santa.org) metamorphoses into the cacophony of spring fair and you'll wonder whether Bizet's Carmen wasn't more real than imagined.

### Sights

#### BARRIO DE SANTA CRUZ

Seville's medieval *judería* (Jewish quarter), east of the cathedral and Alcázar, is today a tangle of atmospheric, winding streets and lovely plant-decked plazas perfumed with orange blossom.

**Hospital de los Venerables Sacerdotes** Gallery
(☎954 56 26 96; www.focus.abengoa.es; Plaza de los Venerables 8; adult/child €5.50/2.75, Sun afternoon free; ⏲10am-2pm & 4-8pm) Once a residence for aged priests, this 17th-century baroque mansion guards what is perhaps

Seville's most typical *sevillano* patio – it's intimate, plant embellished and spirit-reviving. The building's other highlights are its 17th-century church, with rich religious murals, and the celebrated painting *Santa Rufina* by Diego Velázquez, which was procured for a hefty €12.5 million by the on-site Centro Velázquez foundation in 2007. Other roving art exhibitions provide an excellent support act.

### Centro de Interpretación Judería de Sevilla Museum
(☎954 04 70 89; www.juderiadesevilla.es; Calle Ximenez de Enciso; admission €6.50; ☉10.30am-3.30pm, 5-8pm Mon-Sat, 10.30am-6.30pm Sun) A reinterpretation of Seville's weighty Jewish history has been long overdue and what better place to start than in the city's former Jewish quarter. This new museum is encased in an old Sephardic Jewish house in the higgledy-piggledy Santa Cruz quarter, the onetime Jewish neighbourhood that never recovered from a brutal pogrom and massacre carried out in 1391. The events of the pogrom and other historical happenings are catalogued inside along with a few surviving mementos including documents, costumes and books. It's small but poignant.

## EL CENTRO

### Museo del Baile Flamenco Museum
(www.museoflamenco.com; Calle Manuel Rojas Marcos 3; adult/seniors & students €10/8; ☉10am-7pm) The brainchild of *sevillana* flamenco dancer Cristina Hoyos, this museum spread over three floors of an 18th-century palace makes a noble effort to showcase the mysterious art, although at €10 a pop it is more than a little overpriced. Exhibits include sketches, paintings, photos of erstwhile (and contemporary) flamenco greats, plus a collection of dresses and shawls.

### Casa de Pilatos Palace, Museum
(☎954 22 52 98; www.fundacionmedinaceli. org; Plaza de Pilatos; admission ground fl only €5, whole house €8; ☉9am-7pm Apr-Oct, to 6pm Nov-Mar) The haunting Casa de Pilatos, which is still occupied by the ducal Medinaceli family, is one of the city's most glorious mansions. It's a mixture of Mudéjar, Gothic and Renaissance styles, with some beautiful tilework and *artesonado* (ceiling of interlaced beams with decorative insertions). The overall effect is like a poor-man's Alcázar.

The staircase to the upper floor has the most magnificent tiles in the building, and a great golden *artesonado* dome

# Metropol Parasol

Some call him the Ferran Adriá of modern architecture, and it's true, German architect Jurgen Mayer H possesses a strange kind of artistic genius. Who else would have dreamt of constructing a 'flying waffle' in the middle of one of Seville's most traditional shopping squares? Smarting with the audacity of a modern-day Eiffel Tower, the opinion-dividing **Metropol Parasol** (www.metropolsevilla.com; Plaza de la Encarnación) which opened in March 2011 in the Plaza de la Encarnación claims to be the largest wooden building in the world. Its undulating honeycombed roof is held up by five giant mushroomlike pillars earning it the local nickname *Las Setas de la Encarnación*. Six years in the making, the construction covers a former dead zone in Seville's central district once filled with an ugly car park. Roman ruins discovered during the building's conception have been cleverly incorporated into the foundations in the **Museo Antiquarium** (Plaza de la Encarnación; admission €2; ☉10am-8pm Tue-Sat, 10am-2pm Sun), while upstairs on level two you can pay €1.35 to stroll along a surreal panoramic walkway with killer city views.

Seville

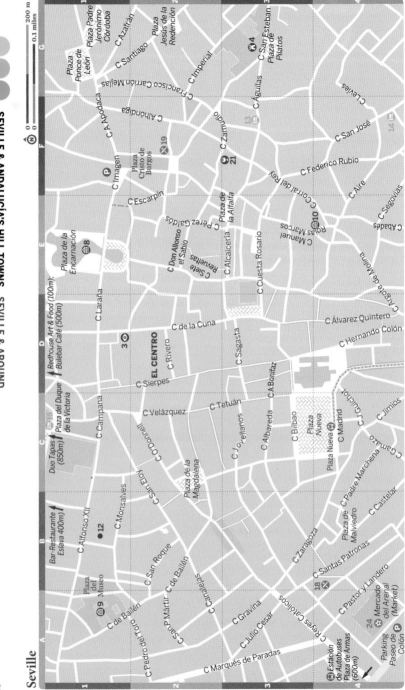

200 m
0.1 miles

**G**
Plaza Padre Jerónimo Córdoba
Plaza Ponce de León
C Azafrán
C Santiago
Plaza Jesús de la Redención
C Imperial
C San Esteban
Plaza de Pilatos
K4
C Águilas
C Levíes

**F**
C A Apodaca
C Alhóndiga
C Francisco Carrión Mejías
Plaza Cristo de Burgos
C Imagen
X19
C Zamudio
C San José
21
C Federal Rubio
C Corral del Rey
C Aire
C Escarpín
Plaza de la Alfalfa
C Pérez Galdós
C Manuel Rojas Marcos
10
C Segovías
C Abades

**E**
Plaza de la Encarnación
8
C Laraña
C Don Alonso el Sabio
C Siete Revueltas
C Alcaicería
C Cuesta Rosario
Redhouse Art & Food (100m);
Bulebar Café (500m)
C Álvarez Quintero
Cargwe de Molina

**D**
C de la Cuna
C Rivero
C Sagasta
C Hernando Colón
EL CENTRO
3
C Sierpes
C Velázquez
C Tetuán
C A Bonfaz

**C**
Duo Tapas (850m)
Plaza del Duque de la Victoria
15
C Campana
C O'Donnell
C Jovellanos
C Albareda
C Bilbao
Plaza Nueva
C Madrid
C Julio César
C J G
C Jimios
C Gamazo
Plaza Nueva

**B**
Bar-Restaurante Eslava (400m)
C Alfonso XII
12
C Monsalves
C San Eloy
Plaza de la Magdalena
C Zaragoza
C Santas Patronas
Plaza de Padre Marchena
C Castelar
18
X

**A**
Plaza del Museo
9
C de Bailén
C Pedro del Toro
San P Martír
C de Bailén
C Canalejas
C Gravina
C Julio César
C Reyes Católicos
C Pastor y Landero
Mercado del Arenal (Market)
24
Estación de Autobuses Plaza de Armas (600m)
Parking Paseo de Colón
C Marqués de Paradas

1
2
3
4

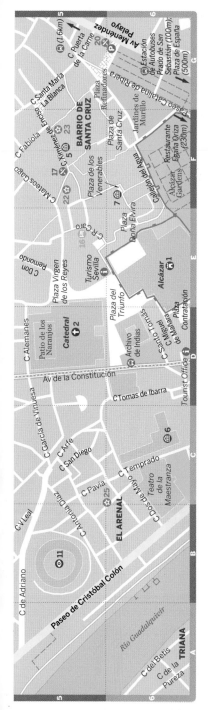

above. Visits to the upper floor, still partly inhabited by the Medinacelis, are guided. Of interest are the several centuries' worth of Medinaceli portraits and a small Goya bullfighting painting.

## EL ARENAL

**Hospital de la Caridad**    Gallery
(Calle Temprado 3; admission €5; ⊙9.30am-1pm & 3.30-7pm Mon-Sat, 9am-12.30pm Sun) A block east of the river is this art gallery that was once a hospice for the elderly, which was founded by Miguel de Mañara, who according to legend was a notorious libertine who changed his ways after seeing a vision of his own funeral procession.

# Don't Miss
# Catedral & Giralda

Seville's immense cathedral, officially the biggest in the world by volume, is awe-inspiring in its scale and sheer majesty. It stands on the site of a great 12th-century Almohad mosque, with the mosque's minaret (the Giralda) still towering beside it. Architecturally, it's an Identikit of High Gothic style and is stuffed with some classic Golden Age art.

www.catedraldesevilla.es

adult/child €8/free

🕑 11am-3.30pm Mon, 11am-5pm Tue-Sat, 2.30-6pm Sun Sep-Jun, 9.30am-2.30pm Mon, 9.30am-4pm Tue-Sat, 2.30-6pm Sun Jul & Aug

## Tomb of Columbus

Inside the **Puerta de los Príncipes** (Door of the Princes) stands the monumental tomb of Christopher Columbus (Cristóbal Colón in Spanish) – the subject of a continuous riddle – containing what were long believed to be the great explorer's bones, brought here from Cuba in 1898.

## Capilla Mayor & Other Chapels

East of the choir is the **Capilla Mayor** (Main Chapel). Its Gothic retable is the jewel of the cathedral and reckoned to be the biggest altarpiece in the world. Begun by Flemish sculptor Pieter Dancart in 1482 and finished by others in 1564, this sea of gilt and polychromed wood holds over 1000 carved biblical figures. The chapels along the southern and northern sides of the cathedral hold riches of sculpture and painting. Near the western end of the northern side is the **Capilla de San Antonio**, housing Murillo's 1666 canvas depicting the vision of St Anthony of Padua; thieves cut out the kneeling saint in 1874 but he was later found in New York and put back.

## Sacrista Mayor

This large room with a finely carved stone dome was created between 1528 and 1547: the arch over its portal has carvings of 16th-century foods. Pedro de Campaña's 1547 *Descendimiento* (Descent from the Cross), above the central altar at the southern end, and Francisco de Zurbarán's *Santa Teresa*, to its right, are two of the cathedral's most precious paintings.

## Giralda

In the northeastern corner of the cathedral you'll find the passage for the climb up to the belfry of the **Giralda**. The decorative brick tower which stands 104m tall was the minaret of the mosque, constructed between 1184 and 1198 at the height of Almohad power. At the very top is El Giraldillo, a 16th-century bronze weathervane representing 'faith' that has become a symbol of Seville.

---

# Catedral & Giralda

RECOMMENDATIONS FROM DARIO GUALTIERI, FOUNDER OF PANCHO TOURS (P249)

**1 TOMB OF COLUMBUS**
Columbus' coffin is held aloft by four figures representing the kingdoms of Aragon, Navarra, León and Castile. At the front, the figures of Castilla and León have their heads held high, while, behind, those of Aragon and Navarra are looking at the floor. Some claim this is because León and Castilla gained far more than Aragon and Navarra from the riches of Latin America first unearthed by Columbus' voyages.

**2 GIRALDA BELLS**
As well as admiring the view at the top of the Giralda, take time to study the tower's enormous bells. They occupy the space where, in pre-Christian times, the muezzins used to tie up their horses while they called the faithful to prayer.

**3 CATHEDRAL ART**
The paintings in the Sala del Pabellón near the cathedral entrance contain some interesting contradictions. Look for the canvas of King Fernando III of Castilla by Murillo that depicts the monarch as San Fernando (he was canonized by Pope Clement X in 1671, 419 years after his death). The saint, dressed in his crown and royal robes, is seen holding a less saintly sword!

**4 PUERTA DEL PERDÓN**
This Moorish gateway – a surviving part of the former mosque that once stood here – has been embellished with Christian imagery. A shield depicting Jesus' 'Cleansing of the Temple' by Miguel Perrin is emblazoned over the horseshoe arch. It's an ironic juxtaposition.

**5 PATIO DE NARANJOS**
The orange tree patio is a legacy of the former mosque where Muslims used to perform their ritual washing before prayer. You can imagine the mountains of shoes that once piled up in the courtyard in the days of the Moorish Caliphate.

# ...dral

'We're going to construct a church so large future generations will think we were mad,' declared the inspired architects of Seville in 1402 at the beginning of one of the most grandiose building projects in medieval history. Just over a century later their madness was triumphantly confirmed.

## WHAT TO LOOK FOR

To avoid getting lost, orient yourself by the main highlights. Directly inside the southern (main) entrance is the grand **tomb of Columbus** ❶. Turn right here and head into the southeastern corner to uncover some major art treasures: a Goya in the Sacristía de los Cálices, a Zurbarán in the **Sacristía Mayor** ❷, and Murillo's shining Immaculada in the Sala Capitular. Skirt the cathedral's eastern wall taking a look inside the **Capilla Real** ❸ with its important royal tombs. By now it's impossible to avoid the lure of **Capilla Mayor** ❹ with its fantastical altarpiece. Hidden over in the northwest corner is the **Capilla de San Antonio** ❺ with a legendary Murillo. That huge doorway almost in front of you is the rarely opened **Puerta de la Asunción** ❻. Make for the **Giralda** ❼ next, stealing admiring looks at the high, vaulted ceiling on the way. After looking down on the cathedral's immense footprint, descend and depart via the **Patio de los Naranjos** ❽.

### TOP TIPS

» **Pace yourself** Don't visit the Alcazar and Cathedral on the same day. There is far too much to take in.

» **Viewpoints** Take time to admire the cathedral from the outside. It's particularly stunning at night from the Plaza Virgen de los Reyes, and from across the river in Triana.

FELIPE RODRIGUEZ/FERNANDEZ/GETTY IMAGES ©

**Capilla Mayor**
Behold! The cathedral's main focal point contains its greatest treasure, a magnificent gold-plated altarpiece depicting various scenes in the life of Christ. It constitutes the life's work of one man, Flemish artist Pieter Dancart.

**Patio de los Naranjos**
Inhale the perfume of 60 Sevillan orange trees in a cool patio bordered by fortress-like walls – a surviving remnant of the original 12th-century mosque. Exit is gained via the horseshoe-shaped Puerta del Perdón.

**Puerta del Perdón**

**Iglesia del Sagrario**

**Puerta del Bautismo**

**Puerta de la Asunción**
Located on the western side of the cathedral and also known as the Puerta Mayor, these huge, rarely opened doors are pushed back during Semana Santa to allow solemn processions of Catholic *hermanadades* (brotherhoods) to pass through.

DMITRY SHAKIN/GETTY IMAGES ©

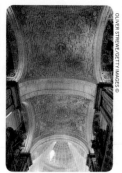

**El Giraldillo**

**Capilla Real**
Keep a respectful silence in this atmospheric chapel dedicated to the Virgen de los Reyes. In a silver urn lie the hallowed remains of the city's Christian conqueror Ferdinand III and his son, Alfonso the Wise.

**Giralda**
Ascend, not by stairs, but by a long continuous ramp, to the top of this 11th-century minaret topped by a Gothic-baroque belfry. Standing 104m tall it has long been the defining symbol of Seville.

⑦

**Sacristía Mayor**
Art lovers will love this large domed room containing some of the city's greatest paintings, including Zurbarán's *Santa Teresa* and Pedro de Campaña's *Descendimiento*. It also guards the city key captured in 1248.

③

④

②

①

**Main Entrance**

**Capilla de San Antonio**
One of 80 interior chapels, you'll need to hunt down this little gem notable for housing Murillo's 1666 painting, *The Vision of St Anthony*. The work was pillaged by thieves in 1874 but later restored.

**Tomb of Columbus**
Buried in Valladolid in 1506, the remains of Christopher Columbus were moved four times before they arrived in Seville in 1898 encased in an elaborately carved catafalque. Or were they? A longstanding debate rages about whether these are actually Columbus' remains or if, in a postdeath mix-up, he still resides in the Dominican Republic.

MARK DAFFEY/GETTY IMAGES ©
OLIVER STREWE/GETTY IMAGES ©
OLIVER STREWE/ GETTY IMAGES ©

VISIONS OF OUR LAND/GETTY IMAGES ©

## ⭐ Don't Miss
## Alcázar

If heaven really *does* exist, then let's hope it looks a little bit like the inside of Seville's Alcázar. Built primarily in the 1300s during the so-called 'dark ages' in Europe, the architecture is anything but dark. Indeed, compared with our modern-day shopping malls and throw-away apartment blocks, it could be argued that the Alcázar marked one of history's architectural high points. Unesco agreed, making it a World Heritage Site in 1987.

From the ticket office inside the **Puerta del León** (Lion Gate) you'll emerge into the **Patio del León** (Lion Patio), which was the garrison yard of the original Al-Muwarak palace. Just off here is the **Sala de la Justicia** (Hall of Justice), with beautiful Mudéjar plasterwork and an *artesonado* (ceiling of interlaced beams with decorative insertions).

Posterity owes Pedro I a big thank you for creating the **Palacio de Don Pedro** (also called the Palacio Mudéjar), the single most stunning architectural feature in Seville.

At the heart of the palace is the wonderful **Patio de las Doncellas** (Patio of the Maidens), surrounded by beautiful arches, plasterwork and tiling. The sunken garden in the centre was uncovered by archaeologists in 2004 from beneath a 16th-century marble covering.

The **Cámara Regia** (King's Quarters), on the northern side of the patio, has stunningly beautiful ceilings and wonderful plaster- and tilework. Its rear room was probably the monarch's summer bedroom.

From here you can move west into the little **Patio de las Muñecas** (Patio of the Dolls), the heart of the palace's private quarters, featuring delicate Granada-style decoration. Indeed, plasterwork was actually brought here from the Alhambra in the 19th century when the mezzanine and top gallery were added for Queen Isabel II.

### NEED TO KNOW

www.alcazarsevilla.org; adult/child €9.50/free; ⊗9.30am-7pm Apr-Sep, to 5pm Oct-Mar

In the 1670s Mañara commissioned a series of works on the theme of death and redemption from Seville's three finest artists of the day – Bartolomé Esteban Murillo, Juan de Valdés Leal and Pedro Roldán – for the church here. The result is a marvellous example of *sevillano* art of El Siglo de Oro (the Golden Age).

### Plaza de Toros de la Real Maestranza    Bullring, Museum
( 954 22 45 77; www.realmaestranza.com; Paseo de Cristóbal Colón 12; tours adult/child €7/3;  half-hourly 9.30am-8pm, 9.30am-3pm bullfight days) In the world of bullfighting Seville's bullring is the Old Trafford and Camp Nou. In other words, if you're selected to fight here then you've made it. In addition to being regarded as a building of almost religious significance to fans, it's also the oldest ring in Spain (building began in 1758) and it was here, along with the bullring in Ronda, that bullfighting on foot began in the 18th century. Interesting guided visits, in English and Spanish, take you into the ring and its museum.

### Museo de Bellas Artes    Gallery
(Fine Arts Museum; Plaza del Museo 9; admission €1.50, EU citizens free;  10am-8.30pm Tue-Sat, 10am-5pm Sun) Housed in the beautiful former Convento de la Merced, Seville's Museo de Bellas Artes does full justice to Seville's leading role in Spain's 17th-century artistic Siglo de Oro. Much of the work here is of the dark, brooding religious type.

## SOUTH OF THE CENTRE

### Parque de María Luisa & Plaza de España    Park
( 8am-10pm) A large area south of the former tobacco factory was transformed for Seville's 1929 international fair, the Exposición Iberoamericana, when architects adorned it with fantastical buildings, many of them harking back to Seville's past glory or imitating the native styles of Spain's former colonies. In its midst you'll find the large Parque de María Luisa, a living expression of Seville's Moorish and Christian past.

Plaza de España, one of the city's favourite relaxation spots, faces the park across Avenida de Isabel la Católica. Around it is the most grandiose of the 1929 buildings, a semicircular brick-and-tile confection featuring Seville tilework at its gaudiest.

On Plaza de América, at the southern end of the park, is Seville's **Museo Arqueológico** (admission €1.50, EU citizens free;  10am-8.30pm Tue-Sat, 10am-5pm Sun), with plenty to interest. Facing it is the **Museo de Artes y Costumbres Populares** ( 954 23 25 76; admission €1.50, EU citizens free;  10am-8.30pm Tue-Sat, 10am-5pm Sun). Both are wheelchair accessible.

## Tours

### Pancho Tours    Cultural Tour
( 664 64 29 04; www.panchotours.com) FREE The best walking tours in the city? Join in and see – they free, although you're welcome to tip the hardworking guide who'll furnish you with an encyclopedia's worth of anecdotes, stories, myths and theories about Seville's fascinating past. Tours kick off daily, normally at 11am – check the website for exact details. Pancho also offers bike tours (€15, Friday and Saturday 10am and 6pm) and nightlife tours (€10 to €15, daily).

## Sleeping

### BARRIO DE SANTA CRUZ

### Hotel Amadeus    Hotel €€
( 954 50 14 43; www.hotelamadeussevilla.com; Calle Farnesio 6; s/d €100/114;  P  ) Just when you thought you could never find hotels with pianos in the rooms anymore, along came Hotel Amadeus. It's run by an engaging musical family in the old *judería* (Jewish quarter) where several of the astutely decorated rooms come complete with soundproofed walls and upright pianos, ensuring you don't miss out on your daily practice.

### Hotel Casa 1800    Luxury Hotel €€€
( 954 56 18 00; www.hotelcasa1800sevilla.com; Calle Rodrigo Caro 6; d €147-210;  @  ) Reigning as number one in Seville's

'favourite hotel' charts is this relatively new Santa Cruz jewel where the word *casa* (house) is taken seriously. This really is your home away from home (albeit a posh one!), with charming staff catering for your every need. Historic highlights include a sweet afternoon-tea buffet, plus a quartet of penthouse garden suites with Giralda views.

### EL CENTRO

#### Hotel Abanico                    Hotel €€
( 954 21 32 07; www.hotelabanico.com; Calle Águilas 17; r from €120;  ) If you want to wake up and know instantly that you're in Seville, book into this central gem where the colourful tilework, wrought-iron balconies and radiant religious art has Seville written all over it.

#### Hotel América                   Hotel €€
( 954 22 09 51; www.hotelamericasevilla.com; Plaza del Duque de la Victoria 9; s/d €69/89;  ) If you like no fuss, then head for the Hotel America, a well-located, professionally run hotel with a business-like

sheen that won't offer you fancy tilework or carnations on your pillow, but will give you all you need to set up a decent sightseeing base.

## Eating

### BARRIO DE SANTA CRUZ

#### Casa Plácido                    Tapas €
(Calle Mesón del Morro 15; tapas €2.50;  12.30-4pm & 8pm-midnight Mon-Thu, to 1am Fri-Sun) A tight-fitting, timeworn bar that hasn't changed much since 1870-something where you can enjoy traditional tapas banged down on the table quicker than you can say *'dos cervezas, por favor'.* Wasn't that just what you came to Seville for?

#### Vinería San Telmo               Tapas, Fusion €€
( 954 41 06 00; www.vineriasantelmo.com; Paseo Catalina de Ribera 4; tapas €3.50, media raciones €10;  1-4.30pm & 8pm-midnight) San Telmo invented the *rascocielo* (skyscraper) tapa, a tower of tomatoes, aubergine, goat's cheese and smoked salmon. If this

and other creative nuggets such as foie gras with quails eggs and lychees, or exquisitely cooked bricks of tuna don't make you drool with expectation then you're probably dead.

### Restaurante Egaña Oriza
Contemporary Spanish €€€
(www.restauranteoriza.com; Calle San Fernando 41; mains €22-32; ⏱1.30-4pm & 8.30-11.30pm Mon-Fri, 8.30-11.30pm Sat) Say Basque and you've got a byword for fine dining these days, so it's not surprising that Basque-run Egaña Oriza is regarded as one of the city's stand-out restaurants. Situated close to the Prado de San Sebastián bus station, this could be your first (and best) culinary treat in Seville. There's an equally posh tapas spot on the ground floor.

## EL CENTRO

### Redhouse Art & Food
International €
( ☎661 61 56 46; www.redhousespace.com; Calle Amor de Dios 7; snacks from €4; ⏱11.30am-

12.30am Tue-Sun; ☎) It's hard to classify Redhouse. With it's mismatched chairs and abstract wall art, its clearly hipster terriotory, yet inside you'll find families, seniors, college geeks and the obviously not-so-hip enjoying a whole variety of food from casual coffee to romantic meals. Whatever you opt for, save room for the best homemade cakes in Andalucía.

### Bar-Restaurante Eslava
Fusion, Andalucian €€
(www.espacioeslava.com; Calle Eslava 3; media raciones €9-13; ⏱12.30pm-midnight Tue-Sat, 12.30-4.30pm Sun) A legend in its own dinnertime, Eslava shirks the traditional tilework and bullfighting posters of tapas-bar lore and delivers where it matters: fine food backed up with equally fine service.

### Los Coloniales
Andalucian €€
(www.tabernacoloniales.es; cnr Calle Dormitorio & Plaza Cristo de Burgos; mains €10-12;

⏱ **12.30pm-12.15am)** The quiet ones are always the best. It might not look like much from the outside, but take it on trust that Los Coloniales is something very special. The quality plates line up like models on a catwalk: *chorizo a la Asturiana,* a divine spicy sausage in an onion sauce served on a bed of lightly fried potato; eggplants in honey; and pork tenderloin *al whiskey* (a whiskey-flavoured sauce).

### Duo Tapas
Tapas, Fusion €€

**(Calle Calatrava 10; tapas €3-4.50, media raciones €9-12; ⏱ 12.30-4.30pm & 8.30pm-midnight)** Missed by the masses who rarely wander north from the Alameda de Hércules, Duo Tapas is 'new school'. But, what it lacks in *azulejos* tiles and illustrious past patrons, it makes up for in inventive tapas with an Asian twist. Alameda trendies swear by its green chicken with rice and spicy noodles.

## EL ARENAL

### La Brunilda
Tapas, Fusion €€

**(☎ 954 22 04 81; Calle Galera 5; tapas €3.50-6.50; ⏱ 1-4pm & 8.30-11.30pm Tue-Sat, 1-4pm Sun)** Seville's crown as Andalucía's tapas capital is regularly attacked by well-armed rivals from the provinces meaning it constantly has to reinvent itself and offer up fresh competition. Enter Brunilda, a new font of fusion tapas sandwiched into an inconspicuous backstreet in the Arenal quarter where everything – including the food staff and clientele – is pretty.

## 🍷 Drinking

### Bulebar Café
Bar, Cafe

**(☎ 954 90 19 54; Alameda de Hércules 83; ⏱ 4pm-late)** This place gets pretty *caliente* (hot) at night but is pleasantly chilled in the early evening, with friendly staff. Don't write off its spirit-reviving alfresco breakfasts that pitch earlybirds with up-all-nighters.

### El Garlochi
Bar

**(Calle Boteros 4; ⏱ 10pm-6am)** Dedicated entirely to the iconography, smells and sounds of Semana Santa, the ubercamp El Garlochi is a true marvel. A cloud of church incense hits you as you go up the stairs, and the faces of baby Jesus and the Virgin welcome you into the velvet-walled bar, decked out with more Virgins and Jesuses.

Roman amphitheatre, Itálica

GUY VANDERELST/GETTY IMAGES ©

# ⭐ Entertainment

### Casa de la Memoria — Flamenco
(📞954 56 06 70; www.casadelamemoria.es; Calle Cuna 6; €18; ⏰shows 7.30pm & 9pm) Neither a *tablao* (show) nor a private *peña* (club), this cultural centre, recently relocated from Santa Cruz to El Centro where it is accommodated in the old stables of the Palacio de la Lebrija, offers what are, without doubt, the most intimate and authentic nightly flamenco shows in Seville.

### Casa de la Guitarra — Flamenco
(📞954 22 40 93; Calle Mesón del Moro 12; tickets adult/child €17/10; ⏰shows 7.30pm & 9pm) Tiny new flamenco-only venue in Santa Cruz (no food or drinks served) where a miscued step from the performing dancers would land them in the front row of the audience. Glass display cases filled with guitars of erstwhile flamenco greats adorn the walls.

### Sevilla de Ópera — Theatre
(📞955 29 46 61; www.sevilladeopera.com; Mercado del Arenal; ⏰shows 9pm Fri & Sat) Seville has served as the fictional setting for countless operas, so it made sense when in 2012 a group of opera singers and enthusiasts decided to initiate the Sevilla de Ópera club. The setting in Arenal market is like a kind of 'Opera *tablao*' with shows designed to make the music more accessible.

### Tablao El Arenal — Flamenco
(www.tablaoelarenal.com; Calle Rodo 7; admission with 1 drink €37, with dinner €72; ⏰restaurant from 7pm, shows 8pm & 10pm) Of the three places in Seville that offer flamenco dinner shows this – ask any local – is the best. A smaller seating capacity (100 compared to 600 at the Palacio Andaluz) offers greater intimacy, although, as a big venue, it still lacks the grit and – invariably – *duende* (flamenco spirit) of the *peñas*.

## ℹ️ Information

Tourist office ( ⏰9am-8pm Mon-Fri, 10am-2pm Sat & Sun, closed holidays) The staff at the

## Detour:
## Itálica

Situated in the suburban settlement of Santiponce, 8km northwest of Seville, **Itálica** (📞955 62 22 66; www.juntadeandalucia.es/cultura/italica; Avenida de Extremadura 2; admission €1.50, EU citizens free; ⏰8.30am-9pm Tue-Sat, 9am-3pm Sun & holidays Apr-Sep, 9am-6.30pm Tue-Sat, 10am-4pm Sun & holidays Oct-Mar) was the first Roman town in Spain. Founded in 206 BC, it was also the birthplace and home of the 2nd-century-AD Roman emperors Trajan and Hadrian. The partly reconstructed ruins include one of the biggest of all the Roman amphitheatres, broad paved streets, ruins of several houses with beautiful mosaics, and a theatre.

Buses run to Santiponce (€1.45, 40 minutes) from Seville's Plaza de Armas bus station, at least twice an hour from 6.35am to 11pm Monday to Friday, and a little less often at weekends. They stop right outside the Itálica entrance.

Constitución office are well informed but often very busy.

Turismo Sevilla (www.turismosevilla.org; Plaza del Triunfo 1; ⏰10.30am-7pm Mon-Fri) Information on all Sevilla province.

## ℹ️ Getting There & Away

### Air

Seville's Aeropuerto San Pablo (www.sevilla-airport.com) has a fair range of international and domestic flights. Iberia (www.iberia.com) flies direct to Barcelona, Madrid and half a dozen other Spanish cities, as well as to London and Paris. Air Europa (www.aireuropa.com) and Vueling (www.vueling.com) fly to Barcelona. Vueling also flies to Paris and Amsterdam.

## Bus

Seville has two bus stations. From the **Estación de Autobuses Plaza de Armas** (www. autobusesplazadearmas.es; Avenida del Cristo de la Expiración) the bus company **Alsa** (www.alsa. es) runs buses to Córdoba (€12, two hours, seven daily), Granada (€23, three hours, 10 daily) and Málaga (€19, 2¾ hours, eight daily); while Damas serves Huelva (€9, 1¼ hours, 18 daily). This is also the main station for **Eurolines** (www.eurolines.es) and international services to Germany, Belgium, France and beyond.

**Comes** (www.tgcomes.es) runs buses from the **Estación de Autobuses Prado de San Sebastián** (Plaza San Sebastián) to Cádiz (€14, 1¾ hours, eight daily) and Jerez de la Frontera (€9, 1¼ hours, seven daily).

## Train

Seville's **Estación Santa Justa** (☎902 43 23 43; Avenida Kansas City) is 1.5km northeast of the centre. Trains go to/from Madrid (€76, 2½ hours, 20 daily), Cádiz (€16, 1 hour 45 minutes, 15 daily), Córdoba (€30, 42 minutes, 30 daily), Huelva (€12, 1½ hours, three daily), Granada (€30, three hours, four daily) and Málaga (€43, two hours, 11 daily).

## 🛈 Getting Around

### To/From the Airport

The airport is 7km east of the city centre on the A4 Córdoba road. A special airport bus marked 'Especial Aeropuerto' runs between the airport and the Plaza de Armas bus station (€4, every 15 minutes, 5.45am to 12.45am, less frequent on Sundays). It stops, among other places, beside the Torre del Oro in the city centre. A taxi costs about €22.

### Car & Motorcycle

Hotels with parking usually charge you €12 to €18 a day for the privilege – no cheaper than some public car parks but at least your vehicle will be close at hand. **Parking Paseo de Colón** (cnr Paseo de Cristóbal Colón & Calle Adriano; per hour up to 10hr €1.20, 10-24hr €14) is a relatively inexpensive underground car park.

# CARMONA

POP 27,950 / ELEV 250M

Perched on a low hill overlooking a wonderful *vega* (valley) that sizzles in the summer heat, and dotted with old palaces and impressive monuments, Carmona comes as an unexpected highlight of western Andalucía.

## ◉ Sights

**Museo de la Ciudad** Museum
(City History Museum; ☎954 14 01 28; www.museociudad.carmona.org; Calle San Ildefonso 1; adult/child €3/free, Tue free; ⊙11am-7pm Tue-Sun, 11am-2pm Mon) Explore the town's interesting history at the city museum, housed in a centuries-old palace, with pieces dating back to Paleolithic times. The sections on the the Tartessos and their Roman successors are highlights: the former includes a unique collection of large earthenware vessels with

Córdoba's Judería (p256)

Middle Eastern decorative motifs, the latter several excellent mosaics.

### Iglesia Prioral de Santa María
*Church*

(📞954 19 14 82; Plaza Marqués de las Torres; admission €3; 🕙9am-2pm & 5.30-7.30pm Mon-Fri, 9am-2pm Sat) This splendid church was built mainly in the 15th and 16th centuries on the site of the former main mosque. The Patio de los Naranjos by which you enter has a Visigothic calendar carved into one of its pillars. Inside, the plateresque altar is detailed to an almost perverse degree, with 20 panels of biblical scenes framed by gilt-scrolled columns.

## Eating

### Casa Curro Montoya
*Tapas €€*

(Calle Santa María de Gracia 13; tapas €2.50; 🕙1.15-5pm & 8.45pm-12.30am Wed-Mon) This friendly, family-run joint opposite the Convento de Santa Clara occupies a narrow hall littered with memorabilia. Long-cultivated family traditions find expression in such items as fresh tuna in a luscious onion sauce, foie-gras-stuffed eggplant and fried *pizcotas*, small sardinelike fish.

## ℹ Information

**Tourist office** (www.turismo.carmona.org; Alcázar de la Puerta de Sevilla; 🕙10am-6pm Mon-Sat, 10am-3pm Sun & holidays) The helpful tourist office is inside the Puerta de Sevilla.

## ℹ Getting There & Away

Monday to Friday, Casal runs hourly buses to Seville from the stop on Paseo del Estatuto, on weekends less often. Two or three buses a day go to Córdoba via Écija from the car park next to the Puerta de Sevilla.

# CÓRDOBA

POP 328,000 / ELEV 110M

Picture a city 500,000 strong, embellished with fine architecture and fuelled by a prosperous and diverse economy.

## If You Like...
# Small Town Life

If you like Carmona's lazy small-town feel (and you will) cruise on by these places for a similar experience:

### 1 ÉCIJA
A stack of Gothic-Mudéjar palaces and churches and a genuine insight into small-town Andalucian life.

### 2 OSUNA
Sleepy and unassuming Osuna has a stash of beautifully preserved Baroque mansions.

### 3 CAZALLA DE LA SIERRA
Attractive White Town with pleasant walks in the woods and some great places to stay.

### 4 LA RÁBIDA, PALOS DE LA FRONTERA AND MOGUER
Three little townships that together helped send Columbus to America.

### 5 NIEBLA
Encircled by ochre-red walls and home to a grotesquely fascinating museum of torture.

Picture universities and libraries filled with erudite artists and wise philosophers. Picture an Islamic caliphate more advanced and civilised than anything else the world had ever known. Picture Córdoba c AD 975.

OK, so this slightly grainy image may be over 1000 years old now, but enough of ancient Córdoba remains to place it in the contemporary top three drawcards of Andalucía. The centrepiece is the gigantic Mezquita, an architectural anomaly and one of the only places in the world where you can worship Mass in a mosque. Surrounding it is an intricate web of winding streets, geranium-sprouting flower boxes and cool intimate patios that are at their most beguiling in late spring.

# Córdoba

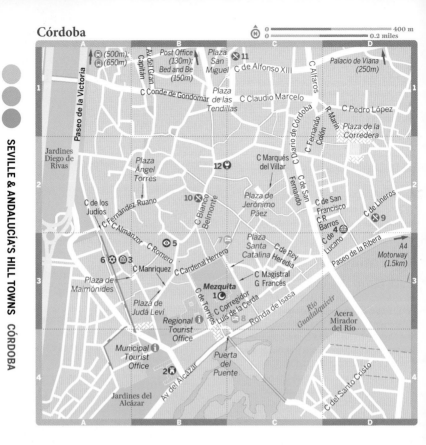

## ◎ Sights & Activities

**Judería**   Historic Neighbourhood

Jews were among the most dynamic and prominent citizens of Islamic Córdoba. The medieval *judería* (Jewish quarter), extending northwest from the Mezquita almost to Avenida del Gran Capitán, is today a maze of narrow streets and whitewashed buildings with flowery window boxes.

The beautiful little 14th-century **Sinagoga** (Calle de los Judíos 20; ⊗ 9.30am-2pm & 3.30-5.30pm Tue-Sat, 9.30am-1.30pm Sun) **FREE** is one of only three surviving medieval synagogues in Spain and the only one in Andalucía. In the late 1400s it became a hospital for hydrophobics. Translated Hebrew inscriptions eroded in midsentence seem like poignant echoes of a silenced society.

In the heart of the *judería,* and once connected by an underground tunnel to the Sinagoga, is the 14th-century **Casa de Sefarad** (www.casadesefarad.es; cnr Calle de los Judíos & Averroes; adult/reduced €4/3; ⊙11am-6pm Mon-Sat, 11am-2pm Sun). Opened in 2008 on the corner of Calles de los Judíos and Averroes, this small, beautiful museum is devoted to reviving interest in the Sephardic-Judaic-Spanish tradition. There is a refreshing focus on music, domestic traditions and on the women intellectuals (poets, singers and thinkers) of Al-Andalus. A specialist library of Sephardic history is housed here, and there's also a well-stocked shop. A program of live music recitals and storytelling events runs most of the year.

### Alcázar de los Reyes Cristianos    Castle

(Castle of the Christian Monarchs; Campo Santo de Los Mártires; admission €4.50, Fri free; ⊙8.30am-8.45pm Tue-Fri, 8.30am-4.30pm Sat, 8.30am-2.30pm Sun; 🚹)
Built by Alfonso XI in the 14th century on the remains of Roman and Arab predecessors, the castle began life as a palace. It hosted both Fernando and Isabel, who made their first acquaintance with Columbus here in 1486. Its terraced gardens – full of fish ponds, fountains, orange trees, flowers and topiary – are a pleasure to stroll and a joy to behold from the tower.

### Centro Flamenco Fosforito    Museum

(☎957 48 50 39; www.centroflamencofosforito.cordoba.es; Plaza del Potro; admission €2; ⊙8.30am-7.30pm Tue-Fri, 8.30am-2.30pm Sat, 9.30am-2.30pm Sun) Possibly the best flamenco museum in Andalucía – which is saying something – this new place benefits from a fantastic location inside the ancient Posada del Potro, an inn named-checked by Cervantes in the novel, *Don Quijote.* Touch-screens, fantastic archive footage and arty displays meticulously explain the building blocks of flamenco and its history, along with the singers, guitarists and dancers who defined it. You'll walk out both enthused *and* wiser.

## Local Knowledge

# Córdoba

BY SEBASTIÁN DE LA OBRA,
EMINENT LOCAL HISTORIAN

### 1 LA MEZQUITA DE CÓRDOBA

Córdoba's Mezquita is one of the most prestigious buildings in Arab-Islamic culture. The interior is indescribably beautiful – a labyrinth of bicoloured columns with horseshoe arches, a forest of palm trees rendered in stone, and brickwork that is most beautiful in the mihrab.

### 2 LA SINAGOGA DE CÓRDOBA

Córdoba's synagogue is richly decorated with Mudéjar art and fragments of the Psalms in Hebrew; women worshipped upstairs, men downstairs. After Jewish people were expelled from Spain, the synagogue served as a school, hermitage, hospital and a brotherhood of shoemakers. It's now one of the few remaining signposts to Spain's Jewish heritage.

### 3 TEMPLO ROMANO DE CÓRDOBA

Away from the heart of tourist Córdoba, the city's spectacular Roman temple is a reminder that Córdoba's fame predates Al-Andalus. Córdoba was the capital of Hispania Ulterior (and later Córdoba Bética), and in the 3rd century was considered the cultural and economic powerhouse of Roman Iberia. The ruins wonderfully evoke this period.

### 4 FERNANDO PERIOD CHURCHES

In the 14th century, churches were built in all the city's neighbourhoods and today provide the focal point for a beautiful route through the city. Thirteen of the 14 churches survive and all share common architectural features – three naves with an apse, rose windows, stone walls and Mozarabic windows. My favourites are the Capilla de San Bartolomé and the Iglesia de Santa Marina.

### 5 CASA DE SEFARAD

This privately run museum and cultural space occupies a 14th-century house and serves as a centre for recovering the heritage and historical memory of Spain's Jewish community. It's home to one of the most prestigious libraries in Andalucía, and hosts concerts of Sephardic and other Andalucian music.

## Don't Miss
# Mezquita

It's impossible to overemphasise the beauty of Córdoba's great mosque, with its remarkably peaceful and spacious interior. The Mezquita hints, with all its lustrous decoration, at a lavish and refined age when Muslims, Jews and Christians lived side by side and enriched their city and surroundings with a heady interaction of diverse and vibrant cultures.

Mosque

☎ 957 47 05 12

www.mezquitadecordoba.org

Calle Cardenal Herrero

adult/child €8/4, 8.30-9.20am Mon-Sat free

🕙 8.30am-7pm Mon-Sat, 8.30-10am & 2-7pm Sun Mar-Oct, 8.30am-6pm Mon-Sat, 8.30am-1.30pm & 3-6pm Sun Nov-Feb

## Patio de los Naranjos & Minaret

Outside the mosque, the leafy, walled courtyard and its fountain were the site of ritual ablutions before prayer. The crowning glory of the whole complex was the minaret, which at its peak towered 48m. The current tower measures only 22m.

## Interior

The main prayer hall consists of 'naves' lined by two-tier arches striped in red brick and white stone. The columns used for the Mezquita were a mishmash of material collected from earlier Visigothic and Roman buildings. Later enlargements of the mosque extended these lines of arches to cover an area of nearly 120 sq metres and create one of the biggest mosques in the world. The arcades are one of the much-loved Islamic architectural motifs. Their simplicity and number give a sense of endlessness to the Mezquita.

## The Cathedral

For three centuries following the Christian Reconquest in 1236, the Mezquita remained largely unaltered save for minor modifications. In the 16th century King Carlos I gave permission for the centre of the Mezquita to be ripped out to allow construction of the Capilla Mayor (the altar area in the cathedral) and *coro* (choir). However, the king was not enamoured with the results: 'You have built what you or others might have built anywhere, but you have destroyed something that was unique in the world.'

## Mihrab & Maksura

Just past the cathedral's western end, the approach to the mihrab begins, marked by heavier more elaborate arches. Immediately in front of the mihrab is the *maksura*, the royal prayer enclosure, with its intricately interwoven arches and lavishly decorated domes created by Caliph Al-Hakam II in the 960s. The decoration of the mihrab portal incorporates 1600kg of gold mosaic cubes, a gift from the Christian emperor of Byzantium, Nicephoras II Phocas.

**Local Knowledge**

# Mezquita

RECOMMENDATIONS BY JOSÉ FABRA GARRIDO, TOUR GUIDE AND OWNER OF BED AND BE (P262).

### 1 EARLY ENTRY
Visit early in the morning. The Mezquita actually allows free entry if you arrive between 8.30am and 9.30pm. There are generally less people around at this time meaning you'll enjoy a more tranquil experience. They usually start ushering early visitors out from 9.20am to make way for the paying hordes.

### 2 PATIO DE NARANJOS
It is always free to enter the Patio de Naranjos, the former ablutions area of the mosque that is today filled with neat lines of orange trees. Don't eat the oranges; they are very bitter. If you sit here people-watching (also recommended), you'll see the occasional tourist biting into one before quickly spitting it out.

### 3 BEST VIEW
The best view of the Mezquita is from the opposite side of Guadalquivir Río. Cross the water on the Roman Bridge, turn left at the Torre de la Calahorra and look back towards the Mezquita from the embankment on the south side. The view is particularly beguiling at night when the building is floodlit.

### 4 MEZQUITA AT NIGHT
It is possible to visit the Mezquita at night when special lights seek out dark corners you might have missed during the daytime. The atmosphere is also very different at this time. The night show is known as 'El Alma de Córdoba' and tickets are more than double daytime rates. Ask about times and availability at the tourist office.

### 5 THE COLUMNS
The hundreds of columns that support the unusual double arches inside the Mezquita were often recycled from old Roman buildings (Córdoba had been capital of the important Roman province of Baetica). They are said to have been inspired by Roman aqueducts.

259

# Mezquita

## TIMELINE

**600** Foundation of the Christian Visigothic church of St Vincent on the site of the present Mezquita.

**785** Salvaging Visigoth and Roman ruins, Emir Abd ar-Rahman I converts the Mezquita into a mosque.

**822–5** Mosque enlarged in reign of Abd ar-Rahman II.

**912–961** A new minaret is ordered by Abd ar-Rahman III.

**961–6** Mosque enlarged by Al-Hakam II who also enriches the **mihrab** ❶.

**987** Mosque enlarged for the last time by Al-Mansur Ibn Abi Aamir. With the addition of the **Patio de los Naranjos** ❷, the building reaches its current dimensions.

**1236** Mosque reconverted into a Christian church after Córdoba is recaptured by Ferdinand III of Castile.

**1271** Instead of destroying the mosque, the overawed Christians elect to modify it. Alfonso X orders the construction of the **Capilla de Villaviciosa** ❸ and **Capilla Real** ❹.

**1300s** Original minaret is replaced by the baroque **Torre del Alminar** ❺.

**1520s** A Renaissance-style cathedral nave is added by Charles V. 'I have destroyed something unique to the world,' he laments on seeing the finished work.

**2004** Spanish Muslims petition to be able to worship in the Mezquita again. The Vatican doesn't consent.

## TOP TIPS

» **Among the oranges** The Patio de los Naranjos can be enjoyed free of charge at any time.

» **Early birds** Entry to the rest of the Mezquita is offered free every morning except Sunday between 8.30am and 9.30am.

» **Quiet time** Group visits are prohibited before 10am, meaning the building is quieter and more atmospheric in the early morning.

**The mihrab**
Everything leads to the mosque's greatest treasure – a scallop-shell-shaped prayer niche facing Mecca that was added in the 10th century. Cast your eyes over the gold mosaic cubes crafted by imported Byzantium sculptors.

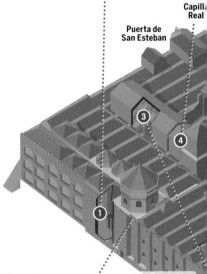

Capill. Real

Puerta de San Esteban

**The maksura**
Guiding you towards the mihrab, the maksura is a former royal enclosure where the caliphs and their retinues prayed. Its lavish, elaborate arches were designed to draw the eye of worshippers towards the mihrab and Mecca.

**The cathedral choir**
Few ignore the impressive *coro* (choir): a late-Christian addition dating from the 1750s. Once you've admired the skilfully carved mahogany choir stalls depicting scenes from the Bible, look up at the impressive baroque ceiling.

**Torre del Alminar**
This is the Mezquita's cheapest sight because you don't have to pay to see it. Rising 93m and viewable from much of the city, the baroque-style bell tower was built over the mosque's original minaret.

**The Mezquita arches**
No, you're not hallucinating. The Mezquita's most defining characteristic is its unique terracotta-and-white striped arches that support 856 pillars salvaged from Roman and Visigoth ruins. Glimpsed through the dull light they're at once spooky and striking.

**Puerta del Perdón**

**Patio de los Naranjos**
Abandon architectural preconceptions all ye who enter here. The ablutions area of the former mosque is a shady courtyard embellished with orange trees that acts as the Mezquita's main entry point.

**Capilla Mayor**
A Christian monument inside an Islamic mosque sounds beautifully ironic, yet here it is: a Gothic church commissioned by Charles V in the 16th century and planted in the middle of the world's third largest mosque.

**Capilla de Villaviciosa**
Sift through the building's numerous chapels till you find this gem, an early Christian modification added in 1277 which fused existing Moorish arches and pillars. It served as the Capilla Mayor until the 1520s.

## Detour:
# Medina Azahara

Even in the cicada-shrill heat and stillness of a summer afternoon, the **Medina Azahara** (Madinat al-Zahra; admission €1.50, EU citizens free; ⏱10am-6.30pm Tue-Sat, to 8.30pm May–mid-Sep, to 2pm Sun) whispers of the power and vision of its founder, Abd ar-Rahman III. The self-proclaimed caliph began the construction of a magnificent new capital 8km west of Córdoba around 936, and took up full residence around 945. Medina Azahara was a resounding declaration of his status, a magnificent trapping of power.

The new capital was amazingly short-lived. Between 1010 and 1013, during the caliphate's collapse, Medina Azahara was wrecked by Berber soldiers. Today, less than a 10th of it has been excavated, and only about a quarter of that is open to visitors.

A new **museum** on the foundation of one of the excavated buildings blends seamlessly with its surroundings and traces the history of the city, with beautifully displayed pieces taken from the site and some amazing interactive displays.

Medina Azahara is signposted on Avenida de Medina Azahara, which leads west out of Córdoba onto the A431.

A taxi costs €37 for the return trip, with one hour to view the site, or you can book a three-hour coach tour for €8.50 through many Córdoba hotels.

---

### Palacio de Viana
Museum

(www.palaciodeviana.com; Plaza de Don Gome 2; admission whole house/patios only €8/5; ⏱10am-7pm Tue-Sat, 10am-3pm Sun Sep-Jun, 9am-3pm Tue-Sun Jul & Aug) This stunning Renaissance palace is set around 12 beautiful patios that are a genuine pleasure to visit in the spring. Occupied by the Marqueses de Viana until a few decades ago, the 6500-sq-metre building is packed with art and antiques. The charge covers a one-hour guided tour of the rooms and access to the patios and garden. It's about 600m northeast of the Plaza de las Tendillas. Or take bus number 6 to Puerta de Sevilla, get off at Plaza de Colón and walk four blocks east.

## 🛏 Sleeping

### Bed and Be
Hostel €

(📞661 42 07 33; www.bedandbe.com; Calle Cruz Conde 22; dm/d with shared bathroom €19/60; ❄🛜) 🅿 Hugely engaging new accommodation thanks in part to the foresight of owner, José, who also runs free evening bike tours around the city. There's an assortment of double and dorm rooms all super-clean and as gleaming white as a *pueblo blanco*. Extra value is added with a kitchen, lounge area, roof terrace and various special events regularly organized by José.

### Hotel Hacienda Posada de Vallina
Hotel €€

(📞957 49 87 50; www.hhposadadevallinacordoba.com; Calle del Corregidor Luís de la Cerda 83; r from €99; 🅿❄@🛜) In an enviable nook on the quiet side of the Mezquita (the building actually predates it), this cleverly renovated hotel uses portraits and period furniture to enhance a plush and modern interior. There are two levels overlooking a salubrious patio and the rooms make you feel comfortable but in-period (ie medieval Córdoba). Columbus allegedly once stayed here.

### Balcón de Córdoba
Boutique Hotel €€€

(📞957 49 84 78; www.balcondecordoba.com; Calle Encarnación 8; r from €197; ❄🛜) Offering top-end boutique luxury, the 10-room Balcón is a riveting place with the obligatory Cordobés patio and roof terrace, plus slick rooms, antique doors, and ancient stone relics dotted around as if it were a wing of the nearby archeological museum. Service doesn't miss a beat and there's a substantial breakfast served as a fruity buffet.

##  Eating

### Salmorejería Umami
Andalucian, Modern €€

(📞957 48 23 47; www.grupoumami.com; Calle Blanco Belmonte 6; mains €14-22; ⏰1-4pm & 8-11.30pm Mon-Sat, 1-4pm Sun) It's new, it's good and it's celebrating what is probably Córdoba's favourite dish, the locally concocted *salmorejo*, a tomato-y version of gazpacho soup that's too thick to drink. The trick (because there's always a trick) is that Umami does a good dozen versions of the recipe including avocado, Thai and green-tea flavours. The main dishes are equally creative.

### Taberna San Miguel El Pisto
Tapas €€

(www.casaelpisto.com/en; Plaza San Miguel 1; tapas €3, media raciones €5-10; ⏰noon-4pm & 8pm-midnight) Brimming with local character, El Pisto is one of Córdoba's best *tabernas* (taverns), in terms of both atmosphere and food. Traditional tapas and *media raciones* (half-rations; small servings) are done perfectly, and inexpensive Moriles wine is ready in jugs on the bar. Be sure to try the namesake item, a sort of ratatouille topped with a fried egg.

### Bodegas Campos
Andalucian €€

(📞957 49 75 00; www.bodegascampos.com; Calle de Lineros 32; tapas €5, mains €13-21; ⏰1.30-4.30pm & 8-11.30pm Mon-Sat, 1.30-4.30pm Sun) One of Córdoba's most atmospheric and famous wine cellar–restaurants, this sprawling hall features dozens of rooms and patios, with oak barrels signed by local and international celebrities stacked up alongside. The bodega produces its own house Montilla, and the restaurant, frequented by swankily dressed *cordobeses,* serves up a delicious array of meals.

##  Drinking

### Cervezas Califa
Brewery

(Calle Juan Valera 3; ⏰12.30-3.30pm & 7.30pm-late) It was probably only a matter of time

Medina Azahara

...he Andalucians came up with
...n microbrewery and here it is.
...ging the hegemony of big-brand
...brewers, Cruzcampo, these enter-
...ads from Córdoba have opened
what they're saying is the region's first
microbrewery (also a brewpub as they
concoct the stuff on the premises).

## ℹ Information

**Municipal tourist office** (☏902 201774; www.
turismodecordoba.org; ☺9am-2pm & 5-7pm)

**Regional tourist office** (Calle de Torrijos 10;
☺9am-7.30pm Mon-Fri, 9.30am-3pm Sat, Sun
& holidays) A good source of information about
Córdoba province; located inside the Palacio de
Congresos y Exposiciones.

## ℹ Getting There & Away

### Bus

The bus station is next to the train station. Each
bus company has its own terminal. **ALSA** (www.
alsa.es) runs services to Seville (€12, 1¾ hours,
seven daily), Granada (€15, 2¾ hours, eight daily),
Málaga (€15 2¾ hours, four daily) and Baeza (€12,
2½ hours, two daily). **Secorbus** (☏902 22 92 92;
www.socibus.es) operates buses to Madrid (€16,
4½ hours, six daily).

### Train

Córdoba's **train station** (☏957 40 02 02;
**Glorieta de las Tres Culturas**) is on the high-
speed AVE line between Madrid and Seville. Rail
destinations include Seville (€30.10, 45 minutes,
every 30 minutes), Madrid (€62.10, 1¾, every
30 minutes), Málaga (€27, one hour, 16 daily),
Barcelona (€115.10, 4½ hours, seven daily). For
Granada, change at Bobadilla.

# WHITE TOWNS

## Arcos de la Frontera

POP 31,500 / ELEV 185M

Choosing your favourite *pueblo blanco*
is like choosing your favourite Beatles
album – they're all so damned good,
it's hard to make a definitive decision.
Pressured for an answer many people
single out Arcos, a larger-than-average
White Town thrillingly sited on a high,
unassailable ridge with sheer precipices
plummeting away on both sides. With the
Sierra de Grazalema as a distant backdrop,
Arcos possesses all the classic White Town
calling cards: spectacular location,
soporific old town, fancy *parador*
(luxurious, state-owned hotel),
and volatile frontier history.

### ◉ Sights

**Plaza del
Cabildo**          Square
The old town captures
multiple historical eras
evoking the ebb and flow
of the once-disputed
Christian-Moorish fron-
tier. Plaza del Cabildo is
the centre of this quar-
ter. Close your eyes to
the modern car park and
focus instead on the fine

Arcos de la Frontera

surrounding buildings (all old) and a verti- ginous **mirador** (lookout) with views over Río Guadalete. The 11th-century **Castillo de los Duques** is firmly closed to the public, but its outer walls frame classic Arcos views. On the plaza's northern side is the Gothic-cum-baroque **Basíllica-Parroquia de Santa María** sporting beautiful stone choir stalls and Isabelline ceiling tracery. On the eastern side, the **Parador Casa del Corregidor** hotel is a reconstruction of a 16th-century magistrate's house. If you think you've already seen every possible jaw-dropping vista in Andalucía, drink this one in – preferably over a *café con leche* (half coffee and half warm milk) and accompanying *torta* (piece of cake). Outside is an equally dramatic mirador at the far end of the plaza.

## 🍴 Eating

### Taberna Jóvenes Flamencos
Andalucian €

( 📞657 13 35 52; www.tabernajovenesfla-mencos.blogspot.com; Calle Dean Espinosa; raciones €6; ⏰noon-late Thu-Tue) You've got to hand it to this new place opening up successfully in the middle of a recession with wonderful flamenco/bull-fighting decor and an easy to navigate menu split in meat, fish, bread, vegetarian and scramble sections – all delicious. Service is impeccable and there are regular outbreaks of flamenco.

## ℹ️ Information

**Tourist office** ( 📞956 70 22 64; Calle Cuesta de Belén 5; ⏰9.30am-2pm & 3-7.30pm Mon-Sat, 10am-2pm Sun) The new tourist office also doubles up as an interpretive centre with various scale models and interesting exhibits on the local history and wildlife.

## ℹ️ Getting There & Away

From the **bus station** ( 📞956 70 49 77; Calle Los Alcaldes), **Los Amarillos** (www.losamarillos.es) and/or **Comes** (www.tgcomes.es) have daily buses (fewer on weekends) to Cádiz (€5.11, one hour, eight daily) and Jerez de la Frontera (€2.64, 45 minutes, 19 daily), Málaga (€17, 3½ hours, two daily) and Ronda (€8.75, two hours, two daily).

## ❤️ If You Like...
## White Towns

If you like the quintessential *pueblos blan-cos* of Arcos de la Frontera and Grazalema, you'll fall instantly in love with the following:

**1  ZAHARA DE LA SIERRA**
Set around a vertiginous crag at the foot of the Sierra de Grazalema, rugged Zahara in Cádiz province hums with Moorish mystery.

**2  VEJER DE LA FRONTERA**
Vejer – the jaw drops, the eyes blink, the eloquent adjectives dry up. Looming moodily atop a rocky hill above the busy N340, 50km south of Cádiz, this placid, yet compact White Town is something very special.

**3  OLVERA**
A White Town par excellence, it is also renowned for its olive oil, striking Renaissance church, and roller-coaster history that started with the Romans.

**4  ZUHEROS**
Rising above the low-lying *campiña* (countryside), Zuheros sits in a dramatic location, crouching in the lee of a craggy mountain and makes a good base for exploring the Parque Natural Sierras Subbéticas.

## Parque Natural Sierra de Grazalema & Around

Of all Andalucía's protected areas, Parque Natural Sierra de Grazalema is the most accessible and best set up for lung-stretching sorties into the countryside. Though not as lofty as the Sierra Nevada, the park's rugged pillarlike peaks nonetheless rise abruptly off the plains northeast of Cádiz, revealing precipitous gorges, wild orchids and hefty rainfall (stand aside Galicia and Cantabria, this is the wettest part of Spain, logging an average 2000mm annually). Grazalema is also fine walking country (the best months are May, June, September and October).

The **Centro de Visitantes** (📞956 70 97 33; Calle Federico García Lorca 1; ⏱9am-2pm & 4-6pm Mon-Sat, 9am-2pm Sun), with limited displays and information, is situated in the village of El Bosque, 20km east of Grazalema village.

## GRAZALEMA

POP 2200 / ELEV 825M

A true mountain White Town, Grazalema looks like it has been dropped from a passing spaceship onto the steep rocky slopes of its eponymous mountain range. Few *pueblos blancos* are as generically perfect as this one, with its spotless whitewashed houses sporting rust-tiled roofs and wrought-iron window bars.

## 🏃 Activities

You're in walking country, so make the most of it. Good hiking info can be pro-

cured at the tourist office. Four of the park's best hikes (including the 12.5km El Pinsapar walk through Spain's best-preserved fir woodland) traverse restricted areas and must be booked ahead at the visitor centre in El Bosque.

**Horizon**                    Adventure Sports
(📞956 13 23 63; www.horizonaventura. com; Calle Corrales Terceros 29, Grazalema; ⏱10am-2pm & 5-8pm Mon-Sat) 🏃 Horizon, a block off Plaza de España, is a highly experienced adventure firm that will take you climbing, bungee jumping, canyoning, caving, paragliding or walking, with English-speaking guides. Prices per person range from around €14 for a half-day walk to over €60 for the 4km underground wetsuit adventure from the Cueva del Hundidero near Montejaque to the Cueva del Gato near Benaoján. Minimum group sizes apply for some activities.

## 🍴 Eating

### Restaurante El Torreón
Andalucian €€

(www.restauranteeltorreongrazalema.com; Calle Agua 44; mains €8-12; ⊙11am-4pm & 7-11pm) This friendly mountain restaurant is where you can take a break from the Cádiz fish monopoly with local chorizo, spinach, soups and the menu speciality, partridge. There's pasta for kids.

## ℹ️ Information

The village centre is the pretty Plaza de España, overlooked by the 18th-century Iglesia de la Aurora. Here you'll find the **tourist office** (☎956 13 20 73; ⊙10am-2pm & 4-9pm), with a shop selling local products.

---

## Ronda

POP 37,000 / ELEV 744M

Perched on an inland plateau riven by the 100m fissure of El Tajo gorge, Ronda is Málaga province's most spectacular town.

It has a superbly dramatic location, and owes its name ('surrounded' by mountains), to the encircling Serranía de Ronda.

## 👁️ Sights & Activities

### La Ciudad
Neighbourhood

Straddling the dramatic gorge and the Río Guadalevín (deep river) is Ronda's most recognisable sight, the towering Puente Nuevo, best viewed from the Camino de los Molinos, which runs along the bottom of the gorge. The bridge separates the old and new towns.

The old town is surrounded by massive fortress walls pierced by two ancient gates: the Islamic Puerta de Almocábar, which, in the 13th century, was the main gateway to the castle; and the 16th-century Puerta de Carlos V. Inside, the Islamic layout remains intact, and its maze of narrow streets now takes its character from the Renaissance mansions of powerful families whose predecessors accompanied Fernando el Católico in the taking of the city in 1485.

## Plaza de Toros
Bullring

(Calle Virgen de la Paz; admission €6.50; ⏱10am-8pm) Ronda's Plaza de Toros is a mecca for bullfighting aficionados. In existence for more than 200 years, it is one of the oldest and most revered bullrings in Spain and has also been the site of some of the most important events in bullfighting history.

Built by Martín Aldehuela, the bullring is universally admired for its soft sandstone hues and galleried arches. At 66m in diameter, it is also the largest and, therefore, most dangerous bullring, yet it only seats 5000 spectators – a tiny number compared with the huge 50,000-seater bullring in Mexico City. In July the ring is used for a series of fabulous concerts, and opera.

The on-site **Museo Taurino** is crammed with memorabilia such as blood-spattered costumes worn by Pedro Romero and 1990s star Jesulín de Ubrique. It also includes photos of famous fans such as Orson Welles and Ernest Hemingway, whose novel *Death in the Afternoon* provides in-depth insight into the fear and tension of the bullring.

Behind the Plaza de Toros, spectacular cliff-top views open out from Paseo de Blas Infante and the nearby Alameda del Tajo park.

## 🍴 Eating

### Bodega San Francisco
Tapas €

(www.bodegasanfrancisco.com; Calle Ruedo Alameda; raciones €6-10; ⏱1.30-5pm & 8pm-1am Wed-Mon) With three dining rooms and tables spilling out onto the narrow pedestrian street, this may well be Ronda's top tapas bar. The menu is vast and should suit the fussiest of families, even vegetarians with nine-plus salad choices. Try the *revuelto de patatas* (scrambled eggs with potatoes and peppers). House wine is good.

### Restaurante Tragabuches
Contemporary Spanish €€€

(📞952 19 02 91; www.tragabuches.com; Calle José Aparício 1; menus €59-87; ⏱1.30-3.30pm & 8-10.30pm Tue-Sat) Ronda's best and most famous restaurant is a 180-degree-turn away from the ubiquitous 'rustic' look and cuisine. Michelin-starred in 1998, Tragabuches is modern and sleek with an innovative menu to match. Choose from three set *menús*. People flock here from miles away to taste the food, prepared by its creative chef.

## ℹ Information

**Municipal tourist office** (www.turismoderonda. es; Paseo de Blas Infante; ⏱10am-7.30pm Mon-Fri, 10.15am-2pm & 3.30-6.30pm Sat, Sun & holidays) Helpful and friendly staff with a wealth of information on the town and region.

Doñana marshes, El Rocío (p269)
SLOW IMAGES/GETTY IMAGES ©

# Detour:
## Parque Nacional de Doñana

Spain's most celebrated and in many ways most important wildlife refuge, the Doñana National Park, created in 1969, is one of Europe's last remaining great wetlands. Covering 542 sq km in the southeast of Huelva province and neighbouring Seville province, this World Heritage Site is a vital refuge for such endangered species as the Spanish imperial eagle. It offers a unique combination of ecosystems and a place of haunting beauty that is well worth the effort of getting to. To visit the national park you must take a tour from the **Centro de Visitantes El Acebuche** ( ☏ 959 43 96 29; ☺ 8am-9pm Apr-Sep, to 7pm Oct-Mar) on the western side of the park, or from El Rocío at the park's northwestern corner, or from Sanlúcar de Barrameda at its southeastern corner.

The village of **El Rocío** overlooks a section of the Doñana *marismas* (marshes) at the park's northwestern corner. The village's sandy streets bear as many hoofprints as tyre marks, and they are lined with rows of verandah-fringed buildings that are empty most of the time. But this is no ghost town: most of the houses belong to the 90-odd *hermandades* (brotherhoods) of pilgrim-revellers and their families, who converge on El Rocío every year in the extraordinary Romería del Rocío festival (p43).

## ℹ Getting There & Away

### Bus

The bus station is at Plaza Concepción García Redondo 2. **Comes** (www.tgcomes.es) has buses to Arcos de la Frontera (€8.75, two hours, two daily), Jerez de la Frontera (€12, three hours, three daily) and Cádiz (€15, two hours, three daily). **Los Amarillos** (www.losamarillos.es) goes to Seville via Algodonales, Grazalema, and to Málaga via Ardales.

### Train

Ronda's **train station** ( ☏ 952 87 16 73; Avenida de Andalucía) is on the line between Bobadilla and Algeciras. Trains run to Algeciras via Gaucín and Jimena de la Frontera. This train ride is incredibly scenic and worth taking just for the views. Other trains depart for Málaga, Córdoba, Madrid, and Granada via Antequera. For Seville, change at Bobadilla or Antequera.

## Jerez de la Frontera

POP 211,000

Stand down all other claimants. Jerez, as most savvy Spain-o-philes know, *is* Andalucía. It just doesn't broadcast the fact in the way that Seville and Granada do. As a result, few people plan their trip around a visit here, preferring instead to jump-cut to the glories of the Giralda and the Alhambra. If only they knew. Jerez is the capital of *andaluz* horse culture, stop one on the famed sherry triangle and – cue the protestations from Cádiz and Seville – the cradle of Spanish flamenco. The *bulería,* Jerez's jokey, tongue-in-cheek antidote to Seville's tragic *soleá,* was first concocted in the legendary Roma *barrios* (neighbourhoods) of Santiago and San Miguel. If you want to unveil the eternal riddle that is Andalucía, start here.

## ◉ Sights

### Alcázar                          Fortress

( ☏ 956 14 99 55; Alameda Vieja; admission excl/incl camera obscura €5/7; ☺ 9.30am-7.30pm Mon-Fri, to 2.30pm Sat & Sun, closes 2.30pm Nov-Feb) Jerez' muscular yet refined 11th- or 12th-century fortress is one of the best-preserved Almohad-era (1140–1212) relics left in Andalucía. It's noted for its octagonal tower, a classic example of Almohad defensive forts.

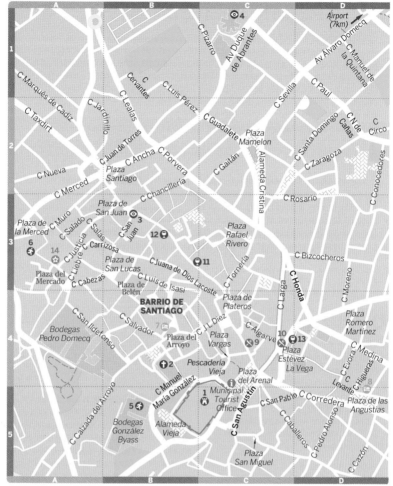

## Catedral de San Salvador
Cathedral

(Plaza de la Encarnación; admission €5; ⊙10am-6.30pm Mon-Sat, Mass 11am Sun) Echoes of Seville colour Jerez' wonderful cathedral, a surprisingly harmonious mix of baroque, neoclassical and Gothic styles. Stand-out features are its broad flying butresses and its intricately decorated stone ceilings. In 2012 the cathedral opened as a musuem showing off its art (including works by Zurbarán and Pa-checo), religious garments and silverware in a series of rooms and chapels behind the main altar.

## Real Escuela Andaluza del Arte Ecuestre
Equestrian Show

( ☎ 956 31 80 08; www.realescuela.org; Avenida Duque de Abrantes; training sessions adult/child €11/6.50, exhibición adult/child €21/13; ⊙training sessions 11am-1pm Mon, Wed & Fri Sep-Jul, Mon & Wed Aug, noon Tue & Thu Sep-Jul, exhibición noon Tue & Thu Oct-Jul, Tue, Thu & Fri

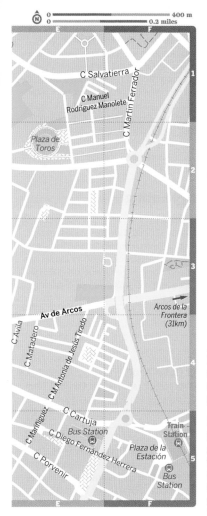

## Jerez de la Frontera

## 🏃 Tours

Jerez is home to around 20 bodegas (cellars) and most are open to visitors, but they're scattered around town and many of them require you to call ahead. The tourist office has up-to-date information.

### Bodegas González Byass    Winery
(Bodegas Tio Pepe; ☎ 956 35 70 16; www.bodegastiopepe.com; Calle Manuel María González 12; tour €12.50, with tapas €16; ☺ tours in English & Spanish hourly 11am-6pm Mon-Sat, to 2pm Sun Oct-Apr) Home of the Tio Pepe brand and one of the biggest sherry houses, handily located just west of the Alcázar. Six or seven tours each are given daily in English and Spanish, and a few in German and French. Reservations can be made online.

### Bodegas Tradición    Winery
(☎ 956 16 86 28; www.bodegastradicion.com; Plaza Cordobeses 3; tours €20; ☺ 9.30am-6.30pm Mon-Fri yr-round, 10am-2pm Sat Mar-Jun) An interesting bodega, not only for its extra-aged sherries (20 or more years old), but because it houses the Colección Joaquín Rivera, a private Spanish art collection that includes important works by Goya, Velázquez and Zurbarán. Tours

**Aug & Sep)** The famed Royal Andalucian School of Equestrian Art trains horses and riders in equestrian skills, and you can watch them going through their paces in training sessions and visit the **Horse Carriage Museum**, which includes an 18th-century Binder Hunting Break. The highlight for most is the official **exhibición** (show) where the handsome white horses show off their tricks to classical music. You can book tickets online for this – advisable for the official shows, which can sell out.

# Jerez' Fertile Flamenco Scene

Explorations of Jerez' flamenco scene ought to start at the **Centro Andaluz de Flamenco** (Andalucian Flamenco Centre; 856 81 41 32; www.centroandaluzdeflamenco.es; Plaza de San Juan 1; 9am-2pm Mon-Fri) FREE, Spain's only bona fide flamenco library where you can pick up information on clubs, performances and singing/dance/guitar lessons. From here you can stroll down **Calle Francos** and visit legendary flamenco bars such as **Damajuana** (www.damajuanacafebar.com; Calle Francos 18; 4.30pm-3am Tue-Sun) and **El Arriate** (Calle Francos 41; 8am-midnight), where singers and dancers still congregate. To the north, in the Santiago quarter, you'll find dozens of small *peñas* (private clubs) all known for their accessibility and intimacy; entrance is normally free if you buy a drink at the bar. The *peña* scene is particularly fertile during the February flamenco festival, which is arguably Andalucía's finest.

of the collection are given three or four times a day.

## 🛏 Sleeping

### Hotel Casa Grande                          Hotel €€
( 956 34 50 70; www.casagrande.com.es; Plaza de las Angustias 3; r €85-105, ste €115-125; P ❄ @ ) This brilliant hotel occupies a carefully restored 1920s mansion. Rooms are spread over three floors and set around a patio, or beside the roof terrace, which has views of Jerez' roof line. All is overseen by the congenial Monika Schroeder, who is a mine of information about Jerez.

### Hotel Bellas Artes                          Hotel €€
( 956 34 84 30; www.hotelbellasartes.com; Plaza del Arroyo 45; d €69-99; ❄ @ 🛜 ) A top-notch palace conversion, the Bellas Artes overlooks the Cathedral of San Salvador from its main terrace and suites. An exquisite carved stone corner pillar graces the sand-coloured neoclassical exterior. Strong interior colours contrast with white marble floors. Free-standing bath-tubs further contribute to an olde-worlde ambience, though rooms have all the mod cons.

## 🍴 Eating

### Albores                          Andalucian €€
( 956 32 02 66; Calle Consistorio 12; mains €8-15; noon-midnight) Among the old favourites in the city centre Albores has added a new edge. Opened in 2013 its tapas and meals provide ideal pairings for the locally concocted sherries. If there's a speciality, it's probably the fish, in particular the tuna *escabeche* (marinated and then poached). It stays open all day and the cakes are homemade.

### El Gallo Azul                          Spanish €€
(Calle Larga 2; raciones from €12; 11.30am-midnight Tue-Sun) Housed in what has become Jerez' signature building, a circular facade emblazoned with a sherry logo, El Gallo Azul (the Blue Cockerel) has a restaurant upstairs and tapas at street level. It's also an excellent perch to enjoy an afternoon coffee and a slice of cake as the city springs back to life after the siesta.

## 🍷 Drinking

### Tabanco El Pasaje                          Bar, Flamenco
( 956 33 33 59; Calle Santa María 8; 11am-3.30pm & 7.30-10.30pm, to 11.30pm Fri & Sat) One of six famous old *tabancos* (food stalls) listed by the town hall, this old drinking house sells plenty of the local plonk (ie sherry) which it serves up with suitably raw flamenco on weekend evenings. Jerez to the very core.

# ⭐ Entertainment

**El Lagá Tio Parrilla**  *Flamenco*
(Plaza del Mercado; show & 2 drinks €25;
🕐10.30pm Mon-Sat) A high quota of Roma
(both performers and clientele) ensures
that this place wins most plaudits for its
regular flamenco *tablaos*. Gutsy shows
rarely end without rousing renditions of
that old Jerez stalwart – the *bulería*.

# ℹ Information

**Municipal tourist office** (📞956 33 88
74; www.turismojerez.com; Plaza del Arenal;
🕐9am-3pm & 5-7pm Mon-Fri, 9.30am-2.30pm
Sat & Sun)

# ℹ Getting There & Around

## Bus

The **bus station** (📞956 33 96 66; Plaza de
la Estación) is 1.3km southeast of the centre.
Destinations include Seville (€8.90, 1¼ hours,
seven daily), Cádiz (€1.72, one hour, nine or more
daily), Arcos de la Frontera (€3.11, 35 minutes,
four daily), and Ronda (€13, 2½ hours, two daily).

## Train

Jerez' **train station** (📞956 34 23 19; Plaza de la
Estación) is an extravagantly-tiled architectural
creation. It's right beside the bus station. Regular
trains go to Cádiz (€5.95, 40 minutes, 15 daily), and
10 or more to Seville (€11, 1¼ hours, 15 daily).

# CÁDIZ

POP 125,000

You could write several weighty university
theses about Cádiz and still fall a mile
short of nailing its essence. Old age accounts for much of the complexity. Cádiz
is generally considered to be the oldest
continuously inhabited settlement in
Europe. Now well into its fourth millen-
nium, the ancient centre is as romantic as
it is mysterious, an ocean settlement surrounded almost entirely by water, where
Atlantic waves crash against eroded
sea walls, municipal beaches stretch for
miles, and narrow streets echo with the
sounds of cawing gulls and frying fish.
Come here for the seafood, surfing, and
the cache of intriguing churches and museums that inflict little, if any, damage on

Cádiz waterfront

JORGE LIZANA PHOTO/GETTY IMAGES ©

# Cádiz

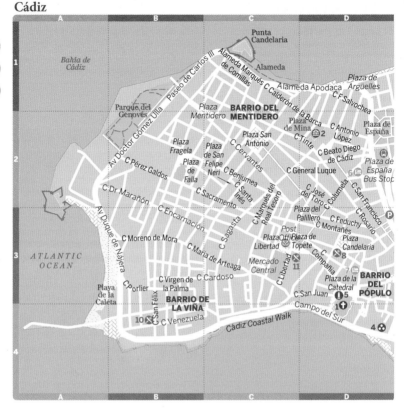

your wallet. More importantly, come here for the *gaditanos* (residents of Cádiz), an upfront and gregarious populace who have made *alegrías* (upbeat flamenco songs) into an eloquent art form.

## ◎ Sights & Activities

**Plaza San Juan de Dios**　　Square
Broad Plaza San Juan de Dios is lined with cafes and is dominated by the imposing neoclassical **ayuntamiento** (town hall) built around 1800. Between here and the cathedral is the Barrio del Pópulo, the kernel of medieval Cádiz and a focus of the city's ongoing sprucing-up program. At the nearby **Roman Theatre** (Campo del Sur; ⊙10am-2.30pm & 5-7pm Wed-Mon) FREE you can walk along a gallery beneath the tiers of seating. The theatre was discovered by chance in 1980.

**Catedral**　　Cathedral
(Plaza de la Catedral; adult/student €5/3, 7-8pm Tue-Fri & 11am-1pm Sun free; ⊙10am-6.30pm Mon-Sat, 1.30-6.30pm Sun) Cádiz' yellow-domed cathedral is an impressively proportioned baroque-neoclassical construction, but by Spanish standards very sober in its decoration. It fronts a broad, traffic-free plaza where the cathedral's ground-plan is picked out in the paving stones. The decision to build the cathedral was taken in 1716 but the project wasn't finished until 1838, by which time neoclassical elements, such as the dome, towers and main facade, had diluted Vicente Acero's original baroque plan. From a separate entrance on Plaza de la Catedral, climb to the top of the **Torre de Poniente** (Western Tower) for marvellous vistas.

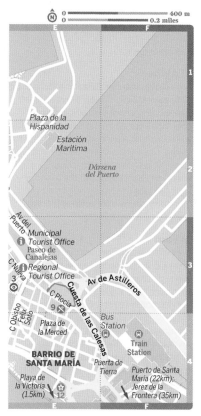

## Cádiz

Tierra. At weekends in summer almost the whole city seems to be out here. Bus 1 (Plaza España–Cortadura) from Plaza de España will get you there or you can walk along the promenade from Barrio de Santa María.

## 🛏 Sleeping

### Hotel Argantonio
Hotel €€

( ☎ 956 21 16 40; www.hotelargantonio.com; Calle Argantonio 3; d/ste incl breakfast €119/222; ❄@🛜) Welcome to a characterful, small-is-beautiful hotel in Cádiz' old quarter. The stand-out features here are the hand-painted doors, beautifully tiled floors that adorn both bedrooms and bathrooms, and the intricate Moorish arch in the lobby. The hotel has three themes: the 1st floor is Mudéjar, the 2nd floor is colonial, and the 3rd floor is a mix.

### Hotel Patagonia Sur
Hotel €€

( ☎ 856 17 46 47; www.hotelpatagoniasur. es; Calle Cobos 11; d €85-105; ❄@🛜) The newest establishment in Cádiz' old town, this sleek gem opened in 2009 and offers clean-lined modernity just steps from the 18th-century cathedral. Bonuses include its sun-filled attic rooms on the 5th floor with cathedral views and a glass-fronted minimalist cafeteria at street level.

### Museo de Cádiz
Museum

(Plaza de Mina; admission €1.50; ⏰2.30-8.30pm Tue, 9am-8.30pm Wed-Sat, 9.30am-2.30pm Sun) The Museo de Cádiz, on one of Cádiz' leafiest squares, is the best museum in the province. The ground-floor archaeology section includes two Phoenician marble sarcophagi carved in human likeness, lots of headless Roman statues, plus Emperor Trajan, with head, from the ruins of Baelo Claudia. The fine-arts collection, upstairs, features a group of 18 superb canvases of saints, angels and monks by Francisco de Zurbarán.

### Playa de la Victoria
Beach

This lovely, wide strip of fine Atlantic sand stretches about 4km along the peninsula from its beginning at the Puertas de

## ✕ Eating

### Freiduría Las Flores          Seafood €

(☎956 22 61 12; Plaza de Topete 4; seafood per 250g €3-8; ⏰9am-4pm & 8pm-midnight) Cádiz' addiction to fried fish finds wonderful expression here. If it comes from the sea, chances are that it's been fried and served in Las Flores as either a tapa, *ración* (large tapas serving) or *media ración* (small tapas serving), or served in an improvised paper cup, fish-and-chips style. You order by weight (250g is the usual order).

### Café Royalty          Cafe €

(☎956 07 80 65; www.caferoyalty.com; Plaza de la Candelaría; snacks €7-10; ⏰11am-11pm) Originally opened in 1912 on the centenary of the 1812 constitution, the Royalty was once a discussion corner for the intellectuals of the day including local boy, Manuel de Falla. The cafe closed in the 1940s, but thanks an inspired renovation by a local *gatidano* it reopened in 2012, 100 years after its initial inauguration.

Its frescoed, mirrored, intricately carved interior is – no word of a lie – breathtaking. Fantastic for brunch or a *merienda* (snack).

### El Aljibe          Tapas €€

(www.pablogrosso.com; Calle Plocia 25; tapas €2-3.50, mains €12-20; ⏰1-5pm & 8pm-midnight) Refined restaurant upstairs and supercool tapas bar downstairs, El Aljibe on its own is almost reason enough to come to Cádiz. The cuisine developed by *gaditano* chef Pablo Grosso is a delicious combination of the traditional and the adventurous – goat's cheese on nut bread with blueberry sauce, courgette and prawn lasagna...you get the drift?

### El Faro          Seafood €€€

(www.elfarodecadiz.com; Calle San Félix 15; mains €15-25; ⏰1-4pm & 8pm-midnight) Ask many *gaditanos* for their favourite Cádiz restaurant and there's a fair chance they'll choose El Faro. Close to the Playa de la Caleta, this place is at once a crammed-to-the-rafters tapas bar and an upmarket restaurant decorated with pretty ceramics. Seafood is why people come here, although the *rabo de toro* (bull's tail stew) has its devotees.

## ★ Entertainment

### Peña Flamenca La Perla          Flamenco

(☎956 25 91 01; www.laperladecadiz.es; Calle Carlos Ollero) The paint-peeled Peña La Perla, set romantically next to the crashing Atlantic surf, hosts flamenco nights at 10pm most Fridays, more so in spring and summer. It's right beside the ocean just off Calle Concepción Arenal in the Barrio de Santa María, entry is free and the audience is stuffed with aficionados. It's an unforgettable experience.

Catedral, Cádiz (p274)
G. LÓPEZ PHOTOGRAFY/GETTY IMAGES ©

# ℹ️ Information

**Municipal tourist office** (Paseo de Canalejas; ⏱️8.30am-6pm Mon-Fri, 9am-5pm Sat & Sun) Handily close to the bus and train stations.

**Regional tourist office** (Avenida Ramón de Carranza; ⏱️9am-7.30pm Mon-Fri, 10am-2pm Sat, Sun & holidays)

# ℹ️ Getting There & Around

## Bus

Comes has regular departures from the **bus station** (📞956 80 70 59; Plaza Sevilla) to Arcos de la Frontera (€6.48, 1½ hours, four daily), El Puerto de Santa María (€1.56, 45 minutes), Granada (€33, 5½ hours), Jerez de la Frontera (€2, one hour), Málaga (€25, four hours), Ronda (€15, two hours), Seville (€8.68, one hour 45 minutes), Tarifa (€8.60, 1½ hours), and Vejer de la Frontera (€5.95, one hour 20 minutes).

## Car & Motorcycle

The AP4 motorway from Seville to Puerto Real on the eastern side of the Bahía de Cádiz carries a €6.30 toll. The toll-free A4 is slower. There's a handily placed underground **car park** (Paseo de Canalejas; per 24hr €9) near the port area.

## Train

From the **train station** (📞902 240202), plenty of trains run daily to/from El Puerto de Santa María (€4.95, 30 minutes, 15 daily), Jerez de la Frontera (€5.95, 35 minutes, 15 daily), Seville (€16 one hour 45 minutes, 15 daily) and Madrid (€74, 4½ hours, three daily).

# Granada & Andalucía's South Coast

**Granada is a meeting point of worlds.** On the one hand it's a city as Spanish as any other, with the requisite tapas bars and carefree, liberal attitude. But this is also a city largely born of Islam. Its old quarter looks, tastes and smells of the exotica of North Africa, while its palaces and gardens recall a bygone age of Moorish magnificence. The feeling of two cultures colliding continues in the green valleys of Las Alpujarras, where white-washed villages with a distinctly Moroccan look sit like early spring snowfall on the lush slopes. Head to the coast, though, and everything changes. This is the land of the infamous Costa del Sol, with its mega-resorts and dirty dancing, although even here cultural and geographic gems can be found, such as the art galleries of Málaga and the crystal clear waters off Cabo de Gata.

Fuengirola, Costa del Sol (p309)

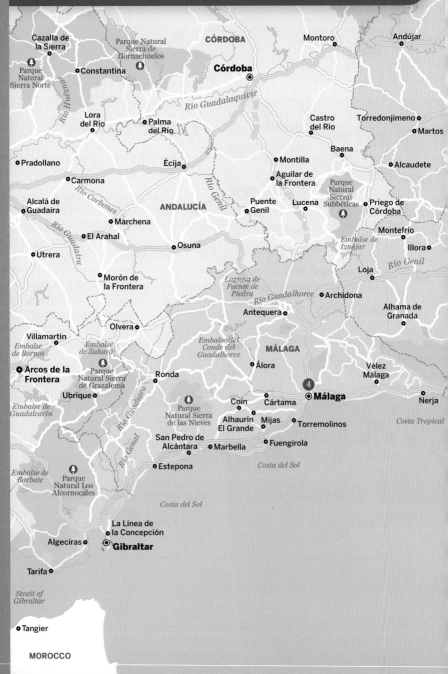

# Granada & Andalucía's South Coast

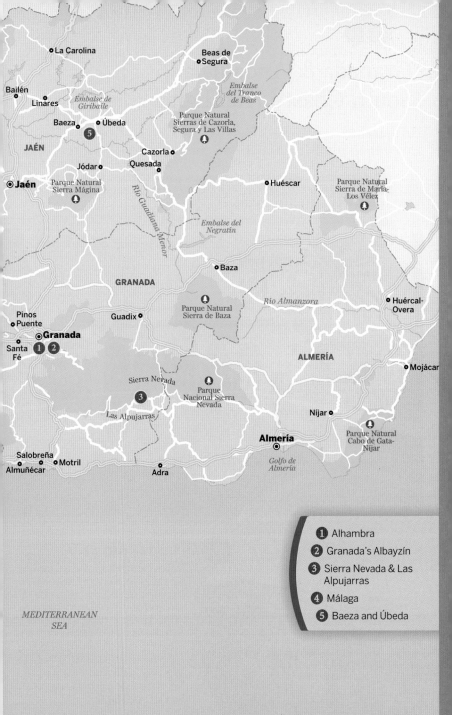

La Carolina

Beas de
Segura

Bailén

Linares

*Embalse de
Giribaile*

*Embalse
del Tranco
de Beas*

Baeza ⑤ Úbeda

Parque Natural
Sierras de Cazorla,
Segura y Las Villas 🌲

JAÉN

Cazorla

Quesada

Jódar

◉ Jaén

Parque Natural
Sierra Mágina 🌲

Huéscar

Parque Natural
Sierra de María-
Los Vélez 🌲

*Río Guadiana Menor*

*Embalse del
Negratín*

GRANADA

Baza

*Río Almanzora*

Huércal-
Overa

Pinos
Puente

Guadix

Parque Natural
Sierra de Baza 🌲

◉ Granada

Santa
Fé

① ②

ALMERÍA

Mojácar

Sierra Nevada

③

Parque
Nacional Sierra
Nevada 🌲

Las Alpujarras

Níjar

Parque Natural
Cabo de Gata-
Níjar 🌲

Salobreña

Almuñécar  Motril

Almería
◉

Adra

*Golfo de
Almería*

*MEDITERRANEAN
SEA*

① Alhambra

② Granada's Albayzín

③ Sierra Nevada & Las
Alpujarras

④ Málaga

⑤ Baeza and Úbeda

N ◉  0              50 km
     0        25 miles

# Granada & Andalucía's South Coast's Highlights

## Alhambra

The Alhambra (p290) is exceptional: the only medieval palace of its type and cultural significance to have survived anywhere in the world. This shining example of the conservation and restoration of heritage buildings displays a harmonious relationship between architecture, the landscape and its refined aesthetic. Fear not the dense crowds and the snaking queues; this is an essential pilgrimage. Palacio del Partal

**1**

## 2 Granada's Albayzín

Cobblestone streets, mosques, palaces, and plazas tinkling with the sound of fountains. Getting lost in Granada's wonderful Albayzín (p297), or old quarter, is as close to a Moroccan dream as you can get this side of Africa. Don't miss the Colegiata del Salvador, a 16th-century church sitting atop the remains of a mosque. Its fusion of Islamic and Christian design perfectly sums up Granada's history.

## Sierra Nevada & Las Alpujarras ③

The icy sentinels of mainland Spain's highest peaks lord it over Las Alpujarras (p310), a jumble of electric green valleys and scorching white, pocket-sized villages that represent some of the most breathtaking scenery in Spain. This is serious walking country, and the hiking trails here come as short and gentle or long and tough as you care to make them. Sierra Nevada

### ④ Málaga

Much maligned Málaga (p299) is the birthplace of Picasso and so therefore it only seems right that it's quietly reinventing itself from mere transit hub for the huge nearby beach resorts to a fully fledged city of art and culture with some impressive art galleries. Throw in the odd Islamic-era palace, a giant cathedral, and the ruins of a lofty castle and you get an altogether delightful, and totally Spanish, city. Plaza del Obispo

### ⑤ Baeza & Úbeda

Way out in the heart of the olive-ribbed countryside in the remote Jaén region, the twin towns of Baeza and Úbeda (p313) might be well off the standard tourist routes, but they reward the adventurous with a fabulous collection of Renaissance beauty that is almost unrivalled in Spain. The highlight is Úbeda's famous chapel, Sacra Capilla del Salvador. Sacra Capilla del Salvador, Úbeda

# Granada & Andalucía's South Coast's Best...

## Old Towns

○ **Albayzín, Granada** Nowhere else in Spain does the Moorish past feel so alive. (p297)

○ **Tarifa** Twisting, whitewashed streets and views to Africa. (p305)

○ **Málaga** Roman amphitheatre, Moorish fort and unfinished Christian cathedral. (p299)

○ **Baeza** A small town with colossal 16th-century architecture. (p313)

○ **Úbeda** Spain's most impressive collection of Renaissance buildings. (p313)

## Beaches

○ **Tarifa** Windsurfing, horse riding and acres and acres of space. (p305)

○ **Cabo de Gata** Hidden coves without the crowds. (p315)

○ **Zahara de los Atunes** Broad expanses of sand on Spain's tuna-fishing coast. (p305)

○ **Los Caños de Meca** The most laid-back beaches in Andalucía – dude. (p305)

○ **Torremolinos** Home to one of Spain's best gay beaches. (p309)

## Museums

○ **Museo Picasso, Málaga** Where better to view Picasso than in the city of his birth? (p299)

○ **Museo Carmen Thyssen, Málaga** Impressive collection of 19th-century Spanish art. (p301)

○ **Museo Ralli, Marbella** Keeping the Costa del Sol cultural with a superb private art gallery. (p309)

○ **Gibraltar Museum** Battles and sieges characterise the Rock's swashbuckling history. (p306)

# Need to Know

## Places to Connect with Nature

- **Sierra Nevada** Mainland Spain's highest mountains and one of Andalucía's two national parks. (p310)

- **Las Alpujarras** Berber-style villages and steep-sided valleys. (p310)

- **Cabo de Gata** Semi-desert landscapes and near pristine beaches. (p315)

- **Straits of Gibraltar** Watch whales and dolphins in the narrows between Europe and Africa. (p306)

### ADVANCE PLANNING

- **Three months before** Plan which festivals you'd like to visit and book accommodation in advance.

- **One month before** Reserve your entry ticket for the Alhambra.

- **Three weeks before** If it's summertime, reserve your beachfront hotel. Book flamenco tickets online.

### RESOURCES

- **Andalucía Te Quiere** (www.andalucia.org) Terrific tourist office site for the entire region.

- **Andalucia.com** (www.andalucia.com) Excellent privately run site on Andalucía.

- **Visit Granada** (www.granadatur.com) Official tourist board website for Granada.

- **Iberianature** (www.iberianature.com) Devoted to Spain's natural world.

- **Holiday in Spain** (www.spain.info) Useful official site.

### GETTING AROUND

- **Air** International airports with intra-Spain connections in Málaga, Granada and Almería.

- **Train** Renfe connects Almería, Granada, Antequera and Málaga. Private line serves Málaga, Torremolinos and Fuengirola.

- **Bus** Portillo buses link the resorts of the Costa del Sol. Alsa buses serve the main cities of Granada, Almería, Jaén and Úbeda.

- **Car** Excellent network of roads.

### BE FOREWARNED

- **Alhambra Tickets** The Alhambra has 6600 daily tickets, but just 2000 are available at the gate.

- **Resort-free coast** If you want to enjoy some quiet time on the coast, avoid the Costa del Sol and head instead to the Cabo de Gata area.

- **Spanish flavour** Coastal cities such as Marbella and Torremolinos burst with tourists, while the city of Málaga retains a strong Spanish flavour.

- **Seasonal closures** Some rural tourist businesses close temporarily in low season (January to February).

**eft:** Antigua Universidad, Baeza (p314);
**bove:** Cabo de Gata (p315)

# Granada & Andalucía's South Coast Itineraries

*Some of the contrasting classics of Andalucía are found on these itineraries. We take you from the Islamic perfection of Granada's Alhambra to chi-chi beach resorts via mountain retreats and a truly bizarre slice of 1950s Britain.*

BAEZA ⑤ ⑥ ÚBEDA

GRANADA ① ①

④ CAPILEIRA
③ BUBIÓN
② PAMPANEIRA

② MÁLAGA

③ MARBELLA

MEDITERRANEAN
SEA

④ GIBRALTAR
TARIFA ⑤

MOROCCO

**5 DAYS**

### GRANADA TO ÚBEDA
## FROM AL-ANDALUS TO THE RENAISSANCE

Any attempt to catch a glimpse of Islamic Al-Andalus just has to begin in ❶**Granada**, which served as the capital of Islamic Spain long after the rest of the country had fallen to the Christian Reconquista. Having had centuries to perfect their distinctive architectural style, Granada's Islamic rulers created the Alhambra, quite possibly one of the most exquisite collection of buildings on earth. You could spend a day in the Alhambra alone, and the Albayzín (Granada's historical and present-day heartbeat), the Capilla Real and the city's wonderful tapas culture deserve another day at least. Getting much more rural but retaining the

Moorish vibe are the snow-drop villages of Las Alpujarras. Start by heading to ❷**Pampaneira** before moving on to explore ❸**Bubión** with its interesting folk museum and finishing in little old ❹**Capileira**. As you explore these slope-hugging villages you'll be watched constantly by the mighty mass of the snow-streaked Sierra Nevada. On day four, head northeast to a drastically different era. The twin towns of ❺**Baeza** and ❻**Úbeda** owe 95% of their heritage to the Renaissance. Use Úbeda as a base for contemplating muscular 16th-century buildings and undulating fields full of olive trees.

 **5**
DAYS

**GRANADA TO TARIFA**
## CRUISING THE COSTA

In ❶ **Granada** sun-bleached streets and splashes of green are overlaid with a sense of having one foot in modern Spain and another planted firmly in the scented alleyways of a Moroccan Medina. And overlooking it all is the sublime Alhambra. Head southwest to ❷ **Málaga**, in which, with its rich history, a party-hard population and Picasso as its favourite son, it's hard not to find something to like. You're now firmly on the Costa del Sol, a place with a reputation for low-budget mass tourism and some serious tack. This may well be the case in places but come to ❸ **Marbella** and you may well find yourself rubbing shoulders

with a glitzy starlet or a high roller in a multimillion Euro yacht. ❹ **Gibraltar** has been British longer than the United States has been American, but even knowing that it comes as a surprise to discover a place that can appear more classically 'British' than Britain. Follow the coast west and you'll come to ❺ **Tarifa**, whose ancient core of sea-salt Moorish white houses contrasts beautifully with the town's modern focus on all things surfy.

View of Granada from Alhambra
ELLEN VAN BODEGOM/GETTY IMAGES ©

# Discover Granada & Andalucía's South Coast

Generalife, Alhambra (p291)
PETE SEAWARD/LONELY PLANET ©

## GRANADA

POP 258,000 / ELEV 685M

Boabdil the Moor wasn't the last departing traveller to shed a farewell tear for Granada, a city of sun-bleached streets and parched earth interspersed with soothing splashes of green, including the woods and gardens that embellish the sultry Alhambra. For those who dig deeper, Granada hides a more elusive allure. This is a place to put down your guidebook and let your intuition lead the way – through mysterious labyrinthine streets and shady Moroccan *teterías* (teahouses).

## ◉ Sights & Activities

### Catedral de Granada      Cathedral
( ☎958 22 29 59; www.catedraldegranada.com; Gran Vía de Colón 5; admission €4; ◷10am-1.15pm & 4-7.45pm Mon-Sat, 2-6pm Sun)
Granada's cavernous cathedral was an Isabel commission, but construction began only after her death, and didn't finish until 1704. The result is a mishmash of styles: baroque outside, by the 17th-century master Alonso Cano, and Renaissance inside, where the Spanish pioneer in this style, Diego de Siloé, directed operations to construct huge piers, white as meringue, a black-and-white tile floor and the gilded and painted chapel. Even more odd, the roof vaults are distinctly Gothic.

### Capilla Real      Historic Building
(www.capillarealgranada.com; Calle Oficios; admission €4; ◷10.15am-1.30pm & 3.30-6.30pm Mon-Sat, 11am-1.30pm Sun) The Royal Chapel adjoins Granada's cathedral and is an outstanding Christian building. Catholic Monarchs Isabel and Fernando commissioned this elaborate Isabelline Gothic–style mausoleum. It was not completed

# Alhambra Admission

Some areas of the Alhambra can be visited at any time without a ticket, but the highlight areas can be entered only with a ticket. Up to 6600 tickets are available for each day. About one third of these are sold at the ticket office on the day, but they sell out early and you need to start queuing by 7am to be reasonably sure of getting one.

It's highly advisable to book in advance (€1.40 extra per ticket). You can book up to three months ahead in two ways:

**Alhambra Advance Booking** ( ☏ 902 88 80 01, for international calls 0034 934 92 37 50; www.alhambra-tickets.es; ⊙9am-8pm)

**Servicaixa** (www.servicaixa.com) Online booking in Spanish and English. You can also buy tickets in advance from Servicaixa cash machines, but only in the Alhambra grounds.

For internet or phone bookings you need a Visa card, MasterCard or Eurocard. You'll receive a reference number, which you must show, along with your passport, national identity card or credit card, at the Alhambra ticket office when you pick up the ticket on the day of your visit.

Buses 30 and 32 (€1.20) both run between Plaza Nueva and the Alhambra ticket office every five to nine minutes from 7.15am to 11pm, or it's an easy and pleasant walk up the Cuesta de Gomérez from Plaza Nueva.

until 1521; they were temporarily interred in the Convento de San Francisco.

### Palacio de los Olvidados    Museum
( ☏ 655 55 33 40; www.palaciodelosolvidados. com; Cuesta de Santa Inés 6; admission €5; ⊙10am-7pm) Lest we forget, the Jews played a vital role in the glorious Nasrid kingdom of Granada that reigned from the 1200s to 1492 built on peaceful Christian, Muslim and Jewish coexistence. The aptly named 'palace of the forgotten', which opened in January 2014 in the Albayzín revisits this oft-ignored Jewish legacy. It's the second and best of Granada's new Jewish-related museums with seven rooms filled with attractively displayed relics (scrolls, costumes and ceremonial artifacts) amassed from around Spain.

### Monasterio de
### San Jerónimo    Monastery
(Calle Rector López Argüeta 9; admission €4; ⊙10am-1.30pm & 4-8pm Mon-Fri, 10am-2.30pm & 4-7.30pm Sat & Sun) One of the most stun-

ning Catholic buildings in Granada is a little out of the centre. At the 16th-century Monasterio de San Jerónimo, where nuns still sing vespers, every surface of the church has been painted – the stained glass literally pales in comparison.

 ## Tours

### Play Granada    Cultural Tour
(segway tour €30) 🌿 The make or break of a good tour is the guide and Play Granada's are truly fantastic. Even if you don't do a tour, you'll see the congenial guides buzzing around Plaza Nueva on their Segways, stopping to chat with anyone and everyone.

 ## Sleeping

### Hostal Molinos    Hotel €€
( ☏ 958 22 73 67; www.hotelmolinos.es; Calle Molinos 12; s/d/tr €53/85/115; ❄ 🛜 ) Don't let the 'narrowest hotel in the world' moniker put you off (and yes, it actually is – and has a certificate from the *Guinness Book*

# ⭐

## Don't Miss
## Alhambra

The Alhambra, once declared Andalucian poet, Federico Lorca, is where
the water from the Sierra Nevada's
bubbling streams 'lies down to die'.
Part palace, part fort, part World Heritage Site, and part lesson in medieval architecture; it is unlikely that,
as a historical monument, it will ever
be surpassed – at least not in the
lifetime of anyone reading this book.

☎ 902 44 12 21

www.alhambra-tickets.es

adult/under 12yr €14/free, Generalife
only €7

🕐 8.30am-8pm 15 Mar-14 Oct, to 6pm
15 Oct-14 Mar, night visits 10-11.30pm
Tue-Sat Mar-Oct, 8-9.30pm Fri & Sat
Oct-Mar

## Palacio Nazaríes

The central palace complex, the Palacio Nazaríes, is the pinnacle of the Alhambra's design. Highlights include the Patio de Arrayanes where rooms look onto the rectangular pool edged in myrtles, and the Salón de Comares, where the marvellous domed marquetry ceiling uses more than 8000 cedar pieces to create its intricate star pattern representing the seven heavens. The adjacent Patio de los Leones (Courtyard of the Lions), built in the second half of the 14th century has as its centrepiece, a fountain that channelled water through the mouths of 12 marble lions. On the patio's north side is the Sala de Dos Hermanas (Hall of Two Sisters) whose dizzying ceiling is a fantastic muqarnas dome with some 5000 tiny cells. A reflecting pool and terraced garden front the small Palacio del Partal (Palace of the Portico), the oldest surviving palace in the Alhambra, from the time of Mohammed III (r 1302–09).

## Generalife

From the Arabic jinan al-'arif (the overseer's gardens), the Generalife is a soothing arrangement of pathways, patios, pools, fountains, tall trees and, in season, flowers. At the north end is the emirs' summer palace, a whitewashed structure on the hillside facing the Alhambra.

## Alcazaba & Christian Buildings

The west end of the Alhambra grounds are the remnants of the **Alcazaba**, chiefly its ramparts and several towers including the **Torre de la Vela** (Watchtower), with a narrow staircase leading to the top terrace. By the Palacios Nazaríes, the hulking Renaissance-era Palacio de Carlos V built in 1527 after the Reconquista clashes spectacularly with its surroundings. Inside, the **Museo de la Alhambra** (⏰8.30am-8pm Wed-Sat, 8.30am-2.30pm Tue & Sun) FREE has a collection of Alhambra artefacts and the **Museo de Bellas Artes** (Fine Arts Museum; non-EU/EU citizen €1.50/free; ⏰2.30-8pm Tue, 9am-8pm Wed-Sat, 9am-2.30pm Sun) displays paintings and sculptures from Granada's Christian history.

> **Local Knowledge**

# Alhambra

BY MARÍA DEL MAR VILLAFRANCA, DIRECTOR OF PATRONATO DE LA ALAMBRA Y GENERALIFE

1 **FACADE OF THE PALACIO DE COMARES**
Unlike many visitors, take the time to contemplate this iconic and perfectly proportioned facade. So many of the Alhambra's signature decorative forms are on display here, including *epigrafía* (inscriptions and calligraphy), *lacerías* (interlocking wooden lengths) and *atauriques* (stylised plant motifs) in plaster and ceramics.

2 **PATIO DE ARRAYANES**
Visit here for the overall majesty, but what's special is the use of water, which is at once decorative and functional. It has the effect of making the porticos seem longer, adding a symbolic dimension and amplifying the sense of light, even as it gives the visitor the feeling that this is not just a garden but an oasis.

3 **PATIO DE LOS LEONES**
My favourite place from which to view this famous patio is from the Sala de Dos Hermanas (Hall of the Two Sisters) on the patio's northern side. This perspective reveals the glorious pinnacle of Nasrid architecture, blending the careful designs of Al-Andalus' most skilled artisans with the wider heritage of oriental art.

4 **PEINADOR DE LA REINA**
The 'Queen's Dressing Room' is like a bridge between the Islamic and Christian periods of the Alhambra. As such, it's an outstanding example of cultural synthesis, where the beautiful decorative art of the Renaissance occupies the heart of an earlier Nasrid tower.

5 **THE SPIRIT OF THE AGE**
Two corners of the Alhambra in particular give a powerful sense of what it was like to live here. The base of the Torre de la Vela conserves that spirit perfectly, while the baths are unique in enabling you to understand the social, cultural and religious practices of Al-Andalus.

# Alhambra

## TIMELINE

**900** The first reference to al-qala'at al-hamra (red castle) atop Granada's Sabika Hill.

**1237** Founder of the Nasrid dynasty, Muhammad I, moves his court to Granada. Threatened by belligerent Christian armies he builds a new defensive fort, the **Alcazaba ❶**.

**1302–09** Designed as a summer palace-cum-country estate for Granada's foppish rulers, the bucolic **Generalife ❷** is begun by Muhammad III.

**1333–54** Yusuf I initiates the construction of the **Palacio Nazaríes ❸**, still considered the highpoint of Islamic culture in Europe.

**1350–60** Up goes the **Palacio de Comares ❹**, taking Nasrid lavishness to a whole new level.

**1362–91** The second coming of Muhammad V ushers in even greater architectural brilliance exemplified by the construction of the **Patio de los Leones ❺**.

**1527** The Christians add the **Palacio de Carlos V ❻**. Inspired Renaissance palace or incongruous crime against Moorish art? You decide.

**1829** The languishing, half-forgotten Alhambra is 'rediscovered' by American writer Washington Irving during a protracted sleep-over.

**1954** The Generalife gardens are extended southwards to accommodate an outdoor theatre.

### TOP TIPS

» **Queue-dodger** Reserve tickets in advance online at www.alhambra-tickets.es

» **Money-saver** You can visit the general areas of the palace free of charge any time by entering through the Puerta de Justica.

» **Stay over** Two fine hotels are encased in the grounds: Parador de Granada (expensive) and Hotel América (more economical).

**Sala de la Barca**
Throw your head back in the anteroom to the Comares Palace where the gilded ceiling is shaped like an up-turned boat. Destroyed by fire in the 1890s, it has been painstakingly restored.

**Palacio de Carlos V**
It's easy to miss the stylistic merits of this Renaissance palace added in 1527. Check out the ground floor Museo de la Alhambra with artefacts directly related to the palace's history.

Mexuar

Patio de Machuca

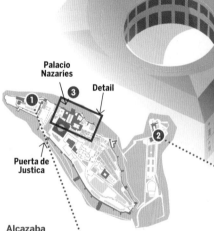

Palacio Nazaríes

Detail

Puerta de Justica

**Alcazaba**
Find time to explore the towers of the original citadel, the most important of which – the Torre de la Vela – takes you, via a winding staircase, to the Alhambra's best viewpoint.

### Patio de Arrayanes
If only you could linger longer beside the rows of *arrayanes* (myrtle bushes) that border this calming rectangular pool. Shaded porticos with seven harmonious arches invite further contemplation.

### Palacio de Comares
The neck-ache continues in the largest room in the Comares Palace renowned for its rich geometric ceiling. A negotiating room for the emirs, the Salón de los Embajadores is a masterpiece of Moorish design.

### Sala de Dos Hermanas
Focus on the *dos hermanas* – two marble slabs either side of the fountain – before enjoying the intricate cupola embellished with 5000 tiny moulded stalactites. Poetic calligraphy decorates the walls.

**Torre de Comares**

**4**

**Patio de Arrayanes**

**Baños Reales**

**Washington Irving Apartments**

**Jardín de Lindaraja**

**5**

**Sala de los Abencerrajes**

**Jardines del Partal**

**Palacio del Partal**

### Patio de los Leones
Count the 12 lions sculpted from marble, holding up a gurgling fountain. Then pan back and take in the delicate columns and arches built to signify an Islamic vision of paradise.

### Generalife
A coda to most people's visits, the 'architect's garden' is no afterthought. While Nasrid in origin, the horticulture is relatively new: the pools and arcades were added in the early 20th century.

*of Records* to prove it), there's plenty of breathing space in Molino's nine rooms, and warm hospitality in its information-stacked lobby. Situated at the foot of the Realejo, it makes an economical central option.

### Carmen de la Alcubilla del Caracol
Historic Hotel €€

( ☎ 958 21 55 51; www.alcubilladelcaracol.com; Calle del Aire Alta 12; s/d €100/120; ❄ @ 🛜 ) This exquisitely decorated place is located on the slopes of the Alhambra.

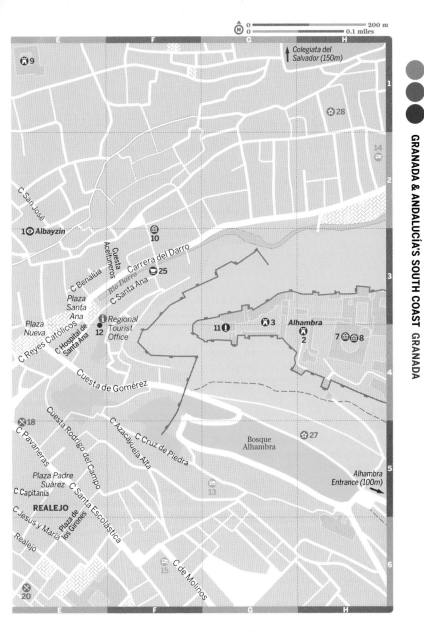

Colegiata del
Salvador (150m)

C San José

1 Albayzín

Cuesta
Aceituneros

C Benalúa

Carrera del Darro

Río Darro

C Santa Ana

Plaza
Santa
Ana

Plaza
Nueva

C Reyes Católicos

C Hospital de
Santa Ana

Regional
Tourist
Office

Cuesta de Gomérez

C Pavaneras

Cuesta Rodrigo del Campo

C Azacaya Alta

C Cruz de Piedra

Plaza Padre
Suárez

C Capitanía

C Santa Escolástica

REALEJO

C Jesus y María

Plaza de
los Girones

Realejo

C de Molinos

Bosque
Alhambra

Alhambra
Entrance (100m)

Alhambra

---

Rooms are washed in pale pastel colours
contrasting with cool cream and antiques.
There are fabulous views and a pretty
terraced garden. Ask for the room in the
tower for a truly heady experience.

### Casa Morisca Hotel

Historic Hotel €€€

(958 22 11 00; www.hotelcasamorisca.
com; Cuesta de la Victoria 9; d/ste €167/220;
❄@⎙) This late-15th-century man-
sion perfectly captures the spirit of the

# Granada

Albayzín. A heavy wooden door shuts out city noise, and rooms are soothing, with lofty ceilings, fluffy white beds and flat-weave rugs over brick floors. The least expensive ones look only onto the central patio with its fountain – cosily authentic, but potentially claustrophobic for some. The hotel is accessible by taxi.

# ✖️ Eating

### Gran Café Bib-Rambla Cafe €
(Plaza Bib-Rambla 3; chocolate & churros €4; ⏰8am-11pm; 👬) Granada's oldest cafe dates back to 1907 when the coffee beans were roasted in the square outside and the milk was brought in daily from surrounding farms. Today, the hot chocolate and churros keep locals coming back.

### Bodegas Castañeda Tapas €
(Calle Almireceros; tapas €2-3, raciónes €6-8; ⏰11.30am-4.30pm & 7.30pm-1.30am) An institution among locals and tourists alike, this buzzing bar doles out hearty portions of food (try a hot or cold *tabla*, or platter; a half order, €6, is ample for two) and dispenses drinks from big casks mounted in the walls. The best choice is a lively, herbaceous *vermut* (vermouth) topped

with soda. Don't confuse this place with Antigua Bodega Castañeda around the corner.

### La Botillería Tapas, Fusion €€
( ☎958 22 49 28; Calle Varela 10; mains €13-20; ⏰1pm-1am Wed-Sun, 1-8pm Mon) La Botillería has established a good reputation for nouveau tapas. It's a streamlined modern place, where you can *tapear* (eat tapas) at the bar or sit down for the full monty Andalucian style. The *solomillo* (pork tenderloin) comes in a rich, wine-laden sauce.

### Arrayanes Moroccan €€
( ☎958 22 84 01; www.rest-arrayanes.com; Cuesta Marañas 4; mains €15; ⏰1.30-4.30pm & 7.30-11.30pm; 🍴) The best Moroccan food in a city that is well known for its Moorish throwbacks? Recline on lavish patterned seating, try the rich, fruity tagine casseroles and make your decision. Note that Restaurante Arrayanes does not serve alcohol.

### Carmela Restaurante Tapas, Andalucian €€
( ☎958 22 57 94; www.restaurantecarmela. com; Calle Colcha 13; tapas €5-10; ⏰12.30pm-midnight) Long a bastion of traditional tapas, Granada has taken a leaf out of

PETE SEAWARD/LONELY PLANET ©

# ⭐ Don't Miss
# Albayzín

On the hill facing the Alhambra across the Darro valley, Granada's old Muslim quarter, the Albayzín, is an open-air museum in which you can lose yourself for a whole morning. The cobblestone streets are lined with gorgeous *cármenes* (large mansions with walled gardens, from the Arabic *karm* for garden). It survived as the Muslim quarter for several decades after the Christian Reconquista in 1492.

Plaza del Salvador, near the top of the Albayzín, is dominated by the **Colegiata del Salvador** (Plaza del Salvador; €0.60; ⊙10am-1pm, 4.30-6.30pm), a 16th-century church on the site of the Albayzín's main mosque; the mosque's horseshoe-arched patio, cool and peaceful, survives at its western end.

The **Arco de las Pesas**, off Plaza Larga, is an impressive gateway in the Albayzín's 11th-century defensive wall. If you follow Callejón de San Cecilio from here you'll end up at the **Mirador San Nicolás**, the Albayzín's premier (and perennially crowded) lookout, with unbeatable views of the Alhambra and Sierra Nevada. Come back here with the world and his wife for sunset, but beware of skilful, well-organised wallet-lifters and bag-snatchers.

Another well-placed lookout is the **Placeta de San Miguel Bajo**, with its lively cafe-restaurants. Close to this square off Callejón del Gallo and down a short lane is the 15th-century **Palacio de Dar-al-Horra** (Callejón de las Monjas), a romantically dishevelled mini-Alhambra that was home to the mother of Boabdil, Granada's last Muslim ruler.

Calle San José meets the top of **Calle Calderería Nueva**, a narrow street famous for its *teterías* (tea rooms), but also a good place to shop for slippers, hookahs, jewellery and North African pottery from an eclectic cache of shops redolent of a Moroccan souk.

Buses 31 and 32 both run circular routes from Plaza Nueva around the Albayzín about every seven to nine minutes from 7.30am to 11pm.

# If You Like...
## Teterías

Granada's *teterías* (tea rooms) have proliferated in recent years, but there's still something exotic and dandyish about their dark atmospheric interiors stuffed with lace veils, stucco, low cushioned seats and an invariably bohemian clientele.

**1 TETERÍA NAZARÍ**
(Calle Calderería Nueva 13) Snuggle down on the misshapen pouffes with the flamenco singers, the earnest art students and the winner of last year's Che Guevara look-a-like contest.

**2 TETERÍA LA CUEVA DE ALI BABA**
(Puente de Espinosa 15) Slightly more refined *tetería* where you can sip wine and pick at tapas overlooking the Río Darr.

**3 TETERÍA DAR ZIRYAB**
( 655 44 67 75; Calle Calderería Nueva 11)
A warm stove and regular live music provide two reasons to duck into the *Arabian Nights* interior of Dar Ziryab where amorous undergraduates share chicambas. Then there's the 40-plus teas, sweet milk shakes and lovely white-chocolate tarts.

**4 TETERÍA KASBAH**
(Calle Calderería Nueva 4; mains €8-12)
Savoury food, ample student-watching potential and amazing stucco make up for the sometimes slow service in Calle Calerería Nueva's biggest and busiest tetería.

**5 ALBAYZÍN ABACO TÉ**
( 958 22 19 35; Calle Alamo de Marqués 5; ) Hidden high up in the Albayzin maze, Abaco's Arabian minimalist interior allows you to enjoy Alhambra views from a comfy-ish floor mat. Health freaks hog the carrot juice; sweet tooths bag the excellent cakes.

Seville's book in this new streamlined restaurant guarded by the statue of Jewish philosopher, Yehuba ibn Tibon at the jaws of the Realejo quarter. Best of the new breed is the made-to-order tortilla and cured ham croquettes the size of tennis balls.

## Drinking

**Botánico** Bar
(www.botanicocafe.es; Calle Málaga 3; 1pm-1am) This eco-chic bar and restaurant dishes up healthy Med-inspired cuisine during the day and morphs into a bar and club at dusk with DJs or live music, mainly jazz and blues, after dark. Named after the peaceful botanical garden across the way, which is worth a stroll around if you are here during the day.

## Entertainment

**Peña de la Platería** Flamenco
(www.laplateria.org.es; Placeta de Toqueros 7)
Buried in the Albayzín warren, Peña de la Platería claims to be the oldest flamenco aficionados' club in Spain. It's a private affair, though, and not always open to nonmembers. Performances are usually Thursday and Saturday at 10.30pm – look presentable, and speak a little Spanish at the door, if you can.

**Casa del Arte Flamenco** Flamenco
( 958 56 57 67; www.casadelarteflamenco.com; Cuesta de Gomerez 11; tickets €18; shows 7.30pm & 9pm) Just what Granada needed. A new small flamenco venue that is neither *tablao* or *peña*, but something in between. The peformers are invariably top-notch; the atmosphere depends on the tourist-aficionado ratio in the audience.

## Information

There's a regional tourist office in Plaza Nueva ( 958 22 10 22; Calle Santa Ana 1; 9am-7pm Mon-Sat, 10am-2pm Sun & holidays).

Municipal tourist office (www.granadatur.com; Plaza del Carmen; 10am-7pm Mon-Sat, 10am-2pm Sun)

## Getting There & Away
### Air

Iberia ( 902 400500; www.iberia.com) flies daily to/from Madrid from Aeropuerto Federico García Lorca (www.aena.es), 17km west of the city. There are also flights to Barcelona and the Canary Islands, and seasonally to Paris.

## Bus

Granada's bus station is inconveniently situated 3km northwest of the city centre. Fortunately, city buses 3 and 33 run from Gran Vía de Colón to and from the bus station every 15 minutes. A taxi costs €7-9. Alsa (www.alsa.es) handles buses in the province and across the region, plus a night bus direct to Madrid's Barajas airport (€33, five hours). Other destinations include Córdoba (€15, 2¾ hours direct, eight daily), Seville (€23, three hours direct, 10 daily), Málaga (€14, 1¾ hours direct, hourly) and Las Alpujarras.

## Train

The train station (☎ 958 24 02 02; Avenida de Andaluces) is 1.5km west of the centre, off Avenida de la Constitución. Four trains run daily to/from Seville (€30, three hours) and Almería (€19.50, 2¼ hours) via Guadix, and six daily to/from Antequera (€11, 1½ hours). Three go to Ronda (€20, three hours) and Algeciras (€30, 4½ hours). For Málaga (€17, 2½ hours) or Córdoba (€36, 2½ hours) take an Algeciras train and change at Bobadilla. One or two trains go to Madrid (€68, four to five hours), Valencia (€32, 7½ to eight hours) and Barcelona (€70, 12 hours).

## ⓘ Getting Around

### To/From the Airport

The airport is 17km west of the city on the A92. Autocares J González (www. autocaresjosegonzalez.com) runs buses between the airport and a stop near the Palacio de Congresos (€3, five daily), with a stop in the city centre on Gran Vía de Colón, where a schedule is posted opposite the cathedral, and at the entrance to the bus station. A taxi costs €18 to €22 depending on traffic conditions and pick-up point.

### Car & Motorcycle

Vehicle access to the Plaza Nueva area is restricted by red lights and little black posts known as *pilonas,* which block certain streets during certain times of the day. If you are going to stay at a hotel near Plaza Nueva, press the button next to your hotel's name beside the *pilonas* to contact reception, which will be able to lower the *pilonas* for you.

## Detour:
# Huerta de San Vicente

**Huerta de San Vicente** (☎ 958 25 84 66; Calle Virgen Blanca; admission only by guided tour in Spanish €3, Wed free; ⊙9.15am-1.30pm & 5-7.30pm Tue-Sun), where Federico García Lorca spent summers and wrote some of his best-known works, is only 1.5km south of the city centre, but still retains the evocative aura of an early-20th-century country villa. Today the modern but handsome Parque Federico García Lorca separates it from whizzing traffic.

To get there, head 700m down Calle de las Recogidas from Puerta Real, turn right along Calle del Arabial, then take the first left into Calle Virgen Blanca.

# MÁLAGA

POP 558,000

The Costa del Sol can seem wholly soulless until you decamp to Málaga, an unmistakably Spanish metropolis curiously ignored by the lion's share of the millions of tourists who land annually at Pablo Ruíz Picasso International Airport before getting carted off to the golf courses and beaches of 'Torrie' and Fuengirola. Their loss could be your gain. Stubborn and stalwart, Málaga's history is as rich as its parks are green, while its feisty populace challenges *sevillanos* as 24-hour party people.

## ⊙ Sights & Activities

**Museo Picasso Málaga**     Museum
(☎ 902 44 33 77; www.museopicassomalaga. org; Calle San Agustín 8; permanent/temporary collection €6/4.50, combined ticket €8; ⊙10am-8pm Tue-Thu & Sun, to 9pm Fri & Sat) The Museo Picasso has an enviable collection

**299**

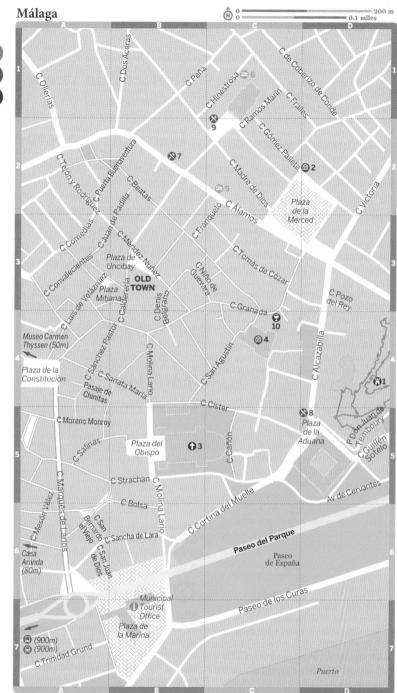

0  _____  200 m
0  _____  0.1 miles

C Ollerías

C Dos Aceras

C Peña

C Hinestrosa

6

C de Cóberizo de Conde

C Ramos Marín

C Fraíles

9

C Gómez Pallete

C Telón y Rodríguez

C Puerta Buenaventura

7

C Beatas

C Madre de Dios

2

C Victoria

C Comedias

C Juan de Padilla

C Méndez Núñez

5

C Álamos

C Franquelo

Plaza de la Merced

C Convalecientes

Plaza de Uncibay

OLD TOWN

C Niño de Guevara

C Tomás de Cózar

C Pozo del Rey

C Luís de Velázquez

Plaza Mitjana

C Calderería

C Denis

C Granada

10

C Alcazabilla

Museo Carmen Thyssen (50m)

C Sánchez Pastor

C San Agustín

4

1

Plaza de la Constitución

C Molina Lario

C Santa María

Pasaje de Chinitas

C Cister

8
Plaza de la Aduana

P Don Juan de Temboury

C Moreno Monroy

C Cañón

C Guillén Sotelo

C Salinas

Plaza del Obispo

3

C Marqués de Larios

C Strachan

C Molina Lario

C Cortina del Muelle

Av de Cervantes

C Bolsa

C Mesón-Vélez

C San Bernardo el Viejo

C San Juan de Dios

C Sancha de Lara

Paseo del Parque

Paseo de España

Casa Aranda (80m)

Municipal Tourist Office

Paseo de los Curas

(900m)
(900m)

Plaza de la Marina

C Trinidad Grund

Puerto

# Málaga

of 204 works, 155 donated and 49 loaned to the museum by Christine Ruiz-Picasso (wife of Paul, Picasso's eldest son) and Bernard Ruiz-Picasso (his grandson), and includes some wonderful paintings of the family, including the heartfelt *Paulo con gorro blanco* (Paulo with a white cap), a portrait of Picasso's eldest son painted in the 1920s.

Don't miss the Phoenician, Roman, Islamic and Renaissance archaeological remains in the museum's basement, discovered during construction works.

## Catedral de Málaga
Cathedral

(☏ 952 21 59 17; Calle Molina Lario; cathedral & museum €3.50; ☉10am-6pm Mon-Sat, closed holidays) Málaga's cathedral was started in the 16th century when several architects set about transforming the original mosque. Of the mosque, only the **Patio de los Naranjos** survives, a small courtyard of fragrant orange trees where the ablutions fountain used to be. It was an epic project plagued with problems and which took some 200 years to complete.

Inside, it is easy to see why it took so long. The fabulous domed ceiling soars 40m into the air, while the vast colonnaded nave houses an enormous cedar-wood choir. Aisles give access to 15 chapels with gorgeous retables and a stash of 18th-century religious art. Such was the project's cost that by 1782 it was decided that work would stop.

One of the two bell towers was left incomplete, hence the cathedral's well-worn nickname, La Manquita (the one-armed lady). The cathedral's **museum** displays a collection of religious items covering a period of 500 years. These include sacred paintings and sculptures, liturgical ornaments, and valuable pieces made of gold, silver and ivory.

## Alcazaba
Castle

(Calle Alcazabilla; admission €2.10, incl Castillo de Gibralfaro €3.40; ☉9.30am-8pm Tue-Sun Apr-Oct) No time to visit Granada's Alhambra? Then Málaga's Alcazaba can provide a taster. The entrance is next to the **Roman ampitheatre**, from where a meandering path climbs amid lush greenery: crimson bougainvillea, lofty palms, fragrant jasmine bushes and rows of orange trees. Extensively restored, this palace-fortress dates from the 11th-century Moorish period and the caliphal horseshoe arches, courtyards and bubbling fountains are evocative of this influential period in Málaga's history.

## Museo Carmen Thyssen
Museum

(www.carmenthyssenmalaga.org; Calle Compañia 10; adult/child €6/free; ☉10am-7.30pm Tue-Sun) One of the city's latest museums opened in 2011 in an aesthetically reno-vated 16th-century palace in the heart of the city's historic centre, the former old Moorish quarter of Málaga. The extensive collection concentrates on 19th-century Spanish and Andalucian art and includes paintings by some of the country's most exceptional painters, including Joaquín Sorolla y Bastida, Ignacio Zuloaga and Francisco de Zurbarán. Temporary exhibitions also focus on 19th-century art.

## Casa Natal de Picasso
Museum

(www.fundacionpicasso.malaga.eu; Plaza de la Merced 15; admission €3; ☉9.30am-8pm) For a more intimate insight into the painter's childhood, head to the Casa Natal de Picasso, the house where Picasso was born in 1881, which now acts as a study foundation. The house has a replica 19th-century artist's studio and small quarterly exhibitions of Picasso's work. Personal

GRANADA & ANDALUCÍA'S SOUTH COAST MÁLAGA

memorabilia of Picasso and his family make up part of the display.

## 🛏 Sleeping

### El Hotel del Pintor
Boutique Hotel €€

(☎ 952 06 09 81; www.hoteldelpintor.com; Calle Álamos 27; s/d €54/69; ❄ @ 🛜) The red, black and white colour scheme of this friendly, small hotel echoes the abstract artwork of *malagueño* (person from Málaga) artist Pepe Bornov, whose paintings are on permanent display throughout the public areas and rooms. Although convenient for most of the city's main sights, the rooms in the front can be noisy, especially on a Saturday night.

### El Riad Andaluz
Guesthouse €€

(☎ 952 21 36 40; www.elriadandaluz.com; Calle Hinestrosa 24; s/d/tr €62/89/119; ❄ @ 🛜) This French-run guesthouse, in the historic part of town, has eight rooms set around the kind of atmospheric patio that's known as a *riad* in Morocco. The

decoration is Moroccan but each room is different, including colourful tiled bathrooms. Breakfast is available.

## 🍴 Eating

### Casa Aranda
Cafe €

(www.casa-aranda.net; Calle Herrería del Rey; churro from €1; 👪) Casa Aranda is in a narrow alleyway next to the market and, since 1932, has been *the* place in town to enjoy chocolate and churros (tubular-shaped doughnuts). The cafe has taken over the whole street with several outlets all overseen by a team of mainly elderly white-shirted waiters who welcome everyone like an old friend (most are).

### El Mesón de Cervantes
Tapas, Argentine €€

(☎ 952 21 62 74; www.elmesondecervantes.com; Calle Álamos 11; mains €13-16; ⏰ 7pm-midnight Wed-Mon) Once a secret, then a whisper, now a loud shout, Cervantes has catapulted itself into Malaga's *numero uno*

restaurant among a grow-
ing number of impressed blog-
gers, tweeters and anyone else with
tastebuds and an internet connection.

### Restaurante
### Garum
Andalucian €€

(📞952 21 84 08; www.garum.com.es; Calle
Alcazabilla 1; mains €12-18; 🕐noon-5pm &
8pm-midnight Tue-Sun) Despite its location
next to the Roman ampitheatre, Garum
specialises in refreshing New Age food
dousing Málaga's signature seafood in
some rich and inventive sauces, mari-
nades and side dishes. Get your tuna
done multiple ways, or settle for your
sardines done simply and covered in the
best extra-virgin olive oil.

### Vino Mio
International €€

(www.restaurantevinomio.com/en; Plaza
Jeronimo Cuervo 2; mains €10-15; 🕐1pm-2am)
This Dutch-owned restaurant has a diverse and interesting menu that includes
dishes like kangaroo steaks, vegetable
stir-fries, duck breast with sweet chilli,
pasta and several innovative salads. Tasty
international tapas, like hummus and
Roquefort croquettes, are also available
to tantalise the tastebuds. The atmosphere is contemporary chic with regular
art exhibitions and live music, including
flamenco.

## 🍷 Drinking

### Bodegas El Pimpi
Bar

(www.bodegabarelpimpi.com; Calle Granada
62; 🕐11am-2am) This rambling bar is an
institution in this town. The interior
encompasses a warren of rooms with a
courtyard and open terrace overlooking
the recently renovated Roman amphitheatre. Walls are decorated with historic
feria posters and photos of visitors, while
the enormous barrels are signed by more
well-known folk, including Tony Blair and
Antonio Banderas. Tapas and meals also
available.

Bodegas El Pimpi (p303), Málaga

QUADRIGA IMAGES/GETTY IMAGES ©

## ⓘ Information

**Municipal Tourist office** (Plaza de la Marina; ☺9am-8pm Mar-Sep, 9am-6pm Oct-Feb) Offers a range of city maps and booklets. It also operates information kiosks at the Alcazaba entrance (Calle Alcazabilla), at the main train station (Explanada de la Estación), on Plaza de la Merced, in front of the main post office (Alameda Principal) and on the eastern beaches (El Palo and La Malagueta).

## ⓘ Getting There & Away

### Air

Málaga's **Pablo Picasso Airport** (www.aena.es), the main international gateway to Andalucía, is 9km southwest of the city centre and underwent a considerable expansion in 2010. It is a major hub in southern Spain serving top global carriers, as well as budget airlines.

### Bus

Málaga's **bus station** (☎952 35 00 61; www.estabus.emtsam.es; Paseo de los Tilos) is just 1km southwest of the city centre. Frequent **Alsa** (☎952 34 17 38) buses travel to Seville (€18 2½ hours, six daily), Granada (€11, 1¾, hourly), Córdoba (€15 three hours, four daily), and Ronda (€9.50, 2½ hours, nine or more daily). Five buses

also run daily to Madrid Airport (€25, six hours). Buses west along the Costa del Sol are handled by **Portillo** (☎952 87 22 62; www.portillo.avanzabus.com).

### Car

Numerous local and international agencies (including Avis and Hertz) have desks at the airport.

### Train

The super-modern Málaga **María Zambrano train station** (www.renfe.es; Explanada de la Estación) – the best in Andalucía – is adjacent to the bus station. Destinations include: Córdoba (€41, one hour, 18 daily), Seville (€43, two hours, 11 daily) and Madrid (€79.50, 2½ hours, 10 daily).

## ⓘ Getting Around

### To/From the Airport

**Taxi** A taxi from the airport to the city centre costs around €16.

**Train** Trains (€1.75) run every 20 minutes from 6.50am to 11.54pm to the Málaga-Renfe Station and the Málaga-Centro station beside Río Guadalmedina. Departures from the city to the airport are every 20 minutes from 5.30am to 10.30pm.

# ANDALUCÍA'S SOUTH COAST

## Tarifa

POP 17,900

Tarifa's tip-of-Spain location has given it a different climate and a different personality to the rest of Andalucía. Stiff Atlantic winds draw in surfers, windsurfers and kitesurfers who, in turn, lend this ancient, yet deceptively small settlement a laidback internationalist image that is noticeably (some would say, refreshingly) at odds with the commercialism of the nearby Costa del Sol.

## ◎ Sights

**Old Town**                                    Old Town

A wander round the old town's narrow streets, which are mainly Islamic origin, is an appetiser for Morocco. The Mudéjar **Puerta de Jerez** was built after the Reconquista. Look in at the small but action-packed **market** (Calle Colón) before wending your way to the mainly 15th-century **Iglesia de San Mateo** (Calle Sancho IV El Bravo; ⊙9am-1pm & 5.30-8.30pm). South of the church, the **Miramar El Estrecho**, atop part of the castle walls, has spectacular views across to Africa, located only 14km away.

## 🎿 Activities

**FIRMM**                                 Whale-Watching

(☏956 62 70 08; www.firmm.org; Calle Pedro Cortés 4; €30; ⊙Apr-Oct) Of the dozens of whale-watching outfits in Tarifa, not-for-profit **FIRMM** is a good bet, not least because its primary purpose is to study the whales, record data and encourage environmentally sensitive tours; unlike other operators, its trips are preceded by an introductory lecture. It also organises camps for children and runs short courses designed for children and families,

## ❤ If You Like...
## Beaches

If you like the beaches around Tarifa, you'll also appreciate the long stretches of white sand northwest along the Costa de la Luz:

**1 ZAHARA DE LOS ATUNES**
Twelve kilometres of uninterrupted sand and very little development next to the beach.

**2 BOLONIA**
A beautiful bay, a long beach, views of Africa, and Baelo Claudia, the most complete Roman town yet uncovered in Spain.

**3 LOS CAÑOS DE MECA**
A bohemian village with fine beaches around the Cabo de Trafalgar, which marks the site of the famous eponymous battle in 1805.

**4 EL PALMAR**
Almost 5km of sand with few buildings and beloved by surfers from October to May and less active beach-lovers the rest of the year.

which include daily boat trips, lectures about oceanography and dune science; multimedia shows, and snorkelling with a marine biologist.

**Club Mistral**                  Windsurfing, Kiteboarding

(www.club-mistral.com; Hurricane Hotel N340) Occupying the spot where the Atlantic meets the Mediterranean, Tarifa's legendary winds have turned the city into one of Europe's premier windsurfing and kiteboarding destinations. The most popular strip is along the coast between Tarifa and Punta Paloma, 10km to the northwest, but you'll see kiteboarders on Tarifa's town beach as well (it's a rather good spectator sport). Club Mistral offers equipment hire and classes (from beginners to experts, young and old).

# Sleeping & Eating

### Hotel Misiana
Hotel €€

(📞 956 62 70 83; www.misiana.com; Calle Sancho IV de Bravo 16; d/ste €95/200; ❄ 🛜 ) Extensively and skilfully refurbished in 2012, Misiana is the best place to stay in Tarifa if you've got the money, courtesy of its exquisite penthouse suite with private roof terrace and Africa views. Talk about taking it to a high level! With their Tarifa whiteness and driftwood decor, the doubles aren't bad either.

### Mandrágora
Moroccan, Arabic €€

(📞 956 68 12 91; www.mandragoratarifa.com; Calle Independencia 3; mains €12-18; ⏲ from 8pm Mon-Sat) Behind Iglesia de San Mateo, this intimate place serves Andalucian-Arabic food and does so terrifically well. It's hard to know where to start, but the options for mains include lamb with plums and almonds, prawns with *ñora* (Andalucian sweet pepper) sauce, and monkfish in a wild mushroom and sea urchin sauce.

## 🛈 Information

**Tourist office** (📞 956 68 09 93; www.aytotarifa. com; Paseo de la Alameda; ⏲ 10am-2pm daily, 6-8pm Mon-Fri Jun-Sep) Near the north end of the palm-lined Paseo de la Alameda.

## 🛈 Getting There & Around

**Bus Comes** (📞 956 68 40 38; www.tgcomes. es; Calle Batalla del Salado 13) operates from the small open lot near the petrol station at the north end of Calle Batalla del Salado. It has regular departures to Cádiz, Jerez de la Frontera, La Línea de La Concepción (for Gibraltar), Málaga, Seville and Zahara de los Atunes.

· · · · · · · · · · · · · · · · · · · · · · · · · · · · · · · · · · · · · · · ·

# Gibraltar

POP 30,000

Red pillar boxes, fish-and-chip shops, bobbies on the beat, and creaky seaside hotels with 1970s furnishing, 'The Rock', as it's invariably known, tends to overstate its underlying Britishness, a bonus for lovers of pub grub and afternoon tea, but a confusing double-take for modern Brits who thought that their country had moved on since the days of stuffy naval prints and Lord Nelson memorabilia. Stuck strategically at the jaws of Europe and Africa, Gibraltar's Palladian architecture and camera-hogging Barbary apes make an interesting break from the tapas bars and white towns of Cádiz province. Playing an admirable supporting role is its swashbuckling local history; lest we forget, the Rock has been British longer than the United States has been American.

# 🎯 Sights & Activities

Pedestrianised Main St has a typically British appearance (including pubs, imperial statues and familiar British shops), though you'll catch Spanish inflections in the shuttered windows, narrow winding side streets and bilingual locals who have a tendency to start their sentences in English and finish them in Spanish.

### Gibraltar Museum
Museum

(www.gibmuseum.gi; Bomb House Lane; adult/ child £2/1; ⏲ 10am-6pm Mon-Fri, to 2pm Sat) Gibraltar's history is swashbuckling to say the least and it quickly unfolds in this fine museum – comprising a labyrinth of rooms large and small – from Neanderthal to medieval to the infamous 18th-century siege. Don't miss the well-preserved Muslim bathhouse and an intricately painted 7th-century-BC Egyptian mummy that washed up here in the late 1800s.

### Upper Rock Nature Reserve
Nature Reserve

(adult/child incl attractions £10/5, vehicle £2, pedestrian excl attractions £0.50; ⏲ 9am-6.15pm, last entry 5.45pm) Most of the upper parts of the Rock (but not the main lookouts) come within the Upper Rock Nature Reserve; entry tickets include admission to St Michael's Cave, the Apes' Den, the Great Siege Tunnels, the Moorish castle, Military Heritage

TRAVEL PIX/GETTY IMAGES ©

Centre, the 100-tonne supergun and the 'Gibraltar: A City Under Siege' exhibition. The upper Rock is home to 600 plant species and is the perfect vantage point for observing the migrations of birds between Europe and Africa.

### Mediterranean Steps     Hike

Not the most well-known 'sight' in Gibraltar, but surely the most spectacular, this narrow, ancient path with steep steps – many of them hewn into the limestone – starts at the park entrance at Jews Gate and traverses around the south end of Gibraltar before steeply climbing the crag on the eastern escarpment. It comes out on the ridge meaning you can descend via the road.

## 🛏 Sleeping

### Bristol Hotel     Hotel €€

( ☎20076800; www.bristolhotel.gi; 10 Cathedral Sq; s/d/tr £63/81/93; P ❄ 🔊 🏊 ) Veterans of bucket-and-spade British seaside holidays can wax nostalgic at the stuck-in-the-'70s Bristol with its creaking floorboards, red patterned carpets and Hi-de-Hi reception staff. Arrivals from oth-er climes will enjoy the attractive walled garden, small swimming pool and prime just-off-Main-St location.

## 🍴 Eating

Goodbye tapas, hello fish and chips. Gibraltar's food is unashamedly British. The staples are pub grub, beer and sandwiches, chippies and stodgy desserts. Grand Casemates Sq has a profusion of cooler, more modern Euro-cafes, though the newest movers and shakers (including some good ethnic places) can be found in Marina Bay's spanking new Ocean Village.

### Clipper     British €€

(78B Irish Town; mains £3.50-9; ⏰8.30am-10pm; 🍴) Ask five....10....20 people in Gibraltar to name their favoure pub and, chances are, they'll say the Clipper – at least for the food. Recipient of a recent modernising refurb that has cleared out some of the stuffy naval decor, the Clipper offers real pub grub in traditionally large portions. Try the chicken tikka masala and don't leave without a dollop of sticky toffee pudding.

### Bistro Madeleine
Cafe, Bistro €

(256 Main St; cakes from £3; ⊙9am-11pm; 🛜🖊)
If you've just polished off steak and ale pie in the pub, have your dessert here, a refined, smoke-free bistro that serves Illy coffee with chunks of English-inspired cake. The toffee and date cake is outstanding.

## ❶ Information

### Electricity

Electric current is the same as in Britain: 220V or 240V, with plugs of three flat pins. You'll thus need an adaptor to use your Spanish plug lead, available for £3 to £4 from numerous electronics shops in Main St.

### Money

The currencies are the Gibraltar pound (£) and pound sterling, which are interchangeable. You can spend euros (except in payphones and post offices), but conversion rates are poor. Change unspent Gibraltar currency before leaving. Banks are generally open from 9am to 3.30pm weekdays; there are several on Main St.

### Telephone

To dial Gibraltar from Spain, you now precede the local number with the code ✒00350; from other countries, dial the international access code, then the Gibraltar country code 350 and local number. To phone Spain from Gibraltar, just dial the nine-digit Spanish number.

### Tourist Information

Gibraltar has several helpful tourist offices, with information booths at the **Airport** (✒20073026; Airport; ⊙Mon-Fri, mornings only) and **Customs House**. (✒20050762; ⊙9am-4.30pm Mon-Fri, 10am-1pm Sat).

**Tourist office** (Grand Casemates Sq; ⊙9am-5.30pm Mon-Fri, 10am-3pm Sat, to 1pm Sun & holidays) Several information desks provide all the information you need about Gibraltar, with plenty of pleasant cafes in the same square where you can read through it all at leisure.

### Visas

To enter Gibraltar, you need a passport or EU national identity card. EU, USA, Canadian, Australian, New Zealand and South African passport-holders are among those who do not need visas for Gibraltar. For further information contact Gibraltar's **Immigration Department** (✒20072500; Joshua Hassan House; ⊙9am-12.45pm Mon-Fri).

Marbella, Costa del Sol

KEN WELSH/GETTY IMAGES ©

## Getting There & Away

### Air

Easyjet (www.easyjet.com) flies daily to/from London-Gatwick and three times a week from Liverpool, while Monarch Airlines (www.monarch.co.uk) flies daily to/from London-Luton and Manchester. British Airways (www.ba.com) flies seven times a week from London-Heathrow.

### Bus

There are no regular buses to Gibraltar, but La Línea de la Concepción bus station is only a five-minute walk from the border.

### Car & Motorcycle

Snaking vehicle queues at the 24-hour border and congested traffic in Gibraltar often make it easier to park in La Línea and walk across the border. To take a car into Gibraltar (free) you need an insurance certificate, registration document, nationality plate and driving licence.

## Getting Around

Bus 5 goes from the border into town (and back) every 15 minutes on weekdays, and every 30 minutes on weekends. The fare is £1.50. Bus 2 goes to Europa Point; buses 4 and 8 serve Caleta Beach.

All of Gibraltar can be covered on foot, if you're energetic. You can also ascend to the upper Rock, weather permitting, by the cable car (Red Sands Rd; 1-way/return £10/12; ⊙9.30am-7.15pm, last cable down 7.45pm Apr-Oct, 9.30am-5.15pm, last cable down 5.45pm Nov-Mar ). For the Apes' Den, disembark at the middle station.

## Marbella

POP 136,000

Marbella is the Costa del Sol's classiest, and most expensive, resort. This inherent wealth glitters most brightly along the Golden Mile, a tiara of star-studded clubs, restaurants and hotels which stretches from Marbella to Puerto Banús, the flashiest marina on the Costa del Sol, where black-tinted Mercs slide along a quayside of luxury yachts.

## If You Like...
# The Costa del Sol

If you like golf, beach-life, wildlife parks and wall-to-wall entertainment, Spain's most touristic coastline could be your bag.

### 1 ESTEPONA
Of the big five resorts on the Costa del Sol, Estepona is the most Spanish in flavor. You don't need a particularly lucid imagination to root out the historic old town here, an attractive tangle of whitewashed streets and well-tended geraniums.

### 2 FUENGIROLA
A genuine Spanish working town that is also unashamedly touristic, Fuengirola attracts mainly Northern Europeans who arrived in the 1960s and stayed after their pony-tails went grey.

### 3 BENALMÁDENA
About 5km west of Torremolinos, Benalmádena has a youthful nightlife, large family-orientated theme parks and a penchant for a style of architecture best described as Gaudí meets Mr Whippy.

### 4 TORREMOLINOS
Chameleonic 'Torrie' was once crowded with lippy 'lager louts', but these days it's known as the most gay-friendly town in Andalucía, awash with rainbow flags and an increasingly legendary clubbing scene.

## Sights & Activities

**Museo Ralli**                    Museum
(Urbanización Coral Beach; ⊙10am-2pm Tue-Sat) FREE This superb private art museum exhibits paintings by primarily Latin American and European artists in bright well-lit galleries. Part of a nonprofit foundation, its exhibits include sculptures by Henry Moore and Salvador Dalí, and vibrant contemporary paintings by Argentine surrealist Alicia Carletti and Cuban Wilfredo Lam, plus works by Joan Miró, Chagall and Chirico.

### Museo del Grabado Español
Museum

(Calle Hospital Bazán; admission €3; ⊙10am-2pm & 5.30-8.30pm) This small art museum in the old town includes works by some of the great masters, including Picasso, Joan Miró and Salvador Dalí, among other, primarily Spanish painters.

## Eating

### El Estrecho
Tapas €€

(Calle San Lázaro; raciones €5-8; ⊙noon-midnight) It's always crammed, so elbow your way to a space in the small back dining room and order from a massive menu that includes tapas such as *salmorejo* (Córdoba-style thick gazpacho). This is one of several great tapas bars on this narrow pedestrian street.

## Information

Tourist office (www.marbella.es; Glorieta de la Fontanilla; ⊙8.30am-8.30pm Mon-Fri, 10am-2pm Sat) Has plenty of leaflets and a good town map.

## Getting There & Around

Buses to Fuengirola (€4.29, one hour) and Estepona (€4.23, one hour) leave about every 30 minutes from Avenida Ricardo Soriano. Other services use the bus station (☑952 76 44 00; Avenida Trapiche), 1.2km north of Plaza de los Naranjos.

Marbella's streets are notoriously traffic-clogged. Fortunately there are a number of pay car parks where you can take refuge on arrival.

## Nerja
POP 22,000

Nerja, 56km east of Málaga, is where the Costa del Sol becomes a little easier on the eye, with more precipitous topography and prettier vistas allowing a peek into the Spain that once was.

The town's pièce de résistance, right in the centre, is the spectacular **Balcón de Europa**, a palm-shaded walkway that protrudes out into the ocean. The new **Museo de Nerja** (☑952 52 72 24; Plaza de España; adult/child €4/2; ⊙10am-2pm & 4-6.30pm Tue-Sun, to 10pm Jul & Aug) traces Nerja's history from cave dwellers to tourist boom and acts as an ideal prelude to a visit to the enormous Cueva de Nerja, 3km north of town.

## Eating

### Oliva
Modern European €€

(☑952 52 14 29; www.restauranteoliva.com; Calle Pintada 7; mains €15-19; ⊙1-4pm & 7-11pm) Single orchids, a drum-and-bass soundtrack and a charcoal grey-and-green colour scheme. In short, this place has class. The menu is reassuringly brief and changes regularly according to what is fresh in season; typical dishes are grilled scallops in a beetroot sauce and sea bass with wasabi, soy and ginger. The toffee pud with hazelnut cream is appropriately sinful and delicious.

## Information

Municipal tourist office (☑952 52 15 31; www.nerja.org; Calle Carmen 1; ⊙10am-2pm & 3-6.45pm Mon-Fri, 10am-2pm Sat & Sun) Just off the Balcón de Europa promenade and lookout point, which has gorgeous coastal vistas.

## Getting There & Away

From the N340 near the top of Calle Pintada, Alsa (www.alsa.es) runs regular buses to/from Málaga (€4.52, 1¼ hours, every 30 minutes), Marbella (€11, 2½ hours, one daily) and Antequera (€9, 2¼ hours, three daily). There are also buses to Almería and Granada.

# SIERRA NEVADA & LAS ALPUJARRAS

True to their name, Spain's highest mountains rise like icy sentinels behind the city of Granada, culminating in the rugged summit of Mulhacén (3479m), mainland Spain's highest peak. The upper reaches of the range form the 862-sq-km Parque Nacional Sierra Nevada, Spain's biggest national park,

KEN WELSH/GETTY IMAGES ©

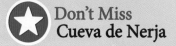

## Don't Miss
## Cueva de Nerja

The **Cueva de Nerja** is the big tourist attraction in Nerja, just off the N340, 3km east of town on the slopes of the Sierra Almijara. The enormous 4km-long cave complex, hollowed out by water around five million years ago and once inhabited by Stone Age hunters, is a theatrical wonderland of extraordinary rock formations, subtle shifting colours and stalactites and stalagmites. Large-scale performances including ballet and flamenco are staged here throughout the summer. About 14 buses run daily from Málaga and Nerja, except Sunday. The whole site is very well organised for large-scale tourism and has a huge restaurant and car park. A full tour of the caves takes about 45 minutes.

### NEED TO KNOW
www.cuevadenerja.es; adult/child €9/5; ⏰10am-1pm & 4-6.30pm, to 10pm Jul & Aug

with a rare high-altitude environment that is home to about 2100 of Spain's 7000 plant species. Andalucía's largest ibex population (about 5000) is here too. The mountains and Las Alpujarras valleys comprise one of the most spectacular areas in Spain, and it offers wonderful opportunities for walking, horse riding, climbing, mountain biking and, in winter, good skiing and snowboarding.

Below the southern flank of the Sierra Nevada lies the 70km-long jumble of valleys known as Las Alpujarras. Arid hillsides split by deep ravines alternate with oasis-like white villages set beside rapid streams and surrounded by gardens, orchards and woodlands.

GRANADA & ANDALUCÍA'S SOUTH COAST PAMPANEIRA, BUBIÓN & CAPILEIRA

## Pampaneira, Bubión & Capileira

POP 1270 / ELEV 1200–1440M

These small villages clinging to the side of the deep Barranco de Poqueira valley, 14km to 20km northeast of Órgiva, are three of the prettiest, most dramatically sited (and most touristy) in Las Alpujarras. Capileira is the best base for walks.

## ⊙ Sights & Activities

All three villages have solid 16th-century Mudéjar churches. They also have small weaving workshops, descendants of a textile tradition that goes back to Islamic times, and plentiful craft shops. In Bubión, get a marvellous glimpse of bygone Alpujarras life at the excellent little folk museum, **Casa Alpujarreña** (Calle Real; admission €2; ☺11am-2pm Sun-Thu, 11am-

2pm & 5-7pm Sat & holidays), beside the church.

Eight walking trails, ranging from 4km to 23km (two to eight hours), are marked out in the beautiful Barranco de Poqueira with little colour-coded posts. Their starting points can be hard to find, but they are marked and described on Editorial Alpina's *Sierra Nevada, La Alpujarra* map. **Nevadensis** ( ☎ 958 76 31 27; www.nevadensis.com), at the information office in Pampaneira, offers hikes and treks, 4WD trips, horse riding, mountain biking, climbing and canyoning, all with knowledgeable guides.

##  Eating

### PAMPANEIRA

**Restaurante Casa Diego**     Andalucian €
(Plaza de la Libertad 3; menu €9, mains €6.50-14; ☺10am-5pm, 7pm-midnight) Sit on the upstairs terrace here across from the magnificent 16th-century stone church

and dine on traditional meals like *conejo a lo cortijero* (rabbit stewed with garlic) and *papas a lo pobre* (fried potatoes, peppers and onions).

## BUBIÓN

**Teide Restaurant**   Traditional Spanish
(📞958 76 30 37; Carretera de Sierra Nevada 2; menús €10; ⏱10am-10.30pm Wed-Mon) Traditional Teide Restaurant has a good *menú del dia*.

## CAPILEIRA

**Bar El Tilo**   Andalucian **€**
(Plaza Calvario; raciones €8; ⏱11.30am-11pm) Capileira's village tavern enjoys prime position on a lovely whitewashed square with a terrace. *Raciones* such as *albóndigas* (meatballs in a tomato sauce) are enormous. There are also cakes and pies made daily.

## ℹ Information

**Punto de Información Parque Nacional de Sierra Nevada** (www.nevadensis.com; Plaza de la Libertad; ⏱10am-2pm & 4-6pm Tue-Sat, to 3pm Sun & Mon, Oct-Mar) Plenty of information about Las Alpujarras and Sierra Nevada; outdoor gear, maps and books for sale.

## ℹ Getting There & Away

**Alsa** (📞958 18 54 80) runs three buses daily from Granada to Pampaneira (€6, two hours), Bubión (€6.08, 2¼ hours) and Capileira (€6.12, 2½ hours).

# BAEZA & ÚBEDA

If the Jaén region is known for anything (apart from olives), it's the twin towns of Baeza (ba-eh-thah) and Úbeda (oo-be-dah), two shining examples of Renaissance beauty. Smaller Baeza has a richness of architecture that defies the notion that there is little of architectural value in Andalucía aprt from Moorish buildings. Here a handful of wealthy fractious families, made rich by the wool trade, left a staggering catalogue of perfectly preserved Renaissance churches and civic buildings.

Úbeda is a slightly different proposition to its little sister, Baeza. Exposed to the cultural influences of the Italian Renaissance and benefiting from the wealth and privilege of the powerful Molina family, the city turned out what are now considered to be some of the purest examples of Renaissance architecture in Spain.

## ◎ Sights

### BAEZA

Baeza's most extraordinary palace, the **Palacio de Jabalquinto** (Plaza de Santa Cruz; ⏱9am-2pm Mon-Fri) `FREE`, was probably built in the early 16th century for one of the Benavides clan. It has a spectacularly flamboyant facade with pyramidal stone studs typical of Isabelline Gothic style, and a patio with Renaissance marble columns, two-tiered arches and an elegant fountain. The **Antigua Universidad** (Old University; Calle del Beato Juan de Ávila; ⏱10am-2pm & 4-7pm Wed-Sun) `FREE` was founded in 1538 and became a fount of progressive ideas that generally conflicted with Baeza's conservative dominant families, often causing scuffles between the highbrows and the well-heeled. Baeza's eclectic **cathedral** (Plaza de Santa María; donations welcome; ⏱10.30am-1pm & 4-6pm Oct-Mar, 10.30am-1pm & 5-7pm Apr-Sep) `FREE` is chiefly in 16th-century Renaissance style, with an interior designed by Andrés de Vandelvira and Jerónimo del Prado.

### ÚBEDA

The purity of Renaissance lines is best expressed in the famous chapel, **Sacra Capilla del Salvador** (Plaza Vázquez de Molina; adult/child €3/1.50; ⏱10am-2pm & 4-7.30pm Mon-Sat, 11.15am-2pm & 5-8pm Sun); the first of many works executed in Úbeda by celebrated architect Andrés de Vandelvira. The classic portal is topped by a carving of the transfiguration of Christ, flanked by statues of St Peter and St Paul. The underside of the arch is an orgy of classical sculpture, executed by French sculptor Esteban Jamete, depicting the Greek gods – a Renaissance touch that would have been inconceivable a few decades earlier.

##  Eating

### BAEZA

**Mesón Restaurante La Góndola** Andalucian €€ (www.asadorlagondola.com; Portales Carbonería 13, Paseo de la Constitución; mains €8-16; ⏱11am-4pm & 8pm-midnight) A terrific local, atmospheric restaurant, helped along by the glowing, wood-burning grill behind the bar, cheerful service and good food. Try *patatas baezanas,* a vegetarian delight that mixes a huge helping of sautéed potatoes with mushrooms.

Sacra Capilla del Salvador, Úbeda

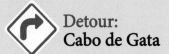

# Detour:
## Cabo de Gata

If you can find anyone old enough to remember the Costa del Sol before the bulldozers arrived they'd probably say it looked a bit like Cabo de Gata. Some of Spain's most beautiful and least crowded beaches are strung between the grand cliffs and capes east of Almería city, where dark volcanic hills tumble into a sparkling turquoise sea. Though Cabo de Gata is not undiscovered, it still has a wild, elemental feel and its scattered fishing villages (remember them?) remain low-key. You can walk along, or not far from, the coast right round from Retamar in the northwest to Agua Amarga in the northeast (61km); but beware – the sun can be intense and there's often little shade.

**Parque Natural de Cabo de Gata-Níjar** covers Cabo de Gata's 60km coast plus a slice of hinterland. The park's main information centre is the **Centro de Interpretación Las Amoladeras** (📞950 16 04 35; 🕐10am-2pm & 5.30-9pm mid-Jul–mid-Sep, to 3pm Tue-Sun mid-Sep–mid-Jul), about 2.5km west of Ruescas.

## ÚBEDA

### Restaurante Antique

Contemporary Andalucian €€€

(📞953 75 76 18; www.restauranteantique. com; Calle Real 25; mains €12-26; 🕐1-4pm & 8-11.30pm Mon-Sat) This place plays on twisting traditional recipes with modern, high-quality cuisine – try its partridge pâté with quinoa and olive-oil marmalade or wild salmon with a creamy leek sauce. The decor is fittingly understated and elegant with simple, stylish decor.

## ℹ Getting There & Away

Alsa (www.alsa.es) runs buses from Baeza to Jaén (€4.46, 45 minutes, eight daily) and Granada (€13, 2-3 hours, nine daily). There are also buses to Córdoba (€11, 2½ hours, two daily) and Seville (€23, 4½ hours, two daily).

There are similar services to Úbeda. Buses between Baeza and Úbeda run every 30 minutes (€1.16, 15 minutes).

# Spain
# In Focus

Gaudí's La Pedrera (p71), Barcelona
KIMBERLEY COOLE/GETTY IMAGES ©

# Spain Today

Plaza Mayor (p186), Madrid

> *many Spaniards are hopeful of what may lie ahead*

**belief systems**
(% of population)

**94** Roman Catholic

**6** Other (mostly Islam)

**if Spain were 100 people**

74 would speak Castilian Spanish
17 would speak Catalan
7 would speak Galician
2 would speak Basque

**population per sq km**

👤 ≈ 30 people

Spain   USA   England

## Economic Crisis

Six years after Spain's economic crisis took hold in late 2008, the country is still reeling. Unemployment, which had dropped as low as 6% as Spain enjoyed 16 consecutive years of growth, now sits stubbornly above 26%, which equates to six million people. The International Monetary Fund (IMF) says that it could be a further five years before that figure falls below 25%. Suicide rates are on the rise, Spain's young professionals are fleeing the country in unprecedented numbers and Oxfam recently predicted that a staggering 18 million Spaniards – 40% of the population – are at risk of social marginalisation within the next decade. And if all of this sounds bad, it's nothing compared with the catastrophic youth unemployment rates which recently topped 57.7%. Old-timers you speak to can't remember a time this bad, with businesses closing their doors forever, including many that weathered civil war and dictatorship down through the decades. And the government's punishing austerity drive is hardly improving the mood of Spaniards.

## A New Politics

One of the most visible responses of Spaniards to the crisis has been to get organised. On 15 May 2011, the *indignados* (those who are indignant) took over the iconic Plaza de la Puerta del Sol in the centre of Madrid in a peaceful sit-in protest. Their popularity maintained by social-media networks, they stayed for months, the forerunner to numerous such movements around the world, including Occupy Wall Street and its offshoots. Driven by dissatisfaction with Spain's major political parties – the Popular Party government is already on the nose due to a major corruption scandal, while the still-disgraced Socialists appear unelectable in the short term having presided over the onset of Spain's catastrophic economic collapse – the 15-M movement (as they are known) has set up social and political grass-roots networks across the country. These community-based networks provide social welfare, prevent the evictions of those unable to pay their mortgages, and agitate for reforms to laws that require defaulting mortgage holders to hand over their homes *and* continue paying off their mortgage. No one quite knows where it will all lead, but many Spaniards are hopeful of what may lie ahead.

TRAVELPIX LTD/GETTY IMAGES ©

## Signs of Hope?

These things are always easier to quantify in hindsight than they are at the time, but there are small signs that Spain's economy is recovering, albeit *very* slowly. After five years of contracting, the economy has begun to grow – yes, it may be at a snail's pace, and yes, it may take another decade to return to the growth rates of the pre-crisis boom years. But economists at Spain's largest banks have predicted that the economy may grow by almost 1% in 2014. Talk to business owners and many will tell you that an imperceptible shift occurred late in 2013. As one restaurant owner told us, 'people started going out to eat again. Maybe everyone just reached a point where they just threw up their hands and said, enough! Whatever the reason, there has been a change, even if it is a small one.' At the very least, the worst seems to have passed. Long may it continue.

Segovia's Roman Acueducto (p226)

CARHOVE PHOTOGRAPHY/GETTY IMAGE

*Spanish history reads like a thriller. The story begins with the great empires of antiquity, then moves on to one of the most enlightened civilisations ever to have ruled on European soil, before the rise of Christendom and its powerful kings and queens transformed Spain forever. Jump forward to the turbulent 20th century and you find a nation convulsed by a fratricidal war, whereafter the country disappeared into the long shadows cast by Francisco Franco for four decades. Since the 1970s, Spain has emerged phoenix-like from dictatorship to become a stable European democracy, although the recent worldwide recession has brought economic challenges.*

## The Phoenicians

To the Ancient Greeks and Romans, the dramatic limestone ridge at Gibraltar, together with Jebel Musa in Morocco, were the Pillars of Hercules and represented the limits of the known world. But the Phoenicians, who came before them, knew differently. From their base on what is now the southern coast of Lebanon, the seafaring Phoenicians were

### 8th century BC

The Phoenicians found Cádiz, which is Europe's oldest continuously inhabited city.

the first of the ancient civilisations to rule the Mediterranean. Not restricted by the narrow Straits of Gibraltar, they continued on along the Atlantic coast and, in the 8th century BC, established the port of Gadir, the site of modern Cádiz in southwestern Andalucía. Around 700 BC the colonists introduced iron-making technology and the Phoenician-influenced culture that developed was very likely the fabled Tartessos, mythologised by later Greek, Roman and biblical writers as a place of unimaginable wealth. Sadly, no traces remain.

## Greeks & Romans

In the 7th century BC, Greek traders arrived along the Mediterranean coast and brought with them several things now considered quintessentially Spanish – the olive tree, the grapevine and the donkey – along with writing, coins, the potter's wheel and poultry. But the Romans, who ruled Hispania (as Roman Iberia was known) for 600 years until the 5th century AD, would go on to leave a far more lasting impression. By AD 50, most of Hispania had adopted the Roman way of life.

Rome gave the country a road system, aqueducts, temples, theatres, amphitheatres and bathhouses, but they began the process of deforestation as they culled the extensive forests that in their time covered half the *meseta* (plateau). Even more than these, their cultural impact was profound. They brought Christianity to Spain, planted olive trees on a massive scale, introduced olive oil production and may even have invented *jamón* (cured ham). The basis of most of the languages still spoken here – Castilian, Catalan, Galician and Portuguese – are versions of the vernacular Latin spoken by Roman legionaries and colonists, filtered through 2000 years of linguistic mutation. The Roman era also saw the arrival of Jewish people in Spain, who were to play a big part in Spanish life for over 1000 years.

## The Celtic North

Around the same time as the Phoenicians brought iron technology to the south, the Celts (originally from Central Europe) brought it – and beer-making – to the north when they crossed the Pyrenees. In contrast to the dark-featured Iberians, the Celts were fair. Celts and Iberians who merged on the *meseta* (plateau; the high tableland of central Spain) are known as Celtiberians. Celts and Celtiberians typically lived in sizable hill-fort towns called *castros*.

### 218 BC
Roman legions arrive in Spain, initiating the 600-year Roman occupation of Iberia.

### AD 711
Muslims invade Iberia from North Africa, overrunning all but Asturias within a few years.

### 10th century
The Cordoban Caliphate reaches its zenith and the city is home to nearly half a million people.

# Islamic Spain

In AD 711 Tariq ibn Ziyad, the Muslim governor of Tangier, landed at Gibraltar with around 10,000 men, mostly Berbers (indigenous North Africans). Within a few years the Muslims (often referred to as Moors) had conquered the whole Iberian Peninsula, except small areas in the Asturian mountains in the north. Their advance into Europe was only checked by the Franks at the Battle of Poitiers in 732.

The name given to Muslim territory on the peninsula was Al-Andalus. Political power and cultural developments centred initially on Córdoba (756–1031), then Seville (c 1040–1248) and lastly Granada (1248–1492). It was during the 10th and early 11th centuries, under the independent Caliphate of Córdoba, that Al-Andalus reached the height of its power and lustre, and became famous for enlightened scholarship (it was through Al-Andalus that much of the learning of Ancient Greece was transmitted to Christian Europe) and religious tolerance. Al-Andalus also developed an extraordinary architectural legacy and developed the Hispano-Roman agricultural base by improving irrigation and introducing new fruits and crops, many of which are still widely grown today. Even in language the Muslims left strong traces and Spanish still contains many words of Arabic origin.

## The Best...
## Roman Ruins

1 Itálica (p253)

2 Tarragona (p109)

3 Segovia (p226)

4 Bolonia (p305)

## The Spanish Inquisition

An ecclesiastical tribunal set up by Fernando and Isabel in 1478, the Spanish Inquisition in Al-Andalus focused first on *conversos* (Jews converted to Christianity), accusing many of continuing to practise Judaism in secret. In April 1492, Isabel and Fernando expelled all Jews who refused Christian baptism. Up to 100,000 converted, but some 200,000 (the first Sephardic Jews) fled into exile. The Inquisitors also carried out forced mass baptisms of Muslims, burnt Islamic books and banned the Arabic language. In 1500, Muslims were ordered to convert to Christianity or leave. Those who converted *(moriscos)* were later expelled between 1609 and 1614.

### 1218
The University of Salamanca is founded by Alfonso IX, King of León, making it the oldest university in the country.

### 1236
Córdoba falls to Fernando III of Castilla, with Seville following 12 years later.

### 1478
Isabel and Fernando, the Reyes Católicos (Catholic Monarchs) establish the Spanish Inquisition.

## The Christian Reconquista

The Christian Reconquest of Iberia began in about 722 at Covadonga, Asturias, and ended with the fall of Granada in 1492. It was a stuttering affair, conducted by Christian kingdoms that were as often at war with each other as with the Muslims. An essential ingredient in the Reconquista was the cult of Santiago (St James), one of the 12 apostles. In 813 the saint's supposed tomb was discovered in Galicia. The city of Santiago de Compostela grew here, to become the third-most popular medieval Christian pilgrimage goal after Rome and Jerusalem. Santiago became the inspiration and special protector of soldiers in the Reconquista, earning the sobriquet Matamoros (Moor-slayer).

By 757, Christians occupied nearly a quarter of the Iberian Peninsula, although progress thereafter was slow. The year 1212, when the combined Christian armies routed a large Muslim force at Las Navas de Tolosa in Andalucía, marked the beginning of the end for Islamic Al-Andalus. The royal wedding of Isabel (of Castilla) and Fernando (of Aragón) in 1469 united two of the most powerful Christian kingdoms, enabling the armies of the Reconquista to make a final push. On 2 January 1492, Isabel and Fernando entered Granada. The surrender terms were fairly generous to Boabdil,

Procession celebrating the Christian Reconquista
MICHAEL TAYLOR/GETTY IMAGES ©

**1492**

Isabel and Fernando capture Granada and the Reconquista is complete. They expel 200,000 Jews who refused baptism.

**1556–98**

The reign of Felipe II marks the zenith of Spanish power.

**1702–13**

The War of the Spanish Succession sees Spain lose Gibraltar and the Low Countries.

## Why Madrid?

When Felipe II chose Madrid as Spain's capital in 1561, it was hardly the most obvious choice. Madrid (population 30,000) was much smaller and less powerful than Toledo and Seville (each with more than 80,000 people) or Valladolid, the capital of choice for Isabel and Fernando. Unlike other cities, however, Madrid was described by one king as 'very noble and very loyal': Felipe II chose the path of least resistance. Another reason was the location: 'a city fulfilling the function of a heart located in the middle of the body,' as Felipe II was heard to say.

the last emir, who was given the Alpujarras valleys south of Granada and 30,000 gold coins. The remaining Muslims were promised respect for their religion, culture and property, but this promise was quickly discarded.

## The Golden Age of Empire

Isabel and Fernando were never going to be content with Spain alone. In April 1492, Los Reyes Católicos (the Catholic Monarchs) granted the Genoese sailor Christopher Columbus (Cristóbal Colón to Spaniards) funds for his long-desired voyage across the Atlantic in search of a new trade route to the Orient. Columbus set off from the Andalucian port of Palos de la Frontera on 3 August 1492, with three small ships and 120 men. After a near mutiny as the crew despaired of sighting land, they finally arrived on the island of Guanahaní, in the Bahamas, and went on to find Cuba and Hispaniola. Columbus returned to a hero's reception from the Catholic Monarchs in Barcelona, eight months after his departure.

Brilliant but ruthless conquistadors followed Columbus' trail, seizing vast tracts of the American mainland for Spain. By 1600 Spain controlled Florida, all the biggest Caribbean islands, nearly all of present-day Mexico and Central America, and a large strip of South America. The new colonies sent huge cargoes of silver, gold and other riches back to Spain. Seville enjoyed a monopoly on this trade and grew into one of Europe's richest cities.

## Two Spains

Spain was united for the first time in almost eight centuries after Fernando annexed Navarra in 1512, and in 1519 Carlos I (Fernando's grandson) succeeded to the Habsburg lands in Austria and was elected Holy Roman Emperor (as Charles V). He ruled

### 1805

Nelson's British ships defeat a Spanish-French fleet at the Battle of Trafalgar.

### 1808-13

Carlos IV abdicates and French occupation begins, with Napoleon's brother, Joseph, on the throne.

### 1872–74

The Second Carlist War begins and the First Republic, a federal union of 17 states, collapses.

all of Spain, the Low Countries, Austria, several Italian states, parts of France and Germany, and the expanding Spanish colonies in the Americas. But the storm clouds were brewing. Colonial riches lined the pockets of a series of backward-looking monarchs; a wealthy, highly conservative Church; and idle nobility. Although some of this wealth was used to foster the Golden Age of art, little was done to improve the lot of ordinary Spaniards and food shortages were rife.

Spain's overseas possessions were ebbing away, but problems at home were even more pressing. In 1812 a national Cortes (parliament) meeting at Cádiz drew up a new liberal constitution for Spain, prompting a backlash from conservatives (the Church, the nobility and others who preferred the earlier status quo) and liberals (who wanted vaguely democratic reforms). Over the next century, Spain alternated between federal republic and monarchy, a liberal-conservative schism that saw the country lurch from one crisis to the next. By the 1930s, Spain was teetering on the brink of war.

## The Spanish Civil War

On 17 July 1936, the Spanish army garrison in Melilla, North Africa, rose up against the left-wing government, followed the next day by garrisons on the mainland. The leaders of the plot were five generals, among them Francisco Franco, who on 19 July flew from the Canary Islands to Morocco to take charge of his legionnaires. The civil war had begun.

Wherever the blame lies, the civil war split communities, families and friends, killed an estimated 350,000 Spaniards (some writers put the number as high as 500,000), and caused untold damage and misery. Both sides (Franco's Nationalists and the left-wing Republicans) committed atrocious massacres and reprisals, and employed death squads to eliminate opponents. On 26 April 1937, German planes bombed the Basque town of Guernica (called Gernika in Basque), causing terrible casualties. The USSR withdrew their support from the war in September 1938, and in January 1939 the Nationalists took Barcelona unopposed. The Republican government and hundreds of thousands of supporters fled to France and, on 28 March 1939, Franco's forces entered Madrid.

## The Best... Civil War Reads

1 *For Whom the Bell Tolls*, Ernest Hemingway

2 *Homage to Catalonia*, George Orwell

3 *Blood of Spain*, Ronald Fraser

4 *The Spanish Civil War*, Hugh Thomas

5 *The Spanish Civil War: A Very Short Introduction*, Helen Graham

6 *Soldiers of Salamis*, Javier Cercas

**IN FOCUS HISTORY**

**1898**
Spain loses Cuba, Puerto Rico, Guam and the Philippines, its last remaining colonies.

**1923–30**
General Miguel Primo de Rivera launches a coup and establishes himself as dictator.

**1936**
The Spanish Civil War begins when General Francisco Franco's rebels rise up against the elected government.

## Franco's Spain

Francisco Franco would go on to rule Spain with an iron fist for almost four decades until his death in 1975. An estimated 100,000 people were killed or died in prison after the war. The hundreds of thousands imprisoned included many intellectuals and teachers; others fled abroad, depriving Spain of a generation of scientists, artists, writers, educators and more. The army provided many government ministers and enjoyed a most generous budget. Catholic supremacy was fully restored, with secondary schools entrusted to the Jesuits, divorce made illegal and church weddings compulsory.

During WWII Franco flirted with Hitler (although Spain watched the war from the sidelines), but Spain was desperately poor to the extent that the 1940s are known as *los años de hambre* (years of hunger). Despite small-scale rebel activity, ongoing repression and international isolation (Spain was not admitted to the UN until 1955), an economic boom began in 1959 and would last through much of the 1960s. The recovery was funded in part by US aid, and remittances from more than a million Spaniards working abroad, but above all by tourism, which was developed initially along Andalucía's Costa del Sol and Catalonia's Costa Brava. By 1965 the number of tourists arriving in Spain was 14 million a year.

Artist's impression of a street battle in Madrid, 1936

**1939**
Franco enters Madrid after 350,000 people die during the Civil War; his dictatorship begins.

**1955**
Spain is admitted to the UN after agreeing to host US bases.

**1959**
ETA is founded with the aim of gaining Basque independence.

But with the jails still full of political prisoners and Spain's restive regions straining under Franco's brutal policies, labour unrest grew and discontent began to rumble in the universities and even in the army and Church. The Basque-nationalist terrorist group Euskadi Ta Askatasuna (ETA; Basque Homeland and Freedom) also appeared in 1959. In the midst of it all, Franco chose as his successor Prince Juan Carlos. In 1969 Juan Carlos swore loyalty to Franco and the Movimiento Nacional, Spain's fascist and only legal political party. Franco died on 20 November 1975.

## Spain's Democratic Transition

Juan Carlos I, aged 37, took the throne two days after Franco died. The new king's links with the dictator inspired little confidence in a Spain now clamouring for democracy, but Juan Carlos had kept his cards close to his chest and can take most of the credit for the successful transition to democracy that followed. He appointed Adolfo Suárez, a 43-year-old former Franco apparatchik with film-star looks, as prime minister. To general surprise, Suárez got the Francoist-filled Cortes to approve a new, two-chamber parliamentary system, and in early 1977 political parties, trade unions and strikes were all legalised and the Movimiento Nacional was abolished. After elections in 1977, a centrist government led by Suárez granted a general amnesty for acts committed in the civil war and under the Franco dictatorship. In 1978 the Cortes passed a new constitution making Spain a parliamentary monarchy with no official religion and granting a large measure of devolution to Spain's regions.

At a social level, Spaniards embraced democracy with all the zeal of an ex-convent schoolgirl. Contraceptives, homosexuality and divorce were legalised, and the Madrid party and arts scene known as *la movida* formed the epicentre of a newly unleashed hedonism that still looms large in Spanish life. Despite challenges such as the brutal campaign by ETA, which killed hundreds in the 1980s, and an unsuccessful

## The International Brigades

The International Brigades never numbered more than 20,000 and couldn't turn the tide against the better armed and organised Nationalist forces. Nazi Germany and Fascist Italy supported the Nationalists with planes, weapons and men (75,000 from Italy and 17,000 from Germany), turning the war into a testing ground for WWII. The Republicans had some Soviet planes, tanks, artillery and advisers, but the rest of the international community refused to become involved (apart from 25,000 French, who fought on the Republican side).

**1975**
Franco dies after ruling Spain for 37 years. King Juan Carlos I succeeds him.

**1977**
Spaniards vote in the first free elections since the 1930s, cementing Spain's return to democracy.

**1986**
Spain joins the European Community (now the EU), having joined NATO in 1982.

## ETA – A Snapshot

The first underground cells of ETA appeared in 1959 at the height of Franco's repression. ETA's founders called for independence, but their primary goal was the promotion of the outlawed Basque language, Euskera. In 1967 the old guard of leaders was ousted during an internal crisis over strategy, and a younger, more militant leadership emerged. On 7 June 1968, ETA killed a Spanish civil guardsman near San Sebastián. After several short lived ceasefires, in October 2011 ETA announced a 'definitive cessation of its armed activity'. According to the Spanish government, more than 800 people have been killed by ETA terrorism in the decades since they were formed, two-thirds of these in the Basque region.

coup attempt by renegade Civil Guards in 1981, Spain's democratic, semifederal constitution and multiparty system have proved at once robust and durable.

## Spain Grows up

The 1980s in particular saw Spain pass a succession of milestones along the road to becoming a mature European democracy. That they took these steps so quickly and so successfully after four decades of fascism is one of modern Europe's most remarkable stories.

In 1982 the left-of-centre Partido Socialista Obrero Español (PSOE; Spanish Socialist Workers' Party) was elected to power, led by a charismatic young lawyer from Seville, Felipe González. During its 14 years in power, the PSOE brought Spain into mainstream Europe, joining the European Community (now the EU) in 1986. They also oversaw the rise of the Spanish middle class, established a national health system and improved public education, and Spain's women streamed into higher education and jobs, although unemployment was the highest in Europe. But the PSOE finally became mired in scandal and, in the 1996 elections, the centre-right Partido Popular (PP; People's Party), led by José María Aznar, swept the PSOE from power.

Upon coming to power, José María Aznar promised to make politics dull, and he did, but he also presided over eight years of solid economic progress. Spain's economy grew annually by an average of 3.4%, and unemployment fell from 23% (1996) to 8% (2006). Not surprisingly, the PP won the 2000 election as well, with an absolute parliamentary majority. Aznar's popularity began to wane thanks to his strong support for the US-led invasion of Iraq in 2003 (which was deeply unpopular in Spain) and his decision to send Spanish troops to the conflict.

**1992**
Barcelona holds the Olympic Games, putting Spain in the international spotlight.

**1996**
The centre-right Partido Popular (PP), led by José María Aznar, wins national elections.

**2004 (11 March)**
Islamic terrorists bomb four commuter trains in Madrid killing 191 people.

# Zapatero's Spain

As the 2004 general election approached, Aznar handed the PP reins to Mariano Rajoy. He was pitted against the PSOE's José Luis Rodríguez Zapatero, who had successfully managed to distance himself from his party's less than pristine past. The PP looked headed for victory, but early on Thursday 11 March 2004, three days before the general election, bombs exploded on four crowded commuter trains in and near Madrid, killing 191 people and injuring 1800; 11 million people poured onto Spain's streets in demonstrations of peace and solidarity the following day. As the evidence mounted that the bombing was the work of Islamic extremists, the government continued to maintain that ETA was responsible, prompting accusations that the PP was attempting to mislead the public (by blaming the bombings on ETA) and thereby escape a backlash for its support for the war in Iraq. Three days after the bombing, the PSOE won the election. Subsequent court cases have established that the bombings were carried out by a local group of North Africans settled in Spain.

Spain's new PSOE government hit the ground running. The Zapatero government quickly pulled Spanish troops out of Iraq. It also legalised gay marriage, made divorce easier, took religion out of the compulsory school curriculum, gave dissatisfied Catalonia an expanded autonomy charter, and declared an amnesty for illegal immigrants. In March 2006, ETA, which wants an independent state covering the Spanish and French Basque Country and Navarra, declared a 'permanent ceasefire', but resumed violence nine months later with a bomb that killed two people at Madrid airport. Zapatero then called off any moves towards dialogue. A year later, parliament also passed the 'Historical Memory Law' designed to officially honour the Republican victims of the civil war and the Franco dictatorship.

The PSOE government won another four years at elections in 2008, but with a vastly reduced majority. However, the early signs of economic crisis quickly contributed to the sense of a government under siege. Zapatero's delay in acknowledging the crisis sealed the government's fate, and it was defeated by the PP, led by Mariano Rajoy, in late 2011. Despite radical austerity measures and a large EU bailout, unemployment is still hovering at around 26% and Rajoy's government faces an uphill task.

## The Best...
## Best History Museums

1 Museo & Cueva de Altamira (p159), Santillana del Mar

2 Museu Nacional Arqueológic de Tarragona (p110), Tarragona

3 Euskal Museoa (p145), Bilbao

4 Museu d'Història de Barcelona (p65)

5 Museo del Teatro de Caesaraugusta (p121), Zaragoza

## 2004 (14 March)

PSOE, led by José Luis Rodríguez Zapatero, wins a surprise election victory.

## 2011

The Popular Party sweeps to power. Spain is gripped by its worst recession in 50 years.

## 2014

After 37 years as king, Juan Carlos I abdicates and passes duties to his son Felipe.

# Family Travel

*Spain is a great place to bring your kids, not least because children are made to feel welcome just about everywhere. Children are such an integral part of Spanish life that you'll see families together in the most unlikely places, such as bars. At fiestas it's common to see even tiny ones toddling the streets at 2am or 3am. Visiting kids like this idea, too – but can't always cope with it quite so readily.*

Accompanied children are welcome at all kinds of accommodation, as well as in many cafes, bars and restaurants. Before you baulk at taking your kids into a bar, remember that Spanish bars are as much hubs of social life as they are places to drink, and with smoking in bars now illegal they've suddenly become even more child-friendly places.

Food and children are two of the great loves for Spaniards and they make for a happy combination in most restaurants. If highchairs aren't available, staff will improvise and you shouldn't be made to feel uncomfortable as your children run amok. As for the food itself, children's menus may be scarce, but Spanish fare is rarely spicy and kids tend to like it. Toddlers are usually fed straight from their parents' plate. When kids get hungry between meals it's easy to zip into the nearest *tasca* (tapas bar) and get them a snack, and there are also sweet shops every few blocks.

For more general information on travelling with children, pick up a copy of Lonely Planet's *Travel with Children* or visit the websites www.travelwithyourkids.com and www.familytravelnetwork.com.

## Sights & Activities

Many child-focused attractions (such as zoos and amusement parks) are often inconveniently located on the outskirts of cities, but most cities and larger towns have swimming pools and plentiful playgrounds. There are also some fabulous parks, including Park Güell in Barcelona and Parque del Buen Retiro in Madrid. Football-addicted youngsters will probably want to visit either FC Barcelona's Camp Nou or Real Madrid's Santiago Bernabéu. Interactive museums are another sure winner, while there's always the obvious appeal of beaches (and all the seaside activities), or the fishy lure of aquariums (seek out Oceanogràfic in Valencia or L'Aquàrium in Barcelona).

Some of Spain's best attractions for children are the CosmoCaixa in Barcelona, Casa de Campo in Madrid, whale-watching in Tarifa and the Alcázar in Segovia.

Wherever you find yourself, your first stop should be the local tourist office where staff can point you in the direction of family-friendly activities.

## The Best...
## Attractions
## for Children

1 CosmoCaixa (p70), Barcelona

2 Casa de Campo (p201), Madrid

3 Whale-watching, (p305), Tarifa

4 Alcázar (p226), Segovia

## Need to Know

**Change facilities** Extremely rare in bars and restaurants

**Cots** Available in midrange and top-end hotels, but reserve in advance

**Health** High health-care standards

**Highchairs** Many restaurants have at least one

**Nappies (diapers)** Widely available

**Strollers** Bring your own

**Transport** Trains are fine; car-hire companies (but not taxis) have car seats

# Flamenco

Flamenco performance, Cádiz

PAUL BERNHARDT/GETTY IMAGES

*Flamenco, Spain's soul-stirring gift to the world of music, provides the ever-present soundtrack to Spanish life. The passion of the genre is accessible to anyone who has heard its melancholy strains in the background at a crowded Spanish bar or during an uplifting live performance. At the same time, flamenco can seem like an impenetrable world of knowledgeable yet taciturn initiates. Where these two worlds converge is in that rare yet famous, almost mystical, moment known as* duende *(spirit), when a performer sends shivers down your spine.*

No one is quite sure where flamenco came from, although it probably owes its origins to a mosaic of ancient sources. Songs brought to Spain by the Roma people were almost certainly part of the mix, wedded to the music and verses of medieval Muslim Andalucía. Some historians argue that the Byzantine chant used in Visigothic churches prior to the Muslim arrival also played its part.

Wherever it came from, flamenco first took recognisable form in the late-18th and early 19th centuries among Roma people in the lower Guadalquivir Valley in western Andalucía. Suitably, for a place considered the cradle of the genre, the Seville–Jerez de la Frontera–Cádiz axis is still considered flamenco's heartland and it's here, purists believe, that you must go for the most authentic flamenco experience. Early flamenco was *cante jondo* (deep song), an anguished form of expression for a people on the margins of society. *Jondura* (depth) is still the essence of flamenco.

## Modern Flamenco Legends

All flamenco performers aspire to the fame enjoyed by Manuel Torre (1878–1933); Torre's singing, legend has it, could drive people to rip their shirts open and upturn tables. One man who undoubtedly achieved this aim was El Camarón de la Isla (whose real name was José Monge Cruz) from San Fernando near Cádiz. El Camarón's incredible vocal and emotional range and his wayward lifestyle made him a legend well before his tragically early death in 1992 at the age of 42.

Paco de Lucía (1947–2014), from Algeciras, was the doyen of flamenco guitarists, with a virtuosity few could match. He was also almost single-handedly responsible for transforming the guitar, formerly the junior partner of the flamenco trinity, into an instrument of solo expression far beyond traditional limits. Such was his skill that De Lucía could sound like two or three people playing together and, for many in the flamenco world, he was the personification of *duende*.

## New Flamenco

Flamenco is enjoying something of a golden age, but part of its appeal lies in a new generation of artists broadening flamenco's horizons. In the 1970s musicians began mixing flamenco with jazz, rock, blues, rap and other genres. At the forefront of the transformation was Enrique Morente (b 1942), a cult figure who enjoys rare popularity among both purists and the new generation of flamenco aficionados. While careful not to alienate flamenco purists, Morente, through his numerous collaborations across genres, helped lay the foundations for Nuevo Flamenco (New Flamenco) and Fusion.

### The Best...
### Flamenco
### Festivals

1 Bienal de Flamenco (p44), Seville (September)

2 Festival de Jerez Jerez de la Frontera (February–March)

3 Festival Internacional de la Guitarra, Córdoba (June–July)

4 Festival Flamenco, Madrid (February)

5 Suma Flamenca, Madrid (May)

## Flamenco Resources

○ **Flama** (www.guiaflama.com) Good for upcoming live concerts.

○ **Duende** (Jason Webster) Chronicles the author's gripping search for the true flamenco spirit.

○ **Camarón** (Director Jaime Chávarri; 2005) A terrific biopic of flamenco legend El Camarón de la Isla.

○ **Bodas de Sangre** (1981) and **Flamenco** (1995) These two Carlos Saura films are flamenco classics; the former is a film version of Federico García Lorca's dramatic play of the same name.

Other genres that have made their way into the repertoire of Nuevo Flamenco include rock (Kiko Veneno and Raimundo Amador), jazz and blues (Pata Negra), Latin and African rhythms (Ketama and Diego El Cigala), reggae, Asian and dance rhythms (Ojos de Brujo), and electronica (Chambao). When it comes to dance, Joaquín Cortés fuses flamenco with contemporary dance, ballet and jazz, accompanied by music at rock-concert amplifications.

## Seeing Flamenco

If you're eager to catch some live flamenco while in Spain, Seville has the widest number of regular, high-quality shows, followed by Jerez de la Frontera, Granada and Madrid.

Aside from widely advertised concerts held in large-scale arenas, the best places for live performances are usually *peñas:* clubs where flamenco fans band together. The atmosphere in such places is authentic and at times very intimate, and is proof that the best flamenco feeds off an audience that knows their flamenco. Most Andalucian towns in particular have dozens of *peñas* and most tourist offices have a list.

The other option is to attend a performance at a *tablao* (flamenco venue), which hosts regular shows put on for largely undiscriminating tourist audiences, usually with high prices and dinner included. The quality of the flamenco in *tablaos* can be top-notch, even if the atmosphere lacks the gritty authenticity of the *peñas*.

Flamenco guitarist, Seville
KARL BLACKWELL/GETTY IMAGES ©

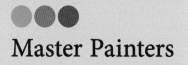

# Master Painters

*The Garden of Earthly Delights* by Hieronymus Bosch, Museo del Prado (p192), Madrid

*Spain's artistic tradition is arguably Europe's most distinguished, and its big names read like a roll-call of Western art history's elite. Although many Spanish artists deserve the term of 'master', we have restricted ourselves to Spain's Big Four. The story begins with Diego Rodríguez de Silva Velázquez and Francisco José de Goya y Lucientes, and 'ends' with two of the towering artistic figures of the 20th century: Pablo Picasso and Salvador Dalí.*

## Velázquez

No painter has come to symbolise Spain's Golden Age of the arts in the 17th century quite like Diego Rodríguez de Silva Velázquez (1599–1660). Born in Seville, Velázquez moved to Madrid as court painter and composed scenes (landscapes, royal portraits, religious subjects, snapshots of everyday life) that owe their vitality not only to his photographic eye for light and contrast but also to a compulsive interest in the humanity of his subjects, so that they seem to breathe on the canvas. His masterpieces include *Las meninas* (Maids of Honour) and *La rendición de Breda* (The Surrender of Breda), both on view in the Museo del Prado.

## Goya

Born into a modest provincial family in the village of Fuendetodos in Aragón, Francisco José de Goya y Lucientes (1746–1828) began

## The Best... Forgotten Art Galleries

1 Fundació Joan Miró (p77), Barcelona

2 Museo de Bellas Artes (p127), Valencia

3 Museo de Bellas Artes (p249), Seville

4 Museo de Bellas Artes (p144, Bilbao

designing for Madrid's Real Fábrica de Tapices (Royal Tapestry Workshop) in Madrid in 1776, but illness in 1792 left him deaf; many critics speculate that his condition was largely responsible for his wild, often merciless style that would become increasingly unshackled from convention. By 1799, Goya was appointed Carlos IV's court painter.

In the last years of the 18th century he painted enigmatic masterpieces such as *La maja vestida* (The Young Lady Dressed) and *La maja desnuda* (The Young Lady Undressed). The arrival of the French and war in 1808 had a profound impact on Goya. Unforgiving portrayals of the brutality of war are *El dos de mayo* (The Second of May) and, more dramatically, *El tres de mayo* (The Third of May).

After he retired to the Quinta del Sordo (Deaf Man's House) in Madrid, he created his nightmarish *Pinturas Negras* (Black Paintings), which now hang in the Museo del Prado. The *Saturno devorando a su hijo* (Saturn Devouring His Son) captures the essence of Goya's genius and *La Romería de San Isidro* and *El Akelarre (El gran cabrón)* are profoundly unsettling.

## Pablo Picasso

Considered by many to be the finest and most influential artist of the 20th century, Pablo Ruiz Picasso (1881–1973) stormed onto the Spanish artistic scene like a thunderclap. Born in Málaga in Andalucía, he moved with his family when still a child to Barcelona. Although he later studied in Madrid's staid Real Academia de Bellas Artes de San Fernando, it was amid the avant-garde freedom of Barcelona's Modernisme that Picasso the artist was formed.

Although best known for his weird and wonderful cubist paintings, Picasso's oeuvre spans an extraordinary breadth of styles as his work underwent repeated revolutions, passing from one creative phase to another. The best place to get an overview is Málaga's Museo Picasso.

His early style began, rather gloomily, with what is known as his Blue Period, then moved on through the brighter Pink Period; Barcelona's Museu Picasso offers an excellent collection of Picasso's early, pre-Cubist years. In 1907 Picasso painted *Les demoiselles d'Avignon,* which was strongly influenced by the stylised masks and wood carvings of Africa, and from there it was a small step to the cubist style (which involved taking objects apart and analysing their shapes), which he pioneered. By the mid-1920s he was even dabbling in surrealism. His most famous painting is *Guernica*.

### Picasso's Guernica

In the first year of the Civil War, Picasso was commissioned by the Republican government of Madrid to do the painting for the Paris Exposition Universelle in 1937. As news filtered out about the bombing of Gernika (Guernica) on 26 April 1937 in the Basque Country (by Hitler's Legión Condor, at the request of Franco), Picasso committed his anger to canvas; it was a poignant memorial to the first use of airborne military hardware to devastating effect. You can see *Guernica* in Madrid's Centro de Arte Reina Sofía (p189).

## Salvador Dalí

Vying with Pablo Picasso for the title of Spain's most original artist is Salvador Dalí. Dalí studied initially in Madrid, where he decided that the eminent professors of Madrid's Real Academia de Bellas Artes de San Fernando were not fit to judge him, and thereafter spent four years romping through the city with poet Federico García Lorca and future film director Luis Buñuel.

But Dalí belongs above all to Catalonia. He was born in Figueres, home now to the Teatre-Museu Dalí, which is one of Spain's most memorable museums thanks to its elevation of art to a form of theatre, which seems such an apt legacy for such a charismatic figure. Dalí spent much of his adult life in Port Lligat, near Cadaques, and left his mark on the Castell de Púbol, near Girona.

Dalí was a larger-than-life figure, but he was also unrelentingly brilliant. He started off by dabbling in cubism, but became more readily identified with the surrealists. His paintings are virtuoso executions brimming with fine detail and nightmare images dragged up from a feverish and Freud-fed imagination.

*La Maja Desnuda* by Francisco Goya, Museo del Prado (p192), Madrid
RICHARD NEBESKY ©

# Spanish Architecture

Detail of the Mezquita (p258), Córdoba

OLIVER STREWE/GETTY IMAGES ©

*Spain's architecture tells the story of the country's past. It is an epic tale that recalls the glories of Al-Andalus and of the sublime Romanesque, Gothic, Renaissance and baroque movements of Christian Spain, before detouring into the Modernisme of Antoni Gaudí and his Catalan cohorts. Spanish architecture's secret has always been one of constant revolution, and therein lies the story of the country's creative future.*

## Islamic Spain

Islamic Al-Andalus was, for much of its nearly 800-year history, one of the most civilised places on earth and its architects were worthy contributors to this ideal. In 756, a mere 45 years after Islamic armies first swept across the Strait of Gibraltar and at a time when Islamic rulers controlled three-quarters of Spain, Abd ar-Rahman I founded Córdoba's Mezquita. More than Spain's oldest surviving Islamic building of significance, the Mezquita was (and is) the epitome of Islamic architecture's grace and pleasing unity of form.

Hundreds of years later, with Islamic sovereignty restricted to Granada's Nasrid emirate, the Alhambra (from the Arabic *al-qala'at al-hamra,* meaning 'red castle'), came to symbolise the last-days decadence of Islamic rule. The only surviving large medieval Islamic palace complex in the world, the Alhambra is at once a palace city and a fortress, with 2km of walls and 23 towers. Within the Alhambra's walls were seven separate palaces, along with mosques, garrisons, houses, offices, baths, a summer residence (the Generalife) and exquisite gardens, but scale is only one element of the Alhambra's charm: the Nasrid architects also refined existing decorative techniques to new peaks of delicacy, elegance and harmony.

Between these two landmarks lie centuries of compelling history, but together the Mezquita and Alhambra give expression to the enduring characteristics of Al-Andalus: enlightened Islam, the opulence of Islamic rule, the imperative to defend against enemies at the gates, and the importance of gardens as a manifestation of earthly paradise. Other significant places where these elements remain include the Alcázar and Giralda in Seville, the Aljafería in Zaragoza, the Alcázar in Jerez de la Frontera, and the Alcazaba and Castillo de Gibralfaro in Málaga.

## Romanesque & Gothic

As the Reconquista gathered momentum, Spanish architects in Christian-controlled territories turned not to the Middle East but to Europe for inspiration. From the 11th century, churches and monasteries in the Romanesque style mushroomed in the north. Many of the finest extant examples are in Catalonia, especially in Girona, the monastery in El Port de la Selva and in the Pyrenean Vall de Boí.

A more elaborate Gothic style, characterised by the use of flying buttresses and other technical innovations, replaced the Romanesque; three of Spain's most important Gothic cathedrals – Burgos, León and Toledo – were all begun in the 13th century. After an interlude known as Isabelline style, pure Gothic returned in the 16th century, perhaps best exemplified by Salamanca's Catedral Nueva and the cathedral in Segovia.

## Renaissance & Baroque

The Renaissance in architecture was an Italian-originated return to classical ideals of harmony and proportion, dominated by columns and shapes such as the square, circle and triangle. Many Renaissance buildings feature elegant interior courtyards lined by two tiers of wide, rounded arcades. To visit Salamanca is to receive a concentrated dose of the most splendid work of plateresque (an early form of Renaissance) style. The university facade, especially, is a virtuoso piece, featuring busts, medallions and a complex

## Mudéjar Architecture

After the Christian Reconquista, the term Mudéjar (from Arabic *mudayan*, meaning domesticated) was given to Muslims who stayed on in areas conquered by the Christians and it came into use as an architectural label. Hallmarks of Mudéjar style include geometric decorative designs, often embellished with tiles, and elaborately carved timber ceilings. *Artesonado* is the word used to describe ceilings with interlaced beams leaving regular spaces for decorative insertions. Another unmistakable Mudéjar feature is the preponderance of brick: castles, churches and mansions all over the country were built of this material. Teruel has an especially rich concentration of Mudéjar architecture.

floral design. Another fine example of the plateresque is the Capilla de Reyes Nuevos in Toledo's cathedral.

The heady frills of baroque are a Spanish speciality, although Cádiz' cathedral is one of only a few almost-complete baroque buildings. Baroque reached new heights of opulence with the Sagrario in Granada's Monasterio de La Cartuja and the Transparente in Toledo's cathedral. Seville is jammed with gems, and the facade superimposed over the Romanesque original in the cathedral of Santiago de Compostela is also notable.

## Modernista Madness

At the end of the 19th century, Catalonia was the powerhouse of the country. Into this optimistic time stepped a group of architects known as the Modernistas. Leading the way was Antoni Gaudí (1852–1926), who sprinkled Barcelona with exotic creations such as his immense, and still unfinished, La Sagrada Família, along with Casa Batlló and La Pedrera.

Gaudí was by no means the only Catalan Modernista master to leave his mark on Barcelona. Lluís Domènech i Montaner (1850–1923), for example, was behind the stunning Palau de la Música Catalana and the Hospital de la Santa Creu i de Sant Pau.

# The Best...
# Modern Temples to Spanish Architecture

1 Ciudad de las Artes y las Ciencias (p128) Valencia

2 Museo Guggenheim (p148), Bilbao

3 Torre Agbar (p70), Barcelona

4 Barajas Airport Terminal 4, Madrid

## Contemporary Creations

More recently, international experts have been buzzing about the energy and creativity surrounding Spanish architecture, and Spanish architects such as Santiago Calatrava (who transformed Valencia and built the Olympic stadium in Athens) are taking the world by storm.

Construction has slowed almost to a halt in Spain since the economic crash, but until recently architects from all over world were clamouring for contracts with Spanish municipal governments, whose programs for urban renewal were some of the most innovative in Europe, and who were funding an extraordinary explosion of architectural ambition.

# Bullfighting

KRZYSZTOF DYDYNSKI/GETTY IMAGES ©

*An epic drama of blood and sand or a cruel blood 'sport' that has no place in modern Spain? This most enduring and controversial of Spanish traditions is all this and more, at once compelling theatre and an ancient ritual that sees 40,000 bulls killed in around 17,000 fights every year in Spain. Perhaps it was best summed up by Ernest Hemingway – a bullfighting aficionado – who described it as a 'wonderful nightmare'.*

## The Basics

The matador (more often called the *torero* in Spanish) is the star of the team. Adorned in his glittering *traje de luces* (suit of lights), it is his fancy footwork, skill and bravery before the bull that has the crowd in raptures, or in rage, depending on his (or very occasionally her) performance. A complex series of events takes place in each clash, which can last from about 20 to 30 minutes (there are usually six fights in a programme). *Peones* (the matadors' 'footmen' whose job it is to test the strength of the bull) dart about with grand capes in front of the bull; horseback picadores (horsemen) drive lances into the bull's withers and *banderilleros* (flagmen) charge headlong at the bull in an attempt to stab its neck. Finally, the matador kills the bull.

If you do plan to attend a bullfight, it's important to understand what you're about to experience. The bull's back and neck are repeatedly pierced by the lances, resulting in quite a lot of blood. The bull gradually becomes weakened through blood loss before the *torero* delivers the final sword thrust. If done properly, the bull dies instantly from this final thrust, albeit after bleeding some time from its other wounds. If the coup de grâce is not delivered well, the animal dies a slow death. The scene can be extremely disturbing.

## When & Where

The bullfighting season begins in the first week of February with the fiestas of Valdemorillo and Ajalvir, near Madrid, to mark the feast day of San Blas. Elsewhere – especially in the two Castillas and Andalucía – *corridas* (bullfights) and *encierros* (running of the bulls through town), as in Pamplona, are part of town festivals. By October, you'd be hard-pressed to find a *corrida* anywhere in the country.

# The Bullfighting Debate

The popular image of Spain would have us all believe that every Spaniard is a die-hard bullfighting fan, but this couldn't be any further from the truth. While bullfighting remains strong in some parts of the country, notably Andalucía, in other areas such as Galicia, Cantabria and other northern regions it's never really been a part of local culture. A recent poll found that just 17% of Spaniards under 25 had any interest in bullfighting, compared with 41% of those aged over 64. Similar polls suggest that three-quarters of Spaniards have no interest in the sport.

Today there's a large, growing antibullfighting movement in Spain. The government has banned children under 14 from attending bullfights, and state-run TV stopped broadcasting live coverage of bullfights for six years in 2006 (this latter decision was overturned by the newly elected Popular Party government in 2012, and live broadcasts of bullfighting resumed on the state-run channel). The bullfighting world was given a further blow when the Catalan government's ban on bullfighting officially became law on 1 January 2012. On the flip side, though, bullfighting does still have some fans in high places. In 2008 around €600 million of public money, including some from European funds, was given to the bullfight breeding industry, and King Juan Carlos is on record as saying: 'The day the EU bans bullfighting is the day Spain leaves the EU'.

That this is a debate at all in Spain owes a little to bullfighting's waning popularity and arguably more to the country's growing integration with the rest of Europe since Spain's return of democracy in the late 1970s. The fall in bullfighting's popularity has fostered some antibullfighting organisations, such as the Madrid-based **Equanimal (www.equanimal. org)**. But the greatest impetus has come from groups beyond Spanish shores, such as the **League Against Cruel Sports** (www.leagueagainstcruelsports.org). For information on creative protests against bullfighting, see www.runningofthenudes.com.

# The Spanish Kitchen

Seafood paella

DAVID SUTHERLAND/GETTY IMAGES ©

*Spanish cuisine is all the rage around the world – and no wonder. Uniquely Spanish ways of eating (such as tapas), the enduring appeal of Spanish staples (including jamón, paella and olive oil) and the astonishing regional varieties partly explain the phenomenon. But sheer culinary excellence wedded to the new wave of innovation that has taken hold in the Basque Country, Catalonia and elsewhere have taken Spanish cuisine to a whole new level.*

## Eating Like a Local

Spanish cuisine is one of Europe's most accessible. But sometimes the first-time visitor can feel so overwhelmed about what to eat, when to eat it and how to order it that they head instead for the nearest tourist restaurant and consequently end up never really experiencing proper Spanish cuisine.

Spaniards are usually so utterly absorbed in having a good time that you're unlikely to stand out if you're unsure what to do. And, despite first impressions, knowing what to do is easy. For a start, take your time to look around at what other people are eating, and don't hesitate to point to someone else's plate when ordering – Spaniards do this all the time. Another important weapon in your armoury is to repeat that well-worn Spanish mantra when entering a bar: '*¿Cuál es la especialidad de la casa?*' ('What's the house speciality?'). Most bars do most things well, but the chances are that locals come here for one or two dishes in particular. Even if you don't understand what the dish is, just go ahead and order it.

## Ways of Eating

Most visitors complain not about the quality of Spanish food but about its timing. Outside of the regular business hours, many bars serve tapas throughout the day. Bocadillos (bread rolls with filling) are another convenient option. Once you do find a bar or restaurant that's open when you're hungry, the typical *carta* (menu) begins with starters such as *ensaladas* (salads), *sopas* (soups) and *entremeses* (hors d'oeuvres). If you can't face a full menu, the *plato combinado* is a meat-and-three-veg dish.

## The Art of Eating Tapas

Too many travellers miss out on the joys of tapas because, unless you speak Spanish, the art of ordering can seem one of the dark arts of Spanish etiquette. Fear not – it's not as difficult as it first appears.

In the Basque Country, Zaragoza and many bars in Madrid, Barcelona and elsewhere, it couldn't be easier. With so many tapas varieties lined up along the bar, you either take a small plate and help yourself, or point to the morsel you want. It's customary to keep track of what you eat. Otherwise, many places have a list of tapas, either on the menu or posted up behind the bar. If you can't choose, ask for *la especialidad de la casa* (the house speciality) and it's hard to go wrong. Another way of ordering tapas is to order *raciones* (literally 'rations'; large tapas servings) or *media raciones* (half-rations; smaller tapas servings). These plates and half-plates of a particular dish are a good way to go if you particularly like something and want a little bit more than a single piece. Remember, however, that after a couple of *raciones* you'll almost certainly be full. In some bars you'll also get a small (free) *tapa* when you buy a drink – but this is very much the exception to the rule.

## The Laws Of Spanish Cooking

The laws of traditional Spanish cooking are deceptively simple: take the freshest ingredients and interfere with them as little as possible.

If simplicity is the cornerstone of Spanish cooking, it's the innovation and nouvelle cuisine emerging from Spanish kitchens that has truly taken the world by storm. Celebrity chefs such as Ferran Adrià and Mari Arzak have developed their own culinary

## Menú del Día

To cap prices at lunchtime Monday to Friday, order the *menú del día,* a three-course set menu that includes water, bread and a drink (usually €10 and up). You'll be given a menu with five or six starters, the same number of mains, and a handful of desserts – choose one from each category. Few working Spaniards have time to go home for lunch and taking a packed lunch is just not the done thing. The *menú del día* allows them to eat home-style food without breaking the bank.

laboratories, experimenting with all that's new, but always with a base rooted in traditional Spanish cuisine.

## Icons of the Spanish Kitchen

The list of signature Spanish dishes and ingredients, not to mention their regional variations, could fill encyclopedias. But if we had to choose just three culinary icons, they would be olive oil, *jamón* (cured ham) and paella.

### Olive Oil

Andalucía is the olive oil capital of the world. There are over 100 million olive trees in Andalucía and a remarkable 20% of the world's olive oil originates in Jaén province. *Aceite de oliva* (olive oil) will appear in just about every dish you order while in Spain – it's a standard base for cooking, is used to dress all manner of salads, and breakfast for many Spaniards includes toasted bread drizzled with olive oil and rubbed with tomato and garlic.

### Jamón

Spaniards are devoted to their cured meats (such as chorizo, *salchichón* and *lomo*), but *jamón* (ham) is Spain's true culinary constant and one of the few things that unites the country. The best *jamón* comes from Andalucía (especially around Jabugo in Huelva province), around Salamanca, and Aragón.

*Jamón serrano* (which accounts for approximately 90% of cured ham in Spain) refers to *jamón* made from white-coated pigs introduced to Spain in the 1950s. *Jamón ibérico* – the more expensive and the elite of Spanish hams – comes from a black-coated pig indigenous to the Iberian Peninsula and a descendant of the wild boar.

### Paella

Easily Spain's best-known culinary export, paella well deserves its fame. The base of a good paella always includes short-grain rice, garlic, parsley, olive oil and saffron. The best rice is the *bomba* variety, which opens out accordion fashion when cooked, allowing for maximum absorption while remaining firm. Paella should be cooked in a large shallow pan to enable maximum contact with the bottom of the pan where most of the flavour resides. The main paella staples are *paella valenciana* (from Valencia, where paella has its roots), which is cooked with chicken, white beans and sometimes rabbit, and the more widespread *paella de mariscos* (seafood paella), which should be bursting with shellfish. In most restaurants, ordering a paella requires a minimum of two people.

For all paella's fame, a *really* good paella can be surprisingly hard to come by in Spanish restaurants. This is partly because saffron is extremely expensive, prompting many restaurants to cut corners by using yellow dye number 2. It's also because many restaurants play on the fact that every second foreign visitor to Spain will order a paella while in the country, but few will have any idea about what a good paella should taste like. Spaniards are much more discerning when it comes to their national dish, so check out the clientele before sitting down.

# Practical Information

Throughout this book, restaurant listings are ordered first by price indicator (starting with €) and then by the author's preference, and the following price ranges refer to a standard main dish:

€      less than €10

€€    from €10 to €20

€€€  more than €20

Restaurant hours in Spain are approximately lunch from 1pm to 4pm, and dinner from 8.30pm to midnight or later.

## Spanish Wine

Spaniards invariably accompany their meal with a Spanish wine.

Probably the most common premium red table wine you'll encounter will be from La Rioja, in the north. Its wine is smooth and fruity, seldom as dry as its supposed French counterpart; look for the 'DOC Rioja' classification on the label and you'll find a good wine.

Not far behind are the wine-producing regions of Ribera del Duero in Castilla y León, Navarra, the Somontano wines of Aragón, and the Valdepeñas region of southern Castilla-La Mancha. The latter is famous for the quantity, rather than quality, of wine it produces, but is generally well priced and remains popular. For white wines, the Ribeiro wines of Galicia are well regarded.

## Regional Variations

The Basque Country and Catalonia are Spain's undoubted culinary superstars. Elsewhere, Andalucía, Aragón, Galicia and much of the Spanish interior are considered the bastions of traditional cuisine, while Madrid has risen above the mediocrity of its home-grown culinary traditions to be the place where you can get the best of regional specialities from around Spain.

In the Spanish interior, meats are a much-loved mainstay. Above all else, these include *cochinillo asado* (roast suckling pig) in Segovia, *cordero asado* (roast lamb) in most of Castilla y León, and the steaks of Ávila, inland Andalucía or the Basque Country. Around the coast, there are few creatures from the sea that Spaniards don't eat, from the Atlantic seafood of Galicia (*pulpo gallego,* or spicy boiled octopus, is the most famous dish) to the fried fish of Andalucía, and the seafood-based rice dishes of Catalonia or the Balearic Islands.

# Survival Guide

Lake in the Picos de Europa (p165)
FLASH PARKER/GETTY IMAGES ©

# A-Z

## Directory

●●●

## Accommodation

Spain's accommodation is generally of a high standard, from small, family-run *hostales* (budget hotels) to the old-world opulence of *paradores* (state-owned hotels).

Officially, places to stay are classified into *hoteles* (hotels; one to five stars), *hostales* (one to three stars) and *pensiones* (basically small private *hostales*, often family businesses in rambling apartments; one or two stars). These are the categories used by the annual *Guía Oficial de Hoteles*, sold in bookshops, which lists almost every such establishment in Spain (except for one-star *pensiones*), with approximate prices. Tourist offices and their websites also have lists of local accommodation options.

Checkout time in most establishments is noon.

### Reservations

Although there's usually no need to book ahead for a room in the low or shoulder seasons, booking ahead is generally a good idea, if for no other reason than to avoid a wearisome search for a room. Most places will ask for a credit-card number or will hold the room for you until 6pm unless you let them know that you'll be arriving later.

### Seasons

Prices throughout this guidebook are generally high-season maximums. You may be pleasantly surprised if you travel at other times. What constitutes low or high season depends on where and when. Most of the year is high season in Barcelona or Madrid, especially during trade fairs that you're unlikely to know about. August can be dead in the cities, but high season along the coast. Winter is high season in the ski resorts of the Pyrenees and low season in the Balearic Islands (indeed, the islands seem to shut down between November and Easter).

Finding a place to stay without booking ahead in July and August in the Balearics and elsewhere along the Mediterranean Coast can be difficult and many places require a minimum stay of at least two nights during high season. Weekends are high season for boutique hotels and *casas rurales* (rural homes), but low season for business hotels (which often offer generous specials) in Madrid and Barcelona. Always check out hotel websites for discounts.

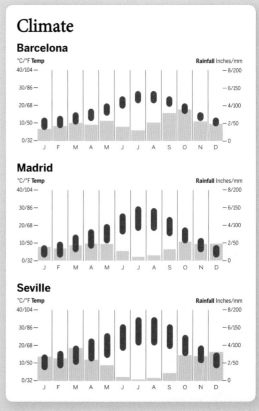

## Climate

### Barcelona

### Madrid

### Seville

## Book Your Stay Online

For more accommodation reviews by Lonely Planet authors, check out http://hotels.lonelyplanet.com. You'll find independent reviews, as well as recommendations on the best places to stay. Best of all, you can book online.

## Price Ranges

Throughout this guidebook, accommodation listings are grouped according to price bracket. Establishments within each bracket are then listed in order of author preference. Each place to stay is accompanied by one of the following symbols (the price refers to a double room with private bathroom):

- o **€** less than €65
- o **€€** from €65 to €140
- o **€€€** more than €140

The price ranges for Madrid and Barcelona are inevitably higher:

- o **€** less than €75
- o **€€** from €75 to €200
- o **€€€** more than €200

## Customs Regulations

Duty-free allowances for travellers entering Spain from outside the EU include 2L of wine (or 1L of wine and 1L of spirits), and 200 cigarettes or 50 cigars or 250g of tobacco.

There are no restrictions on the import of duty-paid items into Spain from other EU countries for personal use. You *can* buy IVA-free articles at airport shops when travelling between EU countries.

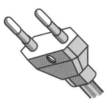

# Electricity

230V/50Hz

240V/50Hz

Electrical plugs in Spain can also be round, but will always have two round pins. The second image is for Gibraltar.

## Food

Throughout this book, restaurants are grouped according to price range (€ to €€€). The order within each of those ranges follows the author's preference. The following price brackets refer to a standard main dish:

- o **€** less than €10
- o **€€** from €10 to €20
- o **€€€** more than €20

# Gay & Lesbian Travellers

Homosexuality is legal in Spain and the age of consent is 13, as it is for heterosexuals. In 2005 the Socialist president, José Luis Rodríguez Zapatero, gave the country's conservative Catholic foundations a shake with the legalisation of same-sex marriages in Spain.

Lesbians and gay men generally keep a fairly low profile, but are quite open in the cities. Madrid, Barcelona, Sitges, Torremolinos and Ibiza have particularly lively scenes. Sitges is a major destination on the international gay party circuit; gays take a leading role in the wild **Carnaval** (www.sitges.com/carnaval) there in February/March. As well, there are gay parades, marches and events in several cities on and around

# Practicalities

- **Currency** Euro

- **Electric current** 220V, 50Hz

- **Smoking** Banned in all enclosed public spaces.

- **Weights & measures** Metric

- **Major newspapers** Centre-left *El País* (www.elpais.com), centre-right *El Mundo* (www.elmundo.es), and right-wing *ABC* (www.abc.es). The widely available *International New York Times* includes an eight-page supplement of articles from *El País* translated into English, or check out elpais.com/elpais/inenglish.html.

- **Radio** Radio Nacional de España (RNE) has Radio 1, with general interest and current-affairs programs; Radio 5, with sport and entertainment; and Radio 3 (Radio d'Espop). Stations covering current affairs include the left-leaning Cadena Ser, or the right-wing COPE. The most popular commercial pop and rock stations are 40 Principales, Kiss FM, Cadena 100 and Onda Cero.

- **TV** Spain's state-run Televisión Española (TVE1 and La 2) or the independent commercial stations (Antena 3, Tele 5, Cuatro and La Sexta). Regional governments run local stations, such as Madrid's Telemadrid, Catalonia's TV-3 and Canal 33 (both in Catalan), Galicia's TVG, the Basque Country's ETB-1 and ETB-2, Valencia's Canal 9 and Andalucía's Canal Sur. Cable and satellite TV is becoming widespread.

the last Saturday in June, when Madrid's **gay and lesbian pride march** (www.orgullogay.org) takes place.

## Useful Resources

In addition to the following resources, Barcelona's tourist board publishes *Barcelona – The Official Gay and Lesbian Tourist Guide* biannually, while Madrid's tourist office has a useful 'Gay & Lesbian Madrid' section on the front page of its website (www.esmadrid.com).

**Chueca** (www.chueca.com) Forums, news and reviews.

**GayBarcelona** (www.gaybarcelona.com) News and views and an extensive listings section covering bars, saunas, shops and more in Barcelona and Sitges.

**Gay Iberia** (Guía Gay de España; www.gayiberia.com) Gay guides to Barcelona, Madrid, Sitges and 26 other Spanish cities.

**Gay Madrid 4 U** (www.gaymadrid4u.com) A good overview of Madrid's gay bars and nightclubs.

**Guía Gay de España** (guia.universogay.com) A little bit of everything.

**LesboNet** (www.lesbonet.org) Lesbian forums, chat and news.

**Night Tours.com** (www.nighttours.com) A reasonably good guide to gay nightlife and other attractions in Madrid, Barcelona and seven other Spanish locations.

**Orgullo Gay** (www.orgullogay.org) Website for Madrid's gay and lesbian pride march and links to gay organisations across the country.

**Shangay** (www.shangay.com) For news, upcoming events, reviews and contacts. It also publishes *Shanguide*, a Madrid-centric biweekly magazine jammed with listings (including saunas and hardcore clubs) and contact ads. Its companion publication *Shangay Express* is better for articles with a handful of listings and ads. They're available in gay bookshops and gay and gay-friendly bars.

## Organisations

**Casal Lambda** (☎ 93 319 55 50; www.lambda.cat; Carrer de Verdaguer i Callís 10; ⏱ 5-9pm Mon-Sat; Ⓜ Uquinaona) A gay and lesbian social, cultural and information centre in Barcelona's La Ribera.

**Colectivo de Gais y Lesbianas de Madrid** (Cogam; ☎ 91 522 45 17; www.cogam.es; Calle de la Puebla 9; ⏱ 10am-2pm & 5-9pm Mon-Fri; Ⓜ Callao or Gran Vía) Offers activities, has an information office and social centre, and runs an information line (☎ 91 523 00 70; ⏱ 10am-2pm Mon-Fri).

**Coordinadora Gai-
Lesbiana Barcelona**
( ☏ 93 298 00 29; www.
cogailes.org; Carrer de Violant
d'Hongria 156; Ⓜ Plaça del
Centre) Barcelona's main
coordinating body for gay and
lesbian groups. It also runs an
information line, the Línia Rosa
( ☏ 900 601601).

**Federación Estatal
de Lesbianas, Gays,
Transexuales & Bisexuales**
( ☏ 91 360 46 05; www.felgtb.
org; 4th fl, Calle de las Infantas
40; ⊘ 8am-8pm Mon-Thu,
8am-3.30pm Fri) A national
advocacy group, based in
Madrid, that played a leading
role in lobbying for the
legalisation of gay marriages.

**Fundación Triángulo**
( ☏ 91 593 05 40; www.
fundaciontriangulo.org; 1st fl,
Calle de Melendez Valdés 52;
⊘ 10am-2pm & 5-8pm Mon-
Fri; Ⓜ Iglesia) One of several
sources of information on
gay issues in Madrid; it has
a separate information line,
Información LesGai ( ☏ 91 446
63 94).

● ● ● ●
# Health
Spain has an excellent health-
care system.

## Availability & Cost
of Health Care

If you need an ambulance,
call ☏ 061. For emergency
treatment, go straight to the
*urgencias* (casualty) section of
the nearest hospital.

*Farmacias* offer valuable
advice and sell over-the-
counter medication. In Spain,

a system of *farmacias de
guardia* (duty pharmacies)
operates so that each district
has one open all the time.
When a pharmacy is closed, it
posts the name of the nearest
open one on the door.

Medical costs are lower
in Spain than many other
European countries, but can
still mount quickly if you are
uninsured. Costs if you attend
casualty range from nothing (in
some regions) to around €80.

## Altitude Sickness

If you're hiking at altitude,
altitude sickness may be a
risk. Lack of oxygen at high
altitudes (over 2500m) affects
most people to some extent.
Symptoms of Acute Mountain
Sickness (AMS) usually de-
velop during the first 24 hours
at altitude but may be delayed
by up to three weeks. Mild
symptoms include headache,
lethargy, dizziness, difficulty
sleeping and loss of appetite.
AMS may become more severe
without warning and can be fatal. Severe symptoms include
breathlessness, a dry, irritative
cough (which may progress to
the production of pink, frothy
sputum), severe headache,
lack of coordination and
balance, confusion, irrational
behaviour, vomiting, drowsi-
ness and unconsciousness.

Treat mild symptoms by
resting at the same altitude
until recovery, usually for a day
or two. Paracetamol or aspirin
can be taken for headaches. If
symptoms persist or become
worse, immediate descent is
necessary; even 500m can
help. Drug treatments should
never be used to avoid descent
or to enable further ascent.

## Hypothermia

The weather in Spain's
mountains can be extremely
changeable at any time of
year. Proper preparation will
reduce the risks of getting
hypothermia: always carry
waterproof garments and
warm layers, and inform
others of your route.

Hypothermia starts with
shivering, loss of judgment
and clumsiness. Unless
rewarming occurs, the
sufferer deteriorates into
apathy, confusion and coma.
Prevent further heat loss by
seeking shelter, wearing warm
dry clothing, drinking hot
sweet drinks and sharing body
warmth.

## Bites & Stings

Nasty insects to be wary of
are the hairy reddish-brown
caterpillars of the pine
processionary moth (touching
the caterpillar's hairs sets off
a severely irritating allergic
skin reaction), and some
Spanish centipedes have a
very nasty but nonfatal sting.

Jellyfish, which have
stinging tentacles, are
an increasing problem
at beaches along the
Mediterranean coastline.

The only venomous
snake that is even relatively
common in Spain is Lataste's
viper. It has a triangular-
shaped head, grows up to
75cm long, and is grey with
a zigzag pattern. It lives in
dry, rocky areas, away from
humans. Its bite can be fatal
and needs to be treated with
a serum, which state clinics in
major towns keep in stock.

## Water

Tap water is generally safe to drink in Spain. If you are in any doubt, ask ¿Es potable el agua (de grifo)? (Is the (tap) water drinkable?). Do not drink water from rivers or lakes as it may contain bacteria or viruses that can cause diarrhoea or vomiting.

## Insurance

A travel-insurance policy to cover theft, loss, medical problems and cancellation or delays to your travel arrangements is a good idea. Paying for your ticket with a credit card can often provide limited travel-accident insurance and you may be able to reclaim the payment if the operator doesn't deliver. Worldwide travel insurance is available at lonelyplanet.com/travel_services. You can buy, extend and claim online anytime – even if you're on the road.

## Internet Access

Wi-fi is almost universally available at most hotels, as well as in some cafes, restaurants and airports; generally (but not always) it's free. Connection speed often varies from room to room in hotels (and coverage sometimes is restricted to the hotel lobby), so always ask when you check in or make your reservation. Some tourist offices may have a list of wi-fi hotspots in their area.

Good internet cafes are increasingly hard to find; ask at the local tourist office. Prices per hour range from €1.50 to €3.

## Legal Matters

If you're arrested, you will be allotted the free services of an abogado de oficio (duty solicitor), who may speak only Spanish. You're also entitled to make a phone call. If you use this to contact your embassy or consulate, the staff will probably be able to do no more than refer you to a lawyer who speaks your language. If you end up in court, the authorities are obliged to provide a translator.

In theory, you are supposed to have your national ID card or passport with you at all times. If asked for it by the police, you are supposed to be able to produce it on the spot. In practice it is rarely an issue and many people choose to leave passports in hotel safes.

The Policía Local or Policía Municipal operates at a local level and deals with such issues as traffic infringements and minor crime. The Policía Nacional (091) is the state police force, dealing with major crime and operating primarily in the cities. The military-linked Guardia Civil (created in the 19th century to deal with banditry) is largely responsible for highway patrols, borders, security, major crime and terrorism. Several regions have their own police forces, such as the Mossos d'Esquadra in Catalonia and the Ertaintxa in the Basque Country.

Cannabis is legal but only for personal use and in very small quantities. Public consumption of any illicit drug is illegal. Travellers entering Spain from Morocco should be prepared for drug searches, especially if you have a vehicle.

## Money

The most convenient way to bring your money is in the form of a debit or credit card, with some extra cash for use in case of an emergency.

### ATMs

Many credit and debit cards can be used for withdrawing money from cajeros automáticos (automatic teller machines) that display the relevant symbols such as Visa, MasterCard, Cirrus etc. Remember that there is usually a charge (around 1.5% to 2%) on ATM cash withdrawals abroad.

### Cash

Most banks and building societies will exchange major foreign currencies and offer the best rates. Ask about commissions and take your passport.

### Credit & Debit Cards

These can be used to pay for most purchases. You'll often be asked to show your passport or some other form of identification. Among the most widely accepted are Visa, MasterCard, American Express (Amex), Cirrus, Maestro, Plus and JCB. Diners Club is less widely accepted. If your card is lost, stolen or swallowed by an ATM, you can call the following telephone numbers toll free to have an immediate stop put on its use: **Amex** (☏ 900 994426), **Diners Club** (☏ 902 401112), **MasterCard** (☏ 900 971231) and **Visa** ( 📞 900 991124, 900 991216).

## Moneychangers

You can exchange both cash and travellers cheques at exchange offices – which are usually indicated by the word *cambio* (exchange). Generally they offer longer opening hours and quicker service than banks, but worse exchange rates and higher commissions.

## Taxes & Refunds

In Spain, value-added tax (VAT) is known as IVA (ee-ba; *impuesto sobre el valor añadido*). Visitors are entitled to a refund of the 21% IVA on purchases costing more than €90.16 from any shop, if they are taking them out of the EU within three months. Ask the shop for a cash back (or similar) refund form showing the price and IVA paid for each item, and identifying the vendor and purchaser. Then present the refund form to the customs booth for IVA refunds at the airport, port or border from which you leave the EU.

## Tipping

Menu prices include a service charge. Most people leave some small change if they're satisfied: 5% is normally fine and 10% extremely generous. Porters will generally be happy with €1. Taxi drivers don't have to be tipped but a little rounding up won't go amiss.

## Travellers Cheques

Can be changed (you'll often be charged a commission) at most banks and building soci-eties. Visa, Amex and Travelex are widely accepted brands with (usually) efficient re-placement policies. Get most of your cheques in fairly large denominations (the equivalent of €100 or more) to save on any per-cheque commission charges. It's vital to keep your initial receipt, and a record of your cheque numbers and the ones you have used, separate from the cheques themselves.

⬤⬤⬤
# Opening Hours

Standard opening hours are for high season only and tend to shorten outside that time.

**Banks** 8.30am to 2pm Monday to Friday; some also open 4pm to 7pm Thursday and 9am to 1pm Saturday

**Central post offices** 8.30am to 9.30pm Monday to Friday, 8.30am to 2pm Saturday (most other branches 8.30am to 8.30pm Monday to Friday, 9.30am to 1pm Saturday)

**Nightclubs** midnight or 1am to 5am or 6am

**Restaurants** lunch 1pm to 4pm, dinner 8.30pm to 11pm or midnight

**Shops** 10am to 2pm and 4.30pm to 7.30pm or 5pm to 8pm; big supermarkets and department stores generally open 10am to 10pm Monday to Saturday

⬤⬤⬤
# Public Holidays

The two main periods when Spaniards go on holiday are Semana Santa (the week leading up to Easter Sunday) and July and/or August. At these times accommodation in resorts can be scarce and transport heavily booked, but other places are often half-empty.

There are at least 14 official holidays a year – some observed nationwide, some locally. When a holiday falls close to a weekend, Spaniards like to make a *puente* (bridge), meaning they take the intervening day off too. Occasionally when some holidays fall close, they make an *acueducto* (aqueduct)! Here are the national holidays:

**Año Nuevo** (New Year's Day) 1 January

**Viernes Santo** (Good Friday) March/April

**Fiesta del Trabajo** (Labour Day) 1 May

**La Asunción** (Feast of the Assumption) 15 August

**Fiesta Nacional de España** (National Day) 12 October

**La Inmaculada Concepción** (Feast of the Immaculate Conception) 8 December

**Navidad** (Christmas) 25 December

Regional governments set five holidays and local councils two more. Common dates:

**Epifanía** (Epiphany) or **Día de los Reyes Magos** (Three Kings' Day) 6 January

**Jueves Santo** (Good Thursday) March/April. Not observed in Catalonia and Valencia.

**Corpus Christi** June. This is the Thursday after the eighth Sunday after Easter Sunday.

**Día de Santiago Apóstol** (Feast of St James the Apostle) 25 July

**Día de Todos los Santos** (All Saints Day) 1 November

**Día de la Constitución** (Constitution Day) 6 December

# Safe Travel

Most visitors to Spain never feel remotely threatened, but a sufficient number have unpleasant experiences to warrant an alert. The main thing to be wary of is petty theft (which may of course not seem so petty if your passport, cash, travellers cheques, credit card and camera go missing). What follows is intended as a strong warning rather than alarmism. In other words, be careful but don't be paranoid.

## Scams

There must be 50 ways to lose your wallet. As a rule, talented petty thieves work in groups and capitalise on distraction. Tricks usually involve a team of two or more (sometimes one of them an attractive woman to distract male victims). While one attracts your attention, the other empties your pockets. More imaginative strikes include someone dropping a milk mixture on to the victim from a balcony. Immediately a concerned citizen comes up to help you brush off what you assume to be pigeon poo, and thus suitably occupied you don't notice the contents of your pockets slipping away.

Beware: not all thieves look like thieves. Watch out for an old classic: the ladies offering flowers for good luck. We don't know how they do it, but if you get too involved in a friendly chat with these people, your pockets almost always wind up empty.

On some highways, especially the AP7 from the French border to Barcelona, bands of thieves occasionally operate. Beware of men trying to distract you in rest areas, and don't stop along the highway if people driving alongside indicate you have a problem with the car. While one inspects the rear of the car with you, his pals will empty your vehicle. Another gag has them puncturing tyres of cars stopped in rest areas, then following and 'helping' the victim when they stop to change the wheel. Hire cars and those with foreign plates are especially targeted. When you do call in at highway rest stops, try to park close to the buildings and leave nothing of value in view. If you do stop to change a tyre and find yourself getting unsolicited aid, make sure doors are all locked and don't allow yourself to be distracted.

Even parking your car can be fraught. In some towns fairly dodgy self-appointed parking attendants operate in central areas where you may want to park. They will direct you frantically to a spot. If possible, ignore them and find your own. If unavoidable, you may well want to pay them some token not to scratch or otherwise damage your vehicle after you've walked away. You definitely don't want to leave anything visible in the car (or open the boot – trunk – if you intend to leave luggage or anything else in it) under these circumstances.

## Theft

Theft is mostly a risk in tourist resorts, big cities and when you first arrive in a new city and may be off your guard. You are at your most vulnerable when dragging around luggage to or from your hotel. Barcelona, Madrid and Seville have the worst reputations for theft and, on very rare occasions, muggings.

Anything left lying on the beach can disappear in a flash when your back is turned. At night avoid dingy, empty city alleys and backstreets, or anywhere that just doesn't feel 100% safe.

Report thefts to the national police. You are unlikely to recover your goods but you need to make this formal *denuncia* for insurance purposes. To avoid endless queues at the *comisaría* (police station), you can make the report by phone (902 102 112) in various languages or on the web at www.policia.es (click on Denuncias). The following day you go to the station of your choice to pick up and sign the report, without queuing.

# Telephone

The reasonably widespread blue payphones are easy to use for international and domestic calls. They accept coins, *tarjetas telefónicas* (phonecards) issued by the national phone company Telefónica and, in some cases, various credit cards. Calling from your computer using an internet-based service such as Skype is generally the cheapest option.

## Collect Calls

Placing *una llamada a cobro revertido* (an international collect call) is simple. Dial ☎99 00 followed by the code for the country you're calling (numbers starting with ☎900 are national toll-free numbers):

**Australia** ☎900 990 061

**Canada** ☎900 990 015

**France** ☎900 990 033

**Germany** ☎900 99 00 49

**Ireland** ☎900 99 03 53

**Israel** ☎900 99 09 72

**New Zealand** ☎900 99 00 64

**UK** for BT ☎900 99 00 44

**USA** for AT&T ☎900 99 00 11, for Sprint and various others ☎900 99 00 13

## Mobile Phones

Spain uses GSM 900/1800, which is compatible with the rest of Europe and Australia but not with the North American system unless you have a GSM/GPRS-compatible phone (some AT&T and T-Mobile cell phones may work), or the system used in Japan. From those countries, you will need to travel with a tri-band or quadric-band phone.

You can buy SIM cards and prepaid time in Spain for your mobile (cell) phone, provided you own a GSM, dual- or tri-band cellular phone. This only works if your national phone hasn't been code-blocked; check before leaving home. Only consider a full contract if you plan to live in Spain for a while.

All the Spanish mobile-phone companies (Telefónica's MoviStar, Orange and Vodafone) offer *prepagado* (prepaid) accounts for mobiles. The SIM card costs from €10, to which you add some prepaid phone time. Phone outlets are scattered across the country. You can then top up in their shops or by buying cards in outlets, such as *estancos* (tobacconists) and newsstands. Pepephone (www.pepephone.com) is another option.

If you plan on using your own phone while in Spain, check with your mobile provider for information on roaming charges, especially if you're using a phone from outside the EU.

## Phone Codes

Mobile (cell) phone numbers start with ☎6. Numbers starting with ☎900 are national toll-free numbers, while those starting ☎901 to ☎905 come with varying costs. A common one is ☎902, which is a national standard rate number, but which can only be dialled from within Spain. In a similar category are numbers starting with ☎800, ☎803, ☎806 and ☎807.

**International access code** ☎00

**Spain country code** ☎34

**Local area codes** None (these are incorporated into listed numbers)

## Phonecards

Cut-rate prepaid phonecards can be good value for international calls. They can be bought from *estancos*, small grocery stores, *locutorios* (private call centres) and newsstands in the main cities and tourist resorts. If possible, try to compare rates. Many of the private operators offer better deals than those offered by Telefónica. *Locutorios* that specialise in cut-rate overseas calls have popped up all over the place in bigger cities.

## Important Numbers

**Emergencies** ☎112

**English-speaking Spanish international operator** ☎1008 (for calls within Europe) or ☎1005 (rest of the world)

**International directory enquiries** ☎11825 (calls to this number cost €2)

**National directory enquiries** ☎11818

**Operator for calls within Spain** 📞 1009 (including for domestic reverse-charge – collect – calls)

# Time

**Time zone** Same as most of Western Europe (GMT/UTC plus one hour during winter and GMT/UTC plus two hours during the daylight-saving period).

**Daylight saving** From the last Sunday in March to the last Sunday in October.

**UK, Ireland, Portugal & Canary Islands** One hour behind mainland Spain.

**Morocco** Morocco is on GMT/UTC year-round. From the last Sunday in March to the last Sunday in October, subtract two hours from Spanish time to get Moroccan time; the rest of the year, subtract one hour.

**USA** Spanish time is USA Eastern Time plus six hours and USA Pacific Time plus nine hours.

**Australia** During the Australian winter (Spanish summer), subtract eight hours from Australian Eastern Standard Time to get Spanish time; during the Australian summer, subtract 10 hours.

**12- and 24-hour clock** Although the 24-hour clock is used in most official situations, you'll find people generally use the 12-hour clock in everyday conversation.

# Tourist Information

All cities and many smaller towns have an *oficina de turismo* or *oficina de información turística*. In the country's provincial capitals you will sometimes find more than one tourist office – one specialising in information on the city alone, the other carrying mostly provincial or regional information. National and natural parks also often have their own visitor centres offering useful information.

**Turespaña** (www.spain.info) is the country's national tourism body, and it operates branches around the world. Check the website for office locations.

# Travellers with Disabilities

Spain is not overly accommodating for travellers with disabilities but some things are slowly changing. For example, disabled access to some museums, official buildings and hotels represents a change in local thinking. In major cities more is slowly being done to facilitate disabled access to public transport and taxis; in some cities, wheelchair-adapted taxis are called 'Eurotaxis'. Newly constructed hotels in most areas of Spain are required to have wheelchair-adapted rooms. With older places, you need to be a little wary of hotels who advertise themselves as being disabled-friendly, as this can mean as little as wide doors to rooms and bathrooms, or other token efforts.

Worthy of a special mention is Barcelona's **Inout Hostel** (📞 93 280 09 85; www.inouthostel.com; Major del Rectoret 2; dm €18; ❄ @ 🛜 ⚓ 🛗 ; 🚇 FGC Baixador de Vallvidrera) 🖋, which is completely accessible for those with disabilities, and nearly all the staff that work there have disabilities of one kind or another. The facilities and service is first-class.

## Organisations

**Accessible Madrid** (www.esmadrid.com) Madrid's tourist-office website has some useful information (type 'Accessible' into the search box). You can download the free, generally outstanding 152-page *Madrid Accessible Tourism Guide;* it covers everything from sights, restaurants and transport to itineraries through the city. The site also allows you to download a list of wheelchair-accessible hotels, and a PDF called 'Madrid Accessible Tourism Guide', a list of wheelchair-friendly restaurants, shopping centres and museums.

**Accessible Travel & Leisure** (📞 01452-729739; www.accessibletravel.co.uk) Claims to be the biggest UK travel agent dealing with travel for people with a disability, and encourages independent travel.

**Barcelona Turisme**
(📞 932 85 38 34; www.barcelona-access.com) Website devoted to making Barcelona accessible for visitors with a disability.

**ONCE** (Organización Nacional de Ciegos Españoles; 📞 91 577 37 56, 91 532 50 00; www.once.es; Calle de Prim 3, Madrid; Ⓜ Chueca or Colón) The Spanish association for the blind. You may be able to get hold of guides in Braille to a handful of cities, including Madrid and Barcelona, although they're not published every year.

**Society for Accessible Travel & Hospitality** (SATH; 📞 212-447-7284; www.sath.org; 347 Fifth Ave at 34th St, New York, USA, Suite 605; 🕐 9am-5pm; 🚇 M34 to 5th Ave, M1 to 34th St, Ⓢ 6 to 33rd St) A good resource, which gives advice on how to travel with a wheelchair, kidney disease, sight impairment or deafness.

●●●
# Visas

Spain is one of 26 member countries of the Schengen Convention, under which 22 EU countries (all but Bulgaria, Cyprus, Ireland, Romania and the UK) plus Iceland, Norway, Liechtenstein and Switzerland have abolished checks at common borders. Bulgaria and Romania were due to become a part of the Schengen Area in January 2014, but their accession was postponed after disagreement among EU-member countries.

The visa situation for entering Spain is as follows:

**Citizens or residents of EU & Schengen countries** No visa required.

**Citizens or residents of Australia, Canada, Israel, Japan, New Zealand and the USA** No visa required for tourist visits of up to 90 days.

**Other countries** Check with a Spanish embassy or consulate.

**To work or study in Spain** A special visa may be required – contact a Spanish embassy or consulate before travel.

●●●
# Women Travellers

Travelling in Spain as a woman is as easy as travelling anywhere in the Western world. That said, you should be choosy about your accommodation. Bottom-end fleapits with all-male staff can be insalubrious locations to bed down for the night. Lone women should also take care in city streets at night – stick with the crowds. Hitching for solo women travellers, while feasible, is risky.

Spanish men under about 40, who've grown up in the liberated post-Franco era, conform far less to old-fashioned sexual stereotypes, although you might notice that sexual stereotyping becomes a little more pronounced as you move from north to south in Spain, and from city to country.

# Transport

●●●
# Getting There & Away

Spain is one of Europe's top holiday destinations and is well linked to other European countries by air, rail and road. Regular car ferries and hydrofoils run to and from Morocco, and there are ferry links to the UK, Italy, the Canary Islands and Algeria.

Flights, tours and rail tickets can be booked online at lonelyplanet.com/bookings.

## Entering Spain

Immigration and customs checks (which usually only take place if you're arriving from outside the EU) normally involve a minimum of fuss, although there are exceptions.

Your vehicle could be searched on arrival from Andorra. Spanish customs look out for contraband duty-free products destined for illegal resale in Spain. The same may apply to travellers arriving from Morocco or the Spanish North African enclaves of Ceuta and Melilla. In this case the search is for controlled substances. Expect long delays at these borders,

# Climate Change & Travel

Every form of transport that relies on carbon-based fuel generates $CO_2$, the main cause of human-induced climate change. Modern travel is dependent on aeroplanes, which might use less fuel per person than most cars but travel much greater distances. The altitude at which aircraft emit gases (including $CO_2$) and particles also contributes to their climate change impact. Many websites offer 'carbon calculators' that allow people to estimate the carbon emissions generated by their journey and, for those who wish to do so, to offset the impact of the greenhouse gases emitted with contributions to portfolios of climate-friendly initiatives throughout the world. Lonely Planet offsets the carbon footprint of all staff and author travel.

especially in summer.

The tiny principality of Andorra is not in the European Union (EU), so border controls remain in place.

## Passport

Citizens of the 27 other EU member states and Switzerland can travel to Spain with their national identity card alone. If such countries do not issue ID cards – as in the UK – travellers must carry a valid passport. All other nationalities must have a valid passport.

By law you are supposed to carry your passport or ID card with you in Spain at all times.

##  Land

Spain shares land borders with France, Portugal and Andorra.

Apart from shorter cross-border services, **Eurolines** (www.eurolines.com) are the main operators of international bus services to Spain from most of Western Europe and Morocco.

In addition to the rail services connecting Spain with France and Portugal, there are direct trains between Zurich and Barcelona (via Bern, Geneva, Perpignan and Girona), and between Milan and Barcelona (via Turin, Perpignan and Girona). For these and other services, visit the 'Internacional' section of the website for **Renfe** (www.renfe.com), the Spanish national railway company.

### Andorra

Regular buses connect Andorra with Barcelona (including winter ski buses and direct services to the airport) and other destinations in Spain (including Madrid) and France. Regular buses run between Andorra and Barcelona's Estació d'Autobusos de Sants (€33.50, three hours).

### France

#### BUS
**Eurolines** (www.eurolines.fr) heads to Spain from Paris and more than 20 other French cities and towns. It connects with Madrid (17¾ hours), Barcelona (14¾ hours) and many other destinations. There is at least one departure per day for main destinations.

CAR & MOTORCYCLE
The main road crossing into Spain from France is the highway that links up with Spain's AP7 tollway, which runs down to Barcelona and follows the Spanish coast south (with a branch, the AP2, going to Madrid via Zaragoza). A series of links cuts across the Pyrenees from France and Andorra into Spain, as does a coastal route that runs from Biarritz in France into the Spanish Basque Country.

TRAIN
The principal rail crossings into Spain pierce the Franco-Spanish frontier along the Mediterranean coast and via the Basque Country. Another minor rail route runs inland across the Pyrenees from Latour-de-Carol to Barcelona.

In addition to the options listed below, two or three TGV (high-speed) trains leave from Paris-Montparnasse for Irún, where you change to a normal train for the Basque Country and on towards Madrid. Up to three TGVs also put you on track to Barcelona (leaving from Paris Gare de Lyon), with a change of train at Montpellier or Narbonne. For more information on French rail services, check out the **SNCF** (www.voyages-sncf.com) website.

There are plans for a high-speed rail link between Madrid and Paris. In the meantime, high-speed services travel via Barcelona. These are the major cross-border services:

**Paris to Madrid** (€198 to €228, 9¾ hours to 17½ hours, five daily) The slow route runs via

Les Aubrais, Blois, Poitiers, Irún, Vitoria, Burgos and Valladolid. It may be quicker to take the high-speed AVE train to Barcelona and change from there.

**Paris to Barcelona** (from €59, 6½ hours, two daily) A recently inaugurated high-speed service runs via Valence, Nimes, Montpellier, Beziers, Narbonne, Perpignan, Figueres and Girona. Also high-speed services run from Lyon (from €49, five hours) and Toulouse (from €39, three hours).

**Montpellier to Lorca** (€79.55, 12 to 13 hours, daily) Talgo service along the Mediterranean coast via Girona, Barcelona, Tarragona and Valencia.

### Portugal

BUS

Avanza (p362) runs daily buses between Lisbon and Madrid (€42.10, 7½ hours, two daily).

Other bus services run north via Porto to Tui, Santiago de Compostela and A Coruña in Galicia, while local buses cross the border from towns such as Huelva in Andalucía, Badajoz in Extremadura and Ourense in Galicia.

CAR & MOTORCYCLE

The A5 freeway linking Madrid with Badajoz crosses the Portuguese frontier and continues on to Lisbon, and there are many other road connections up and down the length of the Spain–Portugal border.

TRAIN

From Portugal, the main line runs from Lisbon across Extremadura to Madrid.

## Bus Passes

Travellers planning broader European tours that include Spain could find one of the following passes useful.

**Busabout** (📞 in the UK 084 5026 7514; www.busabout. com; 7-11 Bressenden Place, London) A UK-based hop-on/ hop-off bus service aimed at younger travellers. Its network includes more than 30 cities in nine countries, and the main passes are of interest only to those travelling a lot beyond Spain (where there are five stops).

**Eurolines** (www.eurolines.com) Offers a high-season pass valid for 15 days (adult/under 26 years €355/300) or 30 days (€465/385). This pass allows unlimited travel between 51 European cities, but the only Spanish cities included are Barcelona, Madrid and Alicante.

**Lisbon to Madrid** (chair/sleeper class from €36/50, nine to 10¾ hours, one daily)

**Lisbon to Irún** (chair/sleeper class €41/56, 14 hours, one daily)

**Oporto to Vigo** (from €14.75, 2¼ hours, two daily)

### 🚢 Sea

Ferries run to Morocco from mainland Spain. Most services are run by the Spanish national ferry company, **Acciona Trasmediterránea** (📞 902 454645; www.tras mediterranea.es). You can take vehicles on most routes.

A useful website for comparing routes and finding links to the relevant ferry companies is www.ferrylines. com.

### Algeria

Acciona Trasmediterránea runs year-round ferries between Almería and Ghazaouet.

### France

A new service operated by **LD Lines** (www.ldlines.co.uk) now sails between Gijón and Saint-Nazaire (15 to 16 hours, three times weekly) for passengers travelling with a car. It continues on to Rosslare in Ireland, stopping for 10 hours in Saint-Nazaire on the way north, and three hours heading south.

### Italy

Most Italian routes are operated by **Grimaldi Lines** (www. grimaldi-lines.com) or **Grand Navi Veloci** (www.gnv.it).

**Genoa to Barcelona** (19 hours, once or twice weekly)

**Civitavecchia (near Rome) to Barcelona** (20 hours, six weekly)

**Livorno (Tuscany) to Barcelona** (20½ hours, weekly)

**Porto Torres (Sardinia) to Barcelona** (12 hours, five to seven times weekly)

**Morocco**

**Tangier to Algeciras** (1½ hours, up to eight daily) Buses from several Moroccan cities converge on Tangier to make the ferry crossing to Algeciras, then fan out to the main Spanish centres.

**Tangier to Barcelona** (24 to 35 hours, weekly)

**Tangier to Tarifa** (35 minutes, up to eight daily)

**Nador to Almería** (six hours, up to three daily)

**UK**

In 2014 LD Lines (p359) inaugurated a new year-round route between Gijón and Poole (25 hours, weekly).

**Brittany Ferries** (☎ 0871 244 0744; www.brittany-ferries. co.uk) runs the following services.

**Plymouth to Santander** (20 hours, weekly, mid-March to October only)

**Portsmouth to Santander** (24 hours, twice weekly)

**Portsmouth to Bilbao** (24 hours, twice weekly)

# Rail Passes

## INTERRAIL PASSES

**InterRail** (www.interrailnet.eu) passes are available to people who have lived in Europe for six months or more. They can be bought at most major stations and student travel outlets, as well as online.

Children's InterRail passes (half the cost of the adult fare) are for children aged four to 11; youth passes for people aged 12 to 25; and adult passes for those 26 and over. Children aged three and under travel for free.

InterRail has a **Global Pass** encompassing 30 countries that comes in four versions, ranging from five days' travel in 10 days to a full month's travel. Check out the website for a full list of prices.

The InterRail **one-country pass** for Spain can be used for three, four, six or eight days in one month. For the eight-day pass you pay €512/326/216 for adult 1st class/adult 2nd class/youth 2nd class.

## EURAIL PASSES

**Eurail** (www.eurail.com) passes are for those who've lived in Europe for less than six months and are supposed to be bought outside Europe. They're available from leading travel agencies and online.

For most of the following passes, children aged between four and 11 pay half-price for the 1st-class passes, while those aged under 26 can get a cheaper 2nd-class pass. The website has a full list of prices, including special family rates and other discounts.

**Eurail Global Passes** are good for travel in 23 European countries; forget it if you intend to travel mainly in Spain. Passes are valid for 15 or 21 consecutive days, or for 10 or 15 days within one month. There are also one-, two- or three-month passes.

The **Eurail Select Pass** provides between five and 15 days of unlimited travel within a two-month period in three to five bordering countries.

Eurail also offers a one-country **Spain Pass** and several **two-country regional passes** (Spain-France, Spain-Italy and Spain-Portugal). You can choose from three to 10 days' train travel in a two-month period for any of these passes. The 10-day Spain Pass costs €455/365 for 1st/2nd class.

As with all Eurail passes, be sure you will be covering a lot of ground to make these worthwhile. To be sure, check the **Renfe** (www.renfe.com) website for sample prices in euros for the places in which you intend to travel.

## Getting Around

Spain's network of train and bus services is one of the best in Europe and there aren't many places that can't be reached using one or the other. The tentacles of Spain's high-speed train network are expanding rapidly, while domestic air services are plentiful over longer distances and on routes that are more complicated by land.

### ✈ Air

Spain has an extensive network of internal flights. These are operated by both Spanish airlines and a handful of low-cost international airlines, which include the following:

**Air Europa** (www.aireuropa. com) Madrid to Ibiza, Palma de Mallorca, Vigo, Bilbao and Barcelona as well as other routes between Spanish cities.

**Iberia** (www.iberia.com) Spain's national airline and its subsidiary, Iberia Regional-Air Nostrum, have an extensive domestic network.

**Ryanair** (www.ryanair.com) Some domestic Spanish routes include Madrid to Palma de Mallorca.

**Volotea** (www.volotea. com) Budget airline; flies domestically and internationally. Domestic routes take in Ibiza, Palma de Mallorca, Malaga, Valencia, Vigo, Bilbao, Zaragoza and Oviedo (but not Madrid or Barcelona).

**Vueling** (www.vueling.com) Spanish low-cost company

with loads of domestic flights within Spain, especially from Barcelona.

### 🚲 Bicycle

Years of highway improvement programs across the country have made cycling a much easier prospect than it once was, although there are few designated bike lanes. Cycling on *autopistas* (tollways) is forbidden. Driver attitudes are not always that enlightened, so beware, and cycling in most major cities is not for the faint-hearted.

If you get tired of pedalling, it is often possible to take your bike on the train. All regional trains have space for bikes (usually marked by a bicycle logo on the carriage), where you can simply load the bike. Bikes are also permitted on most *cercanías* (local-area trains around big cities such as Madrid and Barcelona). On long-distance trains there are more restrictions. As a rule, you have to be travelling overnight in a sleeper or couchette to have the (dismantled) bike accepted as normal luggage. Otherwise, it can only be sent separately as a parcel. It's often possible to take your bike on a bus – usually you'll just be asked to remove the front wheel.

### Hire

Bicycle rental is not as widespread as in some European countries, although it's becoming more so, especially in the case of *bici todo terreno* (mountain bikes), and in Andalucía, Barcelona and popular coastal towns. Costs vary considerably, but expect to pay around €8 to €10 per

hour, €15 to €20 per day, or €50 to €60 per week.

Zaragoza, Córdoba, Málaga and Seville are among those cities to have introduced public bicycle systems with dozens of automated pick-up/drop-off points around the city. These schemes involve paying a small subscription fee, which then allows you to pick up a bicycle at one location and drop it off at another.

### ⚓ Boat

Ferries and hydrofoils link the mainland (La Península) with the Balearic Islands and Spain's North African enclaves of Ceuta and Melilla.

The main national ferry company is Acciona Trasmediterránea (p359). It runs a combination of slower car ferries and modern, high-speed, passenger-only fast ferries and hydrofoils. On overnight services between the mainland and the Balearic Islands you can opt for seating or sleeping accommodation in a cabin.

### 🚌 Bus

There are few places in Spain where buses don't go. Numerous companies provide bus links, from local routes between villages to fast intercity connections. It is often cheaper to travel by bus than by train, particularly on long-haul runs, but also less comfortable.

Local services can get you just about anywhere, but most buses connecting villages and provincial towns are not geared to tourist needs. Frequent weekday services drop off to a trickle, if they operate at all, on

Saturday and Sunday. Often just one bus runs daily between smaller places during the week, and none operate on Sundays. It's usually unnecessary to make reservations; just arrive early enough to get a seat.

On many regular runs (say, from Madrid to Toledo) the ticket you buy is for the next bus due to leave and *cannot* be used on a later bus. Advance purchase in such cases is generally not possible. For longer trips (such as Madrid to Seville or to the coast), and certainly in peak holiday season, you can (and should) buy your ticket in advance. On some routes you have the choice between express and stopping-all-stations services.

In most larger towns and cities, buses leave from a single *estación de autobuses* (bus station). In smaller places, buses tend to operate from a set street or plaza, often unmarked. Locals will know where to go and where to buy tickets.

Bus travel within Spain is not overly costly. The trip from Madrid to Barcelona starts from around €32 one way. From Barcelona to Seville, which is one of the longest trips (15 to 16 hours), you pay up to €102 one way.

People under 26 should inquire about discounts on long-distance trips.

Among the hundreds of bus companies operating in Spain, the following have the largest range of services:

**ALSA** ( 902 422242; www.alsa.es) The biggest player, this company has routes all over the country in

## Beating Parking Fines

If you've parked in a street parking spot and return to find that a parking inspector has left you a parking ticket, don't despair. If you arrive back within a reasonable time after the ticket was issued (what constitutes a reasonable time varies from place to place, but it is rarely more than a couple of hours), don't go looking for the inspector, but instead head for the nearest parking machine. Most machines in most cities allow you to pay a small penalty (usually around €5) to cancel the fine (keep both pieces of paper just in case). If you're unable to work out what to do, ask a local for help.

association with various other companies.

**Avanza** ( 902 020999; www.avanzabus.com) Operates buses from Madrid to Extremadura, western Castilla y León and Valencia via eastern Castilla-La Mancha (eg Cuenca), often in association with other companies.

**Socibus & Secorbus** ( 902 229292; www.socibus. es) These two companies jointly operate services between Madrid and western Andalucía, including Cádiz, Córdoba, Huelva and Seville.

## Car & Motorcycle

Every vehicle should display a nationality plate of its country of registration and you must always carry proof of ownership of a private vehicle. Third-party motor insurance is required throughout Europe. A warning triangle and a reflective jacket (to be used in case of breakdown) are compulsory.

### Automobile Associations

The **Real Automóvil Club de España** (RACE;  900 100992; www.race.es; Calle de Eloy Gonzalo 32, Madrid) is the national automobile club. They may well come to assist you in case of breakdown, but in any event you should obtain an emergency telephone number for Spain from your own insurer or car-rental company.

### Driving Licence

All EU member states' driving licences are fully recognised throughout Europe. Those with a non-EU licence are supposed to obtain a 12-month International Driving Permit (IDP) to accompany their national licence, which your national automobile association can issue, although in practice car-rental companies and police rarely ask for one. People who have held residency in Spain for one year or more should apply for a Spanish driving licence.

### Fuel & Spare Parts

*Gasolina* (petrol) in Spain is pricey, but generally slightly cheaper than in its major EU neighbours (including France, Germany, Italy and the UK).

Petrol is about 10% cheaper in Gibraltar than in Spain and 15% cheaper in Andorra.

You can pay with major credit cards at most service stations.

## Hire

To rent a car in Spain you have to have a licence, be aged 21 or over and, for the major companies at least, have a credit or debit card. Smaller firms in areas where car hire is particularly common (such as the Balearic Islands) can sometimes live without this last requirement. Although those with a non-EU licence should also have an IDP, you will find that national licences from countries such as Aus-

tralia, Canada, New Zealand and the USA are usually accepted without question.

**Atesa** (☏ 902 100101; www. atesa.es)

**Auto Europe** (www. autoeurope.com) US-based clearing house for deals with major car-rental agencies.

**Autos Abroad** (www. autosabroad.com) UK-based company offering deals from major car-rental agencies.

**Avis** (☏ 902 180854; www. avis.es)

**Europcar** (☏ 902 105030; www.europcar.es)

**Hertz** (☏ 91 749 77 78; www. hertz.es)

**Holiday Autos** (☏ 900 838014; www.holidayautos.es) A clearing house for major international companies.

**Ideamerge** (www.ideamerge. com) Renault's car-leasing plan, motor-home rental and much more.

**Pepecar** (☏ 807 414243; www.pepecar.com) Local low-cost company, but beware of 'extras' that aren't quoted in initial prices.

**SixT** (☏ 902 491616; www. sixt.es)

## Insurance

Third-party motor insurance is a minimum requirement in Spain and throughout Europe. Ask your insurer for a European Accident Statement form,

# Road Distances (Km)

| | Alicante | Badajoz | Barcelona | Bilbao | Córdoba | Granada | A Coruña | León | Madrid | Málaga | Oviedo | Pamplona | San Sebastián | Seville | Toledo | Valencia | Valladolid |
|---|---|---|---|---|---|---|---|---|---|---|---|---|---|---|---|---|---|
| Badajoz | 696 | | | | | | | | | | | | | | | | |
| Barcelona | 515 | 1022 | | | | | | | | | | | | | | | |
| Bilbao | 817 | 649 | 620 | | | | | | | | | | | | | | |
| Córdoba | 525 | 272 | 908 | 795 | | | | | | | | | | | | | |
| Granada | 353 | 438 | 868 | 829 | 166 | | | | | | | | | | | | |
| A Coruña | 1031 | 772 | 1118 | 644 | 995 | 1043 | | | | | | | | | | | |
| León | 755 | 496 | 784 | 359 | 733 | 761 | 334 | | | | | | | | | | |
| Madrid | 422 | 401 | 621 | 395 | 400 | 434 | 609 | 333 | | | | | | | | | |
| Málaga | 482 | 436 | 997 | 939 | 187 | 129 | 1153 | 877 | 544 | | | | | | | | |
| Oviedo | 873 | 614 | 902 | 304 | 851 | 885 | 340 | 118 | 451 | 995 | | | | | | | |
| Pamplona | 673 | 755 | 437 | 159 | 807 | 841 | 738 | 404 | 407 | 951 | 463 | | | | | | |
| San Sebastián | 766 | 768 | 529 | 119 | 869 | 903 | 763 | 433 | 469 | 13 | 423 | 92 | | | | | |
| Seville | 609 | 217 | 1046 | 933 | 138 | 256 | 947 | 671 | 538 | 219 | 789 | 945 | 1007 | | | | |
| Toledo | 411 | 368 | 692 | 466 | 320 | 397 | 675 | 392 | 71 | 507 | 510 | 478 | 540 | 458 | | | |
| Valencia | 166 | 716 | 349 | 633 | 545 | 519 | 961 | 685 | 352 | 648 | 803 | 501 | 594 | 697 | 372 | | |
| Valladolid | 615 | 414 | 663 | 280 | 578 | 627 | 455 | 134 | 193 | 737 | 252 | 325 | 354 | 589 | 258 | 545 | |
| Zaragoza | 498 | 726 | 296 | 324 | 725 | 759 | 833 | 488 | 325 | 869 | 604 | 175 | 268 | 863 | 396 | 326 | 367 |

which can simplify matters in the event of an accident. A European breakdown-assistance policy such as the AA Five Star Service or RAC Eurocover Motoring Assistance is a good investment.

Car-hire companies also provide this minimum insurance, but be careful to understand what your liabilities and excess are, and what waivers you are entitled to in case of accident or damage to the hire vehicle.

### Road Rules

#### Blood-alcohol limit
0.05%. Breath tests are common, and if found to be over the limit, you can be judged, condemned, fined and deprived of your licence within 24 hours. Fines range up to around €600 for serious offences. Nonresident foreigners may be required to pay up on the spot (at 30% off the full fine). Pleading linguistic ignorance will not help – the police officer will produce a list of infringements and fines in as many languages as you like. If you don't pay, or don't have a Spanish resident to act as guarantor for you, your vehicle could be impounded, although this is rare.

#### Legal driving age for cars
18 years.

#### Legal driving age for motorcycles & scooters 16
(80cc and over) or 14 (50cc and under) years. A licence is required.

#### Motorcyclists Must use
headlights at all times and wear a helmet if riding a bike of 125cc or more.

**Overtaking** Spanish truck drivers often have the courtesy to turn on their right indicator to show that the way ahead of them is clear for overtaking (and the left one if it is not and you are attempting this manoeuvre).

**Roundabouts (traffic circles)** Vehicles already in the circle have the right of way.

**Side of the road** Drive on the right.

**Speed limits** In built-up areas, 50km/h (and in some cases, such as inner-city Barcelona, 30km/h), which increases to 100km/h on major roads and up to 120km/h on *autovías* and *autopistas* (toll-free and tolled dual-lane highways, respectively). Cars towing caravans are restricted to a maximum speed of 80km/h.

## Local Transport

Most of the major cities have excellent local transport. Madrid and Barcelona have extensive bus and metro systems, and other major cities also benefit from generally efficient public transport. By European standards, prices are relatively cheap.

### Bus

Cities and provincial capitals all have reasonable bus networks. You can buy single tickets (usually between €1 and €2) on the buses or at tobacconists, but in cities such as Madrid and Barcelona you are better off buying combined 10-trip tickets that allow the use of a combination of bus and metro, and

which work out cheaper per ride. These can be purchased in any metro station and from some tobacconists and newspaper kiosks.

Regular buses run from about 6am to shortly before midnight and even as late as 2am. In the big cities a night bus service generally kicks in on a limited number of lines in the wee hours. In Madrid they are known as *búhos* (owls) and in Barcelona more prosaically as *nitbusos* (night buses).

### Metro

Madrid has the country's most extensive metro network. Barcelona has a reasonable system. Valencia, Zaragoza, Bilbao and Seville also have limited but nonetheless useful metro systems. Tickets must be bought in metro stations (from counters or vending machines), or sometimes from *estancos* (tobacconists) or newspaper kiosks. Single tickets cost the same as for buses (between €1 and €2). The best value for visitors wanting to move around the major cities over a few days are the 10-trip tickets, known in Madrid as Metrobús (€12.20) and in Barcelona as T-10 (€10.30). Monthly and seasonal passes are also available.

### Taxi

You can find taxi ranks at train and bus stations, or you can telephone for radio taxis. In larger cities taxi ranks are also scattered about the centre, and taxis will stop if you hail them in the street – look for the green light and/or the *libre* sign on the passenger side of the windscreen. The bigger cities are well populated with taxis, although you might have to wait a bit longer on a Friday or Saturday night. No more than four people are allowed in a taxi.

Daytime flag fall (generally to 10pm) is, for example, €2.40 in Madrid, and up to €2.90 after 10pm and on weekends and holidays. You then pay €1 to €1.25 per kilometre depending on the time of day. There are airport and luggage surcharges. A cross-town ride in a major city will cost about €10 – absurdly cheap by European standards – while a taxi between the city centre and airport in either Madrid or Barcelona will cost €30 with luggage.

## Tram

Trams were stripped out of Spanish cities decades ago, but they're making a timid comeback in some. Barcelona has a couple of new suburban tram services in addition to its tourist Tramvia Blau run to Tibidabo. Valencia has some useful trams to the beach, while various limited lines also run in Seville, Bilbao, Murcia and, most recently, Zaragoza.

## 🚆 Train

**Renfe** ( 📞 902 243402; www.renfe.com) is the excellent national train system that runs most of the services in Spain. A handful of small private railway lines also operate.

You'll find *consignas* (left-luggage facilities) at all main train stations. They are usually open from about 6am to midnight and charge from €4 to €6 per day per piece of luggage.

Spain has several types of trains, and *largo recorrido* or *Grandes Líneas* (long-distance

trains) in particular have a variety of names.

**Alaris, Altaria, Alvia, Arco and Avant** Long-distance intermediate-speed services.

**Cercanías** For short hops and services to outlying suburbs and satellite towns in Madrid, Barcelona and 11 other cities. Called rodalies in Catalonia.

**Euromed** Similar to the Tren de Alta Velocidad Española

(AVE) trains, they connect Barcelona with Valencia and Alicante.

**FEVE (Ferrocarriles de Vía Estrecha)** Narrow-gauge network along Spain's north coast between Bilbao and Ferrol (Galicia), with a branch down to León.

**Regionales** Trains operating within one region, usually stopping all stations.

# Memorable Train Journeys

The romantically inclined could opt for an opulent and slow-moving, old-time rail adventure with numerous options across the peninsula.

Catch the **Transcantábrico** ( 📞 902 555902; www.renfe.com/trenesturisticos) for a journey on a picturesque narrow-gauge rail route, from Santiago de Compostela (by bus as far as O Ferrol) via Oviedo, Santander and Bilbao along the coast, and then a long inland stretch to finish in León. The eight-day trip costs from €2950 per person in high season. The trip can also be done in reverse or in smaller chunks. There are 13 departures from April to October. Check if your package includes various visits along the way, including the Museo Guggenheim in Bilbao, the Museo de Altamira, Santillana del Mar, and the Covadonga lakes in the Picos de Europa. The food is exceptional, with some meals being eaten on board but most in various locations.

The other option is **Al-Andalus** (www.renfe.com/trenesturisticos), which, despite the name, covers a significant proportion of the peninsula, from loops through Andalucía to roots that take the slow route between Madrid and Sevilla, Madrid and Zaragoza, Zaragoza to León, and León to Santiago de Compostela. Options vary from three to five nights. Prices for the six-day/five-night itineraries start at €3125 per person in high season.

The trains don't travel at night, making sleeping aboard easy and providing the opportunity to stay out at night.

A much shorter but nonetheless enchanting train ride is the narrow-gauge train from Palma de Mallorca to Sóller.

# Cheaper Train Tickets

Train travel can be expensive in Spain but there is one trick worth knowing. Return tickets cost considerably less than two one-way tickets. If you're certain that you'll be returning on the same route sometime over the coming months (usually three months is the limit), buy a return ticket and you can later change the return date, which works out a lot cheaper than buying two one-way tickets.

**Talgo and Intercity** Slower long-distance trains.

**Tren de Alta Velocidad Española (AVE)** High-speed trains that link Madrid with Albacete, Barcelona, Burgos, Córdoba, Cuenca, Huesca, Lerida, Málaga, Seville, Valencia, Valladolid and Zaragoza. There are also Barcelona–Seville and Barcelona–Málaga services. In coming years Madrid–Cádiz and Madrid–Bilbao should also come on line.

**Trenhotel** Overnight trains with sleeper berths.

## Classes & Costs

All long-distance trains have 2nd and 1st classes, known as *turista* and *preferente*, respectively. The latter is 20% to 40% more expensive.

Fares vary enormously depending on the service (faster trains cost considerably more) and, in the case of some high-speed services such as the AVE, on the time and day of travel. Tickets for AVE trains are by far the most expensive. A one-way trip in 2nd class from Madrid to Barcelona (on which route only AVE trains run) could cost as much as €139 (it could work out significantly cheaper if you book well in advance).

Children aged between four and 12 years are entitled to a 40% discount; those aged under four travel for free (except on high-speed trains, for which they pay the same as those aged four to 12). Buying a return ticket often gives you a 10% to 20% discount on the return trip. Students and people up to 25 years of age with a Euro<26 Card (Carnet Joven in Spain) are entitled to 20% to 25% off most ticket prices.

If you're travelling as a family, ask for one of a group of four seats with a table when making your reservation.

On overnight trips within Spain on *trenhoteles* it's worth paying extra for a *litera* (couchette; a sleeping berth in a six- or four-bed compartment) or, if available, single or double cabins in *preferente* or *gran clase* class. The cost depends on the class of accommodation, type of train and length of journey. The lines covered are Madrid–A Coruña, Barcelona–Córdoba–Seville, Barcelona–Madrid (and on to Lisbon) and Barcelona–Málaga, as well as international services to France.

## Reservations

Reservations are recommended for long-distance trips, and you can make them in train stations, Renfe (p365) offices and travel agencies, as well as online. In a growing number of stations you can pick up prebooked tickets from machines scattered about the station concourse.

# a b c

## Language

Spanish pronunciation is not difficult as most of its sounds are also found in English. You can read our pronunciation guides below as if they were English and you'll be understood just fine. And if you pronounce 'th' in our guides with a lisp and 'kh' as a throaty sound, you'll even sound like a real Spanish person.

To enhance your trip with a phrasebook, visit **lonelyplanet.com**.

### BASICS

**Hello.**
*Hola.*     o·la

**How are you?**
*¿Qué tal?*     ke tal

**I'm fine, thanks.**
*Bien, gracias.*     byen gra·thyas

**Excuse me. (to get attention)**
*Disculpe.*     dees·kool·pe

**Yes./No.**
*Sí./No.*     see/no

**Thank you.**
*Gracias.*     gra·thyas

**You're welcome./That's fine.**
*De nada.*     de na·da

**Goodbye. /See you later.**
*Adiós./Hasta luego.*     a·dyos/as·ta lwe·go

**Do you speak English?**
*¿Habla inglés?*     a·bla een·gles

**I don't understand.**
*No entiendo.*     no en·tyen·do

**How much is this?**
*¿Cuánto cuesta?*     kwan·to kwes·ta

**Can you reduce the price a little?**
*¿Podría bajar un*     po·dree·a ba·khar oon
*poco el precio?*     po·ko el pre·thyo

### ACCOMMODATION

**I'd like to make a booking.**
*Quisiera reservar*     kee·sye·ra re·ser·var
*una habitación.*     oo·na a·bee·ta·thyon

**How much is it per night?**
*¿Cuánto cuesta*     kwan·to kwes·ta
*por noche?*     por no·che

### EATING & DRINKING

**I'd like ..., please.**
*Quisiera ..., por favor.*     kee·sye·ra ... por fa·vor

**That was delicious!**
*¡Estaba buenísimo!*     es·ta·ba bwe·nee·see·mo

**Bring the bill/check, please.**
*La cuenta, por favor.*     la kwen·ta por fa·vor

**I'm allergic to ...**
*Soy alérgico/a al ... (m/f)*     soy a·ler·khee·ko/a al ...

**I don't eat ...**
*No como ...*     no ko·mo ...

   **chicken**    *pollo*    po·lyo
   **fish**    *pescado*    pes·ka·do
   **meat**    *carne*    kar·ne

### EMERGENCIES

**I'm ill.**
*Estoy enfermo/a. (m/f)*     es·toy en·fer·mo/a

**Help!**
*¡Socorro!*     so·ko·ro

**Call a doctor!**
*¡Llame a un médico!*     lya·me a oon me·dee·ko

**Call the police!**
*¡Llame a la policía!*     lya·me a la po·lee·thee·a

### DIRECTIONS

**I'm looking for (a/an/the) ...**
*Estoy buscando ...*     es·toy boos·kan·do ...

   **ATM**
   *un cajero*    oon ka·khe·ro
   *automático*    ow·to·ma·tee·ko

   **bank**
   *el banco*    el ban·ko

   **... embassy**
   *la embajada de ...*    la em·ba·kha·da de ...

   **market**
   *el mercado*    el mer·ka·do

   **museum**
   *el museo*    el moo·se·o

   **restaurant**
   *un restaurante*    oon res·tow·ran·te

   **toilet**
   *los servicios*    los ser·vee·thyos

   **tourist office**
   *la oficina de*    la o·fee·thee·na de
   *turismo*    too·rees·mo

# Behind the Scenes

## Author Thanks

### Brendan Sainsbury

Thanks to all the untold bus drivers, chefs, hotel receptionists, tour guides and flamenco singers who helped me in this research. Special thanks to José in Córdoba and Dario in Seville for their tips and insights. Kudos, as ever, to my wife Liz and eight-year-old son Kieran for their company on the road.

## Acknowledgments

Climate map data adapted from Peel MC, Finlayson BL & McMahon TA (2007) 'Updated World Map of the Köppen-Geiger Climate Classification', Hydrology and Earth System Sciences, 11, 1633¬44.

Illustrations p74-5, p78-9, p194-5, p246-7, p260-1, p292-3 by Javier Zarracina

Cover photographs
Front: Alcázar fortress and Río Tajo, Toledo, Peter Adams/Getty
Back: Tamariu Castle, Costa Brava, Jose Fuste Raga/Corbis.

## This Book

This 4th edition of Lonely Planet's *Discover Spain* guidebook was researched and written by Brendan Sainsbury. The content was researched and written by Stuart Butler, Anthony Ham, Isabella Noble, John Noble, Josephine Quintero, Regis St Louis and Andy Symington. This guidebook was commissioned in Lonely Planet's London office, and produced by the following:

**Commissioning Editor** Dora Whitaker
**Destination Editor** Jo Cooke
**Product Editor** Elin Berglund
**Senior Cartographer** Anthony Phelan
**Book Designer** Wibowo Rusli
**Assisting Editors** Katie Connolly, Penny Cordner, Kate Evans
**Assisting Cartographer** Corey Hutchison
**Cover Researcher** Naomi Parker
**Thanks to** Sasha Baskett, Ryan Evans, Larissa Frost, Chris Gribble, Jouve India, Kate Mathews, Julia McNally, John Taufa, Amanda Williamson, Tracy Whitmey, Juan Winata

# Index

# How to Use This Book

**These symbols give you the vital information for each listing:**

| | | | | | | | |
|---|---|---|---|---|---|---|---|
| ☑ | Telephone Numbers | ☎ | Wi-Fi Access | ☐ | Bus |
| ☺ | Opening Hours | ☰ | Swimming Pool | ☐ | Ferry |
| ℗ | Parking | ☑ | Vegetarian Selection | Ⓜ | Metro |
| ☻ | Nonsmoking | ☐ | English-Language Menu | Ⓢ | Subway |
| ✳ | Air-Conditioning | ☑ | Family-Friendly | Ⓣ | Tram |
| @ | Internet Access | ☺ | Pet-Friendly | | |

### Look out for these icons:

**FREE** No payment required

🌿 A green or sustainable option

*Our authors have nominated these places as demonstrating a strong commitment to sustainability – for example by supporting local communities and producers, operating in an environmentally friendly way, or supporting conservation projects.*

**All reviews** are ordered in our authors' preference, starting with their most preferred option. Additionally:

**Sights** are arranged in the geographic order that we suggest you visit them, and within this order, by author preference.

**Eating and Sleeping reviews** are ordered by price range (budget, mid-range, top end) and within these ranges, by author preference.

## Map Legend

### Sights
- 🏖 Beach
- 🕌 Buddhist
- 🏰 Castle
- ✝ Christian
- 🕉 Hindu
- ☪ Islamic
- ✡ Jewish
- ❶ Monument
- 🏛 Museum/Gallery
- ⊗ Ruin
- 🍷 Winery/Vineyard
- 🦁 Zoo
- ◉ Other Sight

### Activities, Courses & Tours
- 🤿 Diving/Snorkelling
- 🛶 Canoeing/Kayaking
- ⛷ Skiing
- 🏄 Surfing
- 🏊 Swimming/Pool
- 🚶 Walking
- 🏄 Windsurfing
- ➕ Other Activity/Course/Tour

### Sleeping
- 🛏 Sleeping
- 🏕 Camping

### Eating
- 🍴 Eating

### Drinking
- ☕ Drinking
- ☕ Cafe

### Entertainment
- 🎭 Entertainment

### Shopping
- 🛍 Shopping

### Information
- ✉ Post Office
- ❶ Tourist Information

### Transport
- ✈ Airport
- ⊗ Border Crossing
- 🚌 Bus
- ⊕ Cable Car/Funicular
- 🚲 Cycling
- ⛴ Ferry
- 🚝 Monorail
- ℗ Parking
- Ⓢ S-Bahn
- 🚕 Taxi
- 🚆 Train/Railway
- 🚊 Tram
- Ⓣ Tube Station
- Ⓤ U-Bahn
- Ⓜ Underground Train Station
- ● Other Transport

### Routes
- Tollway
- Freeway
- Primary
- Secondary
- Tertiary
- Lane
- Unsealed Road
- Plaza/Mall
- Steps
- )= = Tunnel
- Pedestrian Overpass
- Walking Tour
- Walking Tour Detour
- Path

### Boundaries
- International
- State/Province
- Disputed
- Regional/Suburb
- Marine Park
- Cliff
- Wall

### Population
- 🔴 Capital (National)
- ◉ Capital (State/Province)
- ● City/Large Town
- ● Town/Village

### Geographic
- 🛖 Hut/Shelter
- 🔦 Lighthouse
- 👁 Lookout
- ▲ Mountain/Volcano
- 🌴 Oasis
- 🏞 Park
- )( Pass
- 🏕 Picnic Area
- 💧 Waterfall

### Hydrography
- River/Creek
- Intermittent River
- Swamp/Mangrove
- Reef
- Canal
- Water
- Dry/Salt/Intermittent Lake
- Glacier

### Areas
- Beach/Desert
- Cemetery (Christian)
- Cemetery (Other)
- Park/Forest
- Sportsground
- Sight (Building)
- Top Sight (Building)

## JOHN NOBLE

**Camino de Santiago & Basque Spain** John, originally from England's Ribble Valley, has lived in an Andalucian mountain village since 1995. He has travelled lengthily all over Spain and helped write every edition of Lonely Planet's *Spain* and *Andalucía* guides. He loves returning to Galicia's green countryside, stone architecture, magnificent coastline and wonderful music, food and wine. The novelty of his latest trip was experiencing Galicia in its winter clothes, disappearing in the fog at Cabo Fisterra and getting stuck in the snow at O Cebreiro.

## JOSEPHINE QUINTERO

**Catalonia & Eastern Spain, Camino de Santiago & Basque Spain** Josephine moved to Spain some 25 years ago, fleeing from the invasion of Kuwait (but that's another story). She still revels in the relaxed way of life in Andalucía and loves to explore the rest of the country, seeking out hidden corners, appreciating the unsung glories and meeting some extraordinary people along the way. During her research, one of the highlights was visiting Zaragoza's fascinating origami museum, another was finally appreciating the appeal of birdwatching, particularly in the magnificent Aragón Pyrenees.

## REGIS ST LOUIS

**Barcelona** Regis first fell in love with Barcelona on a grand journey across Iberia in the late 1990s. Since then he has returned frequently to explore this endlessly fascinating city. Favourite memories from his most recent trip include earning a few scars at a correfoc in Gràcia and watching fearless castellers build human towers at the Santa Eulàlia festival. Regis is also the author of *Barcelona*, and he has contributed to dozens of other Lonely Planet titles. He lives in Brooklyn, New York.

## ANDY SYMINGTON

**Catalonia & Eastern Spain** Andy hails from Australia but has been living in Spain for over a decade, where, to shatter a couple of stereotypes of the country, he can frequently be found huddled in subzero temperatures watching the tragically poor local football team. He has authored and coauthored many Lonley Planet guidebooks and other publications on Spain and elsewhere; in his spare time he walks in the mountains, embarks on epic tapas trails, and co-bosses a rock bar.

## Our Story

A beat-up old car, a few dollars in the pocket and a sense of adventure. In 1972 that's all Tony and Maureen Wheeler needed for the trip of a lifetime – across Europe and Asia overland to Australia. It took several months, and at the end – broke but inspired – they sat at their kitchen table writing and stapling together their first travel guide, *Across Asia on the Cheap*. Within a week they'd sold 1500 copies. Lonely Planet was born.

Today, Lonely Planet has offices in Franklin, London, Melbourne, Oakland, Beijing and Delhi, with more than 600 staff and writers. We share Tony's belief that 'a great guidebook should do three things: inform, educate and amuse'.

# Our Writers

### BRENDAN SAINSBURY

**Coordinating author, Seville & Andalucía's Hill Towns, Granada & Andalucía's South Coast**
Originally from Hampshire, England, Brendan first went to Spain on an InterRail ticket in the 1980s. He went back as a travel guide several years later and met his wife-to-be in a small village in rural Andalucía in 2003. He has been writing books for Lonely Planet for a decade, including several editions of the *Spain* guide. Brendan loves Granada, the writing of Federico García Lorca, cycling along *vias verdes* and attending as many flamenco shows as his research allows.

### STUART BUTLER

**Camino de Santiago & Basque Spain** Stuart's first childhood encounters, in Parque Nacional de Doñana and on family holidays along the north coast, left lasting impressions. When he was older he spent every summer on the Basque beaches, until one day he found himself unable to tear himself away – he has been there ever since. His travels for Lonely Planet, and a wide variety of magazines, have taken him beyond Spain to the shores of the Arctic, the deserts of Asia and the forests of Africa. His website is www.stuartbutlerjournalist.com

### ANTHONY HAM

**Madrid & Around** In 2001, Anthony fell in love with Madrid on his first visit to the city. Less than a year later, he arrived on a one-way ticket, without knowing a word of Spanish or a single person. After 10 years of living in the city, he recently returned to Australia with his Spanish-born family, but he still adores his adopted country as much as the first day he arrived. His most recent Spanish passions, among many, are trying to track down the critically endangered Iberian lynx and sharing stories of Spain's wild places. When he's not writing for Lonely Planet, Anthony writes about and photographs Spain, Scandinavia, Australia and Africa for newspapers and magazines around the world. Read more about Anthony at www.anthonyham.com

### ISABELLA NOBLE

**Camino de Santiago & Basque Spain** Isabella's in-depth investigation of distant northern regions far from her Andalucian home began at the age of 12, and she was thrilled to discover that the two bears of the Senda del Oso are still there a decade later. English/Australian on paper but Spanish at heart, she has lived and travelled in Spain since 1994. Adventures include exploring after-dark Gijón, tackling snowy mountain passes and falling in love with Oviedo. For now, she lives between Andalucía and London.

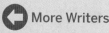 **More Writers** .................................................................................

**Published by Lonely Planet Publications Pty Ltd**
ABN 36 005 607 983
4th edition – Jan 2015
ISBN 978 1 74321 464 0
© Lonely Planet 2015   Photographs © as indicated 2015
10 9 8 7 6 5 4 3 2 1
Printed in China